TRUTH FOR LIFE

A devotional commentary on the Epistle of James

JOHN BLANCHARD

EVANGELICAL PRESS

EVANGELICAL PRESS
16/18 High Street, Welwyn, Hertfordshire, AL6 9EQ, England.

First published 1982
Second edition first published by Evangelical Press 1986

All Scripture references are taken from the New International Version, Hodder & Stoughton, 1979.

By the same author

Read Mark Learn
Right with God
What in the world is a Christian?
Learning and Living
Luke Comes Alive!
How to enjoy your Bible
Pop goes the gospel
Gathered Gold
More Gathered Gold

British Library Cataloguing in Publication Data

Blanchard, John, *1932–*
Truth for life: an exposition of James. — 2nd ed.
1. Bible. N. T. James — Commentaries
I. Title. II. Bible. N. T. James. *English. New International. 1979–*
227′.9107 BS2785.3

ISBN 0-85234-225-X

Typeset by Inset, Chappel, Essex.
Printed in Great Britain by The Bath Press, Avon.

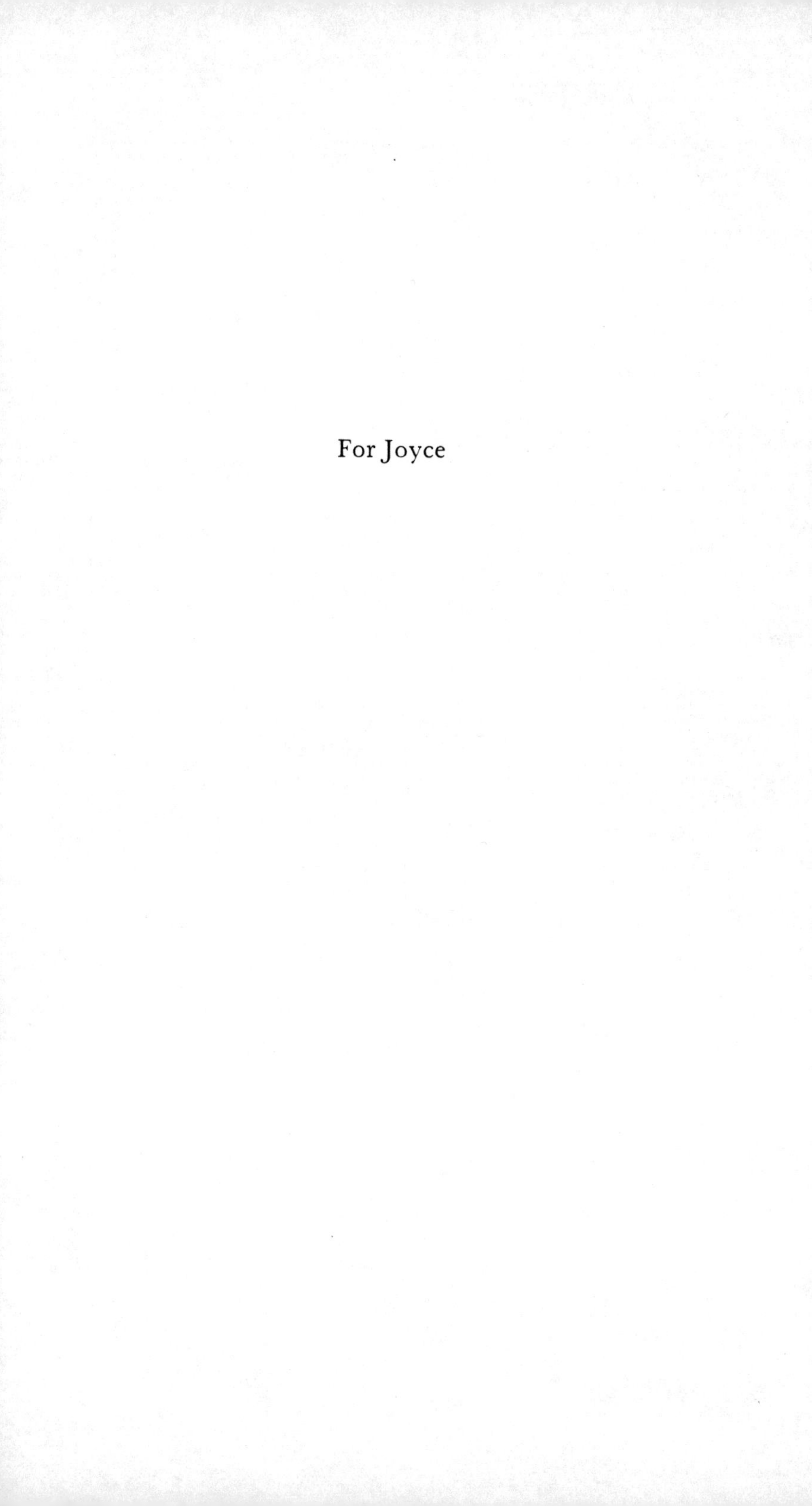

For Joyce

Contents

Preface

The Epistle of James can be read right through in less than eight minutes, yet its message is still powerfully relevant after nearly 2,000 years.

I first 'discovered' James soon after my conversion, and ever since his disturbing words have had a peculiar fascination for me, one which has drawn me to study them again and again with ever-increasing wonder at their content and contemporaneity. My first studies were as a Bible Class leader at Holy Trinity Church, Guernsey in 1958. Then, as a staff evangelist with the National Young Life Campaign, I studied it in broader outline with several NYLC branches in 1961 and 1963. Between 1966 and 1971 I led a large number of houseparties in Europe and elsewhere under the auspices of the Movement for World Evangelization, and again felt drawn to the Epistle of James as the basis for the morning Bible Hour. During this time, I also re-shaped some of the material to produce twenty-nine weekly articles for the *Sunday Companion*. Those articles, later translated for use in Eastern Europe, fuelled the many requests I was already receiving to publish a devotional study on the whole epistle and eventually led to a four-volume series of paperbacks entitled *Not Hearers Only*, published between 1971 and 1974.

Other than preaching occasional sermons from James's letter, I felt sure that that would be the end of the story as far as I was concerned, but I had reckoned without an outstanding new translation of the Bible. All the above studies, spoken and written, were based on the Authorized Version, the only translation I had ever consistently used. In the meantime, however, I had changed to the superb New International Version, which has a genuine claim to being the finest translation of Scripture now available in the English language, and when I came to revise my material for re-publication it was to this version that I turned. The result has been not so much a revision as a revelation! I have been truly amazed at the fresh insights God has graciously given me into the meaning of these familiar chapters, and once more I have been deeply moved by their impact.

As even a relative beginner in the study of the New Testament will know, the Epistle of James is essentially *practical,* and a glance at some of the titles of books devoted to it immediately confirms this: *The Behaviour of Belief* (Spiros Zodhiates), *A Belief that Behaves* (Guy H. King), *Make your faith work* (Louis H. Evans), *Faith that works* (John L. Bird) and *The Tests of Faith* (J. Alec Motyer). It is also warmly *pastoral,* deeply concerned with the average Christian's daily struggle against the pressures of the world, the tug of temptation and the subtle suggestion of compromise. Finally, it is deeply *penetrating,* bringing timeless truth to bear on everyday life in a way that is quite irresistible. Curtis Vaughan is right on the mark when he writes, in the Introduction to his excellent *Study Guide Commentary,* 'Few things would do more to revitalize present-day Christianity than a determined effort on the part of believers to take James seriously and put his teachings into practice.'

It is this kind of conviction that has constantly motivated my interest in these particular pages of Scripture and that has led to the publication of this commentary, which is now appearing in a revised edition.

I would like to express my warmest thanks to Sir Fred Catherwood for his magnanimous foreword and to Sheila Hellberg for her tireless and efficient typing of the manuscript at every stage.

My earnest prayer is that, for all their imperfections, these studies will help many Christians to discover by their obedient response to James's message that, together with every other part of God's precious Word, it is indeed *truth for life!*

John Blanchard
Banstead, Surrey.
(April 1986)

Foreword

by

Sir Frederick Catherwood

Member of the European Parliament

Our generation of Christians needs the Epistle of James as few generations before have needed it. For the permissive culture which is rotting our society has crept into the foundations of the church itself. As the standards of the church crumble, faith and works are coming apart. We profess faith in Christ, but trust to materialism. We say we love our wives as Christ loved the church, but the number of divorces among Christians is rising. And in a world which no longer seems capable of distinguishing free speech from character assassination, we need to be reminded that 'The tongue is a fire, and is set on fire by hell.' So we need to be reminded again that faith without works is dead.

James pulls no punches. It is a practical book which reduces the pretensions of the religious to size. And John Blanchard is a practical man whose commentary is exactly matched to its subject. He has always been nearer to the ordinary Christian than to the institutional church and he has always kept to his deeply held convictions that Christian truth does not change. The man and the subject could not be better matched.

John Blanchard talks of today's society, 'its immorality, its dishonesty, its greed, its selfishness, its violence, its envy, its arrogance, its blasphemy, its cruelty, its materialism, its obsession with pleasure and, above all, its careless or calculated rejection of God'. That is not the way our sycophantic press reflects our society. It is not the way our intellectual leaders like to see the society they have created. But the rottenness of society is now showing through the façade and can no longer be denied. Those in responsible positions who have to deal with the world as it is – trade union leaders, managers, police, politicians – are increasingly pessimistic. They know that something has gone badly wrong, but they cannot put their finger on it. This book puts the finger on it very precisely.

This book is theological in the same way that Christ was theological. It points the reader to God's way simply and directly, but never avoids the problems at the intersection of one great truth with another. James deals with the intersection of the great truths of faith and works. We are saved not by our own deeds but by Christ's sacrifice for our misdeeds. Yet no man whose deeds do not reflect Christ's law can claim to be a Christian. In dealing with this central issue in chapters 17 and 18 John Blanchard shows faultless theological balance. Luther wondered whether James contradicted Paul. John Blanchard says, 'Paul's great theme is that no man can produce justification by the performance of good deeds . . . James's great theme is that no man can prove justification without the performance of good deeds.'

This book is practical, relevant and soundly based in Christian theology. I commend it most warmly to the reader.

Fred Catherwood

1.

To God be the glory!

'James, a servant of God and of the Lord Jesus Christ. To the twelve tribes scattered among the nations: Greetings' (James 1:1).

The opening words of the Epistle of James are at one and the same time perfectly straightforward and powerfully significant. They are straightforward because they follow the common practice of the time, which was for the writer to begin a letter with his own name, the name of the person or persons to whom he was writing and a simple word of greeting. Today, this would be covered by the phrases 'Dear Sir', 'Yours faithfully' and the signature of the sender – and it would be difficult to imagine a formula more ordinary than that! Yet the words we now have before us are far from ordinary, because they tell us three significant things about the man who wrote them. Even more important, they are part of the living Word of God, and as such they have a vitality and relevance far beyond any literature that has only a human author. As we go through this epistle together, let us constantly remember that while it is James who is writing, it is God who is speaking. The Puritan preacher Thomas Watson's advice was this: 'Read the Scripture, not only as history, but as a love-letter sent to you from God.' That approach will never fail to yield rich dividends – not least because that is exactly what the Bible's human authors would wish. The apostle Paul speaks for them all when he thanks God that the Thessalonians received his message to them 'not as the word of men, but as it actually is, the word of God' (1 Thessalonians 2:13).

Now let us turn to this opening verse and see what it has to say about the man who wrote it.

1. He had a lowly consideration of himself
'James, a servant . . .'

If these three words were all that remained of this letter, we would still know that we had the remnant of a remarkable document written by a remarkable man, because the only word he uses to describe himself is the most self-effacing he could possibly have chosen: he says he is 'a servant'. The original word, *doulos*, makes the point even clearer, because it literally means 'a slave'. Slavery was a common social feature in biblical times, and this comment by K. A. Kitchen in *The New Bible Dictionary* gives us a simple summary of what it implied: 'Under the influence of Roman law, a slave was usually considered to be a person (male or female) owned by another, without rights, and – like any other form of personal property – to be used and disposed of in whatever way the owner may wish.' That alone makes it remarkable that James should be content with describing himself as a slave, but his choice becomes even more remarkable when we realize some of the titles he *could* have chosen. After all, he could have written, 'James, the leader of the church at Jerusalem': when Paul had completed his final missionary journey and reported back to the mother church at Jerusalem, Luke records the event by saying that 'Paul and the rest of us went to see James and all the elders were present' (Acts 21:18) – a clear indication that James was the man in charge. He could have described himself as 'James, a pillar of the church': in a biographical note to the Galatians, Paul says that official recognition of his ministry came when 'James, Peter and John, those reputed to be pillars, gave me and Barnabas the right hand of fellowship' (Galatians 2:9). He might have begun his letter, 'James, an apostle': Paul tells the Galatians of an earlier occasion when he went to Jerusalem to meet Peter, and adds, 'I saw none of the other apostles – only James, the Lord's brother' (Galatians 1:19) and although the wording is somewhat ambiguous, there is a distinct possibility that James did by then hold apostolic office. Finally, he could have used the last part of Paul's phrase and opened his letter, 'James, the Lord's brother,' and basked in the reflected glory of having been conceived in the same womb and brought up in the same home as the incarnate Son of God. In the eyes of many people, that would have given him a distinct edge over Peter, John, Matthew and even the mighty Paul. Yet James set all these legitimate alternatives aside and deliberately settled for 'servant'.

Paul's letter to the Romans includes this sobering instruction: 'Do not think of yourself more highly than you ought' (Romans 12:3). How do we face up to a statement like that? How highly do we think we 'ought' to be rated? Few statements in Scripture examine us more closely than that one! The mark of a great man of God is not that he thinks himself great, but rather that he thinks himself utterly insignificant. Paul himself, for all the obvious prominence he had in the early Christian church, was a fine example of this. When the Christians at Corinth quarrelled over the respective merits of Paul and Apollos, whose ministries had been the means of such great blessing in the city, Paul told them that this revealed tragic immaturity and went on, 'What, after all, is Apollos? And what is Paul? Only *servants,* through whom you came to believe – as the Lord has assigned to each his task. I planted the seed, Apollos watered it, but God made it grow. So neither he who plants nor he who waters is *anything*, but only God, who makes things grow' (1 Corinthians 3:5–7). Notice the two words I have emphasized: Paul says he is nothing but a servant and that at the end of the day a servant is nothing!

A few days after a great celebration organized by his friends in November 1888 to mark the fiftieth anniversary of his ordination, Dr Andrew Bonar, that mighty man of God, wrote a lovely letter to a friend who was unable to be present and ended that letter with these words: 'Your affectionate, aged, frail, unworthy, feeble, stupid brother, and fellow-servant of a glorious Master.' One can hardly imagine anyone writing like that today! But do we know anything of that spirit? Is it not true that we are incurably inclined to think of ourselves more highly than we ought? Do we not have an insatiable appetite for appreciation? I fear that many of us do. The Bible has a word for us:

> 'Your attitude should be the same as that of Christ Jesus:
> Who, being in very nature God,
> did not consider equality with God
> something to be grasped,
> but made himself nothing' (Philippians 2:5–7).

As Kenneth Wuest so aptly comments, 'The only person who had the right to assert his rights waived them.'

Yet whenever we assert ourselves, push ourselves forward or adopt an attitude of pride, we are deliberately or ignorantly forgetting that of ourselves we have absolutely nothing of which we *can* be proud. To see ourselves in the right perspective, we need to remember at least two things.

1. *We are owned by God.* Writing to the Christians at Corinth – and to us today – Paul says, 'You are not your own; you were bought at a price' (1 Corinthians 6:19, 20). Surely that should help us to put ourselves in our rightful place! Paul's words are particularly appropriate here because he is using language that would apply to the purchase of a slave, and a slave would not have had the luxury of choosing his own master, dictating the terms of his employment and then asking to be given credit for everything he did. It was the *master* who did the choosing, paid the price, sent the slave to work and had the right to expect loyal and humble obedience. Now see how closely that links in with the words of Jesus to his disciples: 'You did not choose me, but I chose you to go and bear fruit – fruit that will last' (John 15:16). Writing from Cambridge in 1883, the famous missionary C. T. Studd said, 'I had known about Jesus dying for me, but I had never understood that if he had died for me then I did not belong to myself. Redemption means buying back, so that if I belonged to him, either I had to be a thief and keep what wasn't mine, or else I had to give up everything to God. When I came to see that Jesus Christ had died for me, it didn't seem hard to give up all for him.' In the double sense of creation and redemption we are owned by God.

2. *What we owe to God.* In another passage written to the Corinthians, Paul asks, 'What do you have that you did not receive?' (1 Corinthians 4:7.) Have you ever stopped to think that question through? It is a great antidote to arrogance and a great help to humility! Of course, it is easy

to think of the things we *do* owe to God – life and liberty, health and strength, food and shelter, gifts and abilities, every answered prayer, every forgiveness of sin, every true source of joy, our certain hope of heaven. The list is endless; but Paul asks the question the other way round and challenges us to make a list of all the advantages and abilities, blessings and benefits we have that were *not* all given to us by the grace of God. It should take no more than a moment to realize that the answer to Paul's question takes only one word – *nothing*! Frances Ridley Havergal put it like this:

> Not your own, to him you owe
> All your life and all your love.
> Live that ye his praise may show,
> Who is yet all praise above.
> Every day and every hour,
> Every gift and every power,
> Consecrate to him alone,
> Who hath claimed you for his own.

All of this stems from the opening three words of James's letter, which show that he had a lowly consideration of himself.

2. He had a lofty conception of his Saviour
'. . . of God and of the Lord Jesus Christ'.

These words are, of course, true of every Christian, for the reasons we have already seen, but James may deliberately be using them to show that he stands in a direct line of succession to God's Old Testament spokesmen. These are collectively called '[God's] servants the prophets' (2 Kings 17:23); Abraham is referred to as '[God's] servant' (Psalm 105:6); Moses is called 'the servant of the Lord' (Joshua 14:7) and Joshua himself is given exactly the same title (Joshua 24:29). James was content to be called a slave, but his words carry with them the divine authority of the one he served.

Some people have suggested that the original words used here could be translated 'of Jesus Christ, who is God and Lord', but this is not only unnatural but unnecessary, because the deity of Christ depends no more upon this one verse of Scripture than it does upon any other. In his superb commentary on the Epistle of James, Thomas Manton says that, even as they stand, these words show Christ 'as an object of equal honour with the Father; and as the Father is Lord, as well as Jesus Christ, so Jesus Christ is God as well as the Father'. We can certainly not accuse James of giving Christ a minor position here, as he gives him as lofty a title as any other writer in the New Testament.

1. He refers to him as 'the Lord'. The word 'lord' is one of the most common in the whole Bible, the Greek word *kurios*. It occurs over 9,000 times in the Septuagint, the earliest translation of the Old Testament into Greek, and in the overwhelming majority of cases the reference is to God, the sovereign Creator and Lord of the universe. In the New Testament, *kurios* appears in over 700 places. Sometimes it is no more than a term of respect, such as in the parable of the two sons, where one replies to his father's order to go and work in his vineyard with the words: 'I will, sir [*kurios*]' (Matthew 21:30). At other times, it refers to an owner, or someone to whom service was due; but in the vast majority of cases it is used in a much higher sense, and supremely of God himself, such as in the apostle John's glorious vision of 'the Lord [*kurios*] God Almighty' (Revelation 21:22).

There can surely be no doubt as to the sense in which James is using the word here. This is no mere courtesy title, the kind of way in which he might have addressed a friend, an employer, or someone higher up the social scale. This is the language of deity; he is using the word in exactly the same way Thomas did when he saw the risen Christ and cried out, 'My Lord [*kurios*] and my God!' (John 20:28), and in the same way Jude did when he wrote of 'Jesus Christ our only Sovereign and Lord [*kurios*]' (Jude 4). For James, as for every other writer in the New Testament, the only title adequate for Jesus was the name given to God.

William Cowper captured the spirit of this in one of his fine hymns:

> My song shall bless the Lord of all,
> My praise shall climb to his abode;
> Thee, Saviour, by that Name I call,
> The great Supreme, the mighty God.

2. He refers to him as 'Jesus'. If in context the word 'Lord' points towards Christ's deity, then the word 'Jesus' reminds us of his humanity. It is the equivalent of the Old Testament name Joshua and was a common name in biblical times, Paul including in one of his letters greetings from 'Jesus, who is called Justus' (Colossians 4:11). The word 'Jesus' means 'The Lord is salvation', and this is perfectly reflected in the angel's message to Joseph when he said of Mary, 'She will give birth to a son, and you are to give him the name of Jesus, because he will save his people from their sins' (Matthew 1:21). The most stupendous truth the world has ever heard is locked into that one passage of Scripture, because it forges an unbreakable link between Bethlehem and Calvary. Jesus was not, as the title of a famous play puts it, 'the man born to be king'; he was 'the man born to be Saviour'. When the eternal Son of God entered the womb of the virgin Mary and took upon himself the soul and body that make up human nature, he did so not merely to display to a wondering world how life should be lived – though he did that to perfection – but in order to die in the place of sinners, bearing the punishment for their sins and securing salvation for all who put their trust in him. James would gladly join with every Christian in history in singing these words of a fifteenth-century hymn translated by John Mason Neale:

> Jesus is the name we treasure,
> Name beyond what words can tell;
> Name of gladness, name of pleasure,
> Ear and heart delighting well;
> Name of sweetness, passing measure,
> Saving us from sin and hell.

3. He refers to him as 'Christ'. The Greek word *Christos* translates the Hebrew 'Messiah', which literally means 'the Anointed One', and its use refers to the vast number of Old Testament prophecies which told of the time when God would send a great Deliverer into the world. For 400 years the prophets had been silent, but in the person of Jesus all the pieces of the prophetic jigsaw fell into place, so that the whole of the New Testament is an endorsement of

Andrew's ecstatic cry: 'We have found the Messiah' (John 1:41). In his birth, life, death, resurrection and ascension, Jesus fulfilled the promises God had made and untangled the threads of prophecy that ran throughout the Old Testament. In the words of Walter Chalmers Smith:

Earth for him had groaned and travailed
Since the ages first began;
For in him was hid the secret
That through all the ages ran –
Son of Mary, Son of David,
Son of God and Son of Man.

We have done no more than take a glimpse at these names, but even this has been sufficient to show that in using them James had a lofty conception of his Saviour. The question that needs to be asked is whether we share that conception. One of the great glories of evangelical Christianity – indeed one might call it *the* glory of evangelical Christianity – is the doctrine of justification by faith, and by faith alone, on the grounds of the death of the Lord Jesus Christ on Calvary's cross. But doctrine is no substitute for devotion and it is a shameful tragedy when Christians lose their sense of awe and give the impression that they have become pally with Deity. Justification *does* mean that we are right with God, but it does *not* mean that we are equal with him. His ways are still infinitely higher than our ways and his thoughts than our thoughts.

We need to carry this same lofty conception of our Saviour into our evangelism, too. When a friend of mine was still a young preacher he was given a piece of advice that I have never heard bettered: 'Young man, whenever you preach, be sure that you do two things – lift the Saviour high and lay the sinner low.' That advice was never more relevant than now. Some evangelism seems to me to run the risk of suggesting that there are ways in which a sinner can bring himself into the position where he will be acceptable to the Saviour, and then of bringing the Lord down in order to make him accessible to the sinner, so that one is eventually presented with the suggestion that two equals should come to an agreement. Beware of anything that remotely smacks of that kind of thing! Lift the Saviour high! Speak of his glory, his majesty and his power, as well as of his mercy, love and grace. Then lay the sinner low. Show him that he is not just unhappy or unfulfilled, but 'dead in . . . transgressions and sins' (Ephesians 2:1) and in need of a miracle of divine grace if he is ever to receive eternal life. Nothing makes a greater contribution to effective evangelism than high views of God. James had a lofty conception of his Saviour.

3. He had a loving concern for the saints

'To the twelve tribes scattered among the nations: Greetings.'

One of the loveliest pictures the Bible gives of the Christian church is to describe it as 'God's household' (Ephesians 2:19). Regardless of age, background, social status, colour or denomination, all Christians are members of the same family, bound together not by their selfish choice of each other, but by God's sovereign choice of them. Their vertical relationship to God is extended into a horizontal relationship to each other. It is fascinating to see the way in which this is expressed in the New Testament. Writing to the Ephesians, Paul rejoices about 'your faith in the Lord Jesus and your love for all the saints' (Ephesians 1:15). In an almost identical phrase addressed to the Colossians, he thanks God 'because we have heard of your faith in Christ Jesus and of the love you have for all the saints' (Colossians 1:4). There is a lovely rhythm in those relationships – faith in the Saviour; love for the saints. James has it, too, for having acknowledged his allegiance to God and to the Lord Jesus Christ, he immediately demonstrates his concern for his fellow Christians by sending them this letter of encouragement, to 'the twelve tribes scattered among the nations'. Those words suggest two things.

1. The pressing hand of Satan. The people to whom James was writing were 'scattered among the nations'. This translates a Greek phrase which would literally be rendered 'in the dispersion'. In one national disaster after another, countless thousands of Jews had been deported from their native Palestine and were scattered all over the Middle East, eventually becoming known as 'the Dispersion', and it is to Christians within these expatriated communities that James now writes. Commenting on this, Dr Louis E. Evans says, 'Those of the Dispersion were those in captivity, in slavery. Israel and Judah had been taken captive; they had been torn away from friends and country; they had suffered all the indignities of a conquered people. They were starving, homesick, the most loathed of men. Under the heel of the pagan conqueror it would be natural for them to cry out, "Where is God?" James writes to tell them!'

Many of these early Christians would have known something of the pressing hand of Satan. Uprooted from their own familiar surroundings, they lived under the double pressure of being Jews and Christians. Like their great Old Testament heroes, they were 'aliens and strangers on earth' (Hebrews 11:13). Yet this is a picture, and often a parallel, of the experience of God's people in every age. Paul warned the new converts in Asia: 'We must go through many hardships to enter the kingdom of God' (Acts 14:22). The Christian should expect to meet with difficulties, trials, temptations, oppression, misunderstanding and even rejection, to a greater or lesser degree. Anybody who suggests that once a person becomes a Christian his troubles are over is speaking from an empty head and a closed Bible! Jesus told his first disciples quite frankly that 'In this world you will have trouble' (John 16:33), and behind it all is the pressing hand of Satan.

2. The preserving hand of God. James calls his readers 'the twelve tribes'. His letter has become known as one of the 'general' or 'catholic' epistles, in the sense that it was not addressed to specific people known to the writer. We can be virtually certain that James did not have exactly a dozen congregations in mind, each one tracing its corporate ancestry back to one of the twelve tribes of Israel. Instead, he is writing not only to those Jewish Christians who had been driven out from their homeland, but to Gentile converts who as a result of their conversion had become part of what Paul calls 'the Israel of God' (Galatians 6:16). That seems to give added strength to his description of his readers as 'the twelve tribes', because the phrase speaks of unity, preservation, continuity. They may have been 'scattered', but they were still 'the twelve tribes'. They may have been split apart by satanic pressure, but they were held together by divine power! Surely that is a word for today! God's people may be oppressed, they may be persecuted, they may be in the minority, they may find the going hard, they may be ridiculed, they may be thought irrelevant by the world; but they are still 'the twelve tribes', held secure in the preserving hand of God. They are what Peter calls 'a chosen people, a royal priesthood, a holy nation, a people belonging to God' (1 Peter 2:9).

If you are a Christian, then these words – and indeed all of James's words – are for you. You are one of those upon whom God set his saving love. You are one of those whose place Christ took when he laid down his life for his sheep, and therefore one of those of whom he said, 'No one can snatch them out of my Father's hand' (John 10:29). You are one of those who are able to face every trial and difficulty, present or future, in the confidence that 'Neither death nor life, neither angels nor demons, neither the present nor the future, nor any powers, neither height nor depth, nor anything else in all creation, will be able to separate us from the love of God that is in Christ Jesus our Lord' (Romans 8:38, 39).

All of this finds a perfect echo in the very first word that James directly addresses to his hearers – 'Greetings'. The Greek word is *chairein,* which literally means, 'rejoice'! James will have some pretty straight things to say later on; he will not pull his punches when pointing out things that need to be put right in the lives of his readers. But he begins on a note of joy. He encourages his readers to look up, just as Jesus did when he told his hearers: 'Blessed are you when people insult you, persecute you and falsely say all kinds of evil against you because of me. Rejoice and be glad, because great is your reward in heaven' (Matthew 5:11, 12). James will develop this theme later, but his opening word crystallizes it perfectly. Whatever the circumstances, the Christian can rejoice and face the future with confidence, assured of the eternal faithfulness of God.

2.

Trials and temptations

'Consider it pure joy, my brothers, whenever you face trials of many kinds, because you know that the testing of your faith develops perseverance. Perseverance must finish its work so that you may be mature and complete, not lacking anything' (James 1:2–4).

In the Author's Preface to his *Commentary on the Epistle of James,* Professor R. V. G. Tasker writes, 'As part of the New Testament, the Epistle has a permanent message both for the Church as a whole and for each individual Christian . . . it may well be that few books are more relevant to the contemporary situation.' If those words are true of the epistle as a whole, then nowhere is that truth more clearly demonstrated than in the passage we are now going to study, which is a microcosm of everything James writes – vivid, direct, realistic, practical and stimulating. In an age when so much preaching and teaching is sterile, academic or sentimental, we need to hear what James has to say, not least because he gets right to the heart of our present-day situation with such remarkable relevance. Take these verses for instance: what do they have to say to us? I suggest that they say three things.

1. There is a relationship we ought to foster
'. . . my brothers . . .' (v. 2).

It is remarkable to notice that, either directly or indirectly, James calls his readers by this name no fewer than eighteen times and in fact virtually never addresses them in any other way. What a great deal that tells us about the man himself! A leader of the early Christian church, firmly established at the centre of the power base in Jerusalem, he immediately identifies with every one of his anonymous readers. He saw himself as a brother, not a boss. It was common practice for Jews to refer to each other as brothers, but there is no doubt that James is giving the word a much deeper significance. When he calls his readers 'brothers' he has in mind a relationship that is spiritual and not merely national, and the New Testament is crystal clear as to what is the root of that relationship. Writing of the Lord Jesus Christ, the apostle John says that 'To all who received him, to those who believed in his name, he gave the right to become children of God' (John 1:12), while Paul encourages the Christians in Galatia (who were not Jews, but Gentiles), by telling them, 'You are all sons of God through faith in Christ Jesus' (Galatians 3:26). There is nothing here of today's vapid conception of the 'universal brotherhood of man'. Instead, James is speaking of a relationship brought about by living faith in a common Saviour, who had died for their sins and brought them into the family of the forgiven. In a vivid phrase, Augustine of Hippo, one of the most outstanding theologians of all time, said that he and his friend Alipius were 'cemented with the same blood of Christ', and it is nothing less than this relationship that James has in mind here. The word 'brother' is the Greek *adelphos,* which literally means 'one born from the same womb', and the New Testament does not hesitate to employ physical analogy in order to emphasize the inseparability of Christians the one from the other – Paul tells the Christians at Rome: 'Just as each of us has one body with many members, and these members do not all have the same function, so in Christ we who are many form one body, and each member belongs to all the others' (Romans 12:4, 5).

Yet James is not content with establishing doctrinal truth. He wants to see it put into action and his whole letter is evidence of his loving concern for his fellow Christians and his determination to do all he possibly can for their spiritual welfare. No Christian can read the New Testament and escape the responsibility to follow his example. Jesus tells his inner circle of disciples: 'This is my command: Love each other' (John 15:17); Paul writes,

'Therefore, as we have opportunity, let us do good to all people, especially to those who belong to the family of believers' (Galatians 6:10); Peter exhorts us: 'Now that you have purified yourselves by obeying the truth so that you have sincere love for your brothers, love one another deeply, from the heart' (1 Peter 1:22); while John even sees the issue as a test of faith and says, 'We know that we have passed from death to life, because we love our brothers' (1 John 3:14). All James has done so far is to call his readers 'brothers', but already he is stirring us into action. There is a relationship we should foster.

2. There is a reality we ought to face
'. . . whenever you face trials of many kinds . . .' (v. 2).

James is one of the Bible's greatest realists and in writing of life's trials he uses the word 'whenever' and not 'if'! As long as he remains in this world, the Christian will be under pressure of one kind or another and it is highly significant that the down-to-earth James should devote the opening section of his letter to encouraging his readers to face the facts of life. The key word in the phrase we are studying is obviously 'trials', which translates the Greek word *peirasmos.* The root meaning of the word is 'to try, or prove' and the Bible uses it both in a good sense and in a bad one, that is to say, both of trials and temptations. James himself provides us with examples of both uses in the very section we have begun to study, which extends at least as far as verse 15, and the NIV translators seem to have got their choice of words exactly right. Here are the phrases concerned: 'Whenever you face *trials* of many kinds' (v. 2); 'Blessed is the man who perseveres under *trial* . . .' (v. 12); 'When *tempted,* no one should say, "God is *tempting* me." For God cannot be *tempted* by evil, nor does he *tempt* anyone; but each one is *tempted* when, by his own evil desire, he is dragged away and enticed' (vv. 13, 14). The two different words used here point us to the two distinct meanings of *peirasmos. Trials* are sent by God in order to make a person stand; *temptations* are sent by Satan to make a person fall. In testing you, God is aiming at your development; in tempting you, Satan is aiming at your disgrace. Yet it is important to notice that in both cases, the primary sense is the one of putting someone to the test.

Writing in *The New Bible Dictionary,* Dr J. I. Packer says this: 'The biblical idea of temptation is not primarily of seduction, as in modern usage, but of making trial of a person, or putting him to the test; which may be done for the benevolent purpose of proving or improving his quality, as well as with the malicious aim of showing up his weaknesses or trapping him into wrong action.' That being the case, there can be no further doubt that James is dealing with reality here. Trials and temptations are part and parcel of every Christian's daily life and James's 'whenever' gives us the opportunity of hammering out some basic biblical principles that will help us to face the problem. In doing so, I will use the word 'tests' to include both trials and temptations.

1. Tests will not be removed. In a passage that deserves the closest possible study, Paul reminds the Corinthians that temptation is 'common to man' (1 Corinthians 10:13), an inevitable and inescapable experience of life. It is simply no good looking on earth for a situation that only exists in heaven. Just as Christ's coming into the world did not banish temptation universally, so his coming into a person's heart does not banish it personally. While it is marvellously true that as Christians God has 'rescued us from the dominion of darkness and brought us into the kingdom of the Son he loves' (Colossians 1:13), we have not yet been removed from the sphere of Satan's influence. We have been taken out of his rule, but not out of his reach. In the same way, we must expect God-given trials to be part of life; the Bible even dares to say of the perfect man that 'He learned obedience from what he suffered' (Hebrews 5:8).

2. Tests will not be reduced. There is no suggestion in the Bible that life gets easier as a man gets better. We might almost say that the truth is exactly the reverse of this because, as Paul makes clear, 'In fact, everyone who wants to live a godly life in Christ Jesus will be persecuted' (2 Timothy 3:12). Although the primary reference there seems to be to trials, there is no doubt that the same principle applies to temptations. It is no mark of maturity to be unconscious of the devil's activities, or to feel that we can reach a stage in life when we are beyond temptation. In a fine little book *The Gospel in Genesis,* the nineteenth-century preacher, Henry Law, wrote these words about the devil's ceaseless activity: 'He never slumbers, never is weary, never relents, never abandons hope. He deals his blows alike at childhood's weakness, youth's inexperience, manhood's strength and the totterings of age. He watches to ensnare the morning thought. He departs not with the shades of night. By his legions he is everywhere, at all times. He enters the palace, the hut, the fortress, the camp, the fleet. He invests every chamber of every dwelling, every pew of every sanctuary. He is busy with the busy. He hurries about with the active. He sits by each bed of sickness, and whispers into each dying ear. As the spirit quits the tenement of clay, he still draws his bow with unrelenting rage.'

The fact that we cannot expect tests (be they trials or temptations) to be reduced can be proved clearly by remembering that some of the greatest heroes in Scripture faced their greatest tests – and in some cases suffered their heaviest defeats – not at the beginning of their walk with God, but far along the road of discipleship. Moses was the proven leader of God's people and renowned for his humility when he burst into petulant temper; David was established as the greatest king in Old Testament history when he was lured into lust; Peter, the man of rock, had already proved his courage many times before he crumbled into cowardice. Let us face reality! Although God has taken us out of Satan's ownership, he has not yet removed us from his sphere of operation and, although we may be making steady progress in both knowledge and grace, temptation will remain with us until our dying day, with no promise whatever that its power will be lessened.

3. Tests should be recognized. The one point I want to make here can be put in four words: temptation is not sin. How much morbid introspection and negative thinking is cleared away when this simple truth is grasped! No part of Scripture is more constructive or conclusive on this issue than that which describes the Lord Jesus as 'one who has been tempted in every way, just as we are – yet was without sin' (Hebrews 4:15). The wording here is exact and significant. Speaking of the tests we face, James says they are 'of many kinds'; speaking of the tests Jesus faced, the writer to the Hebrews says he was tempted 'in *every* way'. While it is true that some Christians seem to face a more than usual share of trials and temptations, we would not be overstating the case to say that all hell was let loose against Jesus while he lived here on earth. There was not a single avenue of temptation – moral, social, physical, material, mental or spiritual – along which he was not attacked. He was tempted to display himself to the crowds and despair when he was alone. He was tempted in the hour of shining triumph and in the hour of solitary tiredness. He was tempted to be proud, dishonest, selfish, impure and even to distrust his heavenly Father and to worship the devil, 'yet was without sin'. Those four words should give the death-blow to the devil's attempts to persuade sensitive Christians that temptation is sin. It is *not!* Instead, it is an opportunity to prove the power of God.

Before passing on to the next part of the phrase we are studying, we should look at one other word. James is telling us what we should do when we '*face* trials of many kinds'. The English word used here no doubt gives the general sense of what James is saying, but it may just miss one particular element. The Greek word is *peripipto,* which is only used in one other place in the New Testament. This is in the story of the Good Samaritan, where we are told that the man travelling from Jerusalem to Jericho 'fell into the hands of robbers' (Luke 10:30). The attack was not only savage; it was sudden. The traveller was making his way quietly along the road when without a moment's warning he was ambushed. Now this is the word James uses here and in doing so he gives us an advantage over the unfortunate traveller. We have been warned! Peter reinforces this and urges us, 'Be self-controlled and alert. Your enemy the devil prowls around like a roaring lion looking for someone to devour' (1 Peter 5:8). The testing that comes from trial or temptation is likely to hit us without a moment's warning and we should therefore seek to be prepared at all times. Speaking in the House of Commons in 1913 on the subject of naval defence, Winston Churchill said, 'We must always be ready to meet at our average moment anything that any possible enemy might hurl against us at his selected moment.' Outside of Scripture, it would be difficult to imagine better advice than that!

3. There are results we ought to find
'Consider it pure joy . . . because you know that the testing of your faith develops perseverance. Perseverance must finish its work so that you may be mature and complete, not lacking anything' (vv. 2–4).

On the face of it, the opening words here are quite extraordinary; they seem to make no sense at all. In the same breath in which he warns his readers that they will face 'trials of many kinds', James encourages them to 'consider it pure joy'. Surely that is the last thing we should be expected to do? The whole thing seems not so much a paradox as an absurdity. Yet when we read the New Testament we discover again and again the sheer joy that Christians expressed in the moments of their severest trials. When the apostles were flogged for preaching the gospel, we are told that they 'left the Sanhedrin rejoicing because they had been counted worthy of suffering disgrace for the Name' (Acts 5:41); when Paul and Silas were flogged and jailed at Philippi, we are told that even in the middle of the night they were 'praying and singing hymns to God' (Acts 16:25); Paul tells the Corinthians that 'In all our troubles my joy knows no bounds' (2 Corinthians 7:4); and in another astonishing word of testimony he tells the same readers: 'I delight in weaknesses, in insults, in hardships, in persecutions, in difficulties' (2 Corinthians 12:10).

But how could these men possibly rejoice in those circumstances, and how can James tell us to do the same? It is certainly not because we should look upon the tests of life as being a source of joy in themselves; Peter tells his readers that 'For a little while you may have had to suffer grief in all kinds of trials' (1 Peter 1:6). Nor is James glibly suggesting that when faced with trials and temptations we might as well grin and bear it. He is not saying, in the words of one of yesteryear's more banal songs, 'Powder your face with sunshine, put on a great big smile.' James is offering spiritual counsel, not superficial cosmetics. What is more, he is doing so on a perfectly reasonable basis; he says we are to '*consider* it pure joy'. The original word is *hegesasthe,* whose basic meaning is something like 'to lead before the mind'. It is the word used by Paul, who after listing all the religious advantages he had had as the result of his strictly orthodox Jewish background, tells the Philippians, 'But whatever was to my profit I now consider loss for the sake of Christ. What is more, I consider everything a loss compared to the surpassing greatness of knowing Christ Jesus my Lord, for whose sake I have lost all things' (Philippians 3:7, 8). What Paul is saying is that he has come to a settled conclusion after carefully weighing up all the factors involved. This is the word James is using here. He is not asking us to fall about in mindless mirth when under spiritual attack; he is saying that when these tests come we can face them with joy if we think carefully about the results which they can be the means of achieving. But what are these results? James mentions three.

1. Solid proof. '. . . the testing of your faith . . .' As we shall discover as we go further into his letter, James has a constant concern that those who claim to have a living faith should demonstrate that their claim is valid, in other words, that their faith is real. It is precisely this concern that makes him say that the real Christian can find joy in trials and temptations, because they are instruments for proving the validity of his faith. 'Testing' is a word one would have used about assessing the purity of metal. Perhaps a good equivalent today would be the testing of the metal used in the construction of an aircraft to ensure that it is capable of withstanding the pressures and stresses of supersonic flight. Just as the quality of metal cannot be trusted until it has been tested, so there must be 'the testing of faith' before we can be sure that it is the real thing. The first result we should expect from trials and temptations is confirmation that our faith has been proved to be genuine.

2. Steady progress. '[The testing of your faith] develops perseverance.' This follows on naturally from what we have just seen. The testing of faith leads to the development of perseverance. For the Christian, trials and temptations are not only means for proving his faith but for improving his life, and the quality James singles out here is 'perseverance', one that is absolutely vital if he is to make spiritual progress. The Bible calls us to 'run with perseverance the race marked out for us' (Hebrews 12:1) and the obvious picture is not of a quick 100 metre dash, but of a moral marathon, lasting throughout the whole of life. This picture fits in well with what James is saying here, because, as R. V. G. Tasker puts it, 'A Christian must have staying power, and this can be developed only in the face of opposition.'

3. Spiritual perfection. Perseverance must finish its work so that you may be mature and complete, not lacking anything.' This makes it clear that perseverance is not the end of the story, it is only part of the means. The end product is that we might be 'mature and complete, not lacking anything'. God's desire for the Christian is not that he should stagger through life in a series of spiritual fits and starts, flashing out with the odd bright spot here and there and then sinking back into dullness and defeat. God's desire for the Christian is nothing less than that expressed by Jesus: 'Be perfect, therefore, as your heavenly Father is perfect' (Matthew 5:48). This is the spirit caught by James's three-part phrase: 'mature and complete, not lacking anything', a condition which he insists will come about not in a sudden, blinding moment of ecstatic experience, but through steady, lifelong perseverance.

But is such perfection *possible* in this life? The issue is much too complex to discuss in detail here, but the notes from C. Leslie Mitton's fine *Commentary on the Epistle of James* will at least set our thinking in the right direction: 'It is a feature of our common faith that once a man is a Christian his aim should be to become a "perfect" Christian, and though the calling is so high as to be frightening, it is not for us to try to whittle it away in order to make it easier . . . If by perfection is meant the complete elimination of every fault, then it becomes a mocking word, because weakness of temperament and errors of judgement will continue with us to the end. But if by perfection we mean "loving God with all our heart, mind, soul and strength" and "loving our neighbour as ourselves" then this is undoubtedly the aim of every true Christian.'

Yet even that is not the end of the story. The glorious truth is that every Christian in the world is 'predestined to be conformed to the likeness of [God's] Son' (Romans

8:29). Although the concept is utterly beyond our understanding, the day will come when 'we shall be like him, for we shall see him as he is' (1 John 3:2). Equally beyond our understanding is the way in which God is using trials and temptations, problems and pressures, pain and suffering to bring about part of that staggering transformation. The nineteenth-century hymnwriter John Mason Neale put it in these words:

The trials that beset you,
The sorrows ye endure,
The manifold temptations
That death alone can cure:

What are they but his jewels
Of right celestial worth?
What are they but the ladder
Set up to heaven on earth?

O happy band of pilgrims,
Look upward to the skies,
Where such a light affliction
Shall win you such a prize.

3.

The way to get wisdom

'If any of you lacks wisdom, he should ask God, who gives generously to all without finding fault; and it will be given to him. But when he asks, he must believe and not doubt, because he who doubts is like a wave of the sea, blown and tossed by the wind. That man should not think he will receive anything from the Lord; he is a double-minded man, unstable in all he does' (James 1:5–8).

It has sometimes been suggested that the Epistle of James lacks cohesion, that the author jumps haphazardly from one subject to another with no apparent rhyme or reason. One critic says, 'It is difficult, if not impossible, to extract from James a continuous or coherent plan or scheme,' while another suggests that the epistle is 'not so much a chain of thoughts or beads as it is a handful of pearls dropped one by one into the hearer's mind'. I am not sure that I agree! While it is true that the epistle does not contain the vast sweeps of closely argued doctrine that we find, for instance, in Paul's much longer letter to the Romans, it would be perfectly reasonable to see it as containing no more than ten major sections, which seems fair enough in a letter of something approaching 5,000 words, especially as some of those sections themselves are not so totally disconnected from those around them as appears at first sight.

The passage we are now to study gives us a good example of this, because although it seems to deal with at least two new subjects, there is a very definite connection with what went before. James has an interesting technique of linking his teaching together by the deliberate use of identical or similar words, and he does so here. At the end of our last study, we saw him urging his readers to aim for the quality of life where they were 'not *lacking* anything' (v. 4). Now, we see his very next sentence beginning with the words: 'If any of you *lacks* wisdom . . .' (v. 5). In fact, the original connection would have been even more obvious, because the NIV, along with many other versions, unfortunately omits to translate the little Greek word *de* which means 'but'. All of this now takes us into the text, which we can examine under two headings.

1. Both sides of a spiritual problem

'If any of you lacks wisdom, he should ask God, who gives generously to all without finding fault; and it will be given to him' (v. 5).

There is a sense in which this verse gives us a kind of balance sheet of the Christian's earthly situation as he battles against the trials and temptations of life, striving to develop that perseverance that will make him 'mature and complete, not lacking anything', and like all balance sheets, it contains assets and liabilities. Let us look at these in the reverse order.

1. The deficiency of human reasoning. 'If any of you lacks wisdom . . .' It is obvious that the key to understanding what James is saying here is to get at the meaning of the word 'wisdom', and it is equally clear that he means something much more than knowledge, intellectual ability, cleverness or education. Many people with those attributes have found them totally inadequate to deal with life's deepest problems or provide them with the power to deal with spiritual issues. During his education campaign in the nineteenth century, the Earl of Shaftesbury said, 'Education without instruction in religious and moral principles will merely result in a race of clever devils.' Then what is the meaning of 'wisdom' as James uses it here?

In his superb *Commentary,* the nineteenth-century Scottish preacher Robert Johnstone describes the biblical concept of wisdom as 'the grandest and rarest of the acquisitions possible to man', and the Bible itself certainly elevates it to an extraordinarily high position. It says that wisdom is 'better than strength' (Ecclesiastes 9:16) and 'better than weapons of war' (Ecclesiastes 9:18), that it is 'more profitable than silver and yields better returns than gold' (Proverbs 3:14) and that it is not only 'more precious than rubies', but that 'nothing you desire can compare with her' (Proverbs 3:15; 8:11). We shall study James's concept of wisdom later on in the epistle, but for the moment we can encapsulate its meaning like this: wisdom is the God-given insight into our human circumstances and situations that enables a man to see God's will, coupled with a whole-hearted desire to see it done.

That being so, it is obvious that biblical wisdom is something that man desperately needs and equally clear that it is something the unconverted man never has: 'The man without the Spirit does not accept the things that come from the Spirit of God, for they are foolishness to him and he cannot understand them, because they are spiritually discerned' (1 Corinthians 2:14). But we must remember that the Christian is equally incapable of making right judgements by merely human reasoning. Part of the Holy Spirit's ministry in the life of the Christian is to wean him away from trusting only in his rational resources and to make him look and listen for another, higher wisdom. How practical all of this is! You have to make an important decision and two or more courses are open to you. Very carefully you weigh up the pros and cons from a rational viewpoint. The issue seems to lean in one particular direction. So far so good; but unless your ultimate decision is governed by what James later calls 'the wisdom that comes from heaven' (3:17) it will certainly be the wrong one. The same is true in the matter of temptation, seduction to sin: as Spiros Zodhiates puts it in *The Behaviour of Belief,* his comprehensive volume on the Epistle of James, 'Unless there is within us that which is above us, we shall soon yield to that which is about us'! There is a fatal deficiency in merely human reasoning.

2. The sufficiency of divine resources. '. . . he should ask God, who gives generously to all without finding fault; and it will be given to him.' The obvious inference is that God has wisdom to give and Scripture bears this out again and again. To give just one example, Daniel cries out, 'Praise be to the name of God for ever and ever; wisdom and power are his' (Daniel 2:20). Wisdom, in its most perfect sense, is one of God's attributes; God *is* wisdom. But James is not so much concerned with arguing out the doctrine of God's wisdom; what he really wants to get across is that divine wisdom is available to the Christian as he faces life's trials – and what a tremendous encouragement that is! And its truth comes across with even greater impact when we notice that James gives it a triple emphasis.

In the first place he speaks of 'God, who gives'. If the words were translated in their original order, the phrase would read 'the giving God', and would capture exactly the glorious truth that the God we worship is the one of whom the psalmist can rightly say, 'You open your hand and satisfy the desires of every living thing' (Psalm 145:16). Yet this is the language of faith. The unbeliever sees God not with an open hand but with a clenched fist, hard, stern and demanding. The story is told of an old woman who lived alone. She was so poor that she found it difficult to pay the rent to keep a roof over her head. One morning, the local minister called to see her. He knocked at the door several times but as there was no reply he went away. That afternoon, he called again and getting no reply at the door, he looked in at the window. The old woman sat huddled over a few smouldering embers in the fireplace. When she looked up and saw him, she immediately went to the door and welcomed him in. 'I called this morning,' he said, 'but there was no reply.' 'Oh, I heard you knocking,' she answered, 'but I thought you had come to collect the rent.' It is characteristic of the unbeliever to make the same kind of mistake about God; he sees him 'coming to collect', whereas he is always longing to give.

James now adds a second phrase and says that God gives 'generously to all'. The Greek for 'generously' is *haplos,* one of the root meanings of which is 'singleness'. Paul uses the corresponding adverb when exhorting slaves to obey their masters with 'sincerity of heart' (Colossians 3:22) and this helps us to understand James's meaning. God not only gives generously but genuinely, not only with an open hand but with a full heart. To clinch the point, James adds yet another phrase and says that God gives 'without finding fault'. In context, the meaning is that God does not give according to our worthiness or gratitude, nor does he withhold from blessing us because we ask too much or too often. His giving is governed by his nature, not ours. John Calvin suggests that James adds this particular phrase 'lest anyone should fear to come too often to God. Those who are the most liberal among men, when anyone asks often to be helped, mention their former acts of kindness, and then excuse themselves for the future . . . There is nothing like this in God; he is ready to add new blessings to former ones without any end or limitation.'

Here, then, are both sides of a spiritual problem. Basically, man is deficient in wisdom; he simply does not have the necessary resources to cope with life's problems and pressures. But God does and he is willing to give them, continuously, generously and graciously. Then what should man do in such a situation? The answer to that question is obvious and James supplies it: 'he should ask'. That leads us into the remainder of the passage we are studying.

2. Basic secrets of successful prayer

'But when he asks, he must believe and not doubt, because he who doubts is like a wave of the sea, blown and tossed by the wind. That man should not think he will receive anything from the Lord; he is a double-minded man, unstable in all he does' (vv. 6–8).

The phrase 'successful prayer' may sound a little presumptuous, but surely it in no way exaggerates the kind of prayer that James has in mind! After all, he does say that if a man lacking wisdom asks God for it 'it *will* be given to him' (v. 5). If it does sound too simple, it is almost certainly because we are not taking into consideration the conditions which James now mentions.

1. Our prayer must be a fact. 'But when he asks . . .' Notice that James does not say, 'But *if* he asks . . .'! God has promised the result but only if the man in need produces the request. It has been said that 'The real secret of prayer is secret prayer', and if that is over-simplifying things, it does at least get rid of a lot of pious humbug. It is so easy to talk about prayer, to say how much we believe in it, to say how important it is, but the crucial question is this: do we pray? Surely it must be one of the most pathetic paradoxes in Christendom that while we evangelicals set such store by the glorious doctrine of justification by faith and revel in the truth that we have free access to God without the need of any human mediator, it is almost universally true that our prayer meetings are the most poorly attended functions in our church programmes! But let us not be satisfied to generalize. Is the paltry attendance at prayer meetings not a reflection of the private devotional lives of the church members? And is their devotional life not an accurate thermometer of their spiritual health? It has been said that 'What a man is on his knees before God, alone, that he is, and no other.' Where does that put you? Are you so caught up with your other 'Christian activities' that you are making the miserable mistake of confusing programme with progress?

It is said of the saintly Robert Murray M'Cheyne that 'He dwelt at the mercy-seat as if it were his home.' That tribute reminds one of the psalmist's words: 'He who dwells in the shelter of the Most High will rest in the shadow of the Almighty' (Psalm 91:1). An old Arabic translation of the last part of that verse puts it like this: 'will always be in touch with the almightiness of God'. Yet the issue is so vitally important that we can be forgiven for adding two further reasons why we should pray.

The first is that *the way of prayer is open.* When Jesus died on the cross, we are told that 'The curtain of the temple was torn in two from top to bottom' (Matthew 27:51). This was a dramatic visual aid to show that the Old Covenant was at an end and the barrier between God and man removed. The door shut by man's sin was opened by Christ's sacrifice. By his death he bought the right for every Christian to have instant, constant access to the heart of God and to his throne of grace. If only all Christians could grasp this truth! The devil cannot prevent God answering our prayers, so he does all he can to prevent us asking and he often does so by twisting the truth that we are not worthy to ask. Now that certainly is true! If we were only entitled to pray when we were worthy to do so, when we could bring to God a standard of obedience and holiness that entitled us to be answered, then we would never be able to pray at all. The devil knows this perfectly well and all too often he drags the Christian into thinking along these lines: 'What's the use of praying? I feel such a hypocrite. I feel so far away from God. How can I pray when I am backsliding like this? How can God possibly listen to someone like me?' But that kind of thinking is nothing less than the devil's device. The fact of the matter is that however weak, helpless, depressed or sinful you are, however out of touch with God you feel, however long it has been since you feel you really got through to God in prayer, you *can* come to him and you can come *now.* That torn curtain tells you that you need no religious ceremony, no elaborate preparation, no ecclesiastical ritual, no costly sacrifice, no human mediator. The way of prayer is open.

The second reason why we should pray is that *the worth of prayer is obvious.* It is impossible to read the Bible or the biographies of Christian heroes outside of its pages without realizing the obvious worth of prayer. Prayer substitutes man's weakness with God's strength, man's ignorance with God's wisdom, man's emptiness with God's fulness, man's poverty with God's wealth, man's impotence with God's omnipotence. Writing about the effectiveness of prayer, John Chrysostom, the fourth-century Bishop of Constantinople said, 'The potency of prayer has subdued the strength of fire, it has bridled the rage of lions, hushed anarchy to rest, extinguished wars, appeased the elements, expelled demons, burst the chains of death, expanded the gates of heaven, assuaged diseases, dispelled frauds, rescued cities from destruction, stayed the sun in its course, and arrested the progress of the thunderbolt. There is an all-sufficient panoply, a treasure undiminished, a mine which is never exhausted, a sky unobscured by clouds, a heaven unruffled by the storm. It is the root, the fountain, the mother of a thousand blessings'! It is no wonder that towards the end of his letter, James writes, 'The prayer of a righteous man is powerful and effective' (5:16). Not only *can* we come to God in prayer but we *should* come. Our prayer must be a fact.

2. Our prayer must be in faith. 'But when he asks, he must believe . . .' Nobody can read the New Testament with an open mind and fail to see the tremendous premium it places on faith. We are told that 'Without faith it is impossible to please God' (Hebrews 11:6), while Paul in effect sums up the whole philosophy of Christian living when he says, 'We live by faith, not by sight' (2 Corinthians 5:7). On the specific subject of prayer, the New Testament is equally adamant. Jesus says, 'If you believe, you will receive whatever you ask for in prayer' (Matthew 21:22), and again, 'Therefore I tell you, whatever you ask for in prayer, believe that you have received it, and it will be yours' (Mark 11:24).

These promises seem so astonishing that we need to be clear that we understand what James means. Faith is not to be thought of as an additive that somehow gives more impetus to our prayer. It is the essential attitude of heart of the person who prays. We are not to think that we can ask for anything that catches our fancy, add something called 'faith' to our petitions in the way that we would stick a stamp on an envelope and then be sure that our requests will be answered. Nor must we think of faith as a hopeful shot in the dark or a step into the unknown. When the Bible speaks of praying in faith, it does not mean having faith in prayer. Nor does it mean having faith in a proposition. It means having faith in *a person.* Our faith is not to be in the hope that we can pray well enough, nor in the assumption that the theoretical 'laws' of prayer will work if we do. Believing prayer is the prayer of a man utterly convinced of the power, love, grace and mercy and *faithfulness* of God to whom he is praying. My emphasis is deliberate, for there are many times when our prayers can be specifically linked to the promises of God revealed in the Scriptures. In Robert Keen's fine words,

> How firm a foundation, ye saints of the Lord,
> Is laid for your *faith* in his excellent Word!

Without developing it further, this means that the greater our knowledge of God, as revealed in the Bible, the more certain our faith will be. To put it more intimately, the more we know of God's likes and dislikes, the more will our prayers be according to his will – and in the last analysis it is only the prayer that is according to his will that he has pledged himself to answer. In one of his books, E. Stanley Jones shares how this truth came across to him: 'In prayer I seldom ask for *things*; more and more I ask for

God himself, for the assurance that his will and mine are not at cross-purposes, that we are agreed on all major and minor matters. I know then, if this is so, I will get all the things I need.' Looked at in this way, faith becomes not the absence of knowledge, but the application of the knowledge we have. Faith is invisible but it is not irrational because it is faith in a God who is real and who reveals himself to the hungry heart. Our prayer must be in faith.

3. *Our prayer must be firm.* '. . . and not doubt, for he who doubts is like a wave of the sea, blown and tossed by the wind. That man should not think he will receive anything from the Lord; he is a double-minded man, unstable in all he does.' In this passage James is reinforcing by a negative argument what he has already said positively. The word 'doubt' comes from the Greek verb *diakrino* which carries with it the thought of two or more things being separated from each other. With that background, it is not difficult to catch the meaning of the word, nor to apply it to the subject of prayer. Curtis Vaughan says, 'The thought seems to be that when we pray we are not to oscillate between faith and unbelief, trust and distrust, pleading as it were with boldness, but all the time thinking that it is really useless to ask.' Does that ring a mournful bell? The Epistle of James has been likened to a picture-gallery, because he is so fond of using illustrations to drive home the point of what he is teaching. He uses the first of these illustrations here and says that the man whose mind is full of doubt when he prays 'is like a wave of the sea, blown and tossed by the wind'. Let me illustrate the illustration! For some years I lived in the town of Weston-super-Mare, on the west coast of England. The prevailing wind blew in from the Atlantic and whenever it gathered force it used to whip the water in the bay into a foaming frenzy. One only had to look out to sea on a windy day to gain a vivid impression of James's meaning and to realize the sad truth that to pray without real faith and conviction was to pray without power. But what are the winds that can blow a man off course when he comes to pray?

One is the wind of *unsound doctrine.* Paul says that God's purpose for his people is that they should be 'no longer infants, tossed back and forth by the waves, and blown here and there by every wind of teaching and by the cunning and craftiness of men in their deceitful scheming' (Ephesians 4:14). This underlines something we have already seen, and that is that the prayer of faith is firmly based on a knowledge of God's nature and will. There is therefore a direct link between our knowledge of the Scriptures and prayer that is firm in faith.

Another is the wind of *unusual difficulty*. When Paul was on his way to Rome, the ship in which he was travelling ran into a treacherous hurricane from the north-east. After three days, the ship was in danger of breaking up and as one eye-witness reported it, 'We finally gave up all hope of being saved' (Acts 27:20). At that point Paul called everyone together and told them that the previous night an angel had told him that although the ship would run aground, everyone aboard would be saved. Then he added, 'So keep up your courage, men, for I have faith in God that it will happen just as he told me' (Acts 27:25). Paul's faith was not a case of whistling in the dark, nor was it something based on his own human assessment of the circumstances; it was the outcome of his personal relationship with God and of the word that God had spoken to him. God may not send us an angel to show us his chosen way for us to come safely through our trials and temptations, but he has given us the unchanging Scriptures, and the better we know their teaching, the more likely we are to have the firm faith that refuses to be shaken by the storms of life and enables us to pray effectively.

Having shown the conditions for effective prayer, James uses three sad phrases about the man who fails to fulfil them. In the first place, he is *unsuccessful*: James says, 'Let not that man think that he will receive anything from the Lord.' He is like a man making a series of telephone calls through the operator only to have every call met with 'I'm sorry, there's no reply.' Few things are more disheartening to the Christian than a sense of failure in prayer. In the second place, he is *uncertain*: James calls him 'a double-minded man'. The original word is the Greek *dipsuchos,* which James uses again (in the plural) in 4:8. Its literal meaning is 'one who has two souls'. It gives us a pathetic picture of a man who wants the best of both worlds. He wants to trust in God and in himself and finds himself torn in two at the very centre of his being. Finally, he is *unsteady:* James says he is 'unstable in all he does'. Exactly as we should expect, the man with a divided heart leads a distracted life. There is an instability that seeps into everything he does because his life is not controlled by the steadying wisdom that comes from God. No wonder Robert Johnstone describes him as 'a poor, miserable, ignoble character . . . utterly incompatible with the enjoyment of true peace through God's favour and fellowship'.

These verses not only give answers; they raise questions. Do we recognize our lack of wisdom, or are we living on our wits? Are we willing to submit to God's purposes for our lives? Do we pray as we should? Do we have a steady faith, grounded in a growing knowledge of the Word of God? Whatever our honest answers might be, Charles Wesley's words will not be out of place on our lips:

> Come in thy pleading Spirit down
> To us who for thy coming stay;
> Of all thy gifts we ask but one,
> We ask the constant power to pray;
> Indulge us, Lord, in this request;
> Thou canst not then deny the rest.

4.

Lift up your hearts!

'The brother in humble circumstances ought to take pride in his high position. But the one who is rich should take pride in his low position, because he will pass away like a wild flower. For the sun rises with scorching heat and withers the plant; its blossom falls and its beauty is destroyed. In the same way the rich man will fade away even while he goes about his business. Blessed is the man who perseveres under trial, because when he has stood the test, he will receive the crown of life that God has promised to those who love him' (James 1:9–12).

In his spiritual classic *A Serious Call to a Devout and Holy Life* William Law wrote, 'How ignorant . . . are they of the nature of religion, the nature of man and the nature of God, who think a life of devotion to God to be a dull, uncomfortable state, when it is so plain and certain that there is neither comfort nor joy to be found in anything else!' Although James has some stern and uncompromising things to say in the course of his letter, it is interesting to notice that in the opening part of it he repeatedly sounds a note of joy. As we saw, the very first word addressed to his readers – 'Greetings' – actually means 'Rejoice!' Then his very next words are 'Consider it pure joy . . .', even though he writes in the context of trials and temptations. Coming now to verses 9–12, James returns to the same theme, though using different words. He says that a poor Christian should 'take pride' in his position, then that a wealthy Christian should do the same and finally adds, 'Blessed is the man who perseveres under trial.' The point James is daring to make is that joy is meant to be the normal experience of every Christian, whatever his circumstances, because of his unconditional confidence in the overruling power and unchanging goodness of the God in whom he has come to put his trust. The Puritan preacher Walter Cradock once said, 'Take a saint, and put him into any condition, and he knows how to rejoice in the Lord.' James will help us to understand why that should be true! In the passage now before us he takes general issues and focuses them in personal terms by telling us of three people who can lift up their hearts in grateful and confident joy.

1. The man in poverty

'The brother in humble circumstances ought to take pride in his high position' (v. 9).

In any context except a spiritual one, this statement would be quite ridiculous, particularly when we look at the specific words used. The Greek word translated 'in humble circumstances' is *tapeinos,* which literally means 'one who does not rise far above the ground, while the words 'high position' come from the Greek word *hupsos,* which literally means 'height'. Now what an absurdity we seem to have, because if we paraphrase what James is saying, using the primary meanings of these two key words, we arrive at this statement: 'Let the brother who does not rise far above the ground take pride in the height he has reached!' In purely material terms, this makes no sense at all. For most people there is a feeling that happiness goes hand in hand with prosperity, as do misery and poverty. But James is not speaking in material terms; he is speaking about a 'brother', someone who has become a Christian, and what he is saying is that having become a Christian, he should never look at his poverty in the same light again. His material position may not in fact change. He may remain 'not far above the ground' (we might even say 'not far above the breadline!') but in spiritual terms his salvation has raised him to a 'high position'.

James says that the poor convert can 'take pride' in his position. The Greek verb is *kauchastho,* which in its good sense speaks of exuberant rejoicing, such as when Paul says, 'We rejoice in the hope of the glory of God'

(Romans 5:2) and 'We also rejoice in God through our Lord Jesus Christ, through whom we have now received reconciliation' (Romans 5:11). Those quotations already give more than a hint of the high position to which a Christian is raised, but the Bible speaks of many other features of it. Here are just three, chosen because of their special application to a person with very little in the way of this world's goods.

1. He has a new wisdom. It has often been true that poverty and ignorance have gone together, or that limited means have restricted a person's opportunities for education. Many of the very poor early Christians would certainly have lacked the knowledge and sophistication of their richer contemporaries. But as we saw in an earlier study, knowledge and wisdom are not the same thing. In 1860, the philosopher Jeremy Bentham said, 'If we can get universal and compulsory education by the end of the century, all our social and political and moral problems will be solved.' But how wrong he was! Man needs something higher than knowledge before he can conduct his own life along the right lines, let alone make a significant moral and spiritual impact on society. He needs 'wisdom', that is to say spiritual insight, and that wisdom is not a matter of natural education but supernatural revelation.

This is not, of course, to despise education or knowledge. A Christian has a duty to equip himself as thoroughly as he can for his life's work. But even if after the best of his efforts he finds himself at the lower end of the social scale and without the benefits that higher education can sometimes bring, he can rejoice that God has given him the great gift of spiritual insight, 'a wisdom that . . . God destined for our glory before time began' (1 Corinthians 2:7). That wisdom enables him to see his social and material position in its right perspective for the first time. Paul gives a vivid example of this when writing to the Corinthians: 'Were you a slave when you were called? Don't let it trouble you . . . For he who was a slave when he was called by the Lord is the Lord's freedman' (1 Corinthians 7:22). This is exactly the kind of thing that James is saying here. As Robert Johnstone comments, 'Amid the depressing influences of poverty, the Christian is to keep his eye fixed on his *real* dignity, and glory in it. His present low position is merely in external things, and consequently temporary, and is appointed him because his heavenly Father sees poverty to be needful for the good of his soul.' In today's acquisitive age, only biblical wisdom can see things in that light!

2. He has a new wealth. One occasionally reads of poor people, or at least people in quite ordinary circumstances, who suddenly hear that a wealthy relative has died, leaving them a vast fortune. In a moment of time they become millionaires, not because of a lifetime of effort, nor as the result of industrious ingenuity, but simply because they have entered into the benefits of somebody else's death, through which they inherited a fortune. In some instances, it is literally a case of rags to riches. In a spiritual sense, this is what happens when a person becomes a Christian. The Bible says of unconverted people, 'All of us have become like one who is unclean, and all our righteous acts are like filthy rags' (Isaiah 64:6). Even the wealthiest sinner is spiritually bankrupt, devoid of anything that can make a contribution towards his salvation. The poorest Christian, on the other hand, can come to the Bible and read that in Christ he has been 'enriched in every way' (1 Corinthians 1:5). His, too, is a story of rags to riches, but with a much deeper significance.

3. He has a new wardrobe. I remember a time when a friend of mine, although having only a limited income, always seemed to be very well-dressed. I could never understand how she managed it, until one day she told me, 'I have a wealthy friend who keeps on sending me what she buys for herself but then does not bother to wear'! Now as we saw in Isaiah's words, the sinner's wardrobe is pretty pathetic! Even the best moral and spiritual clothing he can find is 'like filthy rags' in God's sight. The Christian, on the other hand, has a new wardrobe. To begin with, he has been given the robe of justification, so that he is clothed with Christ's righteousness. Throughout the rest of his earthly life, and on into eternity, he can claim this glorious promise as his own: 'Blessed are they whose transgressions are forgiven, whose sins are covered. Blessed is the man whose sin the Lord will never count against him' (Romans 4:7, 8). But God also gives the Christian a complete outfit for daily living, namely the potential for living a holy life. Notice the way Paul uses just this kind of language in describing some of the items included in the Christian's wardrobe: 'Therefore, as God's chosen people, holy and dearly loved, clothe yourselves with compassion, kindness, humility, gentleness and patience. Bear with each other and forgive whatever grievances you may have against one another. Forgive as the Lord forgave you. And over all these virtues put on love, which binds them all together in perfect unity' (Colossians 3:12–14). Only the Christian has the resources to be spiritually well-dressed!

To sum up, then: however poor a Christian may be financially or materially, he can rejoice in the fact that God has raised him to a position where he has a new wisdom (the gift of spiritual insight denied even to the wealthiest of unconverted men), a new wealth (unlimited spiritual resources at his disposal because of his union with Christ) and a new wardrobe (the exhilarating potential of pleasing God in his daily life).

2. The man with plenty

'But the one who is rich should take pride in his low position, because he will pass away like a wild flower. For the sun rises with scorching heat and withers the plant; its blossom falls and its beauty is destroyed. In the same way the rich man will fade away even while he goes about his business' (vv. 10, 11).

Here is a man in exactly the opposite circumstances and they can be summed up in one word: he is 'rich'. Now the Bible nowhere condemns riches, but it spells out the dangers of prosperity again and again. It speaks of 'the deceitfulness of wealth' (Matthew 13:22); it says, 'Let not . . . the rich man boast of his riches' (Jeremiah 9:23); it warns that 'The love of money is a root of all kinds of evil' (1 Timothy 6:10); it even says that 'It is hard for a rich man to enter the kingdom of heaven' (Matthew 19:23).

This gives us exactly the biblical background we need to understand what James is saying, which is that the rich convert should rejoice that his conversion has given him an entirely new perspective. There is an implication that his whole outlook on life had been geared to things he could weigh, see, feel, touch, count or take to the bank. Now, he realizes the folly and futility of that kind of thinking. He has been brought into a 'low position', one in which he realizes that, for all of the great reputation his wealth gave him in society (and, no doubt, in his eyes), he was really no more than a hell-deserving sinner, entirely dependent upon the mercy of God for his salvation and for any other blessings of eternal value.

But the rich convert should also have a new perspective on his possessions. When a London newspaper offered a prize for the best definition of money, the winning entrant's definition was 'Money is an article which may be used as a universal passport to everywhere except heaven and as a universal provider of everything except happiness.' This, says James, is what the rich convert ought to realize and he drives home his point with an illustration of a wild flower which looks beautiful for a little while but, under the blazing heat of the Middle East sun, soon 'withers', 'falls' and is finally 'destroyed'. 'In the same way,' James says, 'the rich man will fade away even while he goes about his business.' The man who puts his trust in earthly values and material possessions is a fool, because he is trusting the temporary. By a happy coincidence, the central verse in the Bible is one that says this: 'It is better to take refuge in the Lord than to trust in man' (Psalm 118:8). No man has life in proper focus until he grasps that truth.

In his fine little book *The Tests of Faith* Alec Motyer has such an excellent comment on this whole passage that I can do no better than to quote it at length. Having properly placed the passage in the context of wisdom, he says, 'The poor man is enabled to go on with God in spite of the adverse circumstances of poverty because the wisdom from on high has opened the glories of heaven to him, and he counts them richer than all the trials of earth. And the rich man is enabled to go on with God in spite of the snares and enticements of wealth, because wisdom from on high has opened his eyes to the real state of earthly things, how perishable they are, how unsatisfactory they are in the long run. Wisdom opens the eyes both to the glories of heaven and to the hollowness of earth.'

3. The man under pressure

'Blessed is the man who perseveres under trial, because when

he has stood the test, he will receive the crown of life that God has promised to those who love him' (v. 12).

This statement takes us back in thought to verses 2–4, where James specifically deals with the subject of perseverance, but it also has obvious links with the passage we have just been studying. The poor Christian is under certain pressures because of his poverty and the rich man because of his wealth. In this sense they are both 'under trial'. One is tempted to doubt God because he has so little and the other to desert God because he has so much. Yet James has a final word of encouragement for every Christian under trial and that is that when his last trial is over 'he will receive the crown of life that God has promised to those who love him'. Paul uses similar language when he says that having 'fought the good fight', 'finished the race' and 'kept the faith', he looks forward to 'the crown of righteousness, which the Lord, the righteous Judge, will award to me on that day – and not only to me, but also to all who have longed for his appearing' (2 Timothy 4:8); and so does Peter when he promises his Christian readers that 'When the Chief Shepherd appears, you will receive the crown of glory that will never fade away' (1 Peter 5:4).

James gives no explanation of this 'crown of life' and it would therefore be pointless to speculate. But surely the bare promise is enough to make the Christian long for it? The Bible tells us that when Stephen, the first Christian martyr, was being stoned to death, he 'looked up to heaven and saw the glory of God, and Jesus standing at the right hand of God' (Acts 7:55). The Christian under trial can also look up to heaven and, while his vision will be different it will be no less certain, for the 'crown of life' is something which God himself has promised. Robert Rowland Roberts expressed it like this:

> Far off I see the goal;
> O Saviour, guide me;
> I feel my strength is small;
> Be thou beside me:
> With vision ever clear,
> With love that conquers fear,
> And grace to persevere,
> O Lord provide me.

5.

Sin from start to finish

'When tempted, no one should say, "God is tempting me." For God cannot be tempted by evil, nor does he tempt anyone; but each one is tempted when, by his own evil desire, he is dragged away and enticed. Then, after desire has conceived, it gives birth to sin; and sin, when it is full-grown, gives birth to death. Don't be deceived, my dear brothers' (James 1:13–16).

These verses form a critically important segment of James's opening message on the tests of life, those constant pressures we described in chapter 2 as 'trials and temptations'. As we saw then, he uses one basic word for both – the Greek noun *peirasmos* – which serves to remind us that all trials have in them an element of temptation and all temptations have in them an element of trial. They all raise the question, as Albert Barnes puts it, as to 'whether we have religion enough to keep us'. Yet although they are identified *with* each other, they are not identical *to* each other and the distinction comes across very clearly in the passage before us.

Before we get into the text, three introductory things might be helpful. The first is to notice that the NIV translators have rightly switched from using the words 'trials' (v. 2) and 'trial' (v. 12) to the words 'tempted', 'tempting' and 'tempt' in this passage, capturing exactly the distinction we have just seen. The second is to notice that James also makes an interesting switch, from nouns to verbs, as he moves into an intensely practical area of life. The third is to notice James's words in verse 16: 'Don't be deceived, my dear brothers.' There is no way of telling with certainty whether James intended us to link this on to the end of verse 15 or the beginning of verse 17, but it seems to me that that very word 'deceived' fits so well into the passage before us that this is where it ought to be. James is about to make a crucially important point, and he urges us to be certain that we are crystal clear in our thinking on the issue.

Now to the text, which we can look at under three headings.

1. Definite reality
'When tempted . . .' (v. 13).

The general principle here has already been covered in our study of verse 2, and that is that the tests of life are a matter of 'when' and not 'if'. Here, the primary reference is clearly to temptation, incitement to sin, and James wants us to be in no doubt that it is an experience from which nobody is exempt. There is a very real sense in which all of life is a test, and much of that testing comes in the form of enticement to evil. What is more, we must expect the Christian to be the subject of sharper and subtler temptations than the unbeliever. When a person becomes a friend of God, he becomes an enemy of Satan, and can expect to be attacked at any time, at any level and along any avenue. The Christian who thinks otherwise and who imagines that he will gradually outgrow temptation as he matures in the faith has already fallen into one of the devil's subtlest traps. In Matthew Henry's words, 'The best of saints may be tempted to the worst of sins,' and to face up to that sobering fact is to face up to reality.

2. Defective reasoning
'. . . no-one should say, "God is tempting me." For God cannot be tempted by evil, nor does he tempt anyone' (v. 13).

Woven into everything James has written so far has been the majestic truth of the providence of God. It is God's sovereign use of man's trials to produce maturity and holiness that can cause the Christian to face them with 'pure joy' (verse 2); only a sovereign God can give 'generously to all' (verse 5); only he can reward faithfulness with 'the crown of life' (verse 12). Yet the devil can twist even that truth in man's mind and bring him to the position where he begins to rationalize his failure like this: 'God created all things, so God must have created man's evil impulses and is therefore responsible for the sin in my life.' Appalling as this sounds, it is precisely the line of thinking behind Adam's pathetic attempt to shift responsibility from himself after his fall into sin. Faced with the accusation of having disobeyed God, he blurted out, 'The woman *you put here with me* – she gave me some fruit from the tree . . .' (Genesis 3:12). What a terrifying index it is of the depravity of the human heart that in a moment of crisis, when things go seriously wrong, when a man has a bad moral fall, or makes a fatal mistake, he can not only seek to avoid all personal blame, he can actually flash his fist in God's face and say that *he* is responsible!

But James nails that lie immediately with two swift blows, which draw their power from the nature and character of God. The first statement James makes is that 'God cannot be tempted by evil,' and its relevance to the point is obvious. If God did in fact tempt men to commit sin, he would himself have yielded to the temptation to do so, but James rules the very possibility right out of court. The verb he uses is *apeirastos,* which could be translated 'unversed or unexperienced in evil'. God has no experience of trafficking in evil, his eyes are 'too pure to look on evil' (Habakkuk 1:13) and temptation is a subject not directly related to him in any way. In Thomas Manton's quaint phrase, '[God's] providence is conversant about sin without sin, as a sunbeam lighteth upon a dunghill without being stained by it.' James sums all this up in one simple statement: 'God cannot be tempted by evil', but it is a dazzling diamond of truth, every facet of it sparkling with spiritual brilliance. Think of some of its implications.

1. His person can never be defiled. On my way to speak at a meeting in a town hall in the south of England some years ago, I remember seeing a young man in the foyer and, though I had never seen him before, I remember having a distinct mental impression: 'That man is unclean.' A couple of hours later, when the rally was over and I was leaving the building, a steward told me that a man wanted to speak to me. To my great surprise, he then introduced me to the man I had noticed on the way in! We found a quiet room somewhere and soon he was telling me his story – a girl, a developing friendship and now immorality that had got out of control and was wrecking their lives. I have no idea why I should have been given a sense of the truth about that young man before I ever met him; what I do know is that, in the translated words of a French proverb, 'Sin makes ugly.' It scars and stains, leaving its messy marks on mind and soul and sometimes even on the body. It dims the eye, loosens the grip, defiles the man. But God can never be defiled, because he cannot be tempted by evil. Do we ponder this glorious truth deeply and gratefully enough? It is one thing to grow in our knowledge of God's power and wisdom, but do we grow in our appreciation of his perfect holiness? There can be no real worship until it includes an awesome sense that the one before whom we bow is 'altogether lovely' (Song of Songs 5:16).

2. His purposes can never be deflected. I have long been convinced that the devil is never very worried when Christians make promises to God. He knows perfectly well that the high and holy resolution, made in the emotional heat of the moment, can so easily be deflected into compromise and even into miserable defeat. Even while Peter was promising Jesus, 'I will never disown you' (Mark 14:31), a sharp-eyed maid was coming on duty and the fire was being lit in Caiaphas' courtyard. There would be ways to deflect Peter!

But God's purposes can never be deflected, because he cannot be tempted with evil. When in an hour of darkness for God's people the heathen cried out, 'Where is their God?' (Psalm 115:2), the psalmist's triumphant reply was 'Our God is in heaven; he does whatever pleases him' (Psalm 115:3). The eternal purposes of God can never be deflected. There is no qualifying clause in Paul's statement that God 'works out everything in conformity with the purpose of his will' (Ephesians 1:11). God sometimes moves in the dark, but he is never in the dark as to where he is moving!

3. His perception can never be dulled. Ours can! How many times have we made a wrong decision, adopted a wrong attitude, missed a vital opportunity, because our perception was dulled by sin, and not least by the sin of being out of sensitive touch with God? Yet these things are never true of him! Because he can never be tempted and touched by sin, there is never a moment when he does not know, understand and appreciate our precise circumstances and our exact need. In the words of the psalmist, 'He determines the number of the stars and calls them each by name. Great is our Lord and mighty in power; his understanding has no limit' (Psalm 147:4, 5). Get a grip of that – not just cold, analytical, critical knowledge, but warm, loving, compassionate understanding that is always moving to meet you at the point of your personal need!

4. His power can never be diminished. The Bible faithfully records how directly and devastatingly sin robs men of power. Lot chooses the plain and the people of Sodom (Genesis 13:10–13) and soon he is just a pathetic, unconvincing has-been (Genesis 19:14). Samson breaks his solemn vow and the tiger becomes a toy (Judges 16:25). The disciples, invested with power to cast out evil spirits, are reduced by disobedience from men of wonders to men of words (Mark 9:28, 29).

But the sin that saps the Christian's power can never touch the Christian's God. The ravages of sin cannot affect him because they cannot touch him. God is never weakened, is never 'off-colour' or 'one degree under', is never less than omnipotent. Paul told the Ephesians that the power of God is 'like the working of his mighty strength, which he exerted in Christ when he raised him from the dead and seated him at his right hand in the heavenly realms, far above all rule and authority' (Ephesians 1:19–21), and reminded them that it was precisely *that* power that is now being exercised 'for us who believe' (Ephesians 1:19). What an exhilarating concept that is!

5. His promises can never be devalued. The word devaluation comes home with special force in days of economic difficulty, but it also has permanent spiritual implications. How often have our own promises, to God or man, been devalued by faithless rationalism, clever compromise or some other unworthy means?

How vastly different are the ways of God! At the dedication of the temple in Jerusalem, Solomon's opening words to the congregation were these: 'Praise be to the Lord, who has given rest to his people Israel just as he promised. Not one word has failed of all the good promises he gave through his servant Moses' (1 Kings 8:56). Nearly 3,000 years later, we need not alter a single word of that statement! As we look back over our own lives, think of God's providential dealings with us, marvel at the way in which we were brought to Christ and ponder the provision of our every need, surely we can never dispute the fact that we have a God whose promises can never be devalued?

All of these truths flow from James's single phrase, 'God cannot be tempted by evil', a statement about God's nature. But notice that James now adds a statement about God's character, his nature in action, and says, 'Nor does he tempt anyone.' Once again, we must be absolutely clear about the sense in which James is using the verb here and remember that he is speaking of enticement to evil, not the broader concept of testing. Nobody can deny that God sometimes deliberately places men into situations that are potentially dangerous – the classic case being Jesus himself, who 'was led by the Spirit in the desert, where for forty days he was tempted by the devil' (Luke 4:1, 2), but he never does so with a malevolent purpose. As Thomas Manton puts it, 'God useth many a moving persuasion to draw us to holiness, not a hint to encourage us to sin.' To lay the responsibility for human sin at God's door is defective reasoning. God may call you to endure difficulties, but he will never cause you to experience defeat. The blame lies closer at hand.

3. Decisive responsibility

'. . . but each one is tempted when, by his own evil desire, he is dragged away and enticed. Then, after desire has conceived, it gives birth to sin; and sin, when it is full-grown, gives birth to death' (vv. 14, 15).

As we shall see throughout his letter, James is a brilliant illustrator, drawing vivid pictures to press home the truth of what he is saying. Here, in explaining the origins of sin in a person's life, he uses the pictures of hunting, fishing and childbirth. We can trace the sequence of James's thinking with the help of four words.

1. A condition. '. . . his own evil desire . . .' James is immediately emphatic about where the responsibility lies – he writes about each individual person's '*own* evil desire'. There is no concession here to the kind of thinking which puts the blame for a man's wrong-doing on everyone but himself. Instead, James aligns himself with the rest of the Bible's plain teaching about the reality of original sin and the unpalatable fact that 'The heart is deceitful above all things and beyond cure' (Jeremiah 17:9). There can be no understanding of the universal phenomenon of sin without a recognition of man's total depravity. The Puritan preacher Thomas Browne was not exaggerating when he said, 'Our corrupted hearts are the factories of the devil.'

2. A consideration. '. . . he is dragged away and enticed.' The pictures here are metaphors taken from the worlds of hunting and fishing. The Greek word *exelkomenos* – translated 'dragged away' – is not found anywhere else in the New Testament, and pictures a wild animal being lured from safety into a place where it can be attacked or captured. The word *deleazomenos* – translated 'enticed' – pictures a fish attracted by the glint of something in the water, altering course and closing its mouth on the juicy bait, only to find that it concealed the deadly hook. Both illustrations are powerfully relevant. Inwardly, man has the desire and the potential to sin; outwardly, he is surrounded by enticements, allurements, temptations. As long as he resists these, he is safe, but it is this consideration, this toying with the idea, this allowing of the outward attraction to occupy a place in his mind, that moves him towards the fateful moment.

3. A conception. 'Then, after desire has conceived, it gives birth to sin.' In a vivid change of illustration, James now sees sin as the result of what Alexander Ross has described as an 'unholy marriage' between desire and opportunity, inclination and incitement. It is at this precise moment, when the will joins the desire in yielding to the temptation that the sinful thought or action is born, brought out into the open. This is the moment of what I have called decisive responsibility; as someone has rightly said, 'It takes two to make a successful temptation, and you are one of the two.' This is precisely the point that

James is making and he makes it crystal clear that nobody can escape the personal guilt involved in his acts of sin.

4. A conclusion. '. . . and sin, when it is full-grown gives birth to death.' It is interesting to notice that in the original Greek, the verb 'gives birth' is different from the one James used a moment ago, when he said that desire 'gives birth to sin'. The word used here is *apokuei,* which literally means 'ceases to be pregnant'. Do you see the powerful point of this? Pregnancy is by nature something that *must* cease. It must come to an end and produce the child that has been in the process of gestation during the preceding months. There is an awesome inevitability about pregnancy and this is exactly what James wants to get across to us. Sin always comes to an inevitable end and that inevitable end is what the Bible calls 'death'. The primary meaning of death is separation and the full biblical meaning of death is not only the separation of the soul from the body, but the eternal separation of man from God. This is the terrible, tragic conclusion to which all sin inevitably leads. In Paul's equally chilling metaphor, 'the wages of sin is death' (Romans 6:23).

The lessons from all of this are surely obvious. For the unconverted, there is an urgent warning to turn from sin before it is too late; for the Christian, there is the equally urgent responsibility to share with others the good news that although 'The wages of sin is death . . . the gift of God is eternal life in Christ Jesus our Lord' (Romans 6:23). Only in this glorious gospel is there a solution to man's greatest problem, which is the guilty sinfulness of his own corrupted heart.

6.

Gifts and the Giver

'Every good and perfect gift is from above, coming down from the Father of the heavenly lights, who does not change like shifting shadows' (James 1:17).

Nothing is ultimately more tragic than for a man to have a wrong conception of God, because that one gigantic error will pervade all his thinking and behaviour and at the end of the day point its fatal finger at his destiny. It is presumably for this kind of reason that James moves from the last words we studied to those now before us. In the previous passage, he was at pains to show that God is *not* the source of anything that is evil; now, he says that God *is* the source of everything that is good. Having pointed out error, he now underlines truth. This seems the most natural way of finding a context for this verse and it would accommodate perfectly the views of those who feel that the emphasis of verse 16, 'Don't be deceived, my dear brothers,' should be thrown forwards rather than backwards, as it would give it the sense of needing to be quite sure that one had the right assessment of the nature and character of God.

Now let us turn to the text, from which we can draw truth on three related subjects.

1. Human giving

'Every good and perfect gift . . .'

Literally translated, the original phrase reads: 'Every good *giving* and every perfect *gift* . . .', but most exegetes see this as no more than repetition used as a point of emphasis, and if this is the case, the NIV translators have lost little or nothing in choosing their shorter, more fluent phrase. There is, however, one minority rendering of the opening phrase which reads, 'All giving is good' and I would like to lean on that for a moment because it provides us with a very useful background against which to see the remainder of the verse. The point it makes is that there is a general element of good in all giving. A gift does not have to have a religious or spiritual context in order to have something good about it. Jesus made this clear when he said that 'You, then, though you are evil, know how to give good gifts to your children' (Matthew 7:11). A good gift can be made by a thoroughly bad man and our condemnation of his character ought not to make us automatically cynical about his generosity. Nevertheless, though the act of giving is itself good, all our human gifts are in fact marred in some way or another by our very humanity.

Think of some of the ways in which our giving can be spoilt.

1. It may not be sincere. There is such a thing as giving in order to get, speculating in order to accumulate! There is the kind of giving that is careful, crafty, calculated to fill our pockets rather than to empty them. Giving can sometimes be made to look like generosity when in fact it is ingenuity.

2. It may not be sensible. I remember once staying in a pastor's home over the weekend and, on Sunday morning, as I looked out of my bedroom window, I saw the next-door neighbour loading his golf clubs into his car and then driving off down the road, waving to his little son as he left. Later, I asked the pastor what this man was like. He replied, 'He is very well off, yet the home is not happy. He just lives for the golf course. He gives his wife and son every kind of gadget or toy they ask for, but he deprives them of himself as a husband and father.' Now we cannot condemn him for the gifts he made. There was an element of goodness in them, but his giving was not sensible. It was a pathetic substitute for the giving of himself.

3. It may not be sufficient. We hear an appeal for help, and after thinking about it carefully, we send off our cheque for £1 or £10, or whatever we think we should give. Fine! There is an element of good in that; there might even be generosity in it, perhaps to the point of sacrifice. Yet it is virtually certain that it will not be sufficient; the need at the other end will still not be met.

4. It may not be suitable. Most of us recognize this kind of gift – the presentation cigarette case given to the non-smoker, the shaving soap to the man who has 'gone electric', the sixth set of fruit spoons received as a wedding present! Good gifts, all of them, in the sense that they were generous, but all spoilt because they were not suitable.

Summing up, then, there are two things we can say about human giving: because it is *giving*, there is an element of good about it – 'all giving is good'; but because it is *human* giving, it is marred or limited in some way. It may not be sincere; it may not be sensible; it may not be sufficient; it may not be suitable. One thing is certain, and that is that it is limited by our very humanity. Now we can get to the heart of what James is saying in this verse.

2. Heaven's gifts

'Every good and perfect gift is from above . . . '

The word translated 'perfect' is the Greek *teleion,* which James has already used once, in verse 4. There he wrote that the object of persevering under trial was so that we might be '*mature* and complete, not lacking anything'. Those additional words could virtually be seen as an explanation of the first one and give us exactly the right sense of the word *teleion.* It describes the ultimate, something that cannot be bettered, and that is precisely what James means to say about heaven's gifts. In brilliant contrast to earthly giving, they are always sincere, always sensible, always sufficient and always suitable. They are free from all earthly alloy – perfect in every way. 'Perfect' is one of the Bible's favourite words in describing the nature, character and activity of God and several instances of its use spring immediately to mind.

1. His works are perfect. Addressing the whole assembly of Israel, Moses declared of God, 'He is the Rock, his works are perfect' (Deuteronomy 32:4). Here is one of the great distinguishing marks between something man does and something God does. Man's handiwork may look good on the surface; indeed, the work of a master craftsman might almost look perfect. But the closer you examine it, the more it will reveal those flaws and failures that are in one sense an exposition of the whole of human nature. The closer you examine anything made by man, the more imperfect you see it to be. By contrast, the closer you examine God's handiwork, the more do you see it to be perfect. Take a needle, for instance, one made by the most modern manufacturing process. To the naked eye, it is perfection itself, its smooth surface tapering to an exquisite point. Now put that same needle under a microscope. Immediately you can see that its surface is pitted and scarred and its point no better than a jagged stump. On the other hand, take a common flower. As you stop to admire it by a roadside, you might be tempted to say, 'Just look at that flower. It is perfect!' Now put it under a microscope and take a closer look! The perfection you saw in passing is as nothing compared with the perfection you now see, a miniature world of design and delicacy revealed in all its amazing intricacy. There is the principle: the closer you examine any work of God, the more you see it to be perfect.

Now what are God's greatest works? Surely these – the work of creation and the work of redemption, or, if you prefer, of creation and re-creation.

As far as the work of creation is concerned, listen to the recurring refrain of the first chapter of Genesis: 'God saw that the light was good' (v. 4); 'God saw that it was good' (v. 10); 'God saw that it was good' (v. 12); 'God saw that it was good' (v. 18); 'God saw that it was good' (v. 21); 'God saw that it was good' (v. 25) and finally, as if to underline and emphasize all of these statements, 'God saw all that he had made, and it was very good' (v. 31). God's work of creation was perfect!

And what of God's work of re-creation, of redemption? In an amazing prophecy concerning the Lord Jesus Christ, the prophet Isaiah wrote, 'After the suffering of his soul, he will see the light of life and be satisfied' (Isaiah 53:11). What a staggering sentence! Here we have a statement which says that at the end of time, when man's existence on this planet has finally come to an end, the eternal Son of God will look back on the whole vast enterprise, and especially at his own work of redemption, *and be satisfied!* This can only mean that he will judge his saving work on Calvary's cross to have accomplished everything God intended it to accomplish. Now that is a truly tremendous statement and it says something very important in response to the questions men raise on this issue: 'But what about the heathen who have never heard the gospel?' 'What about Christians who fail in their responsibility to witness faithfully?' 'What about children who die before reaching the age of discretion?' 'What about the mentally incapable?' Now those are vast questions and we dare not attempt to elude or trivialize them, but what we can say is that at the end of the day, God will be completely satisfied that his work of redemption is perfect, complete in every way, utterly beyond the complaint of man. 'His works are perfect!'

2. *His way is perfect.* Again, the words come direct from Scripture – 'As for God, his way is perfect' (Psalm 18:30)– and it is instructive to recall when it was that David wrote them. He had been through a time of great testing and trial, darkness and difficulty, misunderstanding and misery. Saul had hounded him from one place to another. Had David been able to choose out his own way, he would surely have chosen not to go the way of Saul's anger and militancy against him. Yet now he looks back on it all and says, 'As for God, his way is perfect.' What he is saying in effect is this: 'I have gone through the valley of the shadow, through the fire, through the deep waters, through the testing, and now I can see that all of these things have played a part in God's maturing work in my life.'

There comes a time in the life of every Christian when he finds a question-mark in his mind. Circumstances have turned sour, resources have dwindled, pressures have increased, faith has turned to fear and clarity to cloud. It is in times like these that we need to lean on words like this: 'As for God, his way is perfect'! Paulus Gerhardt's words, translated by John Wesley, turn our hearts in exactly the right direction:

> Leave to his sovereign sway
> To choose and to command;
> So shalt thou wondering own his way,
> How wise, how strong, his hand.

Far, far above thy thought
His counsel shall appear,
When fully he the work hath wrought
That caused thy needless fear.

3. His will is perfect. Paul tells us this, when he writes about testing and approving God's 'good, pleasing and perfect will' (Romans 12:2). Of course, this takes us back beyond even God's works and ways and into the hidden counsels of his own heart – and what deep rest the believer has when he meditates on the fact that the will of God, his sovereign, immutable purpose and design, is perfect in every detail and utterly incapable of change or deflection!

4. His Word is perfect. At the beginning of a truly majestic passage about God's Word, David says, 'The law of the Lord is perfect, reviving the soul' (Psalm 19:7), a statement which James emphatically underlines when he calls it 'the perfect law' (1:25). Quite apart from all its other implications, here is one reason why the Bible is never out of date, never out of touch, never out of context. It *is* perfect and remains so in all circumstances, and an acceptance of this truth is the starting point for biblical Christianity. As Dr J. I. Packer puts it, 'To defer to God's Word is an act of faith; any querying and editing of it on our own initiative is an exhibition of unbelief.' It is perfect!

Gathering all of these strands of truth together, we can weave them into this tremendous truth: *nothing good comes except from God and nothing except good comes from God.* His giving and his gifts are perfect in every way. Yet this all leads us back beyond the giving and the gifts to the Giver, which is exactly what James does.

3. The heavenly Giver

'. . . coming down from the Father of the heavenly lights, who does not change like shifting shadows'.

Before getting to the heart of this phrase, it is important to notice that the first verb is a continuous present participle, teaching us that God's good and perfect gifts are continually being poured out. As Spiros Zodhiates delightfully puts it, 'There is a perpetual rain and sunshine of gifts.' God is never less than generous, even when we are less than grateful!

Looking more closely at the rest of the verse, we can discover something about God's name and about his nature.

4. God's name. '. . . the Father of lights . . .' If you look out over a city at night you will see countless thousands of points of light, coming from homes, factories, street lamps, advertising signs and other places, yet all of them having one common source, one parent power. This is the kind of picture James is using here, and it is fascinating to see how it can be developed even beyond the one thing he has in mind.

God is the source of natural light. God's first spoken word recorded in the Bible was 'Let there be light' (Genesis 1:3) and the immediate obedience of the elements showed him to be the source of all natural light throughout the universe. David speaks to God of 'the moon and the stars, which you have set in place' (Psalm 8:3); while Amos even names some of them, and says that God 'made the Pleiades and Orion' (Amos 5:8). It is undoubtedly the natural light produced by the heavenly bodies that James has in mind here, but we can take his point further.

God is the source of intellectual light. When none of the wise men of Babylon could interpret King Nebuchadnezzar's dreams, they were summarily sentenced to death. Daniel, next in line for execution, held a prayer meeting with his companions Hananiah, Mishael and Azariah, and in answer to their prayers, God revealed the secret of the king's dreams to Daniel. The grateful Daniel's immediate response is recorded in the following words: 'Praise be to the name of God for ever and ever; wisdom and power are his. He changes times and seasons; he sets up kings and deposes them. He gives wisdom to the wise and knowledge to the discerning. He reveals deep and hidden things; he knows what lies in darkness, and light dwells with him' (Daniel 2:20–22). No truly wise man glories in his wisdom, but in the God who graciously gives it to him.

God is the source of theological light. Of course, God is the source of the Bible itself, of which the psalmist says, 'Your word is a lamp to my feet and a light for my path' (Psalm 119:105), but we need to go one step further than that and say that even with the light of Scripture burning before us, we would never be able to see it as light unless

God himself revealed its truth to us. This is vividly true of the unbeliever, of whom Paul says, 'The man without the Spirit does not accept the things that come from the Spirit of God, for they are foolishness to him and he cannot understand them, because they are spiritually discerned' (1 Corinthians 2:14). Unless the Holy Spirit makes the truth of the gospel clear to an unconverted person, all the preaching and praying in the world that might be brought to bear upon that person will not bring about his conversion. There must be that sovereign work of the Holy Spirit breaking into that person's darkened mind with the glorious light of the gospel.

Yet the Christian, too, is no less dependent upon the Holy Spirit for the revelation of divine truth from the sacred page, and we do well to remember this. As Evelyn Underhill has said, 'That which we know about God is not what we have been clever enough to find out, but what divine charity has secretly revealed.' It is God alone who is the source of theological light.

God is the source of spiritual light. By this I mean what we could call the practical outworking of the theological light. Peter tells his readers that they are to 'declare the praises of him who called you out of darkness into his wonderful light' (1 Peter 2:9), while Paul says, 'For you were once darkness, but now you are light in the Lord. Live as children of light' (Ephesians 5:8). To become a Christian is to become light instead of darkness, and of that light, the light of eternal life, God is the sole and sovereign source. In the matchless simplicity of the apostle John's words, 'God *is* light; in him there is no darkness at all' (1 John 1:5).

These are just some of the truths that flow from James's statement about God's name, 'the Father of the heavenly lights . . .', a phrase unique in Scripture, yet backed up by biblical teaching from Genesis to Revelation.

2. God's nature. '. . . who does not change like shifting shadows'.

This is a notoriously difficult phrase to translate, and there may be more rhyme than reason for the wording chosen by the NIV; though having said that, it does capture the spirit of what James is saying fairly well. Literally, the original phrase can be rendered 'with whom change or shadow due to turning has no place' and the picture is obviously taken from the natural heavens, to which James has already referred in calling God 'the Father of the heavenly lights'.

The sun gives light, but not always the same amount of light, because it does not always strike the earth at the same angle. The result is a constantly changing cycle – dawn, high noon, twilight, dusk. Again, the turning of earth and sun produce 'shifting shadows', lengthening and shortening as the various factors come into play. The moon too, constantly changes the amount of reflected light it beams to the earth, from the tiniest crescent to its full-globed glory. Then there are the phenomena of the eclipses of both sun and moon, when the light we receive is snuffed out altogether. When you think about it, it is difficult to imagine how James could have chosen a better subject to illustrate his point about 'shifting shadows', and he does so to direct our attention to the one bedrock truth that *God does not change.* Now I suggest that even if that particular truth was not written in Scripture, we would be driven to it by other biblical statements about God. Take the perfect holiness of God, for instance: that alone points to his immutability, his unchangeableness. As A. W. Pink puts it, 'God cannot change for the better, for he is already perfect; and being perfect, he cannot change for the worse.' Other biblical statements about God can be shown to point in exactly the same direction, but we have no need to lean on these inferences, whatever their merit. God himself says with brilliant clarity, 'I the Lord do not change' (Malachi 3:6). It would be impossible to put the truth more succinctly than that! Nor would it ever be possible to conceive of all the glorious implications in our lives of the fact that whatever our changing circumstances, feelings, moods, fears, hopes, desires, resources or powers, God, in Albert Barnes's words, 'is as if the sun stood in the meridian at noonday'.

But let me add one other word. While it is therefore true that life's shadows are never caused by God's turning, they may be caused by ours, by a change in our position. If you stand exactly under a street-lamp, no shadow is cast. Take one step away from the light and you will find a shadow in front of you. Not a very big one, but a shadow nevertheless, and one caused by your turning, or changing your position. Take a few more steps and the shadow grows, more steps and it grows bigger still. Go far enough away and you will be in total darkness. Are there shadows in your life because you have changed position, stepped away from being right under the light of God's revealed will? If there are, then turn back! Turn back to the place of love, trust, submission and obedience and, even as you do so, rejoice in the truth that you are turning back to an unchanging, faithful Father. To recognize this is to revel in the truth of T. O. Chisholm's well-known words:

> Great is thy faithfulness, O God my Father,
> There is no shadow of turning with thee;
> Thou changest not, thy compassions they fail not,
> As thou hast been, thou for ever wilt be!
>
> Great is thy faithfulness! Great is thy faithfulness!
> Morning by morning new mercies I see.
> All I have needed thy hand hath provided;
> Great is thy faithfulness, Lord, unto me!

7.

God's greatest gift

'He chose to give us birth through the word of truth, that we might be a kind of firstfruits of all he created' (James 1:18).

In the last chapter we were concerned, in our study of James 1:17, with the subjects of gifts and giving and with the name and nature of the God who, as James had said earlier, 'gives generously to all' (1:5). Coming now to verse 18, we find James writing about the greatest gift any man can receive from the hand of his Maker, the gift of the new birth which places him into the family of God. Peter rejoices in the same wonderful experience when he says, 'Praise be to the God and Father of our Lord Jesus Christ! In his great mercy he has given us new birth into a living hope through the resurrection of Jesus Christ from the dead' (1 Peter 1:3), and every true Christian will join in the rejoicing!

In the particular edition of the Authorized Version that I used for many years, Ephesians 2 was headed 'What we were by nature and what we are by grace,' and I never tired of reading it through and noting the vivid contrasts between the state of the unbeliever and the state of the believer. Virtually the whole chapter is a development of the two little phrases 'at that time' (Ephesians 2:12) and 'but now' (Ephesians 2:13). The contrasts become even more striking if we set them out like this:

'separate from Christ' (v. 12)	– 'in Christ Jesus' (v. 13)
'excluded from citizenship' (v. 12)	– 'fellow-citizens with God's people' (v. 19)
'foreigners' (v. 12)	– 'members of God's household' (v. 19)
'far away' (.v. 13)	– 'brought near' (v. 13)
'hostility' (v. 16)	– 'peace' (v. 17)

Yet the most startling contrast Paul mentions in that chapter is this: 'But because of his great love for us, God, who is rich in mercy, *made us alive* with Christ even *when we were dead* in transgressions' (Ephesians 2:4, 5). Notice exactly what Paul says has happened to those of us who have become Christians. He does not say merely that we have been spiritually improved, or morally strengthened, or given a new vision or outlook. He does not say (as some still do) that becoming a Christian is a matter of having one's inherent goodness fanned into a flame. Not at all! Paul says that what has happened to us is nothing less than a miracle. We were made alive when we were dead! Anything less than that is less than a biblical appreciation of what God has done for us in bringing us to himself. What is more, it points out man's total inability to bring himself to God. It tells us that no amount of religion, sincerity, church-going, generosity or service can bridge the fatal gap between man and his Maker. As Jesus told the highly religious Nicodemus, 'I tell you the truth, unless a man is born again he cannot see the kingdom of God' (John 3:3), and in the verse now before us, James tells us three things about this stupendous miracle, God's greatest gift to man.

1. The infinity of the new birth
'He chose to give us birth.'

Those words alone are sufficient to tell us that the new birth is something that is essentially infinite. It cannot be contained in terms of earth, time and space, but belongs to heaven, eternity, infinity. Let me focus what I mean in three ways.

1. It is infinite in its being. The story is told of an evangelist visiting a school and being asked by one of the students, 'What was God doing before he created heaven?' The evangelist thought for a moment and then replied, 'I am not sure, but I think he must have been creating hell for people like you who ask questions like that!' I have never been asked that particular question – though I have often used it to buy a little time in answering others! But I have often been asked questions which must seem equally baffling: 'Why did God create the world?', 'Why did God create man?' 'Why did God create *anything*?' Now in facing most questions that begin, 'Why did God . . .?' it is better to keep your mouth shut and be thought a fool than to open it and remove all possible doubt! However, the Bible does in fact give us an answer here. It comes from the lips of the celestial elders, who bow before the throne of God and cry, 'You are worthy, our Lord and God, to receive glory and honour and power, for you created all things, and *by your will* they were created and have their being' (Revelation 4:11). The solitary, simple, sublime reason the Bible gives for the existence of everything in all creation is that it came into being by God's will, because he chose that it should. For the unbeliever, no further explanation is possible; for the believer, no further explanation is necessary.

Then why does God re-create men, bring them to the glorious experience of the new birth of which our verse speaks? James's words give us the answer: 'He chose to give us birth . . .' The only biblical explanation for creation is that God chose to create; the only biblical reason given for re-creation is that God chose to re-create. The initiative, the impulse, the incentive all come from God and are affected by nothing whatever outside of his own perfect will. That is why I am saying that the new birth is infinite in its being – it is wholly rooted in God.

Now I would imagine that most Christians would come at least part of the way here. All Christians would surely agree that their salvation is not the result of their own merit or works or effort. But there are many who would add, 'Now I know that I did not earn my salvation, but without getting too involved in deep and dark theology, doesn't the Bible speak about God's foreknowledge? And doesn't that mean that God saw in advance those who of their own free will would take the initiative of repenting and believing, and then, having seen that these people would take that initiative, he decreed that these would be the people who would be saved?' Now there are many people who think along those lines, and I must confess that there was a time when I not only thought like that, but preached it. Yet, surely, the whole idea is basically unsatisfactory for one simple reason – it places the Creator in the hands of the creature. God's purposes to save men are suspended until men decide that they will be saved. But that makes the grace of God dependent upon the will of man and once grace becomes dependent upon *anything* it ceases to be grace. The very essence of grace is that it is free, independent, sovereign. Nobody makes this clearer than the apostle Paul, who, having said that we were 'chosen by grace' (Romans 11:5), adds, 'And if by grace, then it is no longer by works; if it were, grace would no longer be grace' (Romans 11:6). In an earlier chapter, he emphasized another aspect of the same truth, quoting God's word to Moses that 'I will have mercy on whom I have mercy, and I will have compassion on whom I have compassion' (Romans 9:15) and adding the comment: 'It does not, therefore, depend on man's desire or effort, but on God's mercy' (Romans 9:16).

However much it may be maligned and misrepresented by some, the doctrine of God's unconditional election of individual men and women to salvation is firmly embedded in Scripture, and our biblical duty is not to contest it but to concede it. Commenting on Romans 11:6, W. S. Plumer writes, 'If any say that this doctrine is a high mystery, so it is. Adoration and praise rather than a bold prying curiosity become us on many a theme of revealed truth. Let us bow in aweful submission to [God's] sovereign and adorable will and glorious majesty. Let us not cavil, nor dispute with God.'

The new birth, then, is infinite in its being, in its very essence. It is utterly beyond the ways and will of man.

2. It is infinite in its beginning. That may sound like a contradiction in terms, but let me explain. When we speak of a physical birth we have in mind a moment when independent physical life began – a birthday as we call it. We tend to use the same kind of language about the new birth. When we speak of someone becoming a Christian, our thinking tends to centre around a moment of decision, of response, of faith, of commitment. It hinges on a date on a calendar. But if our thinking ends there, it stops a long way short of the whole truth, which is that although the new birth necessarily takes place in a moment of time, it is set in motion, as it were, before time began. It is infinite in its beginning because its beginning lies in infinity, and

Scripture bears consistent testimony to this fact. The prophet Jeremiah records God as saying, 'Before I formed you in the womb I knew you, before you were born I set you apart; I appointed you as prophet to the nations' (Jeremiah 1:5). Paul extends this same staggering truth to every Christian when he writes, 'For [God] chose us in [Christ] before the creation of the world' (Ephesians 1:4). These two passages alone should be enough to show us that while there is undoubtedly a moment of faith, of personal commitment to Christ, that is merely the outworking of a miracle of regeneration that had its genesis in the eternal will of God before time even began to exist. Here is truth utterly beyond our understanding, but brought within our glad grasp by the gracious ministry of the Holy Spirit. The new birth is infinite in its beginning.

3. It is infinite in its blessing. Locked into the words we are studying is another vital aspect of truth that is often overlooked, and that is the subject of Christian assurance. More Christians than we will ever know still find themselves wrestling with a question that we could frame like this: 'Is it possible for me, at any time, to fall away so badly that I will be rejected by God and be eternally lost?' Now if the answer to that question is 'Yes' the cause would obviously be sin. But if sin causes a believer to be lost, then no believer is ever saved and the argument is reduced to absurdity.

The truth of the matter lies along an entirely different line. The Christian's eternal salvation depends not upon his choice of God but upon God's choice of him. That is where it rests. So much evangelistic preaching and counsel to those young in faith centres around *our* decision, *our* response, *our* faith, and this unhealthy, unbiblical emphasis is a prime cause for the appalling casualty rate in the work of evangelism today. It is also one of the main reasons why so many Christians spend an inordinate amount of time morbidly wondering whether they will manage to hold onto God and make it to heaven. Yet all of this comes from a failure to grasp the truly biblical doctrine of salvation which says that *God chose us* and that our security lies there.

How often one particular verse is misused in this

connection! A professing convert is told to hold on to the words of Jesus that 'Whoever comes to me I will never drive away' (John 6:37), but while those words are undoubtedly true, the real basis of assurance lies in the words that come immediately before these: 'All that the Father gives me will come to me . . .' In a majestic transaction made between the Father and Son before time began, every single one of God's elect people was included in a covenant of redemption infinite in its blessing, eternal in its span. The reason no Christian can be snatched out of the Father's hand is that it was the Father who placed him there! When a person becomes a Christian he does so through God's initiative; not without the preaching of the gospel, not without the offering of Christ, not without repentance, not without faith – but ultimately by divine gift. In David's words, 'The salvation of the righteous comes from the Lord' (Psalm 37:39) and it is this glorious truth that can make us speak of the infinity of the new birth.

2. The instrument of the new birth
'. . . through the word of truth . . .'

This 'word' is obviously the gospel, and Paul uses identical language on at least two important occasions. The first is where he speaks of '. . . the hope that is stored up for you in heaven, and that you have already heard about in the word of truth, the gospel that has come to you' (Colossians 1:5). The second is where he reminds his readers that their faith in Christ came 'when you heard the word of truth, the gospel of your salvation' (Ephesians 1:13). Elsewhere, he even goes so far as to say that the gospel is 'the power of God for the salvation of everyone who believes' (Romans 1:16) and it would surely be impossible to state more clearly than that the indissoluble link between the Word of God and the salvation of man. The Bible is the mighty weapon which the Holy Spirit uses to bring light and life to men in darkness and death – and it is indispensable! W. S. Plumer is not overstating the case when he writes, 'The annals of this world tell us not of one instance where a sinner was converted, sanctified, filled with pious hopes, made willing to suffer in the cause of God, and enabled mightily to triumph over the world, the flesh and the devil, over fears, temptations and death itself, except by the gospel of Christ.' It is the gospel alone which is the word of *truth*; it tells us the truth about God, man, sin, heaven, hell, repentance, faith, life and death. It is completely true, constantly true, convincingly true and convertingly true and nothing can compare with its purity and power.

Let me emphasize this. The longer I continue in full-time Christian service, the more I see of evangelism and of that which goes under the name of evangelism, the more convinced I become of that power that resides only and exclusively in the naked Word of God, and to all of those involved in the ministry of the gospel, and especially those working among people with little or no religious background, I would issue this impassioned cry: 'Never put yourself into the position where you have to evacuate the message in order to accommodate the method!' Unless the Word of God is there, unless your work has about it the authoritative ring of scriptural truth, unmixed with the glamour, glitter and gimmickry of so many modern methods, you have no warrant for claiming for your efforts the promise that 'Faith comes from hearing the message, and the message is heard through the word of Christ' (Romans 10:17). It is the Word of God alone that is the instrument of the new birth.

3. The intention of the new birth
'. . . that we might be a kind of firstfruits of all that he created'.

In this fascinating phrase, James is borrowing language from the Old Testament, where the Israelites were required to 'bring to the priest a sheaf of the first grain you harvest' (Leviticus 23:10). The likelihood is therefore that James's primary use of the metaphor is to state that he and his fellow first-century Christians were tokens of an amazing harvest of Christians to follow in succeeding generations. Paul uses exactly the same picture when describing the risen Christ as 'the firstfruits of those who have fallen asleep' (1 Corinthians 15:20). Yet there is surely a wider application that can be made to include Christians of every age, including our own, and if we do this, two things are immediately suggested.

1. We have a great dignity. The firstfruits constituted something very special, a part of the crop set apart for God in a particular way, and Christians, too, can humbly claim that God has set them apart in a special way from all the rest of humanity. In Paul's words, 'Our great God and Saviour, Jesus Christ . . . gave himself for us to redeem us from all wickedness and to purify for himself a people that are his very own . . .' (Titus 2:13, 14). What a dignity is ours as children of God! We may be pilgrims here on earth, but we are not tramps! We are the people of God and as such have a great dignity.

2. We have a great duty. Privilege and responsibility are always found to be two sides of the same coin and, just as nobody on earth could have a greater privilege than to be a child of God, so no people on earth have greater responsibilities than Christians. Those responsibilities are numerous – we could almost say innumerable – yet two of them in particular spring obviously and biblically to mind.

The first is *gratitude of heart.* Thinking back over our study of this particular verse, how can we be other than grateful to God for all that he has done for us? We were chosen in Christ before the creation of the world, we were raised to spiritual life when we were still dead in our sins and we have been brought to a position of eternal security, 'born again, not of perishable seed, but of imperishable, through the living and enduring word of God' (1 Peter 1:23). It is surely no wonder that Paul tells us that we should be 'overflowing with thankfulness' (Colossians 2:7). Gratitude of heart should be one of the distinguishing marks of a Christian, and, as Andrew Bonar delightfully puts it, 'We should be always wearing the garment of praise, not just waving a palm-branch now and then.'

The second is *godliness of life.* Reminding his covenant people of blessings they had once known, God said, 'Israel was holy to the Lord, the firstfruits of his harvest' (Jeremiah 2:3). Notice the lovely link there – Israel was a holy harvest! The confluence of those two concepts is a striking reminder to us that, as chosen children of God, as his firstfruits, our lives should be marked by a holiness that immediately distinguishes us from the rest of mankind. What is more, that distinctive holiness should flow as a practical demonstration of our gratitude, the two of them blending together in a living anthem of worship. God is never more properly thanked for his goodness than by our godliness.

The more we ponder this one brief sentence in James's letter, the more our hearts should be drawn out in the spirit of these words by Gerhard Tersteegen, translated by John Wesley:

Being of beings! May our praise
Thy courts with grateful fragrance fill;
Still may we stand before thy face,
Still hear and do thy sovereign will;
To thee may all our thoughts arise,
Ceaseless, accepted sacrifice.

8.

Live the life!

'My dear brothers, take note of this: Everyone should be quick to listen, slow to speak and slow to become angry, for man's anger does not bring about the righteous life that God desires' (James 1:19, 20).

In the course of our study of the previous verse in James's letter, we were mountain-climbing in the rarefied heights of God's mysterious and sovereign purposes in choosing a people for himself before the world was created. The merest glance at the verses now before us will tell us that we have suddenly come back to earth, to the plain issues of everyday life. But although this seems to be a violent change, it is in fact a valid pattern and whenever we find these two areas of teaching so close together, we can be sure that there is a specific purpose behind it.

Perhaps the most striking example of this is in John's account of the Last Supper. At one point he says this: 'Jesus knew that the Father had put all things under his power, and that he had come from God and was returning to God' (John 13:3). One only has to read those words through slowly to sense that one is breathing the very air of eternity. Here are conceptions beyond all human invention and understanding. But what comes next? 'So he got up from the meal, took off his outer clothing, and wrapped a towel round his waist. After that, he poured water into a basin, and began to wash his disciples' feet, drying them with the towel that was wrapped around him' (John 13:4, 5). What a staggering transition – from divinity to dirty feet! Yet the lessons which flowed from the incident – Christ's voluntary humiliation, the necessity of his self-sacrifice, the need for obedience to his will, and the call to humble service – could not have been more powerfully illustrated.

Then what is the link between James 1:18 and James 1:19, 20? Surely it is this, that the experience of the new birth is meant to be followed by the expression of a new life. I remember visiting a Bible College in France on one occasion. Glancing over the shoulder of one of the students, I noticed that he had written these words: 'Conversion is the exteriorization of the experience of regeneration.' Now that is quite a mouthful (even in a Bible College!) and I would have thought that the truth could be put a little more simply! Surely what he meant was this: the new life is the outworking of the new birth. Now that is a truth which the Bible affirms again and again, and no writer is more insistent on the point than the apostle Paul. Writing to the Corinthians he says, 'Therefore, if anyone is in Christ, he is a new creation; the old has gone, the new has come!' (2 Corinthians 5:17.) Writing to the Ephesians he says, 'For it is by grace you have been saved, through faith – and this not from yourselves, it is the gift of God – not by works, so that no one can boast. For we are God's workmanship, created in Christ Jesus to do good works, which God prepared in advance for us to do' (Ephesians 2:8–10). Far from conflicting with James on the place of good works in a Christian's life, Paul could not be more closely in agreement. With James he would insist that while we are never saved by *doing* good works, we *are* saved *to do* good works. While it is certainly true that good works without faith are vain and empty as far as salvation is concerned, it is equally true that any profession of faith that does not issue in good works is equally vain and empty. As someone once put it, 'Holiness is the visible part of salvation.' The point is well made: faith, mercy, grace, the new birth – these things are invisible, but you can see holiness, and it proves the reality of the others.

This matter of proving the new birth by a new life is, of course, James's great burden. His great concern is that belief and behaviour should go hand in hand, and in the two verses now before us he touches on three areas of life in which the new birth should express itself. Every Christian, he insists, should be 'quick to listen, slow to speak and slow to become angry'.

The verse begins with an interesting grammatical point in that the Greek word *iste* could be either indicative or imperative. In the indicative, the literal rendering would be 'You [already] know this' and would link verses 18 and 19 with the thought that James's readers already had a grateful grasp of the fact that they had been miraculously born again through 'the word of truth' and would surely wish to live in ways that would show their gratitude. In the imperative, the literal rendering would be 'Know this' or, as the NIV translators have it, 'Take note of this', which would link verses 18 and 19 with the thought that they should be sure that they never forgot the implications of the new birth in terms of their daily lives. Either way, James is concerned that the person who claims to be a Christian should prove to be one by living a transformed life. Three words will help us to hold the teaching of these verses together.

1. Readiness

'Everyone should be quick to listen' (v. 19).

At first thought, it may seem strange that James has given this particular injunction a place of such importance; we might have expected something with a more 'spiritual' sound. But a careful reading of the New Testament will soon correct our thinking, and it is particularly interesting to notice the emphasis that Jesus gave to the point, with his instructions not only to 'consider carefully *what* you hear' (Mark 4:24) but to 'consider carefully *how* you listen' (Luke 8:18).

James's primary intention is obviously connected with the sharing of biblical truth and his longing is that every Christian should have an insatiable appetite for sound doctrine. As Robert Johnstone puts it, he should be 'ready and eager to avail himself of all opportunities of increasing his acquaintance with "the word of truth"'. If that is the general principle, then, of course, it can be opened out and applied in many different ways, but it might be helpful to concentrate on just one, the hearing of the preached word in public. The average Christian in this country probably hears between fifty and a hundred hours of preaching every year, but *how* does he hear? Think for a moment of Jesus' words that 'From everyone who has been given much, much will be demanded' (Luke 12:48). Now apply those words to those who sit week after week under evangelical, biblical teaching. Is there not a solemn responsibility here? Are we eager to listen, and to listen biblically? It sometimes seems to me that, in all the fever of new ideas and all the 'technology' of Christian communication and the sometimes bizarre experimentation in worship and evangelism, we have tended to lose sight of the unique place that preaching occupies in the economy of God. Paul tells us that 'God was pleased through the foolishness of what was preached to save those who believe' (1 Corinthians 1:21) and says elsewhere that 'He brought his word to light through the preaching entrusted to me' (Titus 1:3). Now if that is the kind of store God sets by preaching, what kind of attitude should we have in listening? How often do we listen to preaching either as a duty or even a diversion? How often do we turn to the preacher in the same spirit as Cornelius turned to Peter when he told him, 'Now we are all here in the presence of God to listen to everything the Lord has commanded you to tell us'? (Acts 10:33.) How often do we truly listen to the preaching of the Word of God with hearts solemnly bowed in Samuel's eager attitude: 'Speak, for your servant is listening'? (1 Samuel 3:10.) We dare not pass lightly over those questions!

Of course, James's principle spills over into other areas, such as the reading of helpful Christian literature and listening thoughtfully to the godly counsel and comments of other Christians. Here, too, we should be 'quick to listen'. Even more importantly, we should learn to listen in our times of private devotion, when we turn aside from the world, other Christians, even the members of our own family, and seek God's face in prayer. Is it not true that these so-called 'Quiet Times' are almost filled with the noise of our own voices from beginning to end? How much do we know of quiet, *silent* waiting upon God, listening for his voice, longing for the Holy Spirit to impress upon our open hearts the living truth we need to hear? Here, in the place of private worship, as well as in listening to public preaching, we need to find the spirit of E. May Grimes's hymn:

Speak, Lord, in the stillness,
While I wait on thee;
Hushed my heart to listen
In expectancy.

Speak, thy servant heareth,
Be not silent, Lord;
Waits my soul upon thee
For the quickening word!

The first characteristic that James looks for, then, is readiness, an eager hunger for 'the word of truth'.

2. Reticence

'Everyone should be . . . slow to speak' (v. 19).

When all the exceptions and excuses have been made, and all the 'ifs' and 'buts' accommodated, the plain, unvarnished truth is that basically we talk too much! It is reported that Benjamin Disraeli said of one of his contemporaries, 'He was intoxicated with the exuberance of his own verbosity,' and I am afraid that the disease shows no sign of abating, either among politicians or Christians! The two books most commonly thought of as being the most practical are Proverbs (which someone has cleverly called 'God's transistorized wisdom') and James, and it is surely more than coincidence that they both deal so thoroughly with the matter of speech and that their emphasis is so often on the dangers of speaking too freely.

Here are some examples from Proverbs: 'When words are many, sin is not absent, but he who holds his tongue is wise' (Proverbs 10:19); 'A man of knowledge uses words with restraint, and a man of understanding is even-tempered' (Proverbs 17:27); 'He who guards his mouth and his tongue keeps himself from calamity' (Proverbs 21:23). When we come to James, the words we are now examining are the first mention of a subject he touches on again at 1:26, deals with at length throughout almost the whole of chapter 3 and returns to at 4:11. The rabbis used to have a saying that went something like this: 'Men have two ears but one tongue, that they should hear more than they speak. The ears are always open, ever ready to receive instruction; but the tongue is surrounded with a double row of teeth to hedge it in, and keep it within proper bounds.' The proverb may be uninspired, but it does remind us that something we treat very casually, God treats very seriously. There are surely awesome implications behind Jesus' teaching that 'Men will have to give account on the day of judgement for every careless word they have spoken' (Matthew 12:36). If that was the Bible's only statement on the use of the tongue, we would already know that it is a tremendously important issue, but James's word underlines it for us in one particular way – we are to be 'slow to speak'. Let me sketch out three areas in which this can be applied.

1. We should be slow to speak about ourselves. As the father of five sons, I know that the mark of a child is self-centredness, whereas the mark of a developing character is interest in others. In the spiritual realm, few things are more tragic than to see a Christian – and not infrequently one who is gifted and articulate – whose speech is dominated by the capital 'I'. The initial tragedy lies not in the damage his actual words may do, but in the retarded development they reveal. Whatever his social, ecclesiastical or theological achievements, the man is sadly stunted in his spiritual growth.

What a contrast we have when we turn to the teaching of the Word of God! Of all the passages which touch on the subject, the one that comes most clearly to mind is this: 'Do nothing out of selfish ambition or vain conceit, but in humility consider others better than yourselves' (Philippians 2:3). Boastfulness is never becoming for a Christian, and while this truth covers every part of life, there are three things in particular which the Bible forbids.

We should never boast about *what we are.* This is probably not far from the very context in which James is writing the words we are studying. In verse 18 he has reminded us of the great dignity we have as children of God, the world's true aristocracy. Now that is wonderfully true, but it gives no cause whatever for boasting, for any kind of carnal pride. Paul firmly underlines this in his letter to the Romans. Having stated that righteousness is a gift from God, received through faith in Christ, he asks, 'Where, then is boasting?'

and immediately gives the answer: 'It is excluded' (Romans 3:27), or, as the Amplified Bible puts it, 'excluded, banished, ruled out entirely'. As Archbishop William Temple once said, 'The only thing a man contributes to his salvation is the sin from which he needs to be saved.' That being so, our salvation is a cause for rejoicing, but never for boasting.

We should never boast about *what we have.* When studying the very first verse of James's letter, we had cause to look up a question Paul asked in his first letter to the Corinthians and it is well worth reminding ourselves of it here. The question was this: 'What do you have that you did not receive?' (1 Corinthians 4:7.) The impact of the question is obvious and inescapable in the context of our present study. What do you have in the way of ability, material possessions, influence, spiritual resources or power? Now make a list of all the things that are yours but which you did not receive as a free gift from God. Surely the point is clear! Now if you *did* receive them as a free gift, if they *are* gifts of God's grace, you should never boast about them as if you had acquired them by your own efforts or as the reward of your own ability. That is the thrust of Paul's question. We should never boast about what we have.

We should never boast about *what we do.* Later in the same letter to the Corinthians, Paul makes this point, too, and does so by way of personal testimony. Discussing the rights of an apostle, he positively revels in his God-given office, but adds, 'Yet when I preach the gospel, I cannot boast, for I am compelled to preach. Woe to me if I do not preach the gospel!' (1 Corinthians 9:16.) He shows the same spirit in his letter to the Ephesians, where he writes, 'Although I am less than the least of all God's people, this *grace* was given me: to preach to the Gentiles the unsearchable riches of Christ' (Ephesians 3:8). I suppose we would have to say that 'less than the least' makes pretty poor grammar, but Paul murders the grammar in order to magnify the grace! I must leave you to work out the implications of Paul's words in your own life, but remember that any valid work you do for God, however costly, however faithful, however effective, however efficiently done, is still the outcome of grace. It is nothing to boast about.

These, then, are three things the Bible expressly forbids in the area of speaking about ourselves.

2. *We should be slow to speak about others.* If a man is always boasting about himself, his words very quickly give offence, but there is another arrogant way of speaking that can sometimes pass for knowledge or wisdom. This comes from the kind of people who simply *must* give an opinion on every issue, a judgement on every situation, a verdict on every person brought into the conversation. At the drop of a hat, they appear to be able to give a definitive judgement on every subject under the sun, yet in their pretended omniscience they are ignorantly trampling on James's injunction that every one of us should be 'slow to speak'. This kind of attitude broadens out into many areas, but I want to touch on just one, which can be summed up in one of the most sinister, crippling words in the Christian church – criticism. Few Christians can claim complete exemption from a charge of saying about other people things that are unkind, unjust, untrue, unfair or unloving. We need to bring this whole area under the searchlight of James's command to be 'slow to speak'. There are two obvious reasons why, as James later says on a related issue, 'this should not be' (3:10).

The first is because of *the mischief it starts.* The story is told of a woman who after years of malicious tongue-wagging, became convicted of her sin and went to her minister to ask his advice. He listened carefully to her story, then said, 'If you want a clear conscience, you must take a bag of goose feathers, go around the neighbourhood, and put a goose feather outside the door of every single person you have offended.' Off she went, and a long time later she returned to the minister with an empty bag. 'I have done what you told me,' she said, 'but I feel no better.' 'Of course not', the minister replied, 'because you have only done half the job. What you must now do is to go around and pick all the feathers up again.' Now it so happened that there was a high wind blowing that day, so that when the woman returned hours later, her bag was still empty. Slumping in a chair, she said, 'It's no good. I can't find a single feather. It was easy to put them down, but I can't get even one of them back again.' 'Precisely,' said the minister, 'and in just the same way it was easy to scatter your words of criticism and rumour, but now that they have gone, it is impossible to bring them back.'

The story may be quaint, but the thrust is inescapable. It is so easy to throw away the critical, unkind word, but impossible to control it when it has left our lips. Even as we begin to regret it, it may already be at work, stirring up even more mischief as it is passed from one to another. The Bible has a terribly solemn word about this: 'There are six things the Lord hates, seven that are detestable to him: haughty eyes, a lying tongue, hands that shed innocent blood, a heart that devises wicked schemes, feet that are quick to rush into evil, a false witness who pours out lies and a man who stirs up dissension among brothers' (Proverbs 6:16–19). We should take careful note of the fact that God has a particular loathing of anything that divides Christians from each other, and few things do that more cruelly than barren, negative, unjust criticism. No wonder J. B. Simpson once said, 'I would rather play with forked lightning than speak a reckless word against a servant of Christ.' Spoken words, like a sped arrow, are impossible to retract. Changing the picture, rumour spreads like wildfire, bringing endless harm to countless people. The Bible has precisely the right word for us here: 'Without wood a fire goes out; without gossip a quarrel dies down' (Proverbs 26:20). Let us take that to heart!

The second is because of *the merit it suggests.* The first time I visited the ruins of ancient Corinth I remember being struck by the size of the *bema,* the judgement seat used by Gallio in the story recorded in Acts 18. Looking at this enormous mass of stone, I could not help thinking, 'What a height he had to rise to in order to judge others!' and sometimes the subtle, perhaps unconscious, but terrible truth is that when we are busy criticizing others, we are suggesting that we are above them and above the thing for which we are judging them. As E. Stanley Jones wrote somewhere, 'You may dispense moral judgements so that by the very dispensing of them you judge yourself moral.' When we say a person is careless, are we not implying that we are careful? When we call someone proud, is there not the suggestion that we are humble? When we criticize a man's meanness, are we not implying our own generosity? When we say that another Christian is just a little astray theologically, are we not saying that he does not agree with our impeccable doctrine? Beware of the subtle sins that lurk here!

3. We should be slow to speak about the Lord. This may sound strange at first but I believe that there is an important point that needs to be made here. The Bible certainly says that 'It is with your mouth that you confess and are saved' (Romans 10:10) but that statement must be seen in context and I believe that James's injunction that we should be 'slow to speak' has real application at this point. For instance, it is most unwise to send those who profess conversion straight home to announce their 'salvation' to all and sundry. Surely it would be much wiser to let the life speak before the lips? Again, there is something basically wrong in pushing young converts on to the public stage to give their testimony. Their place is the kindergarten, not the platform. Again, it is a great mistake to encourage every articulate young Christian to go into the ministry. As Thomas Manton says of this word by James, 'It teacheth men not to adventure upon the preaching of the word until they have a good spiritual furniture, or are stored with a sufficiency of gifts. It is not for everyone that can speak for an hour to adventure upon work of teaching.' My advice to any young man thinking about the full-time preaching ministry would be this: do not dare to set foot there until it is impossible for you to do anything else. If you have an alternative, take the alternative! Paul's testimony was 'I am compelled to preach' (1 Corinthians 9:16) and without that divine compulsion there will be no divine anointing.

Mingled into these particular examples I have given is the more general principle that has even wider application and that is the awesome responsibility of speaking about Christian things. It is terribly possible to take the Lord's name in vain by speaking without reason, research or revelation, by speaking not because we have something to say, but because we must say something. Every Christian undoubtedly has a solemn responsibility to share the gospel, to communicate his faith, to play his part in taking the living truth to a dying world, but let him do so with a right understanding of James's cautionary words: 'Everyone should be . . . slow to speak.'

3. Reluctance

'Everyone should be . . . slow to become angry, for man's anger does not bring about the righteous life that God desires' (vv. 19–20).

It is not difficult to see a link between anger and the use of the tongue and in adding this particular warning, James gives us a rule and a reason.

1. A rule. I have deliberately chosen the word 'reluctance' as a heading to this whole section for the specific reason that James does *not* say, 'Everyone should refuse to become angry.' It would not be exaggerating to say that the Bible actually encourages anger, but within certain well-defined limits. The best example of what I mean comes when Paul says, '"In your anger do not sin": Do not let the sun go down while you are still angry' (Ephesians 4:26). It is obvious from this that it is possible to be angry without committing sin – we could quite properly call it 'righteous anger' – but that anger is such a powerful passion that it is likely to get out of control and to become sinful and it is precisely for this reason that James counsels caution.

The Christian must be reluctant to become angry, because the line between righteous anger and personal irritation is sometimes very thin. There is sometimes a very hazy border between defending principles and defending ourselves. Think twice, think three times, count up to ten, put everything possible in the way before you place yourself in a position where there is a danger of your anger spilling over into forbidden territory. As Thomas Manton wrote, 'Anger groweth not by degrees like other passions, but at her birth she is in her full growth. The heat and fury of it is at first, therefore the best cure is deliberation.' The warning is plain and the counsel clear.

2. A reason. There is a specific reason why we should be slow to become angry, and James puts it like this: 'For man's anger does not bring about the righteous life that God desires.' A straightforward rendering of that final phrase would read 'the righteousness of God', but the NIV translators have probably caught the spirit of the sentence well enough. The obvious meaning of what James is saying is that anger that comes from man (that is to say, from his sinful nature) does not reflect the righteousness that comes from God, who is specifically said to be 'compassionate and gracious, *slow to anger,* abounding in love' (Psalm 103:8).

The Christian's over-riding duty is to be Christ-like, to follow his example, reproduce his qualities of life, demonstrating to a cynical, sinful world that he is a child of God, indwelt by the divine nature. A blazing, irrational, uncontrolled temper is no part of that life-style and should therefore be avoided at all costs. Instead, the Christian should seek to bring every part of his life under the continuous control of the Holy Spirit. These words by Katie Wilkinson reflect precisely what his attitude should be.

> May the mind of Christ my Saviour
> Live in me from day to day;
> By his love and power controlling
> All I do and say.

9.

Blueprint for blessing — I

'Therefore, get rid of all moral filth and the evil that is so prevalent, and humbly accept the word planted in you, which can save you' (James 1:21).

This verse is obviously part of a section which runs through at least as far as the end of verse 25, but it says so much within the compass of a very few words that it deserves to be dealt with in a chapter on its own. I have headed the whole section 'Blueprint for Blessing' because that is exactly what it is – verse 25 ends with the specific promise that the person who obeys its teaching 'will be blessed in what he does'.

Looking for a link with what has gone before, we find it in verse 18, where James says that we have been brought to spiritual birth through 'the word of truth', and in verse 19, where the obvious inference is that it is this word to which we should be 'quick to listen'. He now develops his message a little further and lays down two commandments that must be obeyed if the 'word of truth' is to achieve its intended effect in our lives.

1. Something we need to remove
'Therefore, get rid of all moral filth and the evil that is so prevalent.'

The heart of the verse before us comes a little later on, when James instructs us to 'accept the word', but it is important to notice that before that positive command he inserts this negative one. The fact that this is an essential prerequisite to receiving the word (and therefore to being blessed) comes across even more strongly when we translate literally from the original Greek. The phrase would then read like this: 'Therefore, having [already] put off from yourselves . . . ,' which suggests two things. The first is that James almost takes it for granted that his readers will *know* that this must come first and the second is that there can be no effective receiving of the word until it *does* come first. We have no warrant to treat the Bible as an automatic 'blessing-machine'; God has laid down specific conditions which must be obeyed before we can claim the enriching promises he makes.

As we examine this phrase closely we can see that it says three things about sin.

1. Sin's defilement. The higher a man's state of grace, the more is his view of sin. When you hear somebody who is always joking about sin, treating it in an offhand, casual sort of way, you are listening to somebody who is in a lower state of grace than he ought to be. To the unconverted person sin is generally a trifle, to the carnal Christian it is often a trouble, but to the sensitive saint it is always a tragedy.

There can certainly be no difficulty in categorizing James on this issue! With characteristic bluntness he calls sin 'moral filth'. Now we might use that phrase about moral impurity or some such thing, but it is important to notice that James is applying it to the matters he touched on in the previous two verses, namely an unwillingness to listen, sins of the tongue and unrighteous, unjustified anger. Far from passing these things over as being of minor importance, he does not hesitate to describe them as 'moral filth'. Charles Wesley has the same clear recognition of sin's defilement in one of his hymns:

> Purge me from every evil blot;
> My idols all be cast aside;
> Cleanse me from every sinful thought,
> From all the *filth* of self and pride.

Those are telling words! We would probably be very quick to label adultery, rape, homosexuality and the like as 'moral filth'; but are we as ready to see our selfish attitudes and our proud thoughts in the same light and coming under the same condemnation?

2. Sin's depth. James not only speaks of 'moral filth' but of 'the evil that is prevalent'. The original phrase is unusual. The bewildering variety of translations shows something of the difficulty scholars have found in expressing its precise meaning, and the NIV's 'prevalent' may not be the best attempt. The root of that particular word is the same as one used in the story of the feeding of the 4,000, where we read that after everyone had eaten the disciples picked up 'seven basketfuls of broken pieces that were *left over*' (Mark 8:8). It is not difficult to imagine the disciples carefully picking up every last crumb, removing every trace of that extraordinary open-air meal and leaving the area as clean as it was when they found it. Applying this picture to James's words, what he is saying is that we should get rid of every trace of sin that remains, everything in our lives that betrays the continuing presence of the old nature. He is concerned with sin's depth, with the fact that the old nature remains, hidden deep in our personalities, and that unless we exercise unceasing vigilance and discipline it will show itself in hideous, open sin. No Christian can face the battle against sin sanely and scripturally until he comes to a solemn recognition of the depths of indwelling sin in his own heart. Henry Twells had it exactly right when he wrote,

> And none, O Lord, have perfect rest,
> For none are wholly free from sin;
> And they who fain would serve thee best
> Are conscious most of wrong within.

3. Sin's damage. The whole of the phrase infers this, James's point being that unless we do get rid of sin, in whatever form it appears, we shall not be able to receive the life-giving word of God. 'Moral filth' translates the Greek word *rhuparia.* The root of the word is *rhupos* which, when used medically, literally means 'wax in the ear', and when James tells us to get rid of all moral filth he means anything that stops us hearing, receiving and understanding God's Word. I remember leading our family prayers once and reading with my wife and boys part of Acts 5. We reached the incident where Gamaliel came to the defence of the disciples and I asked one of my sons what it was that Gamaliel did. With a worried frown he scoured the Bible-reading notes looking for the magic word. Sensing his difficulty I tried to help the little fellow out by spelling the word – 'd-e-f-e-n-d-e-d'. 'Got it!', he blurted, 'Gamaliel deafened the disciples!' That gorgeous gaffe is a permanent reminder to me of the need to avoid anything that deafens us to what the Bible is saying. It would not be overstating the case to say that the very worst damage that sin can do to the Christian is to deafen him to the teaching of the Word of God. Beware of anything that can tend to become wax in your spiritual ears, preventing you from hearing what it is that God wants to say to you. Whatever it is, it must be recognized, regretted and removed.

James uses a particularly interesting word for the action of removing these hindrances to receiving God's Word. The verb 'get rid' – the Greek *apotithemoi* – is exactly the word you would use for taking off clothing and several New Testament writers use it in exactly the same context as James. Paul says, 'But now you must rid yourselves of all such things as these: anger, rage, malice, slander and filthy language from your lips' (Colossians 3:8); the writer of Hebrews says, 'Let us throw off everything that hinders and the sin that so easily entangles . . .' (Hebrews 12:7); and Peter says, 'Therefore, rid yourselves of all malice and all deceit, hypocrisy, envy and slander of every kind' (1 Peter 2:1). As well as using James's very striking verb for getting rid of sin, it is important that all three passages have something else in common with him – and that is an emphasis on the thoroughness of the work that needs to be done. Paul tells us to rid ourselves of '*all* such things . . .'; the writer of Hebrews to throw off '*everything* that hinders . . .'; Peter to rid ourselves of *all* malice and *all* deceit . . . and slander of *every kind*'. Here, James tells us to get rid of '*all* moral filth and the evil that is so prevalent'. Charles Wesley again captures the spirit of what the Bible is saying on this issue:

> Refining fire, go through my heart,
> Illuminate my soul;
> Scatter thy life through every part,
> And sanctify the whole.

That should be the prayer of every Christian! There must be a recognition that *every* sin is an abomination in God's sight, an offence to his majesty and glory. James makes it very clear that even those sins which we might tend to think of as comparatively 'small' are defiling, deep-rooted and damaging and must be got rid of with ruthless determination.

2. Something we need to receive

'. . . and humbly accept the word planted in you, which can save you.'

Perhaps the simplest way of opening up this phrase is to see it as answering four basic questions about 'receiving' the Word of God. Those four questions would be these: What should we receive? How should we receive it? Where should we receive it? Why should we receive it?

1. What are we to receive? The answer James gives to this question is that we are to receive 'the word', that is to say the Word of God. James's injunction clearly applies to every form of 'receiving' biblical truth, but let me make a comment in one area only, that of reading. Leaving aside all the books, magazines and newspapers that Christians read outside of a purely religious context, how much of our reading is the Word of God itself? It is fatally easy, especially as one's critical faculties become somewhat sharper, to spend a great deal of time reading what other people have written about the Bible and a comparatively small amount of time actually reading the Bible itself. We owe a tremendous debt to generations of godly men who have devoted their lives to the written exposition of Scripture, but we do them and ourselves a serious disservice if we concentrate more on them than on the Bible. Part of the glory of the biblical doctrine of the priesthood of all believers is the ancillary truth that the Holy Spirit can interpret and apply Scripture to the most untutored believer as powerfully and directly as to the greatest expositor or commentator the world has ever known. That being so, every Christian should seek to apply himself earnestly to the study of God's Word, recognizing, in Oscar Feucht's words, that 'Bible reading is not an exceptional thing for the literate Christian. It is part of his response to God.'

2. How are we to receive it? James says we must 'humbly

accept the word' and there is a double emphasis here. The word 'humbly' translates the Greek *en prautes,* and it is virtually impossible to find one English word that will do justice to its meaning. However, the sense of what James is saying is that we must come to Scripture in a submissive, open-minded way, with an eager readiness to learn and with a genuine desire to bring every area of life under its reforming control. David's prayer is a perfect example of this:

> 'Show me your ways, O Lord,
> teach me your paths;
> guide me in your truth and teach me,
> for you are God my Saviour'
> (Psalm 25:4, 5).

That kind of attitude is what Robert Johnstone calls 'childlike docility' and is exactly what James calls for here.

Do we truly come to the Bible like that? Are there not times when we come to it wearing the blinkers of our own pet school of theological thought or doctrinal tradition? Is there not a danger of reading *into* the Bible instead of reading the Bible? Anything that hinders direct access of the untouched Word of God to our open hearts is both disobedient and dangerous. In A. W. Tozer's memorable phrase, 'We must never edit God.'

The added emphasis James gives lies hidden in the word 'accept'. The Greek word is *dexasthe,* which you might use of receiving something or someone with open arms. It is a glad-hearted, welcoming word, which underlines the point that there should be no resistance on our part to *anything* that God is saying to us. As Curtis Vaughan rightly says, 'To receive the word in the fullest sense is so to open the inner self to the influence of God's Word that its truth is transfused into the heart.'

3. Where are we to receive it? 'The answer is inferred by James when he speaks of 'the word *planted in you*'. The Greek word is *emphutos* and this is the only time it occurs in the New Testament. However, the same metaphor occurs in the parable of the sower, where Jesus speaks of the message of the kingdom of God coming to a man as 'seed sown in his heart' (Matthew 13:19), and in Paul's testimony of his evangelistic ministry, where he says, 'I planted the seed' (1 Corinthians 3:6).

The picture, then, is horticultural. James sees the living Word of God as being planted in the heart of the believer and what he urges is that we constantly seek to make the soil of our hearts receptive to it, so that it can germinate effectively and produce godly fruit in our lives. Again, there is a feeling of thoroughness or earnestness here. You cannot grow oak trees in window boxes, nor can we expect to be strong, productive Christians unless the Word of God is allowed to sink its roots deeply into our hearts.

4. Why are we to receive it? The answer James gives to that question is this: 'The word . . . can save you.' At first glance, this seems a strange expression, because it is part of a letter obviously addressed to people who are already Christians, but the mystery is unravelled by realizing that the Bible speaks about salvation in three different senses and tenses. The first is what we could call *salvation in possession,* that once-for-all, unrepeatable, unalterable experience of the new birth, which Paul has in mind when he says, 'It is by grace you have been saved' (Ephesians 2:8). The second is what we could call *salvation in progress,* that gradual process of sanctification that is being hammered out on the anvil of a Christian's developing experience, to which Paul refers when he writes of 'us who are being saved' (1 Corinthians 1:18). The third is what we could call *salvation in prospect,* that full and final deliverance from sin which will be the Christian's experience beyond the grave, which Paul has in mind when he says, 'Since we have now been justified by [Christ's] blood, how much more shall we be saved from God's wrath through him!' (Romans 5:9.)

Now which of these three does James mean? Obviously not the first, the initial experience of the new birth, for that is an unrepeatable experience which his readers already have. It could certainly be the second, the progressive growth in holiness that James is always so anxious to promote. The argument for this is strengthened by reading a very similar passage written by the apostle Peter: 'Therefore, rid yourselves of all malice and all deceit, hypocrisy, envy, and slander of every kind. Like newborn babies, crave pure spiritual milk, so that by it you may grow up in your salvation . . .' (1 Peter 2:1, 2). One of the root meanings of the word 'salvation' is 'health' or 'wholeness', and I have never yet met a sickly Christian whose weakness did not include a lack of disciplined, devoted study of the Word of God. Multitudes of Christians are falling far short of the state of maturity and blessing that ought to be theirs because the Word of God is not taking root deep in their hearts. The Word of God is *able* to nourish them, strengthen them, make them spiritually healthy, but they are refusing to submit to its living power.

The likelihood is, however, that James has in mind the third sense in which the Bible speaks of salvation – the Christian's entrance into heaven. If this is so, what a tremendous commentary his words are on the power of God's Word! Not only is it an instrument powerful enough to repel all Satan's attacks during the Christian's life, but it is even stronger than death. As the psalmist puts it, 'Your word, O Lord, is eternal; it stands firm in the heavens' (Psalm 119:89), and it is this *eternal* word, standing unmoved by all the changing circumstances of time and space, which James exhorts us to receive, to welcome, to bury deep in our hearts, minds and personalities. In the last verse of one of his hymns, Isaac Watts puts into poetry the response of every right-minded Christian:

Thy noblest wonders here we view,
In souls renewed and sins forgiven:
Lord, cleanse my sins, my soul renew,
And make thy Word my guide to heaven.

10.

Blueprint for blessing — II

'Do not merely listen to the word, and so deceive yourselves. Do what it says. Anyone who listens to the word but does not do what it says is like a man who looks at his face in a mirror and, after looking at himself, goes away and immediately forgets what he looks like. But the man who looks intently into the perfect law that gives freedom, and continues to do this, not forgetting what he has heard, but doing it – he will be blessed in what he does' (James 1:22–25).

These four verses carry on the subject which James introduced in verse 21, namely the manner in which we should receive the Word of God. The verses now before us divide naturally into two sections, each one indicating a particular approach to the Bible, and it will help us to get a clear picture of what James is saying if we look at them in turn.

1. The danger of casual observance
'Do not merely listen to the word, and so deceive yourselves. Do what it says. Anyone who listens to the word but does not do what it says is like a man who looks at his face in a mirror and, after looking at himself, goes away and immediately forgets what he looks like' (vv. 22–24).

The key word in these two verses is 'merely'. In our previous study, James exhorts us to be sure that we 'accept the word', and we can never do that unless we make certain that we actually hear it being preached or read it for ourselves. But there is an immediate danger that people will imagine that to 'listen' to the Word of God is enough. Not only do many people think that they are Christians because they go to church, read the Bible and pray, but there are undoubtedly many Christians who fondly imagine that they are making some kind of progress in the Christian life because they go through a regular routine of Bible reading and of listening to preaching. It is precisely this danger that James is anxious to warn us about. Of course he has no objection to people 'listening' to the Word of God – he exhorts us to do that very thing – but his great concern is lest we might '*merely* listen', do nothing else but go through an outward ritual. That is the general drift of what he is saying here, and we can separate his words into two strands.

1. A simple comparison. 'Anyone who listens to the word but does not do what it says is like a man who looks at his face in a mirror.' James is back at his picture-language again and his illustration could not make his point clearer. A man gets up in the morning, dashes to the bathroom, swishes the razor and flannel over his face, throws the comb through his hair, gulps his breakfast and dashes for the train, by which time he has completely forgotten the details of what his face looked like when he glanced in the mirror a few minutes earlier! The comparison is surely simple. The Christian James has in mind comes to his Bible, dashes hurriedly through a brief passage, skims over somebody else's pre-digested notes, bows his head for a moment of prayer and then is off into the mad whirl of business and busyness, with as little detailed understanding of what he has read as the other man had knowledge of the precise delineations of his face.

There may, however, be another vein of truth in James's illustration, one that is unfortunately obscured by the NIV translators. In the original Greek, what the man is said to see in the mirror is not just *to prosopon* ('his face') but *to prosopon tes geneseos autou,* which literally means 'the face of his birth'. Commentators differ widely on the precise significance of the phrase, but there is one minority view that fits in perfectly with the spirit of what James is saying. This is that the word *geneseos* emphasizes something that is natural and temporal as opposed to something spiritual and eternal. If this is the shade of meaning the word is intended to bear here, then James is saying in effect that while a casual glance in the mirror may be sufficient as far as one's natural face is concerned, a casual approach to the reading and study of the Word of God is certainly *not* sufficient, because it deals with the eternal issues of the soul.

But the dangers of this casual approach are not limited to private devotions. The same approach can sometimes characterize the public reading of Scripture. There are times when I have felt that the Bible was being read with less preparation than the notices and with considerably less understanding. I hesitate to use the following illustration because of my part in it, but I do so as a reminder to my own heart of the seriousness of the issue. A year or two after my conversion I was appointed as a lay reader in the Church of England, to Holy Trinity Church, Guernsey. There were two other, more senior, lay readers on the staff, with the result that on most Sundays the responsibilities could be evenly shared out. As it happened, the vicar almost always asked me to read the lessons, following a lectionary which listed the passages appointed to be read on each Sunday of the year. My wife and I lived in a small flat at the time, but I can vividly remember my Sunday morning routine. Immediately after breakfast I would go into the bedroom, lock the door, and begin to prepare for reading the lesson that morning. After a word of prayer I would look up the lesson in the lectionary and read it carefully in the Authorized Version, which we were using in the church. Then I would read it through in every other version I had in my possession, in order to get thoroughly familiar with the whole drift and sense of the passage. Next I would turn to the commentaries. I did not have many in those days, but those I had I used. I would pay particular attention to word meanings and doctrinal implications. When I had finished studying the passage in detail, I would go to the mantelpiece, which was roughly the same height as the lectern in the church and prop up the largest copy of the Authorized Version I possessed. Having done that, I would walk slowly up to it from the other side of the room, and begin to speak, aloud: 'Here beginneth the first verse of the tenth chapter of the Gospel according to St John' (or whatever the passage was). Then I would begin to read aloud the portion appointed. If I made so much as a single slip of the tongue, a single mispronunciation, I would stop, walk back across the room and start again, until I had read the whole passage word perfect, perhaps two or three times. My wife would tell you that there were times when I emerged from the bedroom with that day's clean white shirt stained with perspiration drawn from the effort of preparing one lesson to be read in the church. Does that sound like carrying things too far? Then let me add this: I was told that there were times when after the reading of the lesson people wanted to leave the service there and then and go quietly home to think over the implications of what God had said to them in his Word.

Now you know why I hesitated to tell the story, but I shall never cease to thank God for impressing upon me in that way the importance of a serious approach to the Bible. Beware of coming to God's Word in the same hurried, superficial way that a man glances in his bathroom mirror before dashing to work.

2. A sad consequence. In fact, as we thread our way through these verses, we can pick out three sad consequences experienced by the person who has this casual approach to Scripture.

The first is that *he thinks but does not know:* 'Do not . . . deceive yourselves.' Have you ever noticed how often the Bible warns us about being deceived? It says that we can be deceived by Satan; it tells us that 'he leads the whole world astray' (Revelation 12:9). It says that we can be deceived by other people; Jesus warned, 'Watch out that no one deceives you' (Matthew 24:4). Here, James says that we can deceive *ourselves,* lead ourselves astray, an alarming reminder of the Old Testament statement that 'The heart is deceitful above all things and beyond cure' (Jeremiah 17:9). The word 'deceive' used by James is the Greek *paralogizomenoi,* made up of the preposition *para* ('contrary to') and the verb *logizomenoi* ('to reason'). The meaning, then, is to reason in a way that is contrary to something and in this case contrary to the truth: 'false reasoning' would sum it up exactly. Now what is the false reasoning that James has in mind here? Surely he is thinking of the person who says, 'I read my Bible regularly, I listen to biblical preaching every Sunday: surely I am making progress?' But that is false reasoning and its implications are so deep that it may be the most serious issue in the whole of James's letter. It is perilously possible to deceive ourselves into thinking that we have made spiritual progress, or that some issue has been satisfactorily dealt with just because we have heard (or preached!) the truth on a certain subject. Beware this terrible danger! It is not enough to be able to say, 'I have learned an important truth', unless we can also say, 'The truth I have learned has entered into the bloodstream of my life and changed it for God and for good.' There is a difference between thinking and knowing. There is a difference between reading a menu and eating a meal. There is a difference between reading a prescription and taking medicine. There is a difference between reading the Bible and growing in grace. How easy it is to deceive ourselves on this issue!

The second is that *he looks but does not see.* Turning back to the man in his illustration, James says that as soon as he has turned away from the mirror, he 'immediately forgets what he looks like'. There used to be an advertisement for watches which began by asking two questions. The first ran something like this: 'Are the numerals on your watch Roman, Arabic or some other kind?' Having discovered this, one then read the second question which was '*Without looking at your watch again,* can you say what the exact time is?' As the advertisers expected, I couldn't! I had looked at the face of my watch just a moment before, yet failed to see the most important thing that watch was telling me, which was the time of day.

The application is surely obvious and shows us the second sad consequence of casual Bible reading. We look at the words, but we do not actually see them, or to put it more precisely, we look at the Bible long enough to see the words, but not deeply enough to see the truth. The sad consequence of that kind of thing is that the Word of God will never penetrate to the deep places of life and transform it in the way God desires. The man who reads on the surface will live on the surface and a superficial Christian is a pathetic parody of the truth.

The third is that *he hears but does not act.* James says

that after glancing in the mirror, the man 'goes away'; he leaves it behind and presses on through the day without any further reference to it. Again the application is obvious. The picture is of someone who hears the truth, but after hearing it does nothing about it. The New Testament character we call the 'rich young ruler' was a tragic example of this very thing. He came to the right person, at the right time, with the right question, got the right answer, but still 'went away sad' (Mark 10:22), unwilling to do what Jesus told him. Hearing the truth was not enough; it would only be effective when it found a response in his heart and life.

I remember a young man of twenty-three telling me that he had spent a total of ten years in prisons and approved schools. On one occasion the prison authorities had punished him for some misbehaviour or other by ordering him to write out Psalm 121 a hundred times. He went on to tell me that even that had had no effect on him. 'Perhaps not,' I replied, 'but do you realize that if you had believed and obeyed those words, you would have become a changed man?' Hearing or reading the Word of God is vitally important, but not finally so. Something else is needed. The writer of Hebrews pinpoints this when he says of some of the ancient Israelites, 'The message they heard was of no value to them, because those who heard did not combine it with faith' (Hebrews 4:2). The tragedy that followed was the sad consequence of hearing the Word of God casually, instead of responding to it with the faith that implies submission to the truth. The consequences that follow any Christian's casual observance of God's Word are no less tragic.

2. The development of careful obedience

'But the man who looks intently into the perfect law that gives freedom, and continues to do this, not forgetting what he has heard, but doing it – he will be blessed in what he does' (v. 25).

With the simple conjunction 'but . . .' James now introduces us to someone with a vastly different approach. The person in verse 23 'listens to the word but does not do what it says'; but we find this person 'not forgetting what he has heard, but doing it'. What are the lessons we can learn from the description James gives us?

1. The duty of looking attentively. 'But the man who looks intently into the perfect law that gives freedom, and continues to do this . . .' Taken by itself, this phrase suggests three things that should characterize the Christian's study of the Bible.

The first is *discernment.* James describes the Word of God as 'the perfect law that gives freedom', a phrase he uses again at 2:12. That description alone could give rise to a whole volume of studies, but we must be satisfied at this point with one general line of truth. As we saw in an earlier chapter, the law of God is perfect, which means in theory that if a man kept the law in every detail he would be in perfect spiritual harmony with God and justified in God's sight because of his own obedience. That is the theory, but in practice 'All have sinned and fall short of the glory of God' (Romans 3:23) and 'No one will be declared righteous in [God's] sight by observing the law' (Romans 3:20). Yet the Christian is in the amazing position that all of Christ's perfect obedience to the law is credited to him. Not only is it wonderfully true that all of the believer's sin has been debited to Christ and dealt with by his death on the cross, it is no less wonderfully true that all of Christ's obedience to the law is credited to the believer. This is why Christ is prophetically described as 'the Lord our Righteousness' (Jeremiah 23:6). What could never be done *by* the Christian has been done *for* him. It is at this precise point that we find the practical application of that glorious truth that Christ was 'tempted in every way, just as we are – yet was without sin' (Hebrews 4:15). The sinlessness of Christ is an essential part of God's amazing provision that makes a Christian acceptable in his sight. As Paul says, 'Christ is the end of the law so that there may be righteousness for everyone who believes' (Romans 10:4). The believer has been set free from the place where the law has any power to condemn him; in Paul's own testimony, 'Through Christ Jesus the law of the Spirit of life set me free from the law of sin and death' (Romans 8:2).

But there is another contingent truth which brings us near to the heart of what James is saying here. The Christian is not only free from bondage to the law, he is also free from his natural hatred to it; he now finds that he delights in what he once detested. The law is not now a burdensome outward set of rules and regulations imposed by a distant stranger who threatens dire punishment for every offence. Instead, the law now finds a responsive chord in his heart. He can say with the psalmist David, 'To do your will, O my God, is my desire; your law is within my heart' (Psalm 40:8).

All of this locks in to the point I am making, which is that the Christian should have discernment when he comes to read the Bible, and that discernment should include a biblical understanding of what the law is, where he stands in relation to it, and his potential obedience to it. The Christian is free to obey the law and to know the blessing that comes from obedience. This is not liberty without law, nor is it law without liberty. Instead, as Robert Johnstone says, 'The divine law, as seen by the Christian, exhibits liberty, gives liberty, is liberty.'

The second is *depth.* James describes the person with the right approach to the Bible as 'the man who looks intently'. The Greek word is *parakupsas,* which is made up of two words meaning 'to stoop sideways'. There are two perfect illustrations of its meaning in John's account of the resurrection. He tells us that when Mary of Magdala told him that the tomb of Jesus was empty, he ran to the tomb, 'bent over and looked in . . .' (John 20:5). Later, he describes how Mary 'bent over to look into the tomb . . .' (John 20:11) and it hardly requires a vivid imagination to picture them peering into the semi-darkness, straining to catch a glimpse of anything that might provide answers to the questions that were surging in their hearts. Now this is the word James uses to describe the right approach to the Word of God. We must look at it in depth, determined to miss nothing that the Holy Spirit is willing to reveal to us. I once read that in the Johannesburg area of South Africa, there are at least fifty-five gold mines, some of them nearly 12,000 feet deep, and that men were prepared to go that deep and to bring up to the surface up to four tons of ore in order to find one ounce of gold. I was instantly reminded that David describes the Scriptures as being 'more precious than gold, than much pure gold' (Psalm 19:10). Are we prepared to dig deeply in order to lay hold of its precious truths? Are we determined to find whatever it is that God has for us in his Word? Are we diligent in our study, in our searching? These are the challenges that flow from James's words.

The third is *discipline.* Notice that James not only speaks about a man who 'looks intently into the perfect law that gives freedom'; he specifically adds the phrase, 'and continues to do this'. The addition is important! It is not enough to get serious about Bible study in fits and starts, to have an occasional burst of enthusiasm followed by weeks or months of apathy. The Christian who wants to get somewhere with God must not only look intently into his Word, but continue to do so. When Paul visited Athens a group of Epicurean and Stoic philosophers described him as 'this babbler' (Acts 17:18). The Greek word is *spermologos,* which was used of a grain-eating bird that flitted around here and there, picking up minute trifles and titbits, but never staying anywhere long enough to get its beak into anything solid. The fact that Paul's critics used this word about someone of his massive intellect was a mark of their ignorance, of course, but would the description fit you? Are you satisfied with a few verses or phrases here and there, a few comforting clichés, a thought for the day, a 'little word'? Or is your study of the Word marked by the determined discipline that God has promised to reward? As George Duncan has said, 'God does not reveal the deep things to the casual Christian who drops in for a chat.'

Discernment, depth, discipline – these are the hallmarks of effective, rewarding Bible study.

2. *The delight of living accordingly.* '. . . not forgetting what he has heard, but doing it – he will be blessed in what he does.'

This is the second lesson we can learn from James's description of the person who approaches the Bible in the right way, and the whole thing centres on the phrase 'but *doing* it'. This is the key. The man is not said to be blessed automatically in proportion to the amount of biblical knowledge he accumulates. The blessing comes with his *obedience* to what God has revealed to him. This is a truth on which the Bible is relentlessly insistent: 'By [the ordinances of the Lord] is your servant warned; in keeping them there is great reward' (Psalm 19:11); 'Blessed are they who keep [the Lord's] statutes' (Psalm 119:2); 'Blessed . . . are those who hear the word of God and obey it' (Luke 11:28); 'Now that you know these things, you will be blessed if you do them' (John 13:17); 'Blessed is he who keeps the words of the prophecy in this book' (Revelation 22:7). The Bible's insistence on the relationship between obedience and blessing is inescapable. Notice, too, that in none of these passages is there any indication of precisely *how* an obedient man is blessed. I believe there is a reason for this, namely that when a Christian comes to the Word of God with an open, willing heart, and comes from it with a submissive, obedient will, then he will be blessed in every part of his life, whether consciously or otherwise. He will be blessed in his home, in his family life, in his work, in his Christian service and in the inner recesses of his own soul. The last phrase is important. The greatest blessing of all does not come after obedience, but during it, as part of it. In the mysterious chemistry of God's mercy, a man's very obedience is made a blessing to him and, as John Howe once wrote, 'God is not otherwise to be enjoyed than as he is obeyed.'

This, then, is something of the delight of living accordingly, of constantly reforming one's life according to the teaching of Scripture and the finest summary of all that we have said is given in Scripture itself: 'Blessed is the man who does not walk in the counsel of the wicked or stand in the way of sinners or sit in the seat of mockers. But his delight is in the law of the Lord, and on his law he meditates day and night. He is like a tree planted by streams of water, which yields its fruit in season and whose leaf does not wither. Whatever he does prospers' (Psalm 1:1–3).

11.

False and true religion

'If anyone considers himself religious and yet does not keep a tight rein on his tongue, he deceives himself and his religion is worthless. Religion that God our Father accepts as pure and faultless is this: to look after orphans and widows in their distress and keep oneself from being polluted by the world' (James 1:26, 27).

For many people, few words in the English language have such a dreary connotation as 'religion'. It conjures up a picture of monotonous discipline and dreary routine – what J. B. Phillips somewhere calls 'rites and robes, bells and smells' and seems so utterly irrelevant to the issues of daily life.

Yet this is a tragic caricature of the truth as we find it in Scripture. There we discover a religion that is expressed not in terms of dead formality but living faith, something that is not remotely removed from everyday life but relevantly woven into every aspect of it. It is to the subject of religion that James now turns in these two verses and in a flurry of vivid strokes he paints two striking pictures – one of the false religion in which many are deceived and another of the kind of religion with which God is delighted.

1. False religion condemned

'If anyone considers himself religious and yet does not keep a tight rein on his tongue, he deceives himself and his religion is worthless' (v. 26).

Although we are looking at them separately, it is obvious that the two verses now before us are closely linked with what has gone before and especially with the section beginning at verse 22. Throughout this larger section James has been deeply concerned about the person who fondly imagines that things are right when in fact they are wrong and, as we noticed, the greatest danger he foresaw was that of people who 'merely listen to the word' (v. 22) and deceive themselves into imagining that by this outward act of religious observance they have fulfilled their duty to God and can expect his approval and blessing. James is so anxious to warn us about the dangers of making that tragic mistake that he now goes on to expose and condemn such false religion in three specific ways.

1. A lack of reality. 'If anyone considers himself religious . . . he deceives himself.' By picking these two phrases out from James's opening sentence we can immediately sense the terrible tragedy he is concerned for us to avoid. The word translated 'religious' is the Greek *threskos,* which is not found anywhere else in the Bible. It seems generally agreed that there is no single word in the English language which can capture its precise meaning, but basically it speaks of the outward observance of religious ceremony of one form or another. Here, then, is a man who not only appears to be on the right track, but actually considers himself to be so. He moves in Christian circles, attends the right kind of church, reads the right kind of books, has the right kind of label; but the fact of the matter is that 'he deceives himself'.

How penetratingly the Bible exposes that sort of thing! Paul specifically says that one of the signs of 'the last days' will be that of people 'having a form of godliness but denying its power' (2 Timothy 3:1, 5), while the angel's piercing analysis of the church in Sardis was this: 'You have a reputation of being alive, but you are dead' (Revelation 3:1). The form was there, the name was there, the reputation was there; but there was no life, no reality! Is that not true about so much of our church life today? We have equated busyness with blessing, programme with progress, yet I suspect that so much of it is lacking in reality. The story is told of Arnold Thomas being shown around St Paul's Cathedral. During the tour he asked the guide whether he enjoyed his work. 'Yes,' the man replied, 'but there is only one drawback. I can never get to a place of worship!' Do you see the unconscious truth that may lie hidden in that reply? The man spent his whole life within the four walls of that magnificent shrine, yet never got to a place of worship! Does that have any application in your life? Think of the number of hours you spend in religious observance of one kind or another – at services, Bible studies, rallies, fellowship meetings, prayer meetings and the like. Then ask yourself this: 'How often do I get to a place of worship?' Does that begin to search you, find you out?

One of the inner tests of true worship is this: does it make me sense the presence of God? Joseph Twitchell tells how he went to visit his old friend Horace Bushnell. As he was leaving late at night, his host walked part of the way with him and before turning back said, 'Let us kneel and pray.' Recalling the moments that followed, Twitchell said, 'I was afraid to stretch out my hand in the darkness in case I should touch God!' Do you ever, or often, or often enough, have a similar sense of awe in your religious observance, either in public or in private? It is certainly true that our faith is not to be based on our feelings, but equally true that if our faith is not accompanied by feelings it is suspect. Can we really hope to have a living relationship with the eternal God and remain unmoved? Beware of the danger of slipping into a comfortable routine of outward religion that is lacking in reality.

2. A lack of restraint. '. . . and yet does not keep a tight rein on his tongue'. With characteristic bluntness, James exposes one of the clearest ways in which men reveal the falsity of their faith, the unreality of their religious profession, and that is by the words they speak. Try as he might, a man will eventually betray himself with his mouth, because as Jesus taught so clearly, 'Out of the overflow of the heart the mouth speaks' (Matthew 12:34). Few things give a clearer indication of the state of a man's heart than the words he speaks and the way in which he speaks them, and in the course of his letter James is to return to the subject of the tongue again and again as a means of testing the quality of spiritual life.

The particular fault he diagnoses here is a lack of restraint; he has in mind the person who 'does not keep a tight rein on his tongue'. James is the only New Testament writer to use this particular metaphor (he does so again at 3:2, 3) but it is powerfully appropriate. He sees the tongue as a powerful animal, needing to be restrained, held on a tight rein, kept in check, and sees failure to do so as evidence of a lack of divine grace in the heart. As far as James is concerned, a tongue uncontrolled by the speaker is the sign of a heart uncontrolled by the Saviour.

James is to deal with the use of the tongue at some length later on, but perhaps we should emphasize just one particular point at this stage and that is that the wrong use of the tongue is so easy. As Robert Johnstone puts it, 'Almost before we are conscious that a thought has entered the mind, before we have taken a moment to ponder its nature or the consequences of uttering it, it has leaped into outward life as a spoken sentence.' If that is true of sins of the tongue in general, it is surely true of one area in particular, and that is barren, negative, destructive criticism. In Thomas Manton's phrase, 'Censuring is a pleasing sin, extremely compliant with nature.' We do not have to work hard to find fault in others, to put people down, to get our own back, to stand in judgement on our fellow men – and how often we do so, without any thought of the damage we may be causing! Travelling along the beautiful Sognefjord in Norway on one occasion, I was told that the snow is sometimes so delicately poised on the mountainsides surrounding the fjords that in the spring, when it begins to melt, the sound of a human voice can be sufficient to bring it crashing down in an avalanche of destruction and death. In the same way, there are situations in our lives – at home, at work, in the church, in our social lives – so delicately poised that the sound of a human voice can trigger off an avalanche of pain and sorrow. How many times, even within our relatively closed Christian circles, has God's work been blighted and frustrated by the effects of a carnal, uncontrolled tongue! Each one of us needs to pray with David, 'Set a guard over my mouth, O Lord; keep watch over the door of my lips' (Psalm 141:3), and to remember that one of the marks of falsity in religious profession is a tongue that is lacking in restraint.

3. A lack of results. '. . . his religion is worthless.' The adjective James uses is the Greek word *mataios*, which literally means 'empty of result' and elsewhere in the New Testament there is a perfect example of its use in the same kind of context. When Paul healed a crippled man at Lystra, the crowd went wild with excitement and shouted out, 'The gods have come down to us in human form!' (Acts 14:11.) In the ferment that followed, the priest of Zeus brought bulls and wreaths to the city gates because the crowd wanted to offer sacrifices to Paul and Barnabas, but the apostles shouted, 'Men, why are you doing this? We too are only men, human beings like you. We are bringing you good news, telling you to turn from these worthless things to the living God, who made heaven and earth and sea and everything in them' (Acts 14:15). Here is the same word and the incident at Lystra gives a perfect illustration of its meaning. Paul and Barnabas were insisting that the worship of idols, and of themselves as men, was worthless, because it could produce no positive result. It could never achieve the purpose for which it was ignorantly practised; it could never make a man right with God. Now this is the word that James uses in the verse we are studying. He says that in the matter of a man's relationship with God, superficial religious activity that is marred in the ways we have noticed in this verse is 'worthless'; it can have no results. Let me underline that in two ways.

In the first place, *it is worthless to man.* This is the personal tragedy of it all. The person who acts in the ways we have seen will not get any spiritual benefit from that kind of religion. There may be a lot of activity in it, but there will be no advance. Unless we have a hunger and thirst for reality in our religion, unless we are determined to apply God's Word to our daily lives in godly discipline, there is a terrible danger that we shall settle for the religious roundabout, the organized orbit which fills the diary but not the heart.

In the second place, *it is worthless to God.* To put it bluntly, that sort of thing cuts no ice as far as God is concerned. To the God who searches our hearts, superficial religious observance is utterly worthless. Listen to this devastating indictment of the kind of religion James has in mind:

'Hear the word of the Lord,
  you rulers of Sodom;
listen to the law of our God,
  you people of Gomorrah!
"The multitude of your sacrifices –
  what are they to me?" says the Lord.
"I have more than enough of burnt offerings,
  of rams and the fat of fattened animals;
I have no pleasure
  in the blood of bulls and lambs and goats.
When you come to appear before me,
  who has asked this of you,
  this trampling of my courts?
Stop bringing meaningless offerings!
  Your incense is detestable to me.
New Moons, Sabbaths and convocations –
  I cannot bear your evil assemblies.
Your New Moon festivals and your appointed feasts
  my soul hates.
They have become a burden to me;
  I am weary of bearing them.
When you spread out your hands in prayer,
  I will hide my eyes from you;
even if you offer many prayers,
  I will not listen . . ."'

(Isaiah 1:10–15).

Let us examine ourselves in the light of those words! All outward religious observance that is divorced from a genuine spirit of worship is an abomination in the sight of God, utterly worthless as far as he is concerned. It brings no glory to his name, no joy to his heart. It therefore fails in the very things which should unite to be its first aim. It is surely no wonder that here in James's letter and elsewhere in Scripture false religion is so roundly condemned.

2. True religion commended

'Religion that God our Father accepts as pure and faultless is this: to look after orphans and widows in their distress and to keep oneself from being polluted by the world' (v. 27).

James now turns from the negative exercise of condemning

false religion to the positive exercise of commending true religion, and he does this by giving two illustrations of the kind of outward service that is acceptable to God. Perhaps we need to underline the fact that James is only giving two examples. When he writes, 'Religion that God our Father accepts . . . is this . . .' he is not giving us a definitive description of religion. Instead, he is illustrating the kind of thing he expects to see when a man's religion is real, when his Christianity is genuine.

Yet perhaps another word of introduction is necessary before we look at James's two examples, because the claim he makes for religion characterized by these things is very exalted. He says that this religion is accepted by God as 'pure and faultless'. Now that language sounds very much like the language of justification. It is the kind of language you would expect Paul to use when writing about the great doctrine of justification. But whereas Paul insists that 'A man is justified by *faith* apart from observing the law' (Romans 3:28), James seems to lay the emphasis on a man's *deeds,* his kindness to others and his personal discipline in moral behaviour. Then is this a flaw in James's writing and therefore in the unity and authority of the New Testament? Is he championing a way of salvation different from that preached by Paul, who says, 'For it is by grace you have been saved, through faith – and this not from yourselves, it is the gift of God – not by works, so that no one can boast'? (Ephesians 2:8, 9.) Not at all! The issue of the alleged conflict between Paul and James really comes to a head much later on, rather than in this first chapter, but this verse hints at it, if only by implication. Without taking time or space here to call the evidence, let me just crystallize the position like this: what Paul is saying in places like Ephesians 2 is that justification *never results from* good works; what James is saying, over and over again, is that justification *always results in* good works. We shall develop this theme later on in our studies, but for the time being let us bear this general principle in mind. James sees genuinely good works as being the natural outcome of a spiritual income and his over-riding concern is that those who claim to have a living faith should give evidence of it by living the right kind of religious life. Now we are ready to look at the two examples he gives.

1. Practical helpfulness. '. . . to look after widows and orphans in their distress . . .' This is not only typically down-to-earth writing from James, but completely in tune with his description of God as 'our Father' and in tune, too, with the biblical teaching that sees God as 'a father to the fatherless, a defender of widows' (Psalm 68:5). It is also fascinating to turn back to Isaiah 1 and to continue reading where we left off earlier in this particular study. We saw Isaiah 1:10–15 as a solemn commentary on James 1:26, where false religion was condemned, but if we now read on for two more verses we shall see that they are a commentary on James 1:27, where true religion is commended. Listen to what God goes on to say through the Old Testament prophet:

> 'Your hands are full of blood;
> wash and make yourselves clean.
> Take your evil deeds
> out of my sight!
> Stop doing wrong,
> learn to do right!
> Seek justice,
> encourage the oppressed.
> Defend the cause of the fatherless,
> plead the case of the widow'
> (Isaiah 1:16, 17).

What an amazing unity there is in Scripture, and how inflexibly the Word of God insists that we must show the reality of our faith by the quality of our lives, not least by loving kindness to those in need! As Alec Motyer rightly says, 'Caring love for the helpless is not an accidental or optional manifestation of the new nature, but part of its essence.'

The word translated 'distress' is the Greek *thlipsis,* which has as its primary meaning suffering brought about by the pressure of circumstances. Does that not help to open your eyes to the tremendous range of human need there is in the world today? Is not that word 'pressure' one of the most commonly felt pains in our society? There are people in your neighbourhood, your city, your town, your street, perhaps next door, who are at this very moment under severe pressure of one kind or another. Perhaps it is the pressure of a large family or a low income, the pressure of chronic illness or sudden bereavement, the pressure of unkind discrimination or a fractured relationship, the pressure of mental illness or unemployment. Now James says that true religion will show itself in that kind of situation by the Christian going to the help of the person in need, doing all that he can to alleviate the suffering and ease the pressure. Now think of the people you know near at hand who are in some kind of distress brought about by the pressure of circumstances. Are you doing all that you could, or all that you should, to 'look after' such people? No amount of attendance at church services will absolve you of your responsibility of proving your faith by your works in helping those in need.

2. Personal holiness. '. . . and to keep oneself from being polluted by the world.' This final exhortation completes the picture James has been painting. In discussing the general subject of 'religion' he has so far touched on two areas. The first was what we might call our direct relationship with God, as expressed in outward religious observance, and he dealt with that negatively, showing that that by itself was important but not adequate. The second was what we might call our relationship with others, as seen in our response to those in need. The third area, which completes the picture, is our own moral integrity and it is to this that James now turns.

When he speaks of 'the world', James has in mind humanity at large in its natural state of sinful rebellion against God, exactly as John did when he wrote that 'The whole world is under the control of the evil one' (1 John 5:19). Although by derivation the Greek word used here – *kosmos* – means the ordered world, that is to say a structured and arranged entity, it is often used in the Bible in the sense of the disordered world, a society in moral and spiritual chaos as a result of man's sin. But not only is the world in a state of chaos, it is also in a state of corruption. In an earlier study we saw that James included things like anger and the wrong use of the tongue as 'moral filth' (1:21), a striking indication of the fact that, with other New

Testament writers, he saw sin of every kind not merely as deviation from the truth or an inferior quality of life, but as being inherently polluted and corrupt. This, then, is the world in which we must temporarily live as Christians and to recognize this is to realize that we are in constant danger of becoming polluted by our surroundings. As Thomas Manton put it, 'The world is a dirty, defiling thing. A man can hardly walk here but he shall defile his garments . . . The men of the world are sooty, dirty creatures. We cannot converse with them but they leave their filthiness upon us.' It is a sad commentary on the widespread spirit of compromise abroad among Christians today that many would treat Manton's words as pious overstatement, whereas they are as true today as when they were first written. Let a sensitive Christian think carefully about the common practices of society today – its immorality, its dishonesty, its greed, its selfishness, its violence, its envy, its arrogance, its blasphemy, its cruelty, its materialism, its obsession with pleasure and above all its careless or calculated rejection of God. Can there be any question in his mind that these things are not only polluted but polluting? Can we seriously imagine that we can walk in that kind of atmosphere, breathe in that kind of air every day of our lives and not become affected by it? We would be fools if we did and it is precisely for that reason that James gives us the directive he does here. Nor is he alone in this. Paul tells us, 'Do not conform any longer to the pattern of this world, but be transformed by the renewing of your mind' (Romans 12:2) and John says bluntly, 'Do not love the world or anything in the world', adding the serious warning that 'If anyone loves the world, the love of the Father is not in him' (1 John 2:15).

Now when James says that we are to keep ourselves from being polluted by the world he is not suggesting that we can do so in our own strength. He is not suggesting that whereas salvation is entirely the work of God's grace, sanctification is a matter of man's unaided effort. There is a hidden paradox here, one that comes out in an interesting way towards the end of the little Epistle of Jude. There, the apostle urges his readers, 'Keep yourselves in God's love . . .' (Jude 21), but a moment later writes of God as the one 'who is able to keep you from falling . . .' (Jude 24). This is what we might call one of the mysteries of grace and grace is always a mystery to man's mind because it is foreign to his nature. But however paradoxical it might seem, we must accept what Scripture says. The holiness which can only be accomplished by the power of God will only be accomplished by the care of man. No amount of pre-occupation with the doctrine of God's sovereignty will absolve us from our own searching responsibility.

Then how are we to keep ourselves from being polluted by the world? There are negative and positive answers to that question. *Negatively*, we are to reject its standards: no Christian should take his cue from the moral and ethical standards presented to him by the mass media of radio, television and press, nor by any social grouping of his fellow men. We are to repulse its lies: the world makes many fulsome promises, of happiness, fulfilment and satisfaction, but the truth of the matter is that at the end of the day it can give none of these. The world can no more fulfil a man than a triangle can fill a circle. We are to resist its temptations: the fact that 'everybody is doing it' can easily weaken the Christian's resolve to take a stand on many issues, but temptation in any form must be resisted at every turn. We are to repel its pressures: in a permissive society there are very real pressures to go along with the majority and to abandon the lonely pathway of submission to biblical absolutes, but they must be resolutely turned aside as siren voices. *Positively,* our response also has many facets. In the first place we must give unwearied attention to the Word of God, seeking constantly to reform our lives by obedient submission to its teaching. There is abiding significance in Jesus' words to his heavenly Father: 'Sanctify them by the truth; your word is truth' (John 17:17). Then we must learn to lean constantly on the promises of God's presence, love, grace and power, remembering that it is through what Peter calls his 'very great and precious promises' that we can 'escape the corruption in the world caused by evil desires' (2 Peter 1:4). Then we must constantly remember that we are under divine orders to live godly lives, that we can never for one moment escape the demands placed on us as children of God, a responsibility summed up in the command: 'Be holy, because I am holy' (1 Peter 1:16). We must feed our minds on those things conducive to growth in godliness; in Paul's words, 'Since, then, you have been raised with Christ, set your hearts on things above, where Christ is seated at the right hand of God. Set your minds on things above, not on earthly things' (Colossians 3:1, 2). We must exercise iron discipline not only in matters that are obviously wrong, but in the many areas that are open to question. We must learn to keep at the painful process of obeying the Bible's instruction to 'put to death . . . whatever belongs to your earthly nature' (Colossians 3:5).

Finally, we must cling constantly to God in prayer, in earnest acknowledgement of our own impotence and his omnipotence in overcoming the sinister and satanic powers that are ranged against us. If we do so with a genuine longing to be free from the world's polluting influence, John Wesley's translation of Antoinette Bourignon's words will reflect perfectly the spirit in which we pray:

> Henceforth may no profane delight
> Divide this consecrated soul,
> Possess it thou who hast the right
> As Lord and Master of the whole.

12.

The dangers of discrimination

> *'My brothers, as believers in our glorious Lord Jesus Christ, don't show favouritism. Suppose a man comes into your meeting wearing a gold ring and fine clothes, and a poor man in shabby clothes also comes in. If you show special attention to the man wearing fine clothes and say, "Here's a good seat for you," but say to the poor man, "You stand there," or "Sit on the floor by my feet," have you not discriminated among yourselves and become judges with evil thoughts?'* (James 2:1–4.)

Nothing in the whole Epistle of James is more typical of his teaching than the passage now before us. Here are sound doctrine, pastoral warmth, wise counsel and practical common sense – and all brought to life with the clearest of illustrations. We can helpfully study the passage under four headings.

1. The intimacy that he shared
'My brothers' (v. 1).

James frequently uses this little phrase in the course of his letter and it often marks the introduction of a new subject, or a new slant on the subject with which he is dealing. Yet there seems to me to be more to it than that and that James uses the phrase not merely to focus his readers' interest, but to underline the intimate relationship he had with them. Paul has a lovely example of this in that little gem of a book, the Epistle to Philemon. The background would seem to be that Philemon, a wealthy man living in the city of Colosse, owned a slave called Onesimus. The word 'Onesimus' means something like 'useful', but he ran away and, if the usual inference drawn from verse 18 is correct, stole some of Philemon's property at the same time. Now where would such a man go? The answer is obvious. Certainly not to a small village where every stranger would be recognized; he would go to a big city, where he would be hidden in the crowd. He would want to be anonymous as well as Onesimus! And that is exactly what he did; he went to the great metropolis of Rome, with its teeming masses of people. Then the story took a dramatic, exhilarating turn, as God stepped into the life of this runaway slave. Here was someone who would be loathed by anyone who knew anything about him, yet he was loved by the Lord, who knew everything about him! He tried to run away from identification with individual people by going to the city of Rome and God brought him in touch with the apostle Paul, the key figure in the Christian church! There, in prison, Paul led Onesimus to Christ and then he sent him back to his master with an accompanying letter which we now call the Epistle to Philemon.

The whole letter breathes a beautiful Christian spirit, but nowhere more than where Paul says he is sending Onesimus back to his master 'no longer as a slave, but better than a slave, as *a dear brother*' (Philemon 16). We need to grasp the significance of that! Here is the mighty Paul, who before his conversion was a Hebrew of the Hebrews, a member of the élite tribe of Benjamin and a strict and zealous Pharisee, and now a mighty apostle entrusted by God to receive 'surpassingly great revelations' (2 Corinthians 12:7). He is writing of a man who would be regarded as the scum of the earth, a thieving runaway slave who ran the risk of having his treachery shown by being branded on the forehead. Yet Paul reaches right across the vast social, religious and moral gulf that had separated them and calls him 'a dear brother'! And the reason why he could do such a thing? Because Onesimus was 'a brother *in the Lord*' (Philemon 16). Their relationship was not in terms of the world's vague philosophy about 'the fatherhood of God and the brotherhood of man'; instead, they knew the deep, spiritual intimacy of a fellowship in which 'each member belongs to all the others' (Romans 12:5) and are 'all one in Christ Jesus'

(Galatians 3:28). Now it is this same intimacy, with its built-in facets of equality as well as unity, that James has in mind as he addresses his readers as 'my brothers', and his use of the phrase will become even more significant as we study the next words.

2. The inconsistency that he saw

'. . . as believers in our glorious Lord Jesus Christ, don't show favouritism' (v. 1).

We shall see the details of this inconsistency in a moment, but briefly it was this: people were saying one thing and doing another. Now that was something James could not tolerate. His great concern was that creed and conduct should agree, that belief and behaviour should go together, and here was a situation in which this was not so. What exactly were the ingredients that made up this inconsistency?

1. A profession of faith. His readers are described as 'believers in our glorious Lord Jesus Christ'. This phrase has proved notoriously difficult to translate with certainty. Taken literally from the Greek it would read, 'our Lord Jesus Christ of the glory', and the difficulty has arisen over the exact placing and use of the word 'glory'. Rather than join the commentators' carnival over the point, let us note just one alternative to the phrase used in the NIV, and that is that it should read, 'the Lord Jesus Christ [who is] the Glory'. If this is what James intended, then he is using the word 'glory' not as an adjective to describe Christ, but as a noun to define him. Although this is done nowhere else in the New Testament, it is very close in thought to the statement that 'The Son is the radiance of God's glory and the exact representation of his being' (Hebrews 1:3). In context, there seems little doubt that it is the eternal deity of Christ that James has in mind here and two other New Testament verses will help to underline the relevance of the point.

The first has to do with *his nature.* In the course of his great high-priestly prayer Jesus said, 'And now, Father, glorify me in your presence with the glory I had with you before the world began' (John 17:5). Although he had been born in Bethlehem about thirty years earlier, Jesus reminds his heavenly Father of a glory they had shared for all eternity. This glory was not something that Jesus had acquired. It was part of his eternally divine nature; he was and is the glorious Lord, the Lord of glory!

The second has to do with *his nearness.* In the early part of Old Testament history God had told Moses, 'You cannot see my face for no one may see me and live' (Exodus 33:20) and this principle had remained deeply ingrained in Jewish belief. Yet when Jesus came to earth, John wrote of him, 'The Word became flesh and lived for a while among us. We have seen his glory, the glory of the one and only Son who came from the Father' (John 1:14), and when Philip asked him to show the disciples the Father, Jesus replied, 'Anyone who has seen me has seen the Father' (John 14:9). Here is the amazing truth that in Jesus Christ the eternal God of heaven became a man on earth. In the words of Charles Wesley's magnificent hymn,

Let earth and heaven combine,
Angels and men agree,
To praise in songs divine
The incarnate Deity,
Our God contracted to a span,
Incomprehensibly made man.

Notice how all this bears on the point James is making. Even the glorious deity of the Lord Jesus Christ did not put him at a distance from men. Both by his eternal nature and the perfection of his earthly life he was 'set apart from sinners' (Hebrews 7:26), but in every part of that life he showed himself to be very near to them, regardless of their rank, resources or reputation. Now we can see what James is getting at. He is saying in effect, 'You profess to be followers of Jesus Christ, the one who, even though he was the Lord of glory, lived among men without fear or favour, totally unaffected by men's resources or social standing. But you are *not* following him.' That brings us to the next phrase in our text.

2. The practice of flattery. '. . . don't show favouritism.' 'Favouritism' translates the Greek word *prosopolempsiais,* a combination of the noun 'face' or 'person' and the verb 'to lift up'. This background helps us to bring out its full meaning in the context in which James is using it, which is to show favouritism to certain people because of their position or possessions. Yet this is something the Bible condemns in a number of ways. It is condemned by the very character of God; using exactly the same word as James, Peter said, 'I now realize how true it is that God does not show favouritism' (Acts 10:34). It is condemned by God's instructions to his people; the Israelites were clearly commanded, 'Do not show partiality to the poor, or favouritism to the great' (Leviticus 19:15). Even more precisely to the point here, it was condemned in the life of Jesus, even his enemies having to admit, 'Teacher, we know that . . . you do not show partiality' (Luke 20:21).

Now we can see what James saw! Throughout his earthly life Jesus showed no partiality (the Greek is *prosopon,* the root of the very word James uses); he was never swayed by men's position or possessions. Yet here were those who professed to be his followers acting in exactly the opposite way. As we shall see later, they were flattering the rich and despising the poor. Somebody has said that the difference between flattery and gossip is that gossip is saying behind a person's back what you never say to his face, while flattery is saying to his face what you never say behind his back. In the course of his letter, James condemns both of these; here it is flattery, calculated favouritism, that comes under attack, for the specific reason that it is inconsistent with a profession of faith in the one whose life was utterly devoid of such a thing. When we see people as Jesus saw them, we see them as we should. In Joseph Parker's words, 'He whose eye is filled with Christ never sees what kind of coat a man has on.'

3. The illustration he showed

'Suppose a man comes into your meeting wearing a gold ring and fine clothes, and a poor man in shabby clothes also comes in. If you show special attention to the man wearing fine clothes and say, "Here's a good seat for you", but say to the poor man, "You stand there", or "Sit here on the floor by my feet . . ." ' (vv. 2, 3).

Although the word translated 'meeting' has other uses, we are clearly meant to picture a group of Christians at worship. Two strangers arrive. One is clearly wealthy, as he is dressed in 'fine clothes' and is also wearing 'a gold ring'. Some translations have 'gold rings', which may well be right, as the original Greek word – *chrusodaktulios* – literally means 'gold-fingered'. He had a gem at every joint, a nugget on every knuckle! The other man was just as plainly poor; not only is that very word used of him, but his shabby clothing bears it out. What a contrast these visitors presented – one in rings and the other in rags! Now notice the way they were treated. The rich man was offered 'a good seat', while the poor man was given the alternative of standing somewhere or of sitting on the floor. Here was blatant discrimination of the worst kind, because it was based not on the visitors' moral qualities but on their financial resources. In fact, there were two evils here: indulgence of the rich and indifference to the poor; too much attention being paid to the attractive person and too little to the unattractive.

It is so easy to be guilty of that kind of thing. Some years ago I was sharing the ministry at a Christian conference centre. During the conference, one of the other speakers asked me whether I had ever spoken to a particular member of the staff – a rather simple soul, somewhat over middle-aged, not really very attractive and doing a very menial task. Although the conference had already run for a week, I had to admit that I had not ever said one word to her, at which my colleague said, 'I go out of my way to speak to her every day. You see, most people pass her by.' Most people ignored that lady. They just passed her by and kept to more interesting, more attractive people. But this man went out of his way to spend time with her, to make her feel just as important as anyone else. I have never forgotten that lesson I needed to learn!

Is a jewel less precious because it comes in a plain box? Is a person less important when bound up with what *we* judge to be a limited mind or an unattractive outward appearance? As the Bible bluntly puts it, 'To show partiality is not good' (Proverbs 28:21). One last point here: we must probably assume that these visitors were not believers, but is there not an added dimension to our sin when we despise fellow Christians, those in whom the Lord of glory has deigned to dwell? All of these lessons come out clearly in the illustration James shows.

4. The iniquity he states
'. . . have you not discriminated among yourselves and become judges with evil thoughts?' (v. 4).

We have all seen the kind of competition in which we are asked to spot the number of deliberate mistakes an artist has made in a picture. Here in the picture James has painted, we can see three things that are clearly wrong.

1. A wrong mixture. '. . . have you not discriminated among yourselves . . .?' It has been said that 'The church must be the one place where all distinctions are wiped out. In the presence of God all men are one.' Let us remember that! The ground at the foot of the cross is level. Christians are 'all one in Christ Jesus' (Galatians 3:28) and there is a sense of equality as well as unity built into that particular phrase. In the early days of the Christian church it was sometimes known for a slave to be served by his master at the Lord's table, as a vivid illustration of their equality. Let us never forget that the Christian church is a truly classless society. Yet the precise truth of James's point may lie elsewhere, because the word 'discriminated' is basically the same as the word translated 'doubt' in 1:6, which obviously carries along with it the meaning of inconsistency or uncertainty. What James may be saying is that although these Christians professed to be putting their trust in the Lord, they were in fact also relying on their ability to gain whatever rewards they could by discrimination and flattery.

We need to examine our hearts here! Are we truly living a life of faith? Are we trusting God to honour our honesty, or are we resorting to crafty flattery in the hope of gaining something or another? Are we trying to trust God and man at the same time? If so, then we are using flattery where we are claiming to exercise faith – and that is a wrong mixture.

2. A wrong manner. '. . . and become judges . . .' The word James uses here is perfectly straightforward and the meaning clear. By their very attitude these people had obviously set themselves up as having the right to pass judgement on other people in a manner plainly forbidden by the Word of God. There was a deplorable arrogance in their attitude. A friend of mine who took over a small and rather sluggish church became very burdened with the situation and began distributing literature and doing personal evangelism in the local clubs, public houses and the like. When the church members heard of this, they issued him with an ultimatum: either he stopped doing this kind of thing or he left the church. 'We don't want you going into places like that,' they told him. 'The next thing you know is that some of those people will come to our church, and we don't want them worshipping with us.' Of course, he had no choice but to leave and God honoured his ministry elsewhere. In Britain, at least, it is impossible for a convicted criminal ever to become a judge in a court of law; in the kingdom of God it is never right for a forgiven sinner to set himself up as a critical judge of other men's qualities and characters. Quite apart from his comments in the next few verses, James will return to the subject later (at 4:11, 12). In the meantime, let Paul underline his message to us: 'Therefore let us stop passing judgement on one another' (Romans 14:13). To act as a self-appointed judge is to act in a wrong manner.

3. A wrong motive. '. . . with evil thoughts'. The word 'thoughts' is the Greek *dialogismos,* from which we get our word 'dialogue'. The picture is one of weighing up the pros and cons before coming to a decision and in context the word 'evil' surely tells us what their line of thinking would be. It would be carefully calculated to gain their own selfish ends. Now it is bad enough to find that kind of thing among unconverted people – Jude wrote of those who 'boast about themselves and flatter others for their own advantage' (Jude 16) – but surely it is doubly shameful to find it among Christians!

Let us seriously apply the whole of this passage to our lives, seeking to avoid at all costs the carnal favouritism and careful flattery of which it speaks, and remember that 'Man looks at the outward appearance, but the Lord looks at the heart' (1 Samuel 16:7).

13.

The Lord is King!

'Listen, my dear brothers: Has not God chosen those who are poor in the eyes of the world to be rich in faith and to inherit the kingdom he promised to those who love him?' (James 2:5.)

This verse is part of a segment of teaching that continues through to verse 13, but there may be a particular significance in the opening phrase: 'Listen, my dear brothers.' The first word seems obviously intended to attract his readers' very close attention. It is almost as if he were saying, 'Now listen very carefully while I underline the danger of the kind of behaviour I have been describing.' Not only that, but he then goes on to call his readers 'my *dear* brothers', an even more affectionate term than he used in verse 1, at the beginning of this section. I wonder why? Perhaps it was to reassure them that his anger at the sin they were committing in no way affected his deep personal affection for them. One of the most difficult things in the Christian life is to hold this balance between hatred for sin and love for the person committing it, the balance perfectly exemplified in the Lord Jesus, who was 'full of grace and truth' (John 1:14). It is possible to be passionately concerned for truth and at the same time to be harsh and unloving, or to be so concerned not to hurt anyone's feelings that we compromise to keep the peace. Both Jesus and James show us the way of balance and blessing in this area.

Now what does James have to say in this verse? It has been said time without number that the Epistle of James is a very practical book and, of course, that is true. But we must beware of the dangerous inference that it is not, therefore, a doctrinal book. Nothing could be further from the truth and the robustness of James's theology comes powerfully across in this particular verse. The verse in itself is not a challenge, nor is it a command. It is a statement in the form of a question and it holds together under two general headings.

1. The Sovereign's right

'Has not God chosen those who are poor in the eyes of the world . . .?'

It is vitally important to notice that James argues his case against discrimination not on the grounds that God does *not* choose, but on the grounds that he *does*! This seems quite extraordinary, but its irresistible logic will come through as we recognize that James is basing his argument on a truth which forms part of the bone structure of the whole Bible, and that is God's sovereign right to do precisely what he wishes to do with the whole of his own creation. Remove that truth from the Bible and you are left with a haphazard jumble of religious words; recognize it in the Bible and you have a firm basis for everything else you read. James's words now tell us three things about God's sovereign right to choose out a people for himself and for his own purposes.

1. It is incontestable. 'Has not God chosen . . .?' This is a question to which there can only be one answer! The Bible teems with the truth from Genesis to Revelation. Moses told the children of Israel: 'The Lord your God has chosen you out of all the people on the face of the earth to be his people, his treasured possession' (Deuteronomy 7:6); it is said of Levi and of every priest in the Levitical order: 'The Lord your God has chosen them . . .' (Deuteronomy 18:5); when Saul was announced as king, Samuel said, 'Do you see the man the Lord has chosen?' (1 Samuel 10:24); David's testimony to the people of Israel was 'Yet the Lord, the God of Israel, chose me . . .' (1 Chronicles 28:4); God told his people: 'I have chosen you and have not rejected you' (Isaiah 41:9); and he told Zerubbabel: 'I have chosen you' (Haggai 2:23). The same vein of truth continues in the New Testament. Jesus told his disciples: 'You did not choose me, but I chose you . . .' (John 15:16); Paul assured the Christians at Thessalonica: 'God chose you to be saved' (2 Thessalonians 2:13); Peter told his Christian readers: 'But you are a chosen people . . .' (1 Peter 2:9); and in the last book in the Bible we are told that Christ's eternal triumph will be shared by those who are 'his called, chosen and faithful followers' (Revelation 17:14). This, then, is the rock on which James builds his case – God has chosen.

A great deal is said in Christian circles on the subject of man's free will, but much of it is said without a scriptural understanding that man's will is in bondage to his nature, which is at enmity with God. This means that man's will is not in fact free at all; it is held in bondage. It is free, if you like, to operate or to choose within a certain area, but that area is limited by man's sinful nature. That is why when we say that at our conversion we come freely to Christ (and we can legitimately say that) we mean that we came only because, in the words of the hymnwriter,

> Thou has made us willing,
> Thou hast made us free.

When people come to Christ they come willingly, they come freely, but only because God in his sovereign grace has overwhelmed their sinful nature and made them willing and free to come. Until we understand this we have no true understanding of the miracle of a person's salvation at all. Without that truth, man contributes to his own salvation by exercising his own free will. But is the truth not this – that the only person in the entire universe with free will is God? That, surely, is the incontestable verdict of Scripture. Speaking in a Spirit-filled moment of divine revelation, Nebuchadnezzar said, 'I . . . raised my eyes towards heaven, and my sanity was restored. Then I praised the Most High; I honoured and glorified him who lives for ever. His dominion is an eternal dominion; his kingdom endures from generation to generation. All the peoples of the earth are regarded as nothing. He does as he pleases with the powers of heaven and the peoples of the earth. No one can hold back his hand or say to him: 'What have you done?' (Daniel 4:34–36). There is the clearest possible statement of God's sovereign right and especially of the fact that it is incontestable.

2. It is unconventional. '. . . the poor in the eyes of the world . . .' What an unconventional choice! After all, human choice is always on the grounds of ability, importance, influence, wealth or some other advantage. In James's own illustration, the rich man was received and the poor man rejected. That kind of choice is conventional and carnal; it is man's way of doing things. But God does not work in that way and he often chooses people the world would pass by. When I lived in the Channel Islands, our Youth Fellowship met every Thursday evening on one of the lovely beaches on the north coast of Guernsey. After a hectic swim we would pick teams to play beach cricket. The captains would begin by choosing the fellows, especially those who were good at games. Then they would start choosing the girls, first of all those who were fast runners, then those who were less athletic. Finally, there would be only one person left and she would be told, 'You had better go with that lot'! For quite some time the same person was always left at the end. She was a simple-minded girl and very slow-moving, too, because she was very seriously overweight. She was always the last person to be chosen. In fact, she was not really chosen at all; she was thrown in! Why? Because it was thought that there was nothing whatever that she could contribute to the game. Yet, for all her simplicity, excess weight and a certain unattractiveness, God had chosen her. She was a Christian. We never chose her, but God did!

Paul brings out this whole point quite brilliantly when writing to the Corinthians, 'Brothers, think of what you were when you were called. Not many of you were wise by human standards; not many were influential; not many were of noble birth. But God chose the foolish things of the world to shame the wise; God chose the weak things of the world to shame the strong. He chose the lowly things of this world and the despised things – and the things that are not – to nullify the things that are, so that no one may boast before him' (1 Corinthians 1:26–29). These Christians only had to look around their own congregation to see that God had not chosen them on merit! He chose the foolish to become faithful; the weak to become witnesses; the lowly to become loyal; the despised to become disciples and the world's nobodies to become the Lord's nobility. What an unconventional choice! Yet as Matthew Henry puts it, '[God] is a better judge than we what instruments and measures will best serve the purposes of his glory.'

3. It is unconditional. This is precisely the logic that James is driving home. The Bible teaches that while God does choose, 'God does not show favouritism' (Romans 2:11), that is to say, God chooses without any regard to a person's gifts or goodness or anything else. His choice is totally unconditional and nowhere does this come across more clearly than where we are told that God 'chose us in [Christ] before the creation of the world' (Ephesians 1:4), that is to say, even before we were born. C. H. Spurgeon's comment on this was along these lines: 'It is perfectly obvious that God chose me, because I would never have chosen him, and it is equally clear that he must have chosen me before I was born, because I am sure he would not have chosen me afterwards'! Nowhere in the whole Bible are we given a single hint of a reason outside of himself as to why God should choose to bring certain people to salvation. Even a spiritual giant like Moses could get no further than telling the children of Israel: 'The Lord has chosen you . . . because the Lord loved you' (Deuteronomy 7:6–8). No wonder Paul has to speak of 'this love that surpasses knowledge'! (Ephesians 3:19.)

The story is told of a man who told his minister that he had difficulty in understanding God's statement: 'Jacob I loved, but Esau I hated' (Romans 9:13). The minister agreed that the verse was difficult to understand and asked the man where his particular problem lay. He said, 'In the second part, of course. I can't understand how God could hate Esau.' 'Well my difficulty has always been with the first part,' the minister replied, 'because I can't possibly understand how God could love a crafty, dishonest scoundrel like Jacob!'

In one brief phrase, James has touched depths beyond man's understanding, telling us that God has chosen 'the poor in the eyes of the world'. Not all poor people are chosen, nor does God limit his choice to the poor, but what is clear is that his choice is uncontestable, unconventional and unconditional – and that, the Bible teaches, is the Sovereign's right.

2. The saints' riches

'. . . to be rich in faith and to inherit the kingdom he promised to those who love him'.

It is important to notice James's precise wording here. People were not chosen because they were rich in faith; they were chosen *to be* rich in (or through) faith. Grace is not a reward for faith; faith is the result of grace. What is more, this God-given faith enables the Christian to see more and more of the truth that in Christ he is 'enriched in every way' (1 Corinthians 1:5). We can helpfully follow this through along two lines.

1. The saints' riches here. '. . . to be rich in faith . . .' To use a simple analogy, it is when we put on the spectacles of faith that we are able to see the riches that are ours here on earth, and the greater our faith, the more clearly do those riches come into focus. Here is someone with no more than a *grain* of faith; just enough to see that Christ died in his place and to trust him as his Saviour. Now that person is already richer than the wealthiest sinner in the world, because he possesses eternal life. It does not take a great faith to be a Christian – it takes faith in a great Saviour!

Next we have a person with *growing* faith, someone who sees a bit more. He sees Christ not only as his Saviour, but as the one who enables, guides and strengthens him day by day. Someone has said, 'An incident is only a problem when I have no resources.' The person with growing faith sees more and more of the resources that are his in Christ.

Then think of someone with *great* faith. He sees even further. He sees that all his circumstances are ordained by God for his benefit and blessing. One only has to read the book of Job to find a vivid illustration of the fact that nothing happens outside of the sovereign control of God. But it takes great faith to see that when your world is crumbling, when the sky is dark, when the pressures increase and the problems mount. Yet great faith does see it! It seems that a sovereign God of wisdom and love does not allow a single incident to come into one's life without God's intention that one should be enriched as a result. Great faith enables the Christian to cry with Paul, 'I am convinced that neither death nor life, neither angels nor demons, neither the present nor the future, nor any powers, neither height nor depth, nor anything else in all creation, will be able to separate us from the love of God that is in Christ Jesus our Lord' (Romans 8:38, 39). To know that is to see that even here on earth the poorest saint is richer than the wealthiest sinner.

2. The saints' riches hereafter. '. . . and to inherit the kingdom he promised to those who love him'. When King George VI died quite suddenly in 1952, I vividly remember our newspaper's headline the next day: 'The Queen Flies Home.' Just for a moment, I thought the editor had made a monumental error. Surely we didn't have a queen yet? The king had only died a few hours ago and the coronation would not be until the following year. But I was wrong; we did have a queen. Although the official, public coronation would not be held until much later, the king's eldest daughter Elizabeth, who was in Africa at the time, became queen the moment her father died. The picture is not perfect, but it helps us to see a tremendous truth James is stating here. A better translation of the original would be '*heirs* of kingdom . . .', though, of course, the sense remains the same. Christians are 'heirs of God and co-heirs with Christ' (Romans 8:17) and while they may be rejected in this world they will reign in the next. They are already 'a kingdom and priests to serve . . . God' (Revelation 1:6); their coronation will come later, at the end of time. James's words suggest three things about the kingdom of God which Christians have been called to inherit.

Firstly, *it is supreme because of God's power.* James contents himself with the phrase 'the kingdom', but what vastness lies hidden there! Any reader of history will surely be amazed at the tremendous wealth and power some rulers have gathered unto themselves. Some dynasties have been staggering in their size and influence. Yet the Bible says this about God: 'Surely the nations are like a drop in a bucket; they are regarded as dust on the scales; he weighs the islands as though they were fine dust . . . Before him all the nations are as nothing . . . and less than nothing' (Isaiah 40:15, 17). What a crushing comment! The kingdom of God is supreme because in heaven we shall be beyond the reach of every trial and difficulty, every temptation and sin, every pain and pressure. All our enemies will have been destroyed, all our fears banished, all our doubts removed, all our hopes realized, all our longings fulfilled. Nothing, surely, could be greater than that!

Secondly, *it is sure because of God's promise.* James says that Christians are chosen 'to inherit the kingdom he promised' and there are two words here that have a wonderful sense of certainty about them. The first is 'inherit', which translates the Greek word *kleronomous,* a compound word combining the noun 'a lot, or portion' and the verb 'to possess'. James is not sharing a vague speculation, he is stating an absolute certainty, just as Peter does when he speaks of 'an inheritance that can never perish, soil or fade – *kept in heaven for you*' (1 Peter 1:4). The second word is 'promised'. Now in human terms even that word must be hedged about with 'ifs' and 'buts', because so many factors can come between the promise and the fulfilment. But here is a word of promise given by God himself, of whom the Bible says, 'No matter how many promises God has made, they are "Yes" in Christ' (2 Corinthians 1:20). The Christian can be as certain of arriving in heaven as he is that Christ has already ascended there.

Soon after Adoniram Judson went to Burma as a missionary he was captured by natives who strung him up by the thumbs and then flung him into a filthy prison. Then they asked him, 'And now what of your plans to win the heathen to Christ?', to which Judson replied, 'My future is as bright as the promises of God.' Every Christian can say the same!

Thirdly, *it is sublime because of God's presence.* James says that the kingdom of God is the inheritance promised 'to those who love him'. Quite literally, the original wording would read 'to the ones loving him', and this helps to bring out the point that for the Christian heaven is not a conditional reward but a continuing relationship, though, of course, at a level we will never have known before. There will be no need for faith there, for faith will have been emptied into sight; there will be no need for hope, for hope will have been fulfilled in realization; but there will be love, and heaven for the Christian is to be for ever in the deepest relationship he has ever known, with the one he loves above all else and all others. Heaven will be sublime because of God's presence!

I once had a letter from a little girl who wrote, 'Dear Uncle John, I want to ask you a very serious question. When I get to heaven, will I see my white rabbit?' I am not quite sure what I told that little girl, but I am sure I included the line of thought with which we close this study, and that is that when she reached heaven she would be so caught up with an all-consuming view of the Lord Jesus Christ in all his glory that even the state and location of her white rabbit would assume their correct proportions!

Somebody has said that the most satisfying definition of heaven in the Bible is in Jesus' words: '. . . where I am . . .' (John 14:3). That is a beautiful way of stating a wonderfully precious truth. Anne Ross Cousin caught the same spirit in these words:

> The bride eyes not her garment,
> But her dear bridegroom's face;
> I will not gaze at glory,
> But on my King of grace;
> Not at the crown he giveth,
> But on his pierced hand;
> The Lamb is all the glory
> Of Immanuel's land.

14.

Lessons for life

> *'But you have insulted the poor. Is it not the rich who are exploiting you? Are they not the ones who are dragging you into court? Are they not the ones who are slandering the noble name of him to whom you belong?'* (James 2:6, 7.)

One of the most helpful things ever said to me on the subject of Bible study is that of every passage of Scripture we can ask three questions: What did it mean at that time? What does it mean for all time? What does it mean at this time? We could helpfully apply this formula to these two verses, which at first glance may seem somewhat irrelevant to us today. They clearly meant something at that time, that is to say, when they were originally written. They have a historical context. People were actually doing the things James mentions here. Yet as we study them, we shall see their abiding principles (what they mean for all time) and their practical application to our own lives (what they mean for this time). Let me frame the study into three obvious lessons that James is teaching here.

1. There is a peril we must avoid
'But you have insulted the poor' (v. 6).

The opening words, 'but you', immediately tell us that we must read these words in the context of what has come before. In the previous verses James pointed out that in his infinite grace God had chosen many people who were poor in the eyes of the world to inherit his eternal kingdom: 'But *you*', he now goes on, 'have insulted the poor.' His point of emphasis becomes instantly clear. He was telling his readers that their actions and attitudes were exactly the opposite to God's. The illustration of the two men coming into church was a perfect example of this. They had barely tolerated the poor man, yet it was from among the poor that God chose many to be given the honoured title 'children of God' (1 John 3:1). They had decided that the poor man was not worthy to sit with them in church, yet many poor men were included in those whom 'God raised . . . up with Christ and seated . . . with him in the heavenly realms' (Ephesians 2:6).

It is obviously this alarming difference in approach that James is at pains to point out here and he does so by using the emphatic pronoun '*you*'. He was dismayed to find them behaving in this way and determined to point out the seriousness of what they were doing by showing that in relation to the will of God it was not just a slight deviation but a direct contradiction. We have already seen this to be so in the context of salvation, in that they had rejected as a class a whole group of people from among whom many had been chosen to be fellow-heirs with Christ in the kingdom of God; but if we broaden the picture to take in all that the Bible has to say about God's attitude towards the poor, then the behaviour of James's original readers becomes even more reprehensible. Few things in Scripture are more striking than the number of times it speaks of God's compassion for the poor. Here are some examples taken from just one book: 'From your bounty, O God, you provided for the poor' (Psalm 68:10); 'The Lord hears the needy' (Psalm 69:33); '[God] stands at the right hand of the needy one, to save his life from those who condemn him' (Psalm 109:31); '[God] raises the poor from the dust and lifts the needy from the ash heap' (Psalm 113:7); 'I know that the Lord secures justice for the poor' (Psalm 140:12). James's emphatic 'But *you* . . .' now comes across with even greater force! Insulting the poor was not only contrary to God's special, saving mercy extended to many who lacked this world's riches, but also his general attitude of mercy to all who were in need.

But we can add another factor to the indictment of this kind of behaviour and that is that it is a crime against our common humanity. The Bible says, 'Rich and poor have this in common: The Lord is the Maker of them all' (Proverbs 22:2). As James himself says later, all men (rich and poor) are 'made in God's likeness' (3:9) and as such have the right to be treated with decency and dignity. As Thomas Manton puts it, 'God never made a creature for contempt.' It is in the light of all of this area of truth that James presses home his condemnation of those who 'insulted the poor'.

Writing on these verses in his book *A Belief that Behaves*, Canon Guy H. King called his chapter 'The short-sighted usher' and if we can pin the fault on one man for sake of illustration that seems to me to be a very good definition. The usher was short-sighted. He saw the two visitors only in the immediate context of their material possessions or lack of them. He saw them only in earthly focus and so ran the risk of rejecting someone God would receive and insulting someone God would honour. Taken to its ultimate conclusion, there could hardly be a more terrible sin.

Yet we, too, can suffer from the same miserable myopia. There is a very real danger of developing the kind of philosophy within the church that almost unconsciously excludes from our fellowship, our worship, our service, indeed the whole of our careful interest all those whom we judge to be below our station, or of becoming so concerned with matters of doctrine that we neglect to work it out in love and mercy to those in need. Here is a peril we must avoid, because it is a serious breach of God's law, which commands us to 'show mercy and compassion to one another' (Zechariah 7:9). God has promised a specific blessing to those whose actions here are along the line of his will: 'He who is kind to the poor lends to the Lord, and he will reward him for what he has done' (Proverbs 19:17). This alone would be sufficient reason for agreeing with John Andrew Holmer's comment that 'There is no exercise better for the heart than reaching down and lifting people up'!

2. There is a pressure we must anticipate

'Is it not the rich who are exploiting you? Are they not the ones who are dragging you into court?' (v. 6.)

James now brings another argument to bear on the situation and, as C. L. Mitton puts it, shows that their preferential treatment of the rich was 'not only a disgrace to their profession as Christians', but also 'a mark of something less than good sense'. In essence he tells his readers that their actions were not only sinful but senseless, because they were flattering the very people who were persecuting them. James puts his argument in the form of two questions, one general and one specific. The general one is this: 'Is it not the rich who are exploiting you?' The verb is another of those compound Greek words, *katadunasteuousin,* the middle part of which is the root of our English word 'dynasty'. The only other time the word is used in the New Testament gives us an illustration of its meaning, when Peter tells us that Jesus 'went around doing good and healing all who were *under the power* of the devil' (Acts 10:38). The picture is one of cruel oppression, the callous exercise of superior power. It is not difficult to prove James's claim that Christians were under this kind of pressure. Going through the Acts of the Apostles, I have found about fifty instances of Christians being persecuted for their faith, by beating, stoning, scourging and imprisonment, as well as by slander and abuse of one kind or another.

James's second question is more specific: 'Are they not the ones who are dragging you into court?' The emphatic use of the word 'they' suggests that the rich people being foolishly flattered were in a position to take direct and personal legal action against the Christians and again there is ample evidence to support this. It was the wealthy Sadducees who 'seized Peter and John, and . . . put them in jail' before putting them on trial (Acts 4:1–3); Saul of Tarsus, armed with official authority from the high priest at Jerusalem, was on his way to Damascus, 'breathing out murderous threats against the Lord's disciples' and determined to 'take them as prisoners to Jerusalem' (Acts 9:1, 2) when he was miraculously converted, and he later admitted, 'On the authority of the chief priests I put many of the saints in prison, and when they were put to death, I cast my vote against them' (Acts 26:10). No wonder that in commenting on this section John Calvin says that it seems odd to honour one's executioners and in the meantime to injure one's friends! But why did rich or influential people persecute the Christians? We can certainly find three obvious reasons.

1. The gospel hit at their positions. This would be particularly true of those who held high religious positions in the land. The Christian gospel of salvation by grace and through faith would sweep away the rituals, ceremonies and sacrifices that provided the grist to their ministerial mills. This explains precisely why 'the chief priests and the teachers of the law' had constantly been 'looking for some way to get rid of Jesus' (Luke 22:2).

2. The gospel hit at their pockets. When Paul exorcised a spirit of divination from a slave-girl at Philippi, her owners 'seized Paul and Silas and dragged them into the market-place to face the authorities' because they 'realized that their hope of making money was gone' (Acts 16:19). Later, there was the incident at Ephesus, the headquarters of those who worshipped the goddess Artemis. We are told that a silversmith called Demetrius 'brought in no little business for the craftsmen' by making religious paraphernalia. Recognizing that he would instantly lose the custom of people who became Christians, he called the craftsmen and related tradesmen together and warned them that because of Paul's preaching there was a double danger: 'not only that our trade will lose its good name, but also that the temple of the great goddess Artemis will be discredited . . .' (Acts 19:27). The order in which the dangers are mentioned is significant! Needless to say, his hearers were incensed and soon the whole city was in an uproar and Paul's associate evangelists, Gaius and Aristarchus, were dragged into the amphitheatre to face a public trial. When the gospel threatened to hit at people's pockets, then the gospel and those who preached it must go.

3. The gospel hit at their pride. Many of the early Christians were poor and before their conversion had contracted debts with rich money-lenders. Hearing their debtors claim spiritual richness and liberty would no doubt anger the lenders, who thought only in materialistic terms, and as they often had corrupt judges in their pockets they would find it very easy to turn the screw on the Christians. There may well be more than a hint of this in Jesus' statement that 'It is hard for a rich man to enter the kingdom of heaven' (Matthew 19:23). The gospel says that in obtaining favour with God, money is meaningless and that was something these proud and wealthy men could not stomach.

How does all of this apply to us today? When Paul wrote about 'the offence of the cross' (Galatians 5:11) his phrase had a meaning far beyond its immediate context. There is a general principle we must accept because it points to a particular pressure we must anticipate. The cross will always be an offence to the natural man. Man wants the results of the cross but never its requirements. He wants the happiness that it brings, but not the holiness that it demands; the comforts that it offers, but not the cost that it involves. Any preaching and way of life that takes all of the pride, arrogance, wealth and authority of man and lays it in the dust is never likely to be universally popular. There is a pressure we must anticipate. If we preach the kind of message and live the kind of life that takes man down off his self-made pedestal and lays him in the dust before an omnipotent and sovereign God, then it is not going to be popular, and we are going to be pressurized. Jesus himself made this crystal clear: 'If you belonged to the world, it would love you as its own. As it is, you do not belong to the world, but I have chosen you out of the world. That is why the world hates you. Remember the words I spoke to you: "No servant is greater than his master." If they persecuted me, they will persecute you also' (John 15:19, 20). There is the pressure we must anticipate. We must not excite it, but we must expect it. As John Newton said, 'Can the servant expect or desire peace from the avowed enemies of his Master? We are to follow his steps; and can we wish, if it were possible, to walk in a path strewed with flowers when his was strewed with thorns?'

3. There is a profanity we must abhor

'Are they not the ones who are slandering the noble name of him to whom you belong?' (v. 7.)

This was the climax of their crime. They not only dragged the Lord's people into court, they dragged the Lord's name into contempt, the Pharisees even going so far as to suggest that Jesus performed his miracles of healing 'by Beelzebub, the prince of demons' (Matthew 12:24). No wonder James points out the stupendous folly of toadying to men to whom Christ was no more than a swear word! James's phrase suggests two things.

1. A great dignity. '. . . the noble name of him to whom you belong'. The NIV translators have chosen the word 'noble' for the Greek *kalos,* which is normally rendered 'good', but does carry with it the sense of being better than others – a reminder to the Christian that the Lord Jesus has 'the name that is above every name' (Philippians 2:9). The Saviour we worship has a name invested with all the dignity of deity. The phrase 'him to whom you belong' captures the spirit of the original Greek, even though it is hardly a precise translation of the words, which would be better rendered '[the noble name] which was called upon you'. It seems to stem from the ancient Jewish custom of calling their children by the name of their ancestors, as when the dying Jacob laid his hands upon Ephraim and Manasseh with the words: 'May they be called by my name' (Genesis 48:16). It is interesting that the only other time the phrase occurs in the New Testament is when James reminds the council at Jerusalem of God's prophecy through Amos about 'all the Gentiles who *bear my name*' (Acts 15:17). All of these renderings help to fill out the general sense of Christians being intimately identified with the one to whom they belong, whose children they are. The reference might in fact be to their baptism, which must be '*in the name* of the Father and of the Son and of the Holy Spirit' (Matthew 28:19). If this is so, then James is saying that these rich and ruthless men were not only despising Christians and dragging them into the law courts, they were also slandering the noble name of the triune God which was called upon their victims when they made their open profession of faith.

But there is also a practical application here. If we claim to be God's children, then we should behave in godly ways; if we bear the name of Christ, we have an inescapable obligation to be Christ-like. What is more, the quality of our lives should be such that we have no need to wear badges announcing what we believe and to whom we belong. We may be pilgrims in this world, but we are not tramps. As Christians we bear about with us the noble name of Christ and 'Everyone who confesses the name of the Lord must turn away from wickedness' (2 Timothy 2:19).

2. A great danger. 'Are they not the ones who are

slandering . . .?' This would seem to settle the question as to whether the people James had in mind were Christians or not, for surely no Christian would slander the name of Christ? Surely we are out of danger here? Not at all! Paul tells Christians to behave in such a way 'that God's name and our teaching may not be slandered' (1 Timothy 6:1). We may be guilty of behaving in such a way that we cause others to commit a sin we would never dream of committing ourselves! When the German philosopher Friedrich Nietzsche became interested in Christianity he began to move among Christian people, listening to what they were saying, watching what they were doing. His conclusion was this: 'These Christians will have to look a lot more redeemed before I can believe in it.' So Nietzsche went back to his philosophical searching and eventually became the spiritual father of Nazism and the forerunner of what has come to be known as 'God-is-dead theology'.

That is obviously a very striking example, but it warns us never to underestimate the power of personal influence, and especially of its effect in spiritual terms. We need to guard against any inconsistency of life that turns people away from God, from Christ, from the gospel, or that becomes a factor in leading them to a position where they blaspheme the name we bless. The Rev. H. R. L. 'Dick' Sheppard, of St Martin-in-the-Fields, London, who used to be a renowned 'soap box' orator at Hyde Park Corner, once said, 'If anything emerged from that ancient war of words it was this, that the greatest hindrances to the spread of Christianity are the unsatisfactory lives of professing Christians.' To be an accessory before the crime is a serious offence in the realm of law and it is even more serious in the realm of grace! There is an inescapable challenge in these words of Jesus: 'He who is not with me is against me, and he who does not gather with me scatters' (Matthew 12:30).

In the light of that truth let us aim to make our lives such as will not drive people from Christ, but draw them to him and 'make the teaching about God our Saviour attractive' (Titus 2:10). It was exactly this longing that was expressed by Joachim Lange in these words translated by John Wesley:

Lord, arm me with thy Spirit's might,
Since I am called by thy great name;
In thee let all my thoughts unite,
Of all my works be thou the aim;
Thy love attend me all my days,
And my sole business be thy praise.

15.

The Christian and God's law — I

> *'If you really keep the royal law found in Scripture, "Love your neighbour as yourself," you are doing right. But if you show favouritism, you sin and are convicted by the law as law-breakers. For whoever keeps the whole law and yet stumbles at just one point is guilty of breaking all of it. For he who said, "Do not commit adultery," also said, "Do not murder." If you do not commit adultery but do commit murder, you have become a law-breaker'* (James 2:8–11).

In studying these particular verses, we need to keep in mind that they form part of a segment of teaching that begins at verse 1 and ends at verse 13 and in which James is condemning behaviour towards our fellow men that is based on worldly or material considerations. At this point, he examines such behaviour in direct relationship to God's law and in the particular verses now before us gives us a description of that law and a disclosure of some of its fundamental teaching.

1. How the law is described

'If you really keep the royal law found in Scripture, "Love your neighbour as yourself", you are doing right' (v. 8).

Many suggestions have been advanced as to why James uses this unique phrase 'the royal law'. In what ways can we say that this is a valid description?

1. Its source is royal. At one particular point during our coronation service a Bible is handed to the monarch with these words: 'We present you with this Book, the most valuable thing this world affords. Here is wisdom, *this is the Royal Law.* These are the lively oracles *of God.*' My italics bring out the point! The Bible is royal because it has God as its Author. Nearly 4,000 times in the Old Testament alone, 700 times in the Pentateuch, forty times in one chapter, that claim is made. 'God said', 'God spoke', 'the word of the Lord came', 'the Lord commanded' – this is the language of the Old Testament from beginning to end. Incidentally, if these statements are false, then the Bible is surely the most evil and perverse book ever written, because it tells nearly 4,000 blasphemous lies about its origin in its first section alone! In the New Testament, we find about 600 quotations from the Old, all of them taken as being divinely authoritative; and when the New Testament speaks about itself, notice the terms it uses. Paul told the Corinthians, 'If anybody thinks he is a prophet or spiritually gifted, let him acknowledge that what I am writing to you is the Lord's command' (1 Corinthians 14:37); Peter urged his readers to recall 'the command given by our Lord and Saviour through your apostles' (2 Peter 3:2); John claimed to be writing nothing less than 'the word of God' (Revelation 1:2). In the plainest possible way, the Bible claims to be the royal law, because the King of kings is its Author.

In the People's Bible, published in 1895, Joseph Parker said this: 'The Bible stands alone. Other books are as trees which men have planted, and trimmed, and pruned with periodic care; but the Bible belongs to that forestry of thought, event, direction and sovereignty which human hands never planted – a church built and aisled and lighted in a way beyond the ways of man.' That is wonderful oratory and glorious truth! The Bible stands alone. Its source is royal.

2. *Its subjects are royal.* There is a very real sense in which God's law is meant for every man. It is relevant to every person on the face of the earth, regardless of their knowledge or experience of God. Everyone must reckon as much with God's spiritual law as they must with his physical laws, such as the law of gravity. Nobody can say, 'I do not believe in God and will have nothing to do with the law of gravity'; at least, he may say that, but he dare not live by it! Just as the man who defies the law of gravity will end up breaking

his neck, so the man who defies God's spiritual law will end by damning his soul. In that sense, nobody can ignore God's law; it cannot be set aside. Yet God's law has at least two distinct purposes that we can usefully mention here.

The Bible *helps unbelievers to find Christ.* Writing to the Galatians about their new-found faith Paul says, 'Before this faith came, we were held prisoners by the law, locked up until faith should be revealed. So the law was put in charge *to lead us to Christ*' (Galatians 3:24). Paul is saying that in their unconverted days the Bible's purpose was to reveal their guilt, the terrible truth of their rebellion against God and the utter helplessness of their position, and then to show them that their only hope of salvation lay in accepting God's free gift of salvation in Christ. The Bible points unbelievers to Christ; it shows the provision God has made for them to be 'rescued . . . from the dominion of darkness and brought . . . into the kingdom of the Son he loves' (Colossians 1:13).

The Bible *helps believers to follow Christ.* One of the most powerful evidences of the Bible's unity is the fact that every part of it points to Christ. Jesus himself made it clear that this was true of the Old Testament, saying, 'These are the Scriptures that testify about me' (John 5:39), while the whole of the New Testament is a record of his life and of the teaching committed to his apostles. Every part of the Bible from Genesis to Revelation – law and gospel, psalm and prophecy, narrative and epistle – was written for the blessing, benefit, guidance, comfort, encouragement and strengthening of the children of God, so that they might be 'conformed to the likeness of his Son' (Romans 8:29). The purpose of the Bible for the believer is to enable him to walk the royal road of righteousness. In William Gurnall's words, 'The Christian is bred by the Word, and he must be fed by it.'

3. Its standards are royal. The Bible is not only rightly described as royal because it was given by the King of all kings, but because it is in itself the king of all laws, supreme in both its purity and its power. As Ezekiel Hopkins put it, 'The Bible is the statute-book of God's Kingdom, wherein is comprised the whole body of the heavenly law, the perfect rules of a holy life, and the sure promises of a glorious one.'

But notice that James singles out one particular part of Scripture to describe as 'the royal law' and that is the command: 'Love your neighbour as yourself.' Why does he do that? When Jesus was asked to name the greatest commandment in the law, he replied, '"Love the Lord your God with all your heart and with all your soul and with all your mind". This is the first and greatest commandment. And the second is like it: "Love your neighbour as yourself".' Jesus then added these very significant words: 'All the Law and the Prophets hang on these two commandments' (Matthew 22:37–40). In the first part of his reply, Jesus summarized the first four of the Ten Commandments, those that have to do with our relationship to God. The second part of his reply was a summary of the last six of the Ten Commandments, those that deal with our relationships with one another. Now we can see what James is saying. He says that the command 'Love your neighbour as yourself' is 'the royal law' because it perfectly encapsulates the way in which God requires us to behave towards our fellow men. It sets a royal standard for children of the King! Obviously those who 'really keep' this law are 'doing right'; but James's inference is that his readers were *not*, because they were making distinctions between rich people and poor; they were picking and choosing those towards whom they acted favourably. But the Bible sets a higher standard than that. Biblical love demands that regardless of who people are, regardless of what they believe, regardless of how they behave, regardless of their attitudes or actions towards us, we will constantly seek to act towards them in ways deliberately calculated to bring about their greatest good. That is the biblical meaning of love and when men begin to act like that, things happen!

In his book *Through the Valley of the Kwai*, Ernest Gordon tells of the amazing transformation that took place in a Japanese prisoner of war camp in Burma between Christmas 1942 and Christmas 1943. In 1942 the camp was a sea of mud and filth. It was a scene of gruelling, sweated labour and brutal treatment by the Japanese guards. There was hardly any food and the law that pervaded the whole camp was the law of the jungle, every man for himself. Twelve months later, the ground of the camp was cleared and clean. The bamboo bed slats had been de-bugged. Green boughs had been used to rebuild the huts and on Christmas morning 2,000 men were at worship. What had happened? During the year a prisoner had shared his last crumb of food with another man who was also in desperate need. Then he had died. Among his belongings they found a Bible. Could this be the secret of his life, of his willingness to give to others and not to grasp for himself? One by one the prisoners began to read it. Soon the Spirit of God began to grip their hearts and change their lives and in a period of less than twelve months there was a spiritual and moral revolution within that camp. It was lifted from disgrace to dignity by the royal standards of the Word of God. When the Bible begins to be lived, men begin to be lifted. God's Word is royal in its source, its subjects and its standards.

2. What the law discloses

'But if you show favouritism, you sin and are convicted by the law as law-breakers. For whoever keeps the whole law and yet stumbles at just one point is guilty of breaking all of it. For he who said, "Do not commit adultery," also said, "Do not murder." If you do not commit adultery but do commit murder, you have become a law-breaker' (vv. 9–11).

James now moves from an indication of what the law is to an indication of what it says, but notice that he is still relentlessly nailing down this one particular sin of 'favouritism', this calculated partiality in personal relationships and behaviour.

1. The guilt over which we should mourn. A casual reader might feel that in hammering away at this business of favouritism James is making a very large mountain out of a very small molehill. After all, he admits that courtesy and kindness were at least being shown to some; was selectivism really as serious as all that? Yes it was! And the particular words James uses drive the point home. There are two main Greek words for sin in the New Testament: *hamartia*, which means 'missing the mark' and *paraptoma,* which means 'trespassing' or stepping over the line, and James considers the matter with which he is dealing serious enough to bring in both of these concepts. 'But if you show favouritism,' he says, 'you sin *[hamartian]* and are convicted by the law as law-breakers *[parabatai]*.' Surely it is significant that James uses both words to condemn this kind of behaviour! Favouritism is not trivial; it is intolerable. As C. L. Mitton puts it, 'It is an affront to God, not an amiable weakness.' No sin is to be regarded as small, because the God who forbids all sin is so great. Minimizing sin is a device of the devil. Beware of falling into the trap!

James then develops the matter of the seriousness of sin by saying that 'Whoever keeps the whole law, and yet stumbles at just one point is guilty of breaking all of it.' The logic here is irresistible. James is not saying that the man who commits one sin is held to be guilty of committing every other sin, nor is he saying that to break one part of the law is to break every other part of the law. What he *is* saying is that because the law of God is an entity, a unity, even one sin results in the law as a whole being broken. This is the crushing truth that has to be faced by the unconverted person who is hoping to cancel out his bad deeds by his good ones. As Paul told the Galatians, even the man who tries to obtain God's favour by religious observance is 'obligated to obey *the whole law*' (Galatians 5:3). Earlier in the same letter he wrote, 'All who rely on observing the law are under a curse, for it is written: "Cursed is everyone who does not continue to do *everything* written in the book of the Law"' (Galatians 3:10). Notice the 'everything'! The man seeking to get right with God under his own steam is in a hopeless position, because he would need to keep every single part of the law of God throughout his entire life.

But there is a lesson here for the Christian, too, and that is that he is not allowed to pick and choose his virtues. The law of God is not like an examination paper which says, 'Only six questions out of ten need to be attempted'! The law of God is not like a pile of stones, from which you can remove one without anyone noticing its loss. It is like a pane of glass – one crack and the whole pane is broken. We could use other analogies – one severed link and the whole chain is broken; one puncture and the whole tyre is flat; one leak and the boat is sunk. In the light of this kind of teaching, which of us can honestly claim to be living as we should? As John Trapp once put it, 'If the best man's faults were written in his forehead, it would make him pull his hat over his eyes'!

In exactly the manner we have come to expect of him, James next backs up his principle (v. 10) with an illustration (v. 11). The phrases 'he who said' and 'also said' bring James's picture into even clearer focus, because they make the point that the commands 'Do not commit adultery' and 'Do not murder' were both spoken by the same God and were therefore integral parts of the one law. It would be absurd for a murderer to claim that he had not broken the law because he had not committed adultery! In fact, James's point is so obvious that one might be tempted to leave it there and 'go on to the next bit'. But we dare not do that without reminding ourselves of what Jesus said about these two particular sins in the course of the Sermon on the Mount. After reminding the people of the commandment 'Do not commit adultery', Jesus told them that it meant much more than a prohibition of the outward act of fornication and that 'Anyone who looks at a woman lustfully has already committed adultery with her in his heart' (Matthew 5:27, 28). Likewise in underlining the commandment 'Do not murder', Jesus said that 'anyone who is angry with his brother' was likewise 'subject to judgement' (Matthew 5:21, 22).

Now one can surely say that it would be an astonishing thing to find a Christian committing murder; but can we say that we are never angry, bitter or resentful? Must we not all plead 'Guilty' when the commandment is expressed as Jesus did? And what about adultery? I know of nothing more heart-breaking than the way in which this loathsome leprosy has touched Christian homes in this generation, wrecking marriages by the thousand. Yet before we catch up our righteous robes and say that at least we are free from that particular sin, let us remember what Jesus said about it. Can we truthfully plead 'Not Guilty' to the charge of the lustful look, the impure thought, the provocative manner or the unwise association? And these are only some of the applications of just two of the Ten Commandments!

Where would we stand if we could hold in our minds the full implication of every one of them? No doubt we may be able to claim innocence here and there; we may be better in certain areas than others; we may have succeeded where some have failed – but the fact is that James has found us out. As far as the law of God is concerned, whenever we sin we are 'guilty of breaking all of it'. The law discloses the guilt over which we should mourn.

2. The grace over which we should rejoice. John Calvin once wrote, 'James seems more sparing in proclaiming the grace of Christ than it behoved an apostle to be', and you may well be asking where we find grace in these verses. I would certainly have to admit that it is not stated explicitly, but I have come to the conclusion that it is suggested irresistibly. We have been studying a section which shows us all to be law-breakers, guilty, every time we sin, of violating God's law. If we are in any way sensitive to the Holy Spirit's voice at this point, we find ourselves utterly exposed in the sight of God and crying out with the psalmist: 'Do not bring your servant into judgement, for no one living is righteous before you' (Psalm 143:2) and asking, 'If you, O Lord, kept a record of sins, O Lord, who could stand?' (Psalm 130:3.) How can we possibly go on as Christians when we realize that even at our best we fall so far short of what God commands us to be?

We need to be very clear in our thinking here and to recognize our precise relationship to God in the matter of his law. As Christians we are under a most searching moral obligation to keep it in every part, yet at the same time we may dare to say this: that just as we were not saved by our obedience before our conversion, so we are not kept saved by our obedience after conversion. This is because the question of being saved, of being justified, is not a matter of law at all, but of grace, through faith. It is a matter, as Paul expressed it for himself, of 'not having a righteousness of my own that comes from the law, but that which is through faith in Christ – the righteousness that comes from God and is by faith' (Philippians 3:9). Here, surely, is truth that helps us to see something of the wonder of God's grace! God does not lower his standards for us when we become Christians. He does not excuse our sins and failures. Yet the fact remains that in terms of our justification we are still treated as being 'in Christ' (2 Corinthians 5:17). As far as the Christian's justification is concerned, the penalty due for his every sin, from birth to death, has been paid once for all in the death of Christ, while the life of Christ, in all of its perfect obedience to the law, is the only life God takes into account. Could there be anything more wonderful than that? How the Christian should continually rejoice at the glorious grace of God! In the words of Samuel Davies,

> Great God of wonders! all thy ways
> Are matchless, godlike and divine;
> But countless acts of pardoning grace
> Beyond thine other wonders shine.
> Who is a pardoning God like thee?
> Or who has grace so rich and free?

16.

The Christian and God's law — II

'Speak and act as those who are going to be judged by the law that gives freedom, because judgement without mercy will be shown to anyone who has not been merciful. Mercy triumphs over judgement!' (James 2:12, 13.)

This is the second of two studies over which we have put the general heading 'The Christian and God's law'. In the previous passage (vv. 8–11) James showed us that God's 'royal law' convicts us all and that, even as Christians, we break God's law every time we commit sin of any kind. Yet we also saw, by implication rather than direct statement, God's amazing grace in the justification of the believer, placing him into a position in which all his disobedience – past, present and future – is debited to Christ's account and all of Christ's perfect obedience to the law is credited to the believer. There are dimensions here that many Christians have failed to grasp. They think of salvation mainly in terms of forgiveness, but while forgiveness is certainly a part of salvation, it is *only* a part. The glory of the biblical doctrine of justification is that the Christian is eternally 'in Christ'. Recognizing this, he can turn to a holy God in the spirit of these words by Isaac Watts:

The best obedience of my hands
Dares not appear before thy throne;
But faith can answer thy demands,
By pleading what my Lord hath done.

But does this mean that a Christian can live carelessly? If his past, present and future sin all comes within the scope of his justification, can the Christian live just as he pleases? Far from it! No Christian can afford to be careless and James now turns to this issue as he brings in the subject of judgement. Three main headings will give us an overall picture of what he is saying in these two verses.

1. The reckoning we must face

'. . . those who are going to be judged by the law that gives freedom . . .' (v. 12).

I have deliberately picked these words out from the body of the text at this point because I believe it will be helpful to the rest of our study if we consider them first. Notice two things here.

1. A firm statement. '. . . those who are going to be judged . . .' The first thing to be clear about is that this is an *inclusive* statement and not an *exclusive* one. While the Bible teaches that for some people there will be 'no condemnation' (Romans 8:1), it does not say that for anyone there will be no judgement; in fact, it says exactly the opposite. Speaking of the moment when he would dispense final judgement, Jesus said, 'When the Son of Man comes in his glory, and all the angels with him, he will sit on his throne in heavenly glory. *All the nations* will be gathered before him, and he will separate the people *one from another* . . .' (Matthew 25:31, 32). Paul wrote of a day when 'we will *all* stand before God's judgement seat' (Romans 14:10) and said elsewhere that 'We must *all* appear before the judgement seat of Christ' (2 Corinthians 5:10). Here is a firm biblical basis for our thinking on the subject of eternal judgement and there is a special word in it for two groups of people.

There is *a warning to the unbeliever who thinks he will be excused.* Thomas Adams once wrote, 'Alas! that the farthest end of all our thoughts should be the thought of our ends,' and that is certainly true of the average unbeliever. He lives year in, year out with scarcely a serious thought about judgement, heaven or hell. One of the psalmists has captured perfectly the attitude this kind of person has to these issues: 'He says to himself, 'God has forgotten; . . . and never sees . . . He won't call me to account' (Psalm 10:11, 13). Yet that man is living under a deadly delusion, because nothing could be further from the truth. Psychologist William James once said that every physical sensation and every contact a man has with the outside world leaves a permanent trace on a thousand million cells in the human brain. What a sobering thought! Everything that you say and do and think leaves its trace and mark on a thousand million cells in the human make-up. Down there in the nerve complexities and cells and fibres and molecules of the human chemistry, everything that you have said, been and done is recorded permanently – and will the God who made those recording instruments forget what is recorded?

Notice that the psalmist speaks of the unbeliever's delusion covering the past, the present and the future. As far as *the past* is concerned, he says, 'God has forgotten'; but he is wrong. The Bible says otherwise and warns us that 'God will call the past to account' (Ecclesiastes 3:15). God is going to ask for the records, he is going to examine the books. He is going to require every thought that has ever entered a man's mind, every word that has passed his lips, every action that has occupied his body. God has *not* forgotten. Here, too, is the lunacy of the man who does give some thought to these things, but relies on resolutions. He says, 'I am concerned that one day I will have to face a God of judgement. I know that I am a sinner and that I deserve to be damned. I will simply have to put things right. I will try harder. I will clean up my life. I will stop committing some of those things I know to be downright sinful. I will try to be kinder to my children, my parents, my workmates. I will go to church and start reading the Bible.' Now those resolutions may be commendable, but they cannot alter the fact that 'God will call the past to account' and no man can escape judgement by making resolutions, nor even by keeping them.

As far as *the present* is concerned, the unbeliever says, 'God never sees.' He lives under the delusion that God is either morally blind or limited in his knowledge. This might particularly apply to sins of the heart, mind, attitude or spirit. Because he is able to hide these things from other people, the unbeliever thinks he can hide them from God. But the Bible says that 'Nothing in all creation is hidden from God's sight. Everything is uncovered and laid bare before the eyes of him to whom we must give account' (Hebrews 4:13). Here again, the unbeliever is hopelessly deluded.

As far as *the future* is concerned, the unbeliever says, 'God won't call me to account.' Here there may be an extra strand in his line of thinking and for millions of people it goes something like this: 'Surely the Bible says that God is love? Then how can a God of love possibly reject anybody and send him to hell? I imagine that God might give me some kind of temporary punishment for my sins, but surely at the end of the day a God of love will be bound to forgive me and to receive me into heaven?' Yet that kind of thinking is monumental folly and leads a man straight to hell, because for the unconverted the Bible speaks not of probation, nor of purgatory; instead, it says that 'They will go away to eternal punishment' (Matthew 25:46). No amount of interpretative sleight of hand can remove this solemn truth from the pages of Scripture. The wicked must face the judgement of a holy God whose eyes are 'too pure to look on evil' (Habakkuk 1:13) and the result of that judgement is inevitable. James's words, then, are a warning to the unbeliever who thinks he will be excused. But they have another message.

There is *a warning to the believer who thinks he will not be examined.* Paul makes it clear that the appearance of Christians at the judgement seat of Christ will be 'that each one may receive what is due to him for the things done while in the body, whether good or bad' (2 Corinthians 5:10). There is no question, no possibility, of the Christian being rejected, refused entrance to heaven, because that issue has already been dealt with. As we saw in an earlier study, an inheritance in God's eternal kingdom has already been 'promised those who love him' (2:5) and God will never go back on his word. But the Christian must beware of misapplying that glorious truth and of imagining that on the Day of Judgement his life will not be subject to examination. It will! No less than with the unbeliever, God will sift and weigh every thought, every motive, every word, every action. On that day, the Bible says, the Christian's work will be 'shown for what it is, because the Day will bring it to light. It will be revealed with fire, and the fire will test the quality of each man's work. If what he has built survives, he will receive his reward. If it is burned up, he will suffer loss; he himself will be saved, but only as one escaping through the flames' (1 Corinthians 3:13–15). These are solemn words! The fact that the Christian can face the Day of Judgement secure in the knowledge that he will not be rejected does not mean that he is to think of it in terms of a glorified prizegiving. It will be a judgement, not a jamboree, and while there will certainly be what the Bible calls 'reward' for those things that had been pleasing to God, there will with equal certainty be 'loss' for those things which had grieved him. No truth in Scripture has more practical relevance for the Christian than this, that on the Day of Judgement every moment of his life will come under the searching scrutiny of a holy God; he is 'going to be judged'. Not only that, but this truth has an urgent relevance. The phrase 'going to be' translates the Greek *mellontes,* which literally means 'being about to be', and there is no escaping its impact here. Every Christian should live every moment of every day as if he was on the brink of judgement, as if that day was his last opportunity for what the old theologians used to call 'amendment of life'. For believer and unbeliever alike, then, James has this firm statement – they are 'going to be judged'.

2. A fixed standard. '. . . by the law that gives freedom'. When Abraham was pleading with God for the godly minority living in Sodom, he made a statement absolutely pivotal in our understanding of what is going to happen on the Day of Judgement: 'Will not the Judge of all the earth do right?' (Genesis 18:25.) Here is the answer to all those legitimate questions about the destinies of children who die in infancy, those people who never hear the gospel during their lifetime or those who hear it imperfectly or in a very limited way. We could tie ourselves in knots trying to answer those questions on the basis of some kind of human reasoning, but we have no need to do so, because the Bible makes it clear that in the case of every single individual human being who has ever drawn breath on the face of our planet, God will do what is right in his perfect sight. This is what I mean by 'a fixed standard'. God will judge men by the fixed standard of his own revelation. To some, that will have been no more than the light of nature; to others, the law of Moses; to others, the light of the gospel – yet that standard can rightly be called 'fixed' because it is rooted in God himself. As James is writing to Christians, and as Christians will be judged in the light of the gospel, it is obviously the gospel that he now describes as 'the law that gives freedom'. The phrase seems almost paradoxical: how can a law bring in liberty? In what sense can we say as Christians that the gospel has set us free? Here are just three answers to the crucial question.

In the first place, *we are free from the law's covenant.* This was a covenant of works in which God said, 'Keep my decrees and laws, for the man who obeys them will live by them' (Leviticus 18:5). But the law which demands perfection simply shows us our imperfection. In Paul's words, 'Therefore no one will be declared righteous in [God's] sight by observing the law; rather, through the law we become conscious of sin' (Romans 3:20). It was the Jews' ignorance of this basic truth that broke Paul's heart: 'For I can testify about them that they are zealous for God, but their zeal is not based on knowledge. Since they did not know the righteousness that comes from God and sought to establish their own, they did not submit to God's righteousness. Christ is the end of the law so that there may be righteousness for everyone who believes' (Romans 10:2–4). What vivid phrasing there is here! Knowing their need to be in a right relationship with God, the Jews blindly 'sought to establish their own'; they enslaved themselves to the treadmill of rituals, ceremonies and laws, in the hope that God would accept them on the basis of their own efforts. But they had missed the glorious truth that 'Christ is the end of the law' for everyone who puts their trust in him, because he perfectly fulfilled all the conditions of the law on their behalf. Christ abolished the law as a means of justification, not by destroying it, but by fulfilling it, and all who trust in Christ are free from the law's covenant.

In the second place, *we are free from the law's curse.* There is an excellent, if unconscious, illustration of this in Bruce Hunt's book *For a Testimony*. During the Second World War, Hunt was captured by the Japanese, taken to Manchuria and tried on some trumped up charge or another.

We break into the story as he is waiting for the verdict. The court made its decision and the verdict was read in Japanese and then interpreted into Korean, and it came across to Bruce Hunt like this: 'You are without crime.' Hunt asked, 'Is this a suspended sentence?' 'No,' said the guard, 'this is a suspended judgement. It means that they have not found you guilty and if for two years you do not get into trouble, then everything will be all right.' Hunt then asked why was it a suspended judgement? The guard explained that while the court had not found him guilty, neither had they declared him not guilty. The judgement one way or the other had been left hanging. If nothing came up within the next two years, then the case would be dropped. It now all depended on how the prisoner behaved. If he behaved well for a certain period of time, then the case would be dropped. But if during that period of time he should do something that offended the authorities, then all that he had done in the past would be brought up against him again.

Now that is an illustration by contrast; our liberty as Christians means much more than that. The Bible says, 'Christ redeemed us from the curse of the law by becoming a curse for us' (Galatians 3:13). God's judgement against our sin is not a suspended sentence; instead, that judgement has been meted out in full in the death of Christ. It is there, on the cross, that we find the majesty and miracle of our justification, in that God showed himself 'to be just and the one who justifies the man who has faith in Jesus' (Romans 3:26). The Christian is freed from the curse of the law because Christ was made a curse for him. His suffering is my release; his death is my life; his hell is my heaven. In the words of Charitie Lees De Chenez,

> Because my sinless Saviour died,
> My guilty soul is counted free;
> For God, the Just, is satisfied
> To look on him and pardon me!

In the third place, *we are free from the law's compulsion.* To the unbeliever, the law is an outward thing, pressing against him and making demands he has no wish to fulfil.

But under the new covenant of the law of liberty all that has been changed. The Old Testament prophesied it like this: '"The time is coming," declares the Lord, "when I will make a new covenant with the house of Israel and with the house of Judah. It will not be like the covenant I made with their forefathers when I took them by the hand to lead them out of Egypt, because they broke my covenant, though I was a husband to them," declares the Lord. "This is the covenant I will make with the house of Israel after that time," declares the Lord. "I will put my law in their minds and write it on their hearts. I will be their God, and they will be my people"' (Jeremiah 31:31–33). The difference is obvious and the Christian has entered into this new experience. He can say with the psalmist, 'To do your will, O my God, is my desire; your law is within my heart' (Psalm 40:8). He no longer views the law as an outward, almost hostile thing, but something written in the depths of his own personality.

J. Stuart Holden in his book *Chapter by Chapter through the Bible* says this: 'The law of liberty is the law of love. Christ makes men good, not by outward restraint but by inward restraint; not by inspired fear, but by infused passion. It is the glory and transcendence of the gospel that it creates an instinct of obedience in forgiven souls. We find complete enfranchisement in complete enslavement. His people are made free to do his will; and under its sway become too free to want to do any other.' It is precisely that 'instinct of obedience' that tells the Christian that he has been set free from the law's compulsion and brought into the liberty of longing to do God's will. Yet it is his use of that liberty for which the Christian will one day be judged. This, James is teaching us here, is the reality we must face.

2. The responsibility we should feel
'Speak and act . . .' (v. 12).

These words bring us from the general to the particular. The reality of final judgement is not something that calls for approval, it calls for action; and in one crisp phrase James puts his finger on two areas where action is called for.
1. Our words. 'Speak . . .' It is absolutely typical of James to bring this in first. He has already touched on the use of

the tongue (1:19, 20) and will have a great deal to say about it later (e.g. 3:1–12; 4:11–12). Here, he writes in the context of the Day of Judgement and his words are an irresistible reminder of Jesus' warning that 'Men will have to give account on the day of judgement for every careless word they have spoken' (Matthew 12:36). If this is true of our careless words, how much more is it true of those we have carefully and deliberately used – including criticism, flattery, lying, exaggeration and slander?

2. Our works. '. . . and act . . .' In words that could have been written by James himself, John wrote, 'Dear children, let us not love with words or tongue but with actions and in truth' (1 John 3:18). As we shall see in the next section we study, James has a passionate concern that Christians should practise what they preach; here, he stresses the importance of this by placing it in the context of judgement to come. An Anglican bishop, in giving his final charge to candidates on the eve of their ordination, used to say to them, 'Tomorrow I shall say to you, "Wilt thou . . .? Wilt thou . . .? Wilt thou . . .?" But always remember that the day is coming when Another will say to you, "Hast thou . . .? Hast thou . . .? Hast thou . . .?"' Responsibility brings accountability. What is more, it is important to realize that in this phrase 'Speak and act . . .' both verbs are in the present continuous tense, with the clear implication that we should *always* speak and act as those who are 'going to be judged'. The fact that God is going to take every word and action into account then means that we should take them into account now. This is the responsibility we should feel.

3. The relationship we shall find

'. . . because judgement without mercy will be shown to anyone who has not been merciful. Mercy triumphs over judgement!' (v. 13).

Put very simply, the relationship we shall find is the one between the quality of our lives and the measure of God's judgement. As someone once put it, 'What we weave in time we wear in eternity.' Paul has a phrase about 'the kindness and sternness of God' (Romans 11:22) and both of these are reflected here.

1. The sternness of God. '. . . because judgement without mercy will be shown to anyone who has not been merciful.' The key phrase here is surely 'anyone who has not been merciful'. Here is a man who has shown no mercy in his own life. He has constantly turned a blind eye to the needs of others and a deaf ear to the cries of the poor, the sick and the homeless in society. His life has been centred on self. Now what can we say of such a man? Surely this: a man without mercy is a man without love, a man without love is a man without grace and a man without grace is a man without God. John puts the same truth in the form of a question: 'If anyone has material possessions and sees his brother in need but has no pity on him, how can the love of God be in him?' (1 John 3:17.) The man who is merciless and pitiless is clearly not a Christian because, in Thomas Manton's words, 'It is a sin most unsuitable to grace.' For him, there will not be judgement without justice, but there will be judgement without mercy, reflecting the sternness of God.

2. The kindness of God. 'Mercy triumphs over judgement!' This is a difficult phrase to translate, but perhaps we can helpfully weave two strands of meaning together. The first is that the man who knows in his heart that he has been changed from a self-centred sinner into someone who shows genuine mercy to others can approach the Day of Judgement with confidence, knowing that for him, in R. V. G. Tasker's words, 'The sting of the final judgement will be found to have been already drawn.' There is, of course, no suggestion here that the man's works of love and mercy are the *grounds* of his confidence; rather they are proofs of that greater mercy already shown to him. The second strand of meaning is this: although not even the finest Christian deserves to stand in God's presence, although every Christian has continually fallen short of God's glory in his daily life, God's mercy will triumph over the judgement that would otherwise overwhelm his people. When the saintly Puritan theologian Thomas Hooker lay on his deathbed in 1647, somebody said to him, 'Brother, you are going to receive the reward of your labours,' to which Hooker replied, 'Brother, I am going to receive mercy.' John Greenleaf Whittier put it like this:

I have but thee, my Father; let thy Spirit
Be with me then to comfort and uphold:
No gate of pearl, no branch of palm I merit,
Nor street of shining gold.

Suffice it if – my good and ill unreckoned,
And both forgiven through thy abounding grace –
I find myself by hands familiar beckoned
Unto my fitting place.

There, from the music round about me stealing,
I fain would learn the new and holy song,
And find at last, beneath thy trees of healing
The life for which I long.

17.

Faith and deeds — I

'What good is it, my brothers, if a man claims to have faith but has no deeds? Can such faith save him? Suppose a brother or sister is without clothes and daily food. If one of you says to him, "Go, I wish you well; keep warm and well fed," but does nothing about his physical needs, what good is it? In the same way, faith by itself, if it is not accompanied by action, is dead. But someone will say, "You have faith; I have deeds." Show me your faith without deeds, and I will show you my faith by what I do. You believe that there is one God. Good! Even the demons believe that — and shudder' (James 2:14–19).

The central thrust of the whole of the Epistle of James is crystallized in the section we shall study in the next two chapters. The theme of verses 14–26 is faith and deeds and the whole epistle is a series of variations on that theme.

But not only is this section central to an understanding of everything else James says; it has itself been subject to the most widespread misunderstanding. This is why. In verse 17, for instance, James says that 'Faith by itself, if it is not accompanied by action, is dead'; in verse 20 he says that 'Faith without deeds is useless'; in verse 24 he claims that 'A person is justified by what he does and not by faith alone'; while in verse 26 he states that 'Faith without deeds is dead.'

Now on the surface, those statements seem to run clean contrary to the great biblical doctrine of justification by faith and especially to Paul's insistence on that glorious truth. After all, Paul says, 'For we maintain that a man is justified by faith apart from observing the law' (Romans 3:28); whereas James says that 'A person is justified by what he does and not by faith alone.' Now if Paul and James *are* in conflict then the whole of the New Testament is in ruins, and the authority and unity of the Bible destroyed. It was for this very reason that Martin Luther described the Epistle of James as 'a right strawy epistle' – though he did admit that it was 'full of profitable and precious matter'! But *are* they in conflict? The best way to answer that question is to get down to a close examination of what James says in verses 14–19. Three things form the structure of this passage.

1. There is a false claim

'What good is it, my brothers, if a man claims to have faith but has no deeds? Can such faith save him? Suppose a brother or sister is without clothes and daily food. If one of you says to him, "Go, I wish you well; keep warm and well fed", but does nothing about his physical needs, what good is it?' (vv. 14–16). **'You believe that there is one God. Good! Even the demons believe that – and shudder'** (v. 19).

It would be no exaggeration to say that the whole of this passage and therefore the entire thrust of this epistle, hinges on the word 'claims' in verse 14. The verb in the original Greek is *lego*, which means 'to say', but the NIV's perfectly legitimate alternative gives us an immediate clue to what James is getting at. He produces a hypothetical man who *claims* to be a Christian. But having made that claim, the man has no supporting evidence; he has 'no deeds', nothing to show that his claim is valid. Then James is surely right to ask the question: 'Can such faith save him?' It is vitally important to understand that James is *not* arguing whether or not a man is saved through faith; his real question is whether we must automatically assume that what we might call 'spoken faith' is in fact saving faith. Surely the new birth is followed by new life? How can a man be converted if he is not changed? That is a contradiction in terms. That is James's line of argument and it is one with which Paul would certainly have been in complete agreement, because it was he who wrote, 'Therefore, if anyone is in Christ, he is a new creation; the old has gone, the new has come!'

(2 Corinthians 5:17.) The trouble with the man James introduces is that there is none of that vital evidence. In fact, as he listened to this man saying, 'I am a Christian,' James came to the conclusion that three things were missing.

1. No compassion for others. 'Suppose a brother or sister is without clothes and daily food. If one of you says to him, "Go, I wish you well; keep warm and well fed," but does nothing about his physical needs, what good is it?' As usual, James puts his point in a picture. He speaks of 'a brother or sister' in need, and while this could refer to anybody, he almost certainly has in mind a fellow Christian. This gives added force to his illustration. Christians have a special responsibility to their fellow believers. Paul says, 'Therefore, as we have opportunity, let us do good to all people, especially those who belong to the family of believers' (Galatians 6:10). The Christian church is not a closed shop and Christians should extend their love to all in need, but charity begins at home!

Next, we are told the specific needs of the person concerned – 'without clothes and daily food'. The first phrase translates the Greek *gymnos*, which could also mean 'poorly clothed', but this is a mere technicality. The simple fact was that here was a person in desperate and urgent need. Now (as he obviously intends us to do) let us read James's professing Christian into the picture. What does he have to offer to this needy visitor? Words! 'Go, I wish you well; keep warm and well fed.' But are they of any use? Will words keep the needy person's back warm or his stomach filled? Of course not! And James's whole point is that the kind of faith that stops at words is just as worthless. James is not saying that any person with good deeds is saved, but that the person without them is not. As Thomas Manton puts it, 'The poor will not thank you for your good wishes, neither will God for saying you have faith'!

Back in the Old Testament, that astonishing man Job was able to say this: 'If I have denied the desires of the poor or let the eyes of the widow grow weary, if I have kept my bread to myself, not sharing it with the fatherless . . . if I have seen anyone perish for lack of clothing, or a needy man without a garment, and his heart did not bless me for warming him with the fleece from my sheep, if I have raised my hand against the fatherless, knowing that I had influence in court, then let my arm fall from the shoulder, let it be broken off at the joint' (Job 31:16–22). Could you dare to say the same thing? Have you the same concern for compassion as for creeds? What a challenge this is to heartless orthodoxy, and what a contrast to the man in James's illustration, a man with no compassion for others!

2. No communion with God. 'You believe that there is one God. Good! Even the demons believe that – and shudder.' Although he does not directly relate it to him, we can safely assume that James intends this to represent this man's statement of faith. We might do better to translate it, 'You believe that God is one', which more accurately represents the basic article of Jewish faith, 'The Lord our God, the Lord is one' (Deuteronomy 6:4). Nothing could be more orthodox than that and James's first comment reflects this. 'Good'! he says; but then adds the devastating comment: 'Even the demons believe that – and shudder.' This is certainly a startling statement, but it has a great deal of biblical warrant. We are told that when two demon-possessed men met Jesus they cried out, 'What do you want with us, Son of God?' (Matthew 8:29.) At Capernaum, an evil spirit possessing a man in the synagogue cried out, 'What do you want with us, Jesus of Nazareth? Have you come to destroy us? I know who you are – the Holy One of God!' (Mark 1:24.) Later, we are told that when evil spirits saw Jesus they fell down before him and cried out, 'You are the Son of God' (Mark 3:11).

These and other instances underline precisely the point that James is making here, which is that there are no atheists in hell. Even the evil spirits 'believe' in the sense of knowing a certain amount of biblical truth. After all, those we have mentioned acknowledged the deity of Christ before some of his disciples! There is no shadow of doubt that in this sense the devil himself is a 'believer'. He believes in the eternal existence and power of the one true God, he believes in the deity of Christ, in his virgin birth, perfect life, substitutionary death, glorious resurrection and certain return to the earth. Surely nothing could more vividly demonstrate the difference between a faith that merely consists of mental assent to certain facts and the faith that brings a man into communion with God?

But why can we say that this man had no communion with God? Because of James's comment: 'Even the demons believe that – and *shudder*.' This particular word, used nowhere else in the New Testament, is a translation of the Greek *phrissousi*, whose basic meaning is to have a rough surface. However, it is the kind of word one would use to describe certain aspects of horrified reaction and the Amplified Bible has caught the picture when it says that the demons' reaction to their knowledge about God is to 'shudder in terror such as to make a man's hair stand on end and contract the surface of his skin'! But is that what saving faith does? Does trust in Christ make a person terrified of God? The Bible teaches exactly the opposite: 'Therefore, since we have been justified through faith, we have peace with God through our Lord Jesus Christ' (Romans 5:1). Faith that goes no further than the head can never bring peace to the heart and it is quite clear that the man of whom James is writing had no communion with God.

3. No conversion from self. 'Can such faith save him?' By giving no answer, James means that the answer is 'No'! Let me emphasize once more that James is *not* denying that a man is saved through faith. Instead, he is making it clear that it is not enough for a man to *say* he has faith if the evidence of his life proves otherwise. When Philip was preaching in Samaria, a man called Simon, who had previously practised sorcery, 'believed and was baptized' (Acts 8:13). Later, when Peter and John visited the area, Simon was amazed at the power of their ministry and offered to pay them if they would give him the same power. Peter's reply was direct and devastating: 'May your money perish with you, because you thought you could buy the gift of God with money! You have no part or share in this ministry, because your heart is not right before God . . . you are full of bitterness and captive to sin' (Acts 8:20–23). Here was a man who not only 'believed', but persuaded the church to baptize him, yet his subsequent actions showed him to be unconverted, captive to sin and self, his life still dominated by the capital 'I'. The Bible says, in testing genuine Christian experience, 'The only thing that counts is faith expressing itself through love' (Galatians 5:6). In other words, the way to test a profession of faith is to see whether there is evidence of communion with God, compassion for others and conversion from self. The man James had in mind failed at all three points.

2. There is a foolish compromise

'But someone will say, "You have faith; I have deeds." Show me your faith without deeds, and I will show you my faith by what I do' (v. 18).

This has always been a notoriously difficult verse to interpret with certainty, mainly because of the original absence of punctuation, but our NIV text illustrates one obvious explanation by dividing the verse into two parts.

1. The argument. 'But someone will say, "You have faith; I have deeds."' Here is a snatch of conversation between two people discussing this whole question of genuine Christian experience and the gist of what one of them is saying is this: 'You have a great concern for doctrine, and theology; you place a great emphasis on "faith", on being quite sure of what you believe. Well, that's fine, but you see I am what I would call a practical Christian. For me, Christianity means trying to live up to the Ten Commandments and the Sermon on the Mount. But surely we are both right? We are just different kinds of Christians, that is all. Your Christianity majors on the things you believe, mine majors on the things I do. Surely there is room for both of us?' Now that is the argument, and it is still alive today. But doctrinal indifference is never the answer to doctrinal differences and at the end of the day this kind of argument only succeeds in clouding the issue, not clearing it.

2. The answer. 'Show me your faith without deeds, and I will show you my faith by what I do.' It is probably best to take these words as James's own reply to the argument we have heard and it is obvious that he rejects the suggested compromise out of hand. He does so by throwing out a challenge: 'Show me your faith without deeds.' It may help to understand exactly what James means by putting the first part of his challenge in the form of a question: 'In what other way can you possibly demonstrate to me that your faith is genuine except by living the kind of life that proves it to be so?' The challenge remains relevant today. It is not enough for a person to give mental assent to doctrine, nor even to be a church member. What Jesus said about false prophets is equally true about false professors: 'By their fruit you will recognize them' (Matthew 7:20). It has been cleverly said that genuine faith is like calories; you can't see them, but you can see their results!

The second part of James's answer is to say, 'I will show you my faith by what I do.' Now we need to be crystal clear at this point that James is *not* saying that good deeds automatically mean that a person has genuine, saving faith. To give an extreme illustration, among those involved in humanitarian work all over the world today are some who deny the very existence of God. James's point is not that the presence of deeds proves the presence of faith, but that the absence of deeds proves the absence of faith. In his own case, what he is saying in effect is this: 'I claim to have faith, and if that faith is called into question, then by the grace of God I am able to point to a changed life as evidence that my claim is genuine.'

Two men were arguing over this very point of faith and deeds while they were being rowed across a river. The oarsman was a Christian and asked whether he could join in the discussion. Given permission, he said, 'Let us assume that one of these oars is faith and the other one is deeds. We'll take the "deeds" oar out of the water and just use "faith".' As a result, of course, the boat went around in circles. After a while he said, 'Perhaps we have got the wrong one. We'll put the "faith" oar in the boat and just use "deeds".' The result, of course, was the same. They still went around in circles. Finally, he put both oars in together and the boat made straight for the shore. Biblical Christianity has precisely that kind of balance. Only the person with faith and deeds working in perfect harmony is heading in the right direction.

3. There is a firm conviction

'In the same way, faith by itself, if it is not accompanied by action, is dead' (v. 17).

This phrase lies at the centre of the passage we have been studying, but we can helpfully look at it here, not only because it provides us with a concise summary of the passage we have been studying, but also because in verse 26 James himself uses a very similar phrase in his own conclusion to the whole section. In the text, this phrase comes immediately after the illustration of the man Alec Motyer has described as an 'armchair philanthropist', the man who offered someone in desperate need nothing but words. It is 'in the same way' that faith without action is dead. Idle faith is as useless as idle words.

James is to develop this theme in the next passage, but before we leave this one it will be helpful to notice that the supposed conflict between Paul and James is already evaporating. Paul's great theme is that nobody can procure salvation by the works of the law; James's great theme is that nobody can prove their salvation except by works of love. There is no disagreement here. Indeed, when Paul wrote of those who 'claim to know God, but by their actions they deny him' (Titus 1:16) he was exactly on James's wavelength!

We shall develop this line of thought in our next study. For the moment, our concern should be to examine our hearts on the issues involved and to pray that our lives might 'please [the Lord] in every way: bearing fruit in every good work, growing in the knowledge of God' (Colossians 1:10).

18.

Faith and deeds — II

'You foolish man, do you want evidence that faith without deeds is useless? Was not our ancestor Abraham considered righteous for what he did when he offered his son Isaac on the altar? You see that his faith and his actions were working together, and his faith was made complete by what he did. And the scripture was fulfilled that says, "Abraham believed God, and it was credited to him as righteousness," and he was called God's friend. You see that a person is justified by what he does and not by faith alone. In the same way, was not even Rahab the prostitute considered righteous for what she did when she gave lodging to the spies and sent them off in a different direction? As the body without the spirit is dead, so faith without deeds is dead' (James 2:20–26).

As we noted in our last study, this passage concludes the section containing the central theme of the whole Epistle of James. Without taking time to recapitulate the argument so far, let me remind you of this one important point: James is not challenging the person who claims to be a Christian because of the *presence* of good deeds in his life; he is challenging the person who claims to be a Christian in spite of the *absence* of good deeds in his life. Now let us turn to the passage itself and notice the three ways in which James deals with the subject in these verses.

1. How he introduces it

'You foolish man, do you want evidence that faith without deeds is useless'? (v. 20.)

The opening comment is hardly a compliment! The adjective translates the Greek *kene*, which literally means 'empty', and the kind of person James has in mind is someone with a lot to say but little to show. In spiritual matters, as elsewhere, it is often empty vessels that make the greatest sound! Eloquence and ignorance can often go together, and without the enlightening of the Holy Spirit men will always remain in spiritual darkness. When Peter made his great confession of faith, 'You are the Christ, the Son of the living God,' Jesus told him, 'Blessed are you, Simon son of Jonah, for this was not revealed to you by man, but by my Father in heaven' (Matthew 16:16, 17). The biblical principle is clear: 'The man without the Spirit does not accept the things that come from the Spirit of God, for they are foolishness to him and he cannot understand them, because they are spiritually discerned' (1 Corinthians 2:14). This is as true for the Christian as for the non-Christian, and no amount of Bible study will result in a living apprehension of the truth unless the Holy Spirit reveals it to you. William Gurnall once said that trying to understand the Bible without the Holy Spirit's help was like trying to open a locked door with the wrong key; you will just end up 'pottering . . . to little purpose'!

The question James has for the spiritually ignorant windbag is this: 'Do you want evidence . . .?' The important word here is 'want'. The original word is *theleis* which carries with it a sense of determined purpose. What an incisive question this now becomes! Some people ask questions about the Christian faith because they want to believe, but others because they want to disbelieve, and it is this kind of quibbling questioning and arid argument that James is challenging. He will not tolerate the attempt to substitute argument for action, because he sees what lies behind it, which is an unwillingness to forsake sin for righteousness. As Jesus said, 'Everyone who does evil hates the light, and will not come into the light for fear that his deeds will be exposed' (John 3:20). The insincere enquirer does not want to know the truth, he does not want to understand, he does not want to accept Christ – because he does not want to forsake his sin. But there is also a challenge here for the Christian. Are you honestly willing to know the Word of God, to understand all its implications in your life and to obey whatever God says to you through it? You dare not ignore the issue.

He is seeking to establish the one clear principle that a claim to be a Christian without the evidence of a good life is a false claim. Does a person who thinks otherwise really want evidence? Then let him listen to what James has to say!

2. How he illustrates it

'Was not our ancestor Abraham considered righteous for what he did when he offered his son Isaac on the altar? You see that his faith and his actions were working together, and his faith was made complete by what he did. And the scripture was fulfilled that says, "Abraham believed God, and it was credited to him as righteousness," and he was called God's friend. You see that a person is justified by what he does and not by faith alone. In the same way, was not even Rahab the prostitute considered righteous for what she did when she gave lodging to the spies and sent them off in a different direction?' (vv. 21-25.)

To prove his point, James draws on the stories of Abraham and Rahab, two people mentioned in the 'Hall of Fame' in Hebrews 11.

1. Abraham the patriarch. James's reference to him as 'our ancestor' ('father' would be a more usual translation of *pater*) has a double meaning. Physically he is the father of the ethnic Israel, and spiritually he is the father of all Christians, who form the new 'Israel of God' (Galatians 6:16). As Paul put it earlier in the same letter, 'Those who believe are children of Abraham' (Galatians 3:7). This means that converted and unconverted Jews alike could all identify with James's use of Abraham as an illustration.

Many incidents in the life of Abraham showed him to be a man of faith, but James concentrates on the one recorded in Genesis 22, when, in obedience to God's command, he placed his son Isaac on the altar and was prepared to offer him up as a sacrifice. The whole crux of James's argument is now put in the form of a question: 'Was not . . . Abraham considered righteous for what he did . . .'? To say that the answer to that question is important is putting it mildly – it is all-important, because it raises several other questions. What does James mean? Is he really saying that God declared Abraham righteous (that is to say, that Abraham was justified) *because* of what he did on Mount Moriah? Then is that not exactly the opposite of what Paul says? And is James not rejecting faith as the means of a man's salvation? If the answer to each of these secondary questions is 'Yes', then the answer to the primary question is 'No' – and James's biblical integrity is in ruins. Strange as it may seem, the clue to understanding this crucially important passage is to see it not from the perspective of deeds, but from the perspective of faith. As soon as we begin to look at these verses from this angle, four things stand out.

Faith's principle. '[Abraham's] faith and his actions were working together.' That one statement begins to take some of the heat out of the argument, because James is uniting 'faith' and 'actions', not dividing them. This is the language of co-operation, not conflict. What is more, James is agreeing precisely with the Bible's statement that '*By faith* Abraham, when God tested him, offered Isaac as a sacrifice' (Hebrews 11:17). The story is well-known: God had promised Abraham that his descendants would be as numerous as the stars in the sky. Yet when Abraham was well over a hundred years old, God told him to take his only son, Isaac, and put him to death as a sacrifice. All of Abraham's hopes lay in the body of that boy, yet such was his unflinching faith that he immediately set about the task, fully prepared to see Isaac killed and to leave the consequences with God. This is precisely the framework in which James invites us to see that '[Abraham's] faith and his actions were working together.' His faith was the energizing force that moved him to action; his actions were the energetic evidence of his faith. This is what we can call the principle of faith: it is not something that is arid, dead, fruitless. Faith works! When disbelieving Jews sought to claim that they were members of God's family by saying, 'Abraham is our father,' Jesus told them, 'If you were Abraham's children, then you would do the things Abraham did' (John 8:39) – in other words, they would be obedient to God's commandments.

Faith's proof. '. . . and his faith was made complete by what he did.' Again, this seems dangerous ground, because James seems to be implying that Abraham's faith was defective in some way until the incident at Mount Moriah. But the explanation comes when we look at the way Paul uses an almost identical word. Writing of the time when God refused to remove the unidentified thorn in the apostle's flesh, Paul says that God's word to him was 'My grace is sufficient for you, for my power is made perfect in weakness' (2 Corinthians 12:9). Now it is obvious that God's power was not created by Paul's weakness, nor was it in any way increased by it. What happened was that God's power was revealed in Paul's weakness. The weaker Paul became, the more obvious it was that God's power was the secret of his amazing life and ministry. Now that is the kind of word James is using here. He is saying that Abraham's faith was brought out into the open and proved to be real by this staggering act of obedience. When a man over a hundred years old is prepared to kill his only son when he has been told that he will have millions of descendants, one can surely assume that that man's faith is something more than an empty profession!

Faith's promise. 'And the scripture was fulfilled that says, "Abraham believed God, and it was credited to him as righteousness."' The crucially important thing to notice here (and the death-blow to those who suggest that James is claiming that Abraham was made right with God as the result of his works rather than through faith) is that James is quoting *not* from the incident at Mount Moriah, but from one that happened about thirty years earlier. It was then, when God made his astonishing promise about the number of descendants Abraham would have, that 'Abraham believed the Lord, and he credited it to him as righteousness' (Genesis 15:6). The apostle Paul, in seeking to underline his great theme that justification is through faith alone, deliberately speaks of 'the faith that our father Abraham had before he was circumcised' (Romans 4:12), that is to say, he goes back to Genesis 15; James, seeking to show the reason for Abraham's amazing act of obedience, goes back to exactly the same place! Abraham's willingness to sacrifice Isaac did not improve his justification, nor add to it, nor contribute to it, nor alter it in any way, for none of these things could ever be done. Justification is a full, perfect, complete, unalterable act of the grace of God in the heart of man and is received by faith and by faith alone. This is faith's promise and Abraham had received it.

We can now see what James meant by saying that when Abraham offered Isaac 'the scripture was fulfilled'. As Matthew Poole has it, 'Things are said to be fulfilled when they are most clearly manifested,' and that is exactly the point here. There had been other occasions when Abraham had shown that he was a man whose trust was in the living God, but the incident at Mount Moriah wrote it in headlines across the world's history.

Faith's privilege. '. . . and he was called God's friend.' This truly astonishing title is confirmed elsewhere in Scripture: Jehoshaphat speaks to God of 'Abraham your friend' (2 Chronicles 20:7) and God himself refers to 'Abraham my friend' (Isaiah 41:8), though without any elaboration as to the reason why such a wonderful title should be given. That silence is significant, because for God to call a man his friend is utterly beyond human reasoning. There is a sense of divine initiative about it that lies entirely in the realm of grace, which can only be received through faith, 'and this not from yourselves' (Ephesians 2:8). Our thinking in this area is usually the other way round and we have hymns such as 'What a Friend we have in Jesus!' and 'Thou art the sinner's Friend'. Now both of those statements are wonderfully true, but the point being made here is surely even more wonderfully true: Abraham was God's friend. Nor is this glorious fact limited to that one man in history. Jesus told his disciples, 'I no longer call you servants . . . Instead, I have called you friends' (John 15:15). God-given faith in Christ brings the Christian into a living relationship with him, a relationship in which there can be communion and communication utterly unknown to the unbeliever. Faith's privilege is not only that we can share our secrets with God, but that he is willing to share some of his with us! When, as a Christian, you come to the Bible and God speaks to you through it, he is doing so as a friend. That is a glorious part of faith's privilege. Now let us turn to James's other illustration of his central point that genuine faith is faith that acts.

2. *Rahab the prostitute.* There would seem to be three good reasons why James introduces Rahab as his second witness. In the first place, *her condition was so sinful.* Listening to James's argument so far, some people might have objected that his choice of an example was almost unfair. They might have said, 'How can we be expected to match up to Abraham, when you think of God's special dealings with him and the extraordinary promises that were made to him? We are such ordinary people by comparison. It is no good giving us Abraham as an example. He is so far above us that we can't identify with him at all.' James's answer is to go right to the bottom of the social barrel and to quote the case of a prostitute alongside that of the patriarch. In doing this he showed that even from those who come from the lowest reaches of society, or have the deepest scars of past sin, God insists on good works as evidence of genuine faith. And that demand is perfectly reasonable, because with every demand he makes he also gives the dynamic to meet it: 'His divine power has given us everything we need for life and godliness through our knowledge of him who called us by his own glory and goodness' (2 Peter 1:3). No Christian can plead background, environment or anything else as an excuse for not living a godly life. After all, Rahab had been a prostitute.

In the second place, *her confession was so similar.* It is obvious that Rahab had become a believer. We are not told how or when, but she clearly confessed her faith when telling Joshua's spies, 'The Lord your God is God in heaven above and on the earth below' (Joshua 2:11). How similar to the confession quoted by James earlier in the chapter we are studying: 'There is one God'! (v. 19.) James's argument may be this: 'Rahab made a confession of faith very similar to yours. But was it her confession that proved she was a genuine believer? No, it was not.' She was considered righteous for what she *did.* Exactly as with Abraham, her actions proved the reality of her faith.

In the third place, *her confirmation was so straightforward.* The confirmation of Rahab's faith was certainly not easy – she put her own life at risk in harbouring the Israelite spies – but it was simple, straightforward: 'By faith the prostitute Rahab, because she welcomed the spies, was not killed with those who were disobedient' (Hebrews 11:31). She was prepared to be identified with the people of God. She put her own life in jeopardy in order to save the lives of two fellow believers. A woman who had ruined her life with lust at its lowest now revealed her faith by love at its highest. The grace of God at work in her life transformed her and the reality of her spiritual experience was made strikingly clear by her daring act of loyalty to the people of God in their great need.

In the passage we have been studying, James has introduced his point and then illustrated it. There is one thing left to notice.

3. How he insists on it

'As the body without the spirit is dead, so faith without deeds is dead' (v. 26).

In the whole section running through verses 14–26 we have been studying what we might call James's 'magnificent obsession', the bedrock biblical truth that belief and behaviour must go together, that creed and conduct are twins, that profession with the lips must be backed up by proof in the life. James insists on this principle; there are no exceptions to it and there is no escaping from it, and the whole of this passage is cemented together with this great truth: 'What good is it, my brothers, if a man claims to have faith but has no deeds? Can such faith save him?' (v. 14); 'In the same way, faith by itself, if it is not accompanied by action, is dead' (v. 17); '. . . faith without deeds is useless' (v. 20); and now, to round off the whole section, 'As the body without the spirit is dead, so faith without deeds is dead.'

Generations of commentators have wrestled with the difficulties of getting at James's precise meaning here, yet perhaps a simple illustration will take us to the heart of it. If you were to discover a man lying on the ground and did not know whether he was dead or alive, you could find out by holding a mirror to his face. If marks of condensation appeared on the mirror you would know he was alive, but if none appeared you would know he was dead. James says that if a person claims to be a Christian, then that claim can be tested by bringing him face to face with the

Word of God. If there is a positive reaction, the claim is real; if nothing appears, then the claim is false. Without delving into the intricacies of the imagery James is using, that certainly captures its spirit. In his original creation, God joined body and spirit together; in the new creation he joins faith and deeds together. What God has joined, we dare not put asunder.

So we come to the end of the central section in the Epistle of James, and if we have grasped what he is saying we can see that there is no substance whatever in the suggestion that he is at odds with the teaching of Scripture in general and of the apostle Paul in particular. Put in a nutshell, Paul's great theme is that no man can *produce* justification by the performance of good deeds (and he mainly has in mind the observance of religious rules); James's great theme is that no man can *prove* justification without the performance of good deeds (and he mainly has in mind obedience to God's moral law). Much of the difficulty has occurred because of a failure to understand that Paul and James use the term 'righteousness' (or 'justification') in different, but not contradictory ways. Paul uses the word to speak of *God's declaration* that he has accepted a man on the exercise of faith; James uses it to speak of *man's demonstration* that his faith is genuine and that he has been accepted. Thomas Manton puts it like this: 'In Paul's sense a sinner is absolved, in James's sense a believer is approved; and so most sweetly, and for aught I can see, without exception the apostles are agreed.'

Yet it is not enough that Paul and James should be seen to agree with each other. The important thing is that *our* lips and lives should agree, that what *we* profess is borne out in *our* lives. An exposition of the truth is no substitute for an exhibition of it. This is James's unflinching challenge that probes and penetrates and demands a response. As William Gurnall has it, 'Say not that thou hast royal blood in thy veins, and art born of God, except thou canst prove thy pedigree by daring to be holy.'

May God give us the grace to prove what we profess!

19.

The sanity of humble service

> *'Not many of you should presume to be teachers, my brothers, because you know that we who teach will be judged more strictly. We all stumble in many ways'* (James 3:1, 2a).

The Puritan preacher Thomas Brooks once wrote, 'We know metals by their tinkling, and men by their talking.' I rather think that James would have agreed with that, because in an epistle which majors on the practical outworking of Christian faith, he deals with matters concerning the use of the tongue on no fewer than six occasions and does so more forcefully than any other writer in the New Testament. This makes it no coincidence that his longest section on the subject (3:1–12) comes immediately after his keynote statement on the whole theme of his epistle.

Although it may seem somewhat arbitrary, a case can be made for making a break, or at least taking a pause, after the first sentence in verse 2, as I have done here. Looking at the segment of text this gives us, we can see two things James gives his readers – past and present!

1. Pointed instructions

'Not many of you should presume to be teachers, my brothers . . .' (v. 1a).

The instruction itself seems clear and concise, but of course its immediate application would have hinged on the meaning of the word 'teachers'. It is a word used about sixty times in the New Testament, sometimes of specific individuals and sometimes of a whole group or class of people. To give an example of each: Jesus called Nicodemus 'Israel's teacher' (John 3:10), while Jesus himself had spent one memorable occasion 'in the temple courts, sitting among the teachers, listening to them and asking them questions' (Luke 2:46).

There are perhaps three uses of the word which have a claim to be the particular one James has in mind here. The first is a special office within the Christian church. Paul says that within the church 'God has appointed first of all apostles, second prophets, third teachers . . .' (1 Corinthians 12:28) and that in bestowing gifts upon the church, Christ 'gave some to be apostles, some to be prophets, some to be evangelists, and some to be pastors and teachers . . .' (Ephesians 4:11). On the other hand, James may mean any position within the church that involved teaching the Scriptures. The third, and totally different, possibility is that James had in mind what John Calvin called 'self-constituted censors and reprovers of others', in which case he is touching on a subject to which he will refer later, at 4:11, 12. Interestingly enough we can give space to each of these possible meanings by seeing here two warnings that James may be giving.

1. A warning against carnal ambition. The office of teacher in the early Christian church was akin to the office of rabbi in the Jewish church and it is therefore not difficult to appreciate one of its greatest dangers. The very word 'rabbi' comes from the Hebrew word *rab*, meaning 'great', and rabbis were usually held in very high esteem. It has even been said that if a man's father and his rabbi were captured by enemies and only one of them could be ransomed, the man would be duty bound to ransom the rabbi and leave his father in captivity! Some rabbis were certainly godly and humble men, but it is not difficult to see that the fawning and flattery of their followers often proved more than flesh and blood could stand, with the result that many others became insufferably proud. This is how Jesus saw those who did: 'Everything they do is done for men to see: They make their phylacteries wide and the tassels on their garments long; they love the place of honour at banquets and the most important seats in the synagogues; they love to be greeted in market places and to have men call them "Rabbi"' (Matthew 23:5–7). Commenting on that devastating indictment, Matthew Henry says, 'For him that is taught in the Word to give respect to him that teaches is commendable enough in him that gives it; but for him that teaches to love it, and demand it, is sinful and abominable; and instead of teaching he has need to learn the first lesson in the school of Christ, which is humility.'

It is not difficult to see how the office of teacher in the infant church would inherit some of the exalted status of that of the rabbi in the Jewish church, and it is even less difficult to see one of the dangers this brought about: people began to hanker after the position because of the prestige that went with it. There is no question that that sort of thing happened, because Paul warned Timothy about those who 'want to be teachers of the law, but they do not know what they are talking about or what they so confidently affirm' (1 Timothy 1:7). This point about carnal ambition is brought out by the NIV's use of the word 'presume' in the verse we are studying. James was not suggesting that properly qualified teachers should resign, but that people should beware of wanting to leap into the limelight. As Andrew McNab comments, 'There seems to have been an eagerness on the part of many to speak in public, and a failure to recognize that the fundamental qualification for teaching is learning.' Mark that! The man who ceases to learn has no right to teach.

Of course, we must be careful not to over-react against what James is saying here. He is not suggesting that there is need for little teaching in the church. Exactly the opposite was the case then, and remains so now. An American pastor once told me, 'We are suffering now for what happened in this country a few years ago, when anybody with a bright tie, a flashy pair of socks and a big Bible could get a job as an evangelist.' In Britain, too, we have a surfeit of the superficial and a dearth of depth. There is a crying need for those who will devote themselves earnestly to the study and teaching of the Word of God and those whom the Lord has qualified to do so are under an urgent obligation to 'fan into flame the gift of God' (2 Timothy 1:6). Indeed, the same applies to every Christian. Pray that the Holy Spirit will energize the gift God has given you, that it might be used to his glory and the blessing of others.

But it is the negative note of warning that comes directly

through James's words here and it is a word sorely needed for today. There is a shameful amount of striving and scheming and wriggling going on in the Christian church – people fighting to be president of this, chairman of that, director of the other – and all of it stinks of self. If there is one thing worse than social climbing in the world, it is ecclesiastical climbing in the church. Thomas Brooks was certainly not exaggerating when he wrote these words: 'Ambition is a gilded misery, a secret poison, a hidden plague, the engineer of deceit, the mother of hypocrisy, the parent of envy, the original of vices, the moth of holiness, the blinder of hearts, turning medicines into maladies and remedies into diseases. High seats are never but uneasy, and crowns are always stuffed with thorns'!

The Bible has a beautiful corrective for all this, though it comes in a quite different context. When Jeremiah was prophesying dire disaster for the nation, his private secretary, Baruch, broke down under the pressure of the prospect. He longed for easier times, happier days and, no doubt, the kudos that would come from being the right-hand man of a popular prophet instead of a messenger of doom. But God sent a message to Baruch, one which is riveting in its relevance here: 'Should you then seek great things for yourself? Seek them not' (Jeremiah 45:5). The message is obvious: 'Seek great things by all means. Seek them for God, seek them for the Lord Jesus Christ, seek them for the Holy Spirit, seek them for the benefit of God's people, seek them for the lost. But do *not* seek them for yourself.' Here is a warning against carnal ambition.

2. A warning against critical attitudes. This obviously has a primary application to people in positions of authority and it should remind us of one simple fact: leadership, even when God-given, is not necessarily a sign of worthiness, let alone of superiority. Even Paul admitted that he did 'not even deserve to be called an apostle' (1 Corinthians 15:9). Nor, in God's sight, is the holding of an office or the exercise of a ministry something which we have earned and for which we can take credit. To quote Paul again, 'Although I am less than the least of all God's people, *this grace was given me*: to preach to the Gentiles the unsearchable riches in Christ' (Ephesians 3:8). Notice the words

I have emphasized! Even God-ordained leadership in the church is a grace, not a gong. Whatever degrees, or titles, or positions we may hold, whatever pleasant praises men might heap upon us, the fact remains that none of these things make us superior, giving us the right to adopt critical, censorious attitudes towards our fellow Christians.

Again, the Bible supplies us with the necessary corrective, by showing us that all teaching, preaching and leadership are ministries – and the root meaning of 'to minister' is 'to serve'. It is exactly in this spirit that Peter writes to church elders, 'Be shepherds of God's flock that is under your care . . . not lording it over those entrusted to you, but being examples to the flock' (1 Peter 5:2, 3). There is a call here for a beautiful balance in the exercising of any office within the church. There will need to be biblical correction, but not barren criticism; discipline, but not domination; authority, but not autocracy; leadership, but not lordship. All Christians, and especially those called to any position of leadership within the church, must beware of the dangers of self-assumed superiority.

So much for James's pointed instructions – a warning against carnal ambition and a warning against critical attitudes. Yet he does not give these instructions in a vacuum. He now turns to reasons why we should obey his instructions and heed his warnings.

2. Powerful incentives

'. . . because you know that we who teach will be judged more strictly. We all stumble in many ways' (vv. 1b, 2).

In backing up the instructions he has given, James adds two powerful incentives or motives.

1. A warning that our judgement is not trivial. '. . . because you know that we who teach will be judged more strictly.' We saw something of James's teaching on the subject of judgement when we were studying chapter 2:12, 13. Now he returns to it, but with specific reference to those who teach the Scriptures to others. These people, he says, 'will be judged more strictly'. Let us get to his meaning in three stages.

The first thing to say is that there is no hint here of the possibility of a born-again church leader being eternally lost because of the misuse of his ministry. As with every other Christian, he can claim the promise made by the Lord Jesus: 'I tell you the truth, whoever hears my word and believes him who sent me has eternal life and will not be condemned; he has crossed over from death to life' (John 5:24). It is tragically possible for the strongest Christian to fall *in* grace, but totally impossible for the weakest Christian to fall *from* grace.

The second thing to say is that James is clearly underlining what he said earlier about the fact that Christians will not be exempt from an assessment of their lives on the Day of Judgement, and in doing this he is echoing Paul's warning that 'Each of us will give an account of himself to God' (Romans 14:12). Assurance of our justification must never be allowed to blunt the impact of those words. As James Denney once put it, 'The things we have done in the body will come back to us, whether good or bad. Every pious thought and every thought of sin, every secret prayer and every secret curse; every unknown deed of charity and every hidden deed of selfishness; we will see them all again and though we have not remembered them for years and perhaps have forgotten them altogether, we shall have to acknowledge that they are our own and take them to ourselves. Is that not a solemn thing to stand at the end of life?'

It is clear from Scripture that as well as the division between heaven and hell, there are degrees of punishment and reward, and that these will depend on the light we have received, the opportunities we have had and the privileges we have been given. James now applies this truth to the matter of holding office in the church. The person who claims the ability to teach others the meaning of Scripture will not only be judged as to the content of his teaching, but as to the conduct of his own life. The 'expert' will be judged by the kind of standard one should expect from an expert; the leader will be judged against the qualities one would expect to find in a leader; and the man who professes to be superior will be judged on the basis that he should have been so! Notice, too, that James says, '*We* who teach will be judged more strictly.' He is including himself in this. There will be no exceptions on that great day. The mind of God is so perfectly tuned that every single one of us will be judged in precise relationship to the offices we have held, the claims we have made and the duties we have exercised. Is that not a motive that should kill at heart this striving, this carnal ambition, this longing to lord it over other people, this passion for power, this critical attitude? We are going to be judged and here is a warning that our judgement is not trivial.

2. The wonder that our judgement is not total. 'We all stumble in many ways.' We shall see this statement as a second incentive or motive to wean us away from carnal ambition or superior, critical attitudes when we see it in the context of what James has been saying about the Day of Judgement. Every word in this little phrase is vitally important. Let us look at them in turn. 'We all . . .' translates the Greek *hapantes*, which literally means 'each and every one of us without exception'. Not only does James once again identify himself completely with the teaching he is giving, but he warns us that none of us will be excused from judgement because none of us is exempt from sin. The verb 'stumble' comes from the Greek *ptaio*, the same word James used when speaking about the hypothetical man who 'keeps the whole law, and yet stumbles at just one point' (2:10). The NIV's choice here is a good one: the picture is not of the Christian deliberately setting out to commit premeditated sin, but of him being tripped up as he is walking along the pathway of life. However, this does not mean that he can treat this kind of thing as a 'little sin'; every sin the Christian commits is reprehensible, because it is sin for which he is responsible. If I stumble over something lying in the road, it is because I am being careless and not keeping my eyes open. Finally, the phrase 'in many ways' is the one Greek word *polla*, which can also mean 'many times'. Now let us look at the whole sentence in one piece. When we adopt critical attitudes towards other people, from a position of church leadership or otherwise, it is a classic case of the pot calling the kettle black, because, to paraphrase James's statement, each and every one of us, without exception, often stumbles into sin in many different ways.

No right-minded Christian can possibly argue with that, but let me try to apply this in an intensely personal way, and do so in the light of the Day of Judgement. Suppose you were to sin – in word, thought, attitude or action – just once a day. In one week that would amount to seven sins; in a year 365; in ten years 3,650; and in fifty years 18,250. But surely you sin more often than that? Suppose it was once an hour. In one day that would be twenty-four; in a week 168; in a year 8,736; in ten years 87,360; and in fifty years 436,800. Now take another look at your life, this time in the light of the perfect purity of the Word of God and of the life of the Lord Jesus Christ. Dare you say that you do not fall short of the glory you see there once a minute? In a day that comes to 1,440; in a week 10,080; in a year 524,160; in ten years 5,241,600; and in fifty years 26,208,000! But even that does not take us anywhere near the end of the story, because the Bible teaches us that 'All have sinned and *fall* short of the glory of God' (Romans 3:23), that is to say, we continue to do so, every moment of every day. When we grasp that, when we are overwhelmed with the enormity of our guilt and the multiplicity of our disobedience, we can only marvel that on the Day of Judgement God's mercy will triumph over judgement, so that instead of rejecting us out of hand, he will welcome us into his holy presence for ever, seeing us 'without stain or wrinkle or any other blemish, but holy and blameless'! (Ephesians 5:27.) It was a recognition of this amazing truth that moved Augustus Toplady to write:

A debtor to mercy alone,
Of covenant mercy I sing;
Nor fear, with thy righteousness on,
My person and offering to bring.
The terrors of law and of God
With me can have nothing to do;
My Saviour's obedience and blood
Hide all my transgressions from view.

In the light of that, what is the spirit in which we should hold office in the church – as a pastor, Sunday School teacher, Bible Class leader, elder, deacon, committee member? How should we exercise our office? And what should our attitude be towards our fellow Christians? I think we know the answers! Then let us live them out!

20.

Taming the tongue — I

'If anyone is never at fault in what he says, he is a perfect man, able to keep his whole body in check. When we put bits into the mouths of horses to make them obey us, we can turn the whole animal. Or take ships as an example. Although they are so large and are driven by strong winds, they are steered by a very small rudder wherever the pilot wants to go. Likewise the tongue is a small part of the body, but it makes great boasts' (James 3:2b–5a).

We ended our last study overwhelmed at the wonder of God's amazing grace, by which he will receive us into heaven in spite of the fact that our earthly lives continually fall short of his glory. We must begin this study in exactly the same spirit, not merely because my division of the two passages is somewhat arbitrary, but because James is about to deal in depth with an area in which our failure is so frequent – the use of the tongue. The whole section goes through to the end of verse 12, but it will be helpful to treat this passage as an introduction to the detailed development that is to follow. The verses before us present us with a dual responsibility.

1. We must realize a practical fact

'If anyone is never at fault in what he says, he is a perfect man, able to keep his whole body in check' (v. 2b).

A superficial reading of these words could lead one to the conclusion that James is contradicting himself. After all, he has just admitted that 'We all stumble in many ways'; now he speaks of someone being 'a perfect man'. Is he seriously suggesting that such a man exists on the earth, or is he advocating a short-cut to perfection by the right use of the tongue? Certainly not! That would be at variance with the whole tenor of the Bible's teaching on sanctification, as well as being at odds with what James himself says elsewhere. Three biblical concepts can be brought together in penetrating the surface of what James is saying.

1. Mystery. Whatever we might think of some people's views on 'perfectionism', there is no escaping the fact that the Bible commands us to be perfect. The all-embracing edict given to the children of Israel was 'You must be blameless before the Lord your God' (Deuteronomy 18:13), while the Sermon on the Mount could be summed up in the uncompromising command: 'Be perfect, therefore, as your heavenly Father is perfect' (Matthew 5:48). There seems no room for manoeuvre there! Yet the Bible makes it equally clear that not a single person in the world *is* perfect. John says bluntly, 'If we claim to be without sin, we deceive ourselves and the truth is not in us' (1 John 1:8), while Paul, towards the end of his remarkable life, writes of the ultimate in Christian experience and then adds, 'Not that I have already obtained all this, or have already been made perfect' (Philippians 3:12).

Christian biography down the years has confirmed this, and underlined the seeming paradox that the closer a man walks with God, the more conscious he is of his sin. Here is something of this element of mystery. God is fitting the believer for heaven, but the closer he gets to it, the more he realizes that he is not fit to enter. No amount of moral or spiritual improvement can qualify a Christian for heaven, yet every Christian is certain to get there. A Christian is commanded to grow in grace, but his eternal standing before God does not depend in the slightest degree on whether that growth is vague or vigorous. Satan is a defeated enemy, yet he is permitted by a sovereign God to attack the Christian again and again and even to win one victory after another. These things are a mystery, but because God has sovereignly ordained them, we can only bow in humble submission and accept that in some way beyond our understanding these are the ways in which God's grace can be most magnificently displayed. Our old nature is not removed at conversion, nor refined after it. Instead, it remains, with the result that throughout the Christian's life his old nature and the indwelling Holy Spirit are 'in conflict with each other' (Galatians 5:17). All of this forms part of the mystery, what we might call the paradox of perfection. Everywhere in the Bible we find it demanded; nowhere in the world do we find it demonstrated. Human nature being what it is, man finds himself tempted to rationalize this situation in one way or another. He either lessens his view of what God requires of him, in order to accommodate his weaknesses and failures, or he slackens his efforts to be holy because God's standards seem so incapable of attainment. As we shall see, the biblical answer lies elsewhere.

2. *Maturity.* This concept brings us directly to the text of what James is saying. His words immediately follow his confession that we all stumble in many ways and it is surely not surprising to find him immediately going on to mention the use of the tongue, because it is here above all that man's weakness is betrayed. When Paul lists what Thomas Manton calls 'the anatomy of wickedness in all the members of the body', he places a heavy emphasis on sins of speech:

> 'Their throats are open graves;
> their tongues practise deceit.
> The poison of vipers is on their lips.
> Their mouths are full of cursing and bitterness'
> (Romans 3:13, 14).

When I worked in the Law Courts in Guernsey I became very familiar with a document called a 'crime sheet', which listed the cases to appear before the magistrate. It contained the names and addresses of all the accused and listed their alleged crimes of assault, theft, drunkenness and so on. On the biblical crime sheet the tongue is one of the accused and the list of offences is enormous – dishonesty, unkindness, flattery, impurity, blasphemy, pride, criticism, exaggeration, temper, greed, slander, boasting and many others. What can we say as we read through that terrible list? Even more important, what should we do?

In the first place, *we must be realistic.* By that, I mean that we must face up to the simple fact that, however far we have gone in the Christian life, we are not beyond committing a single one of these sins. Some years ago, I was watching skiers coming down Mount Kellogg, near Pinehurst, Idaho. After a while, one of them (obviously a novice) came very gingerly down the slope, then suddenly fell head over heels right in the middle of the ski run. Turning to a friend, I said, 'You must get quite a lot of that among beginners.' 'Yes', he replied, 'and you never get so expert that you can't do it!' My mind went immediately to Paul's warning: 'So, if you think you are standing firm, be careful that you don't fall' (1 Corinthians 10:12). We can never become so 'expert' in Christian living that we are incapable of stumbling, of falling into sin. We must be realistic.

In the second place, *we must be resolute.* By that, I mean that we should always be aiming to improve. If I had returned to Mount Kellogg two years later, I would not expect to see that same man falling with the same frequency. I would realize that he was still *capable* of falling, but I would hope that he would have learned a great deal in the meantime, not only about the slope itself, but also about the art of skiing. This is where James's word 'perfect' comes in. The Greek word is *teleios,* which means one who reaches maturity or attains a goal, and this should be the resolute aim of every Christian. It is significant that at one point Paul specifically relates this concept to our thinking: 'Brothers, stop thinking like children. In regard to evil be infants, but in your thinking be adults *[teleioteta]*' (2 Corinthians 14:20). In our thinking, our attitudes, our behaviour and not least in our speech, God wants us to be adults, not infants, and this should be the resolute determination of every Christian. So far, then, we have the concepts of mystery and maturity.

3. Mastery. James says that the man who is faultless in speech is 'able to keep his whole body in check'. As we have already noted, James is not even hinting that such a paragon of virtue exists, but his point is clear. A man able to control his tongue is surely able to control the rest of his body, because the tongue is the most uncontrollable part of the human anatomy – so that *if* (the question is hypothetical), says James, a man could have complete mastery over the use of his tongue, he would surely be 'a perfect man', because everything else would be controlled too.

Throughout this whole section, James is going to use one argument and illustration after another to impress upon us the need to control our tongues. Not only is his teaching explicitly repeated throughout the Bible, but there are several places which seem to me to make the same point by implication. After Cain had killed Abel, God asked him, 'Where is your brother Abel?', to which Cain replied, 'I don't know' (Genesis 4:9). Is it not significant that the first recorded words spoken by man after his expulsion from Eden formed a lie? When Isaiah had his extraordinary vision of the glory of God, he cried, 'Woe to me! I am ruined! For I am a man of unclean lips . . .' (Isaiah 6:5). Is that not an admission that he had most frequently failed in the things he had said? Peter wrote of the Lord Jesus, 'He committed no sin, and no deceit was found in his mouth' (1 Peter 2:22). Did he add the reference to speech because it was Christ's perfection there that had made the deepest impression on the quick-tongued Peter? We can be quite certain that James is not suggesting that we can become holy in bits and pieces, nor that once we have mastered our tongues no further discipline is required elsewhere. Instead, he is hammering home the point that if a Christian is to grow in grace he will need to pay constant and particular attention to the things he says. And because he has no power of his own to deal with the situation, he will continually need to pray with the psalmist, 'Set a guard over my mouth, O Lord; keep watch over the door of my lips' (Psalm 141:3).

2. We must recognize a powerful force

'When we put bits into the mouths of horses to make them obey us, we can turn the whole animal. Or take ships as an example. Although they are so large and are driven by strong winds, they are steered by a very small rudder wherever the pilot wants to go' (vv. 3–5a).

Exactly as we have come to expect, James reinforces his argument by illustration, and the two he uses here are so clear that they hardly need any comment. The surging power of an impetuous horse can be brought under control by the use of a tiny piece of metal placed in its mouth. A large ship – even one of today's supertankers displacing thousands of tons! – can be turned in whichever direction the pilot chooses, and he does so by controlling the movements of the comparatively tiny rudder.

It is important to notice that James is not speaking about the wickedness of the tongue, nor of the evil results it can bring about; he will come on to those things in the next passage we shall study. After all, a bit does not have an evil effect on a horse, nor does a rudder on a ship. But these things do have a powerful effect, and it is this truth that James is getting across here. After giving the illustrations of the bit and the rudder he says, 'Likewise the tongue is a small part of the body, but it makes great boasts.' It is difficult to know whether James is using the phrase 'makes great boasts' in a good sense or a bad one. We normally think of boasting in terms of pride and arrogance, that is to say, in an evil sense, but the word 'likewise' does link back to the illustrations about the bit and the rudder and James's point about them was not that their influence was evil, but powerful. Perhaps we could usefully cover both angles in closing this part of our study.

1. The tongue can have an evil influence. The Bible is certainly clear on this: 'Your tongue plots destruction; it is like a sharpened razor, you who practise deceit' (Psalm 52:2); '. . . violence overwhelms the mouth of the wicked' (Proverbs 10:11); '. . . a harsh word stirs up anger' (Proverbs 15:1). We dare not minimize the evil influence the tongue can have. It can break marriages, divide families, wreck churches, destroy reputations, breed distrust and motivate violence.

2. The tongue can have an excellent influence. We could sum up the Bible's teaching on this by quoting the opening part of a verse at which we have just been looking: 'The mouth of the righteous is a fountain of life . . .' (Proverbs 10:11). What an expressive phrase that is! Who can possibly measure the amount of goodness and blessing that has poured from men's lips? Think of all the love, comfort, encouragement, wisdom and inspiration that has been given. Think of those who have boldly spoken the truth even at the risk of their own lives, and of others who have uprooted tyrants from their thrones by the power of their words. Mary Queen of Scots once said that she was more afraid of the tongue of John Knox than of 10,000 fighting men! Above all, think of the millions of times the human tongue has been used to preach the glorious gospel of salvation and of the countless numbers of people who have been brought into the kingdom of God through listening to the sound of a human voice.

But not only does the tongue have a powerful influence; it has a lasting influence. There is a remarkable story told about a New England farmer by the name of Luke Short. He reached a hundred years of age fit and well and was sitting in his field meditating one day when he suddenly remembered a sermon that John Flavel had preached eighty-five years earlier in Dartmouth, England, before Luke Short had left for America. As he turned Flavel's words over in his mind, they came to him with such power that he was converted on the spot! It would be difficult to find a more vivid illustration, both as an encouragement and a warning.

The Bible says, 'The tongue of the righteous is choice silver' (Proverbs 10:20). May God give us precious metal in our mouths!

21.

Taming the tongue — II

'Consider what a great forest is set on fire by a small spark. The tongue also is a fire, a world of evil among the parts of the body. It corrupts the whole person, sets the whole course of his life on fire, and is itself set on fire by hell. All kinds of animals, birds, reptiles and creatures of the sea are being tamed and have been tamed by man, but no man can tame the tongue. It is a restless evil, full of deadly poison. With the tongue we praise our Lord and Father, and with it we curse men, who have been made in God's likeness. Out of the same mouth come praise and cursing. My brothers, this should not be. Can both fresh water and salt water flow from the same spring? My brothers, can a fig tree bear olives, or a grape-vine bear figs? Neither can a salt spring produce fresh water' (James 3:5b–12).

This passage is the second part of a major section in the Epistle of James, in which he is dealing with the use of the tongue. In the previous passage he wrote generally about the tongue's place in a person's life and emphasized the powerful influence it could exercise. Now he is to develop these themes by showing us some of the things of which the tongue is capable.

1. The tongue is capable of terrible injury

'Consider what a great forest is set on fire by a small spark. The tongue also is a fire, a world of evil among the parts of the body. It corrupts the whole person, sets the whole course of his life on fire, and is itself set on fire by hell. All kinds of

animals, birds, reptiles and creatures of the sea are being tamed and have been tamed by man, but no man can tame the tongue. It is a restless evil, full of deadly poison' (vv. 5b–8).

We have already seen that James is a master illustrator, and in this passage he gives full rein to his gift, using one metaphor after another to press his teaching home. In this opening part he likens the tongue to two powerful forces.

1. A spreading blaze. 'Consider what a great forest is set on fire by a small spark. The tongue also is a fire, a world of evil among the parts of the body. It corrupts the whole person, sets the whole course of his life on fire, and is itself set on fire by hell.' The word 'forest' is the Greek *hule*, which could equally well mean a pile of dead wood, and either translation would fit James's point here, which is to remind us that even the tiniest spark can lead to the most terrible result. During World War II I was evacuated to the Isle of Islay in the Western Hebrides of Scotland, where two other young refugees joined me on a remote farm. One of the jobs we were given was to take the ashes out of the farmhouse fire and dump them in a low-lying, wet place to make absolutely sure that all the embers were put out. But boys will be boys and our one aim was to keep them alive and to have some fun with them. I can vividly remember one occasion when we took one small ember from the ashes, wrapped it around with cardboard, held it cupped against the wind, and ran with it up the side of a nearby mountain. We put the little ember down in some very dry heather and blew until it caught alight. Then we deliberately started to spread it a little bit further. We had seen heather fires put out before and decided to see how big a frontage of fire we could allow to get going before putting it out. When we had about five yards of frontage it still looked quite small, so we let it grow to ten yards, then fifteen, then twenty. Suddenly that fire was raging out of control, sweeping through acres of heather with devastating speed, and I can still remember cowering in the farmhouse looking up with absolute horror as the whole of the mountain roared into flame. Every farmer for miles around rushed in to help in controlling the blaze, which almost literally consumed the whole mountain. As far as the eye could see there was nothing but flame and smoke. It was terrifying – and it began with a little ember that could be cupped in a little boy's hand! The Bible says, 'A scoundrel plots evil, and his speech is like a scorching fire' (Proverbs 16:27) and adds, 'As charcoal to embers and as wood to fire, so is a quarrelsome man for kindling strife' (Proverbs 26:21). All of this is a vivid reminder to us that the tongue is capable of terrible injury and it is the theme of this destructive power that James now develops by drawing our attention to four specific things that are true about the tongue.

The first is *the suggestion of its potential:* 'The tongue is . . . a world of evil among the parts of the body.' The point about potential comes across in the two most obvious ways of interpreting what James means by calling the tongue 'a world of evil'. The word he is using is *kosmos*, which can mean the whole universe in general, or the whole world order of things as it now is, wrecked by sin and in opposition to God. If James has the first of these in mind, then the picture is one of vastness and variety, implying that the tongue is capable of committing every sin under the sun. That is certainly true! Go through the Ten Commandments, for instance, and you will see that the tongue can be involved in breaking every one of them. No wonder Thomas Manton suggests that 'Most of a man's sins are in his words'! There is no end to the trouble the tongue can cause. However, if James has the second use of *kosmos* in mind, then he is saying that it is a microcosm of mischief, a living embodiment of the fallen world's sinful characteristics. One way or the other, there is no escaping the suggestion of its potential.

The second is *the stain of its pollution:* 'It corrupts the whole person . . .' The verb here comes from the Greek *spilo*, which literally means to stain by spotting and again makes James's meaning clear. Just as a rotten apple in a basket of good ones contaminates the rest, so a contaminated tongue has a polluting effect which spreads like a dirty stain into other areas. It is precisely because so many sins begin with words that the Bible says, 'Do not let your mouth lead you into sin' (Ecclesiastes 5:6).

The third is *the sphere of its penetration:* 'It . . . sets the whole course of his life on fire . . .' This is a notoriously difficult phrase, but the NIV captures its meaning well. The word 'course' is the Greek *trochos*, which means 'wheel', and the wheel was an ancient symbol of the whole cycle of life from birth to death. James is therefore not only saying that there is no part of life which the tongue cannot affect, but that there is no time in life when it cannot do so. In John Calvin's words, 'The vice of the tongue spreads and prevails over every part of life. It is as active and potent for evil in old age as ever it was in the days of our youth.'

Driving through Czechoslovakia late one night I was held up at a railway crossing. After a few minutes, a goods train came rumbling through the darkness, and as it reached the level crossing I noticed that one of its wheels was literally red-hot; it was blazing from hub to rim. I sat there mesmerized, wondering what the train's cargo was, and knowing that at any moment between then and the end of the journey that wheel of fire might suddenly spark off the most appalling disaster. So it is with the tongue. Its penetration extends throughout a man's life.

The fourth is *the source of its power:* '. . . and is itself set on fire by hell.' James seems to be using the word 'hell' here as a synonym of the devil, in the sense that Jesus did when accusing the Pharisees of turning a man into 'twice as much a son of hell as you are' (Matthew 23:15). As Matthew Poole comments, 'The tongue being the fire, the devil, by the bellows of temptation, inflames it yet more and more and thereby kindles the fire of all mischief in the world.' That seems clear enough, but we must not see the tongue as something infected in isolation. James is merely identifying one part of the whole human personality that has been invaded by the devil, a disaster that can move Paul to cry out, 'I know that nothing good lives in me, that is, in my sinful nature' (Romans 7:18). Isaac Watts put this truth about man's total depravity in these words of a hymn that is seldom sung today:

> Lord I am vile, conceived in sin,
> And born unholy and unclean;
> Sprung from the man whose guilty fall
> Corrupts the race and taints us all.

No wonder the tongue is capable of terrible injury! And this means that yours is! You may have reached a stage in your Christian life when you feel that there are some sins you are unlikely to commit, but be sure to settle in your mind that there is no sin of which you have become spiritually incapable. The tongue is like a spreading blaze, liable to break out at any time. This is the first picture James uses.

2. A savage beast. 'All kinds of animals, birds, reptiles and creatures of the sea are being tamed and have been tamed by man, but no man can tame the tongue. It is a restless evil, full of deadly poison.' At the time of creation, God commanded man, 'Rule over the fish of the sea and the birds of the air and over every living creature that moves on the ground' (Genesis 1:28). That God-given dominion, confirmed after both the Fall and the Flood, has been exercised ever since and James is stating a simple fact when he says that creatures from all four categories he mentions are still under subjection to man. Yet that straightforward observation is made in order to point out a tragic contrast: 'but no man can tame the tongue'. No statement in the Bible puts man's power into such precise perspective. He can tame the tiger but not the tongue! He can destroy all the creatures James mentions, and even domesticate some of them, but his tongue, by comparison so small and accessible, remains beyond his control. Yet we must underline the fact that the tongue must not be seen in isolation here, as if it is the only part of man that is out of control. The same applies to his hands, his feet, his eyes, his mind. The untamed tongue is a vivid example of man's latent inability which finds him crying out, 'For what I do is not the good I want to do; no, the evil I do not want to do – this I keep on doing' (Romans 7:19). As Sir Winston Churchill once said, 'The power of man has grown in every sphere except over himself.'

James now adds two additional words about the uncontrollability of the tongue. In the first place, he speaks of its *disorderly passion*; he describes it as 'a restless evil'. The adjective here is the Greek word *akatastaton*, which could well be translated 'ungovernable'. One of the most exciting things I can remember about life on that farm in

Islay was the breaking in of a horse. For little boys it really was a terrifying experience to see a young horse brought in from the field, never having had a saddle on its back, or a bit in its mouth. Strong men would coax it into the yard and eventually manoeuvre it into a horse-box. But I have seen a young horse lash and kick so violently that the horse-box just collapsed like matchwood. Here was an unruly passionate animal and it had to be broken in. On the other hand, there was an old farm horse called Bob who was so tame and so docile that we were able to put a lump of sugar right into its mouth with no danger at all. There was no fear that Bob would ever break out again. Now you can never say that about the tongue. It is a restless evil; it is always liable to break out. Nobody is able to say, 'I am now in perfect control of my tongue, it will never let me down again, never wound anyone again, never criticize anyone again, never grieve the Holy Spirit again.'

In the second place, James speaks about its *deadly poison*; in fact, he uses exactly that phrase: '. . . it is full of deadly poison'. The language is very similar to that of the psalmist who wrote of evil men, 'They make their tongues as sharp as a serpent's; the poison of vipers is on their lips' (Psalm 140:3). The imagery is obvious, but it is also interesting to notice that the Greek word translated 'poison' – *ios* – is translated by the word 'rust' at 5:3, giving us a picture of corrosion as well as poisoning. When the Bible tells us that the words we use can be capable of such terrible injury, it is hardly surprising to find it adding that 'The tongue has the power of life and death' (Proverbs 18:21).

2. The tongue is capable of treacherous inconsistency

'With the tongue we praise our Lord and Father, and with it we curse men, who have been made in God's likeness. Out of the same mouth come praise and cursing. My brothers, this should not be. Can both fresh water and salt water flow from the same spring? My brothers, can a fig tree bear olives, or a grape-vine bear figs? Neither can a salt spring produce fresh water' (vv. 9–12).

In these verses, James says two things about inconsistency, once more using illustrations from nature to make his point clear.

1. It is impossible in the natural world. 'Can both fresh water and salt water flow from the same spring? My brothers, can a fig-tree bear olives, or a grape-vine bear figs? Neither can a salt spring produce fresh water.'

Part of God's promise to the Israelites before they entered the promised land was this: 'For the Lord your God is bringing you into a good land – a land with streams and pools of water, with springs flowing in the valleys and hills' (Deuteronomy 8:7). Natural springs remain common in the Middle East today, some producing fresh water and others salt water, but none producing both! The thing is impossible, says James. In the same way, it is equally impossible for a fig-tree to produce grapes, or a grape-vine figs. In spite of all the cosmic ravages brought about by the Fall, there is basic law and order in nature and in the instances James mentions inconsistency is impossible.

2. It is improper in the spiritual world. 'With the tongue we praise our Lord and Father, and with it we curse men, who have been made in God's likeness. Out of the same mouth come praise and cursing. My brothers, this should not be.' Notice how clearly James makes his point about inconsistency. He begins by saying that it is with the tongue that 'we praise our Lord and Father'. This happy admission will prevent us from thinking that James thinks of the tongue as being so totally evil in its activities that we would be better off without it! Every Christian should rejoice that he is able to use his tongue in the same way as the godly psalmist who cried out, 'I will extol the Lord at all times; his praise will always be on my lips' (Psalm 34:1) and rejoice even more in the knowledge that the offering of 'a sacrifice of praise' is one of the specific things of which we are told that 'God is pleased' (Hebrews 13:15, 16). No wonder Isaac Watts could write these words:

> Sweet is the work, my God, my King,
> To praise thy name, give thanks and sing;
> To show thy love by morning light,
> And talk of all thy truth at night.

But now comes the inconsistency. With the same tongue 'we curse men, who have been made in God's likeness. Out of the same mouth come praise and cursing.' What shameful inconsistency! Man is not merely to be thought of as being in some way superior to the beasts of the field. He bears a unique relationship to God. He is capable of rebirth and restoration into God's likeness. In spite of his depravity, he retains that dignity. Man still has what John Wesley called 'an indelible nobleness, which we ought to reverence in ourselves and others'. Yet we use our tongues to 'curse' the crown of God's creation! James's word is not limited in meaning to the literal calling down of curses on people. It takes in all the bitter, callous, unkind, critical, spiteful, angry, harsh words that we can sadly use about our fellow men. A friend once told me that one of the most challenging sermons he had ever heard was called 'Ten minutes after the benediction'. It spoke of those who moved in moments from the gloria to gossip, from creed to criticism, from worshipping God to wounding men. Can we plead 'Not Guilty' to that sort of thing? That is the kind of inconsistency James is attacking and it is little wonder that he adds, 'My brothers, this should not be.' The thing is not only inconsistent, it is iniquitous.

Has James overdone it in taking up so much space in warning us about the use of the tongue? Surely not. No sensitive Christian ought to be able to read his words without a sense of shame, mingled with a longing to know in his own life God's answer to the psalmist's prayer:

> 'May the words of my mouth and the meditation of my heart
> be pleasing in your sight,
> O Lord, my Rock and my Redeemer'
> (Psalm 19:14).

22.

Wisdom is for living

> *'Who is wise and understanding among you? Let him show it by his good life, by deeds done in the humility that comes from wisdom'* (James 3:13).

A first glance at these words might give the impression that after his lengthy section on the use and misuse of the tongue, James is now switching to an entirely new subject. He would, of course, be perfectly entitled to do so, but a closer look shows that his words are still flowing in the same general direction. The roots of this particular verse lie deep in the heart of what we saw to be the keynote section of the whole epistle (2:14–26) where James insisted that genuine faith proved itself by the quality of a person's life. In his typical down-to-earth fashion, he immediately used the tongue as an illustration of the need for this truth to be applied in practical, everyday life, and especially by those claiming or clamouring to be Christian leaders. Now, in a section of teaching that goes right through to the end of verse 18, he challenges his readers to test the genuineness of their Christian faith and the quality of their Christian living in the light of another vitally important concept, that of *wisdom.*

We tend to use the word 'wisdom' in a somewhat careless way today, but its origins and history are vastly different. Put at its highest, wisdom is nothing less than one of the attributes of God: 'To God belong wisdom and power; counsel and understanding are his' (Job 12:13). Seen in this light, the word carries with it the sense that God has complete knowledge of everything, that all of his actions are perfect and that his judgement on every issue in the universe is infallible. H. B. Smith has called God's wisdom 'that attribute of God whereby he produces the best possible results with the best possible means'. It is fascinating to discover that even outside of biblical history and data wisdom was associated with deity. The great Socrates, who died about 400 B.C., refused to be called *sophos* – the Greek word for 'wise' – because he felt that such a claim would be blasphemous. Instead, he preferred the name *philosophos*, which means 'a lover of wisdom'. Yet the Bible teaches that the wisdom of God is one of his communicable attributes, that there is a measure of wisdom which God intends his people to have and instructs them to seek, and it is to this point that James now speaks. In order that his words can be applied to us directly, let us see them as making two specific demands upon us.

1. The excellence we ought to seek
'Who is wise and understanding among you?'

The first thing to say about this question is that there may be a direct link here with verse 1. If we took the teaching on the tongue (vv. 2–12) as an elongated parenthesis, we could certainly see the force of putting these two phrases together: 'Not many of you should presume to be teachers, my brothers . . . Who is wise and understanding among you?' James may therefore be introducing a deliberate deterrent to those who were pushing themselves into positions of prominence in the church, though his teaching has much wider application. In James's test, the excellence we ought to seek is a combination of two things. For reasons that will become obvious, let us look at them in reverse order.

1. Intelligence. The NIV has chosen 'understanding' to translate the Greek *epistemon*, the kind of word one would use about an expert in a particular sphere. It speaks of a person who has gained technical knowledge as the result of careful observation and study. There is an implication here that we dare not miss! Nowhere does the Bible suggest that a person with a high IQ is spiritually superior as a result, but it does impress upon each one of us the importance of learning all that we can in order to be better qualified for living the Christian life. Notice how this comes across in the New Testament.

The most important commandment is 'Love the Lord your God with all your heart and with all your soul and with all your *mind* and with all your strength' (Mark 12: 30); the way to avoid conformity to the spirit of this world is to be 'transformed by the renewing of your *mind*' (Romans 12:2); part of the secret of holiness is to 'prepare your *minds* for action' (1 Peter 1:13). Every Christian has an inescapable responsibility to use whatever ability God has given him to appropriate spiritual truth. There has never been a time in the history of the world when God's people have had such readily available material to help them in their study of his Word, yet indolence, indiscipline and laziness have made pygmies out of many who should be giants. If this is true of so many 'ordinary' Christians, it is an even greater tragedy when it is in any way true of those who are meant to be teaching others. While on holiday in Germany, C. H. Spurgeon was looking out of his hotel window, watching people coming to draw water from a pump in the street. After a while he realized that one man had returned several times. Eventually, Spurgeon discovered the reason – this man was a local water-seller and because he was distributing the water to others, he needed to come back to the source again and again. So in Christian teaching, we can only share with others what we have stored ourselves, and that will require from us the disciplined determination to gain an increasing knowledge of the things of God.

2. Insight. If understanding or knowledge can be explained or suggested by the word 'intelligence', then wisdom can be explained or suggested by the word 'insight', and it is interesting to notice how often the two concepts are linked together in the Bible. Here are some examples: 'But where can wisdom be found? Where does understanding dwell?' (Job 28:12); 'Get wisdom, get understanding' (Proverbs 4:5); 'Buy the truth and do not sell it; get wisdom, discipline and understanding' (Proverbs 23:23); 'Who is wise? He will realize these things. Who is discerning? He will understand them' (Hosea 14:9). It is also interesting to notice that in all these instances, wisdom is mentioned first. That is no coincidence, because although they are closely related, wisdom is greater than knowledge; it has a deeper dimension.

This does not, of course, mean that wisdom comes from God but knowledge does not. When we were studying James's description of God as 'the Father of the heavenly lights', we included the fact that God is the Father of intellectual light, that is to say, the light of knowledge. Every discovery that a person makes about the material universe in which he lives is the result of God graciously allowing him to see something of the vast treasury of his creation. There is no area of human discovery which is not first an area of divine revelation. Knowledge, in other words, is a gift from God.

Yet even outside of a religious context, it is possible to have knowledge without wisdom. As Charles Caleb Colton put it, 'It is better to have wisdom without learning, than to have learning without wisdom; just as it is better to be rich without being the possessor of a mine, than to be the possessor of a mine without being rich.' But the Christian is not faced with alternatives: he is given the privilege of possessing both of the virtues we are discussing and should therefore cry out to God with the great King Solomon, 'Give me wisdom *and* knowledge . . .' (2 Chronicles 1:10). Perhaps the best way of pointing out the superiority of wisdom is to remind ourselves once more that the Bible repeatedly shows wisdom as being God-centred. This becomes strikingly clear when we discover that nowhere in the Bible is wisdom attributed to an unbeliever. Surely that is significant? According to the Bible's teaching, an unbeliever can be knowledgeable, intelligent, clever and shrewd, but 'The fear of the Lord is the beginning of wisdom' (Psalm 111:10). As Dr. J. I. Packer puts it, 'Not until we have become humble and teachable, standing in awe of God's holiness and sovereignty . . . acknowledging our own littleness, distrusting our own thoughts, and willing to have our minds turned upside down, can divine wisdom become ours.' This leads us to say two things about our possession of true wisdom.

The first is that *it begins with conversion.* The Bible describes a Christian as being 'in Christ' and at one point Paul says that God has placed us 'in Christ Jesus, who has become for us wisdom from God – that is, our righteousness, holiness and redemption' (1 Corinthians 1:30). This is a striking example of the place that wisdom occupies in biblical thinking. Would we have put those last four nouns in that order? Would we not tend to put 'wisdom' at the end, after those other magnificent biblical words 'righteousness', 'holiness' and 'redemption'? Yet not only does Paul put it first, he goes so far as to say that it includes the other three. The wisdom of God is embodied in Christ, and when we receive him as Saviour, we receive the righteousness, holiness and redemption he came to secure for his people. Another way of putting this is to say that only when we become God-centred through our relationship to Christ do we have our first experience of true wisdom. No man can have a right understanding of the great issues of human experience until he is 'in Christ'.

The second is that *it grows through communion.* Put as simply as possible, development of knowledge centres around activity of mind, while development of wisdom centres around attitude of heart. One comes through looking around, the other through looking up. Knowledge is extended by observation, wisdom by meditation. This is how the psalmist puts it:

> 'Oh, how I love your law!
> I meditate on it all day long.
> Your commands make me wiser than my enemies,
> for they are ever with me.
> I have more insight than all my teachers,
> for I meditate on your statutes'
> (Psalm 119:97–99).

God has given us all the written directions we will ever need on this earth in his infallible Word, which is a reflection of his own character, and we will grow in wisdom only as we immerse ourselves in it and allow its truth to permeate every part of our lives. And to do that is not merely to become more familiar with written words, but to enter into a deeper relationship with God himself. To quote J. I. Packer again, 'The kind of wisdom that God waits to give to those who ask him is a wisdom that will bind us to himself, a wisdom that will find expression in a spirit of faith and a life of faithfulness.' That is the excellence we ought to seek and it leads us straight on to James's second point.

2. The evidence we ought to show

'Let him show it by his good life, by deeds done in the humility that comes from wisdom.'

This is vintage James! The language he likes is the kind of language that can be seen so clearly that it never has to shout. In effect, he is saying this: 'Do you claim to have wisdom and understanding? Then let me see the evidence. I can hear your words; let me see your works.' The impact of what James is saying comes across even more forcefully when we notice that his phrase 'let him show' is precisely the one he used in the passage we described as the keynote of the whole epistle. There he said, '*Show me* your faith without deeds, and *I will show you* my faith by what I do' (2:18). The root verb James uses is *deixon,* which basically means to exhibit or display, and the tenor of his language is identical in both places. If a man claims to have faith, then let him display it by living a transformed life; if a man claims to have wisdom, then let him display that wisdom by the way he lives. As Curtis Vaughan comments, 'The true test of wisdom is works, not words.' In the remainder of the sentence we are studying James suggests that true wisdom will show itself in two ways.

1. It will be general. 'Let him show it by his good life . . .' Christianity is not just a collection of religious ideas, nor is it merely a matter of performing religious ceremonies. True Christianity pervades every part of what a man is and does and in practical terms it produces what James calls a 'good life'. James refuses to let us escape from this! In Robert Johnstone's words, 'We have here again what may be described as the central thought of this epistle, that where religion has real saving hold of a mind and heart, it cannot from its nature but powerfully influence the outward life; and that the more a Christian has of true wisdom and spiritual knowledge, the more manifestly will his life *at all points* be governed by his religion.' My italics are intentional! The trouble with some Christians is that they seem to be suffering from spiritual measles; they are sanctified in spots. Their lives are a disappointing mixture of the occasionally marvellous and the often mediocre. And in a Christian this is disappointing, because it shows a lack of wisdom, which at the end of the day means a lack of obedience to the clear directions for living which God is longing to give him day by day through his Word and by his Spirit. True wisdom, then, will pervade the whole life; it will be general.

2. It will be gentle. '. . . by deeds done in the humility that comes from wisdom.' Here, James moves from the general to the particular and says that true wisdom will manifest itself in a very specific way. The Greek word *prautes* has been called 'the untranslatable word' and virtually every English Bible uses a number of variations to try to express its meaning. In this instance, the NIV translators have chosen 'humility', which is certainly in the right general area, but hardly captures the precise quality that is meant. Older English versions of the Bible almost always used 'meekness', but that word is now so widely misinterpreted as meaning weakness, that we probably need another to take its place. 'Gentleness' would be a good word to use – yet it is a particular kind of gentleness, one that can almost only be explained by way of illustration. It is first of all a quality rooted in such a conviction about the overruling sovereignty of a wise and loving God that it accepts his dealings and dispositions without resistance. But it is also a quality that accepts without retaliation the insults and injuries caused by one's fellow men, recognizing that these, too, are under God's providential control.

The perfect example of this was 'the meekness and gentleness of Christ' (2 Corinthians 10:1) which Peter illustrates like this, when telling Christians how to react under unjust pressure: 'To this you were called, because Christ suffered for you, leaving you an example, that you should follow in his steps. "He committed no sin, and no deceit was found in his mouth." When they hurled their insults at him, he did not retaliate; when he suffered, he made no threats. Instead, he entrusted himself to him who judges justly' (1 Peter 2:21–23). What a perfect pattern! Jesus did not answer violence with violence, anger with anger, insult with insult. Instead, he gently committed his cause to God, knowing that he was in complete control. How differently we act at times! We are so occupied with self, so concerned about our reputation. We dissipate so much nervous energy fighting off every pinprick that might damage our ego or spoil our 'image'. Yet all that energy is a sign of spiritual weakness, because it betrays a lack of the biblical wisdom whose sole concern is obedience and which is content to leave the consequences to God.

Some years ago I came across a man I shall never forget. He was a Latvian, short, stocky and enormously strong. As a young man, while living in Siberia, he became seriously ill, and vowed that if he recovered he would give his life to God. Miraculously, his health was restored and soon afterwards he came across a New Testament. After a while he was converted and immediately felt that he ought to share the challenge of the Word of God with his widowed father, especially as his father was at that time living in sin with a German countess. As best he could, he told his father that he had become a Christian and then urged him to turn from sin. His father was furious and began to persecute him. Every evening, when he came in from working in the fields, his father would ask him, 'Are you still a Christian?' When he said he was, his father ordered him to strip and lie face down on the floor. He would then beat him with the buckle end of a leather belt until his back was raw and bleeding. As he told me of this, my friend said, 'While I was working in the fields, I used to ask God to help me to bear the pain I knew was coming without fear or resentment, and while I lay on the floor being whipped, I would think of all those people who had laid down their lives for Christ and pray, "Thank you, Lord, for allowing me the privilege of this small sacrifice." '

Now that is meekness, gentleness – the ability not to use the power at one's disposal because of the conviction that in God's overruling providence these terrible things would in some way be used for his glory. This man was one of the strongest men I have ever met, yet he allowed himself to be mutilated by an old man he could have murdered. Here was someone who had learned the biblical lesson that 'Those who suffer according to God's will should commit themselves to their faithful Creator and continue to do good'! (1 Peter 4:19.)

The personal application of all this is surely obvious. In all the turmoil of today's world, in all the stresses and strains of life, in all your responsibilities at work, at home and in your social life, in all of that complexity of human relationships that go to make up this thing we call 'life', hold fast to the three great truths that shine out from Peter's description of Christ and his later lesson on facing difficulties: God is the Creator, so stands at the beginning of things; God is faithful, so stands at the centre of things; God is the Judge, so stands at the end of things. To face life with these convictions is to stand on the high road to victory. In his marvellous little book *The Knowledge of the Holy* A. W. Tozer puts it like this: 'To believe actively that our heavenly Father constantly spreads around us the providential circumstances that work for our present good and our everlasting well-being, brings to the soul a veritable benediction. Most of us go through life praying a little, planning a little, jockeying for position, hoping but never being quite certain of anything, and always secretly afraid that we will miss the way. This is a tragic waste of truth and never gives rest to the heart. There is a better way. It is to repudiate our own wisdom and take instead the infinite wisdom of God. Our insistence on seeing ahead is natural enough, but it is a real hindrance to our spiritual progress. God has charged himself with full responsibility for our eternal happiness and stands ready to take over the management of our lives the moment we turn in faith to him.' There is the secret of true wisdom, and wisdom is for living!

23.

Wisdom from hell

> *'But if you harbour bitter envy and selfish ambition in your hearts, do not boast about it or deny the truth. Such "wisdom" does not come down from heaven but is earthly, unspiritual, of the devil. For where you have envy and selfish ambition, there you find disorder and every evil practice'* (James 3:14–16).

As we saw in our previous study, true wisdom is God-orientated. It begins at conversion, because no man has life in its right perspective until he comes to the Lord Jesus Christ in repentance and faith and puts God at the very centre of his life. Not only that, but it grows through communion, it develops and deepens with discipleship. This true wisdom shows itself generally in every part of a man's life and especially in that wise gentleness that comes from a proper conception of God as the Creator who stands at the beginning of things, as the Faithful One who overrules the present, and as the Judge who is utterly in control of the future. Only when we have that conception of God can we approach all of the tangled web of our human relationships and structures in the right way. Only then do we have that wise gentleness that does not always have to be asserting itself, that is not always thinking of 'here', 'now' and 'mine', but is content to rely upon God's wisdom, faithfulness and love. Yet for the very reason that wisdom is such a wonderful quality, we should expect there to be a forgery in circulation. There is, and James warns us about it by telling us three distinct things.

1. The significance of its motives

'But if you harbour bitter envy and selfish ambition in your hearts, do not boast about it or deny the truth' (v. 14).

In this opening phrase of James's teaching on the subject of wisdom, there are two specific parts closely linked together.

1. The corruption that is noted. 'But if you harbour bitter envy and selfish ambition in your hearts . . .' Notice the last words first! It has been said that 'The heart of man's problem is the problem of man's heart'; and when James begins to expose false wisdom, he begins at the centre of things and not on the circumference. This is because of his unerring insight into the human personality, and in particular his clinical understanding of the fact that outward actions are the result of inward attitudes. He sees a direct connection between the fruit and the root, the signs and the source, and never hesitates to point it out. Here he sees two evil motives lurking behind actions that are the practical expression of false wisdom.

The first is *'bitter envy'*. The word 'envy' is the Greek *zelos*, which can sometimes have a perfectly good meaning and be translated 'zeal'. A clear example of this is when Jesus drove out the moneychangers from the temple courts at Jerusalem and the disciples remembered the messianic prophecy: 'Zeal for your house will consume me' (John 2:17). However, its main New Testament use is the bad meaning given to it as one of the 'acts of the sinful nature', namely 'jealousy' (Galatians 5:20). That word alone carries enough sinister connotations, but James adds the adjective 'bitter'. The Greek word is *pikros*, which comes from a root meaning 'to cut' or 'prick'. When James speaks of 'bitter envying' he is speaking of the kind of jealousy that cannot bear someone else's popularity or success and, given the opportunity, will do anything it can to humiliate and degrade that person, regardless of who may get hurt in the process.

The story is told of two men who lived in a certain city. One was envious and the other covetous. The ruler of the city sent for them and he said that he wanted to grant them one wish each, with this proviso, that the one who chose first would get exactly what he asked for, while the other man would get exactly twice what the first had asked for himself. The envious man was ordered to choose first, but immediately found himself in a quandary. He wanted to choose something great for himself, but realized that if he did so the other would get twice as much. He thought for a while and then he asked this – that one of his eyes should be put out.

That may sound an extravagant example, but let us beware of any danger signals in this area. One of the most honest prayers ever prayed by a minister of the gospel was surely the one which admitted, 'Lord, I would sooner your work was not done at all than done by someone better than I can do it.' That was a horrible prayer, but am I not right in calling it honest? Is it not true that even Christians are capable of descending to that level? Was John Calvin not right to warn us of 'minds so infected with the power of malignity that they turn all things into bitterness'? Let us beware of the tiniest trace of this vile spirit!

The second is *'selfish ambition'*. This translates the single Greek word *eritheia*, which has a fascinating history. Part of its background was political, when it was used of a person willing to do anything to get himself elected to office. If this gives us something of its colour, it is also instructive to notice its connection with the word 'jealousy'. These treacherous twins are found together several times in the New Testament; they are both listed in the 'acts of the sinful nature', which are said to include 'jealousy' and 'selfish ambition' (Galatians 5:20), while Paul was deeply concerned lest in the spiritually deficient church at Corinth he would find 'jealousy' *(zelos)* and 'factions' *(eritheia)*. They are found together because the Bible is true to life. A man who seems unusually concerned with the demotion of others is usually concerned with the promotion of himself. It is not difficult to think of the sort of person who will do anything, say anything, lobby anybody in order to get somewhere in the church. Yet this carnal drive for dominance can sometimes be mistaken for commendable drive and enthusiasm. It is precisely at this point that James speaks to us, because his concern is not with what other people think, but what is in our hearts. James majors on motives! The Bible tells us that 'The Lord is a God who knows, and by him deeds are weighed' (1 Samuel 2:3). What a telling phrase that is! Men can only watch our actions; God weighs them, searching our hearts for the motives that lie behind all we do.

2. The correction that is needed. '. . . do not boast about it or deny the truth.' These words help to bring home with even greater force James's point about envy and selfish ambition being matters of the heart. A man *knows* when his zeal is fired by personal ambition, or when he has achieved something by dishonourable means, and James now warns such a person not to compound his sin by boasting about it, because to boast will be to 'deny the truth'. There is another example of James's devastating insight into the human heart. As A. W. Tozer says, 'Hardly anything else reveals so well the fear and uncertainty among men as the length to which they will go to hide their true selves from each other and even from their own eyes.' Yet unless we are utterly out of touch with God we know the truth; we know when we have done something or got somewhere by our own carnal efforts. We know because the Holy Spirit rebukes us and we should never cease to praise God for this part of his ministry.

There may well be a special word here for preachers, teachers and leaders in the church, with James linking all of this passage back to verse 1. Phillips Brooks once described preaching as 'truth expressed through personality', but who can tell how much impact is lost when the personality does not match up to the preaching, when the preacher is out of touch with God? It is always easier to condemn sin in others than to conquer it in ourselves. Let those of us who preach and teach strive at all costs to avoid pretence and hypocrisy in our ministry! In particular, let us search our hearts for any trace of envy or selfish ambition and when we find it root it out. We need to live more and more in the spirit of these words by William Boyd-Carpenter:

> For sins of heedless word and deed,
> For pride ambitious to succeed;
> For crafty trade and subtle snare
> To catch the simple unaware;
> For lives bereft of purpose high,
> Forgive, forgive, O Lord, we cry.

2. The source of its menace

'Such "wisdom" does not come down from heaven but is earthly, unspiritual, of the devil' (v. 15).

The more one studies the Epistle of James, the more one comes to appreciate the way in which the Holy Spirit gave him such deep insight into spiritual truth as it affects daily life and then the ability to convey all of this in such a devastatingly direct way. This verse is a perfect example of what I mean, because in the space of a handful of words James says four things about the source of the kind of false wisdom he has been describing.

1. It 'does not come down from heaven'. The word 'heaven' supplies the obvious meaning of the original Greek word *anothen*, which literally means 'from above', and which James used at 1:17. There is nothing godly about this so-called wisdom; it has none of the fragrance of heaven about it.

2. It is 'earthly'. Paul uses the same word when he speaks of those whose mind 'is on earthly things' (Philippians 3:19). Commenting on that phrase, J. A. Motyer wrote, 'At the very centre of their being, where their life finds its direction, where their attitudes and tendencies are fashioned which subsequently influence decisions and govern likes and dislikes – at this vital centre the world and its ways are the whole object of attention.' That vividly captures the practical effect of what James is saying here. This kind of wisdom never gets out of the pull of earth's gravity.

3. It is 'unspiritual'. Two other passages of Scripture will help to bring James's meaning into focus here. Jude uses a very similar word when speaking of those who 'follow mere natural instincts' (Jude 19), while Isaiah describes the Holy Spirit as 'the Spirit of wisdom and of understanding' (Isaiah 11:2), that is to say, the one who alone can give true wisdom, clear insight, right attitudes. The challenge to the Christian is to ask whether his attitudes and actions are truly directed by the Holy Spirit, or whether they are motivated by nothing more than natural instinct. Every Christian has been gifted by the Holy Spirit in one way or another; the real question is whether he is using those gifts in a spiritual or an unspiritual way. There is a great difference between gifts and graces. In *The Work of the Holy*

Spirit, Octavius Winslow writes, 'It is a remarkable fact . . . that the Corinthian church, the most distinguished for its possession of the gifts of the Spirit, was at the same time the most remarkable for its lack of the sanctifying graces of the Spirit. It was the most gifted, but at the same time the least holy community gathered and planted by the apostles.' Mark that carefully! Ability is no yardstick of spirituality.

4. It is 'devilish'. The primary reference of the word is to demons or evil spirits and that alone should cause us sobering concern. As the tide of the gospel recedes in Great Britain we are being forced to recognize the half-forgotten reality of multitudes of evil spirits in the world today – spirits of impurity, hatred, rebellion, disorder and, in the context of what James is saying, spirits which defy Christ and defy self. Yet all of these demons are agents of Satan, the author of all sin and therefore of the false wisdom of which James is speaking. We could go further and say that the fall of Satan was the greatest example of false wisdom the universe has ever known. Jonathan Edwards once said, 'Although the devil be exceedingly crafty and subtle, yet he is one of the greatest fools and blockheads in the world, as the subtlest of wicked men are. Sin is of such a nature that it strangely infatuates and stultifies the mind.' We may find it amusing to hear the devil called a blockhead, but this is a matter for learning and not for laughter. It is no light or little thing when Satan so corrupts the Christian's thinking that he follows false wisdom, something the Bible uncompromisingly describes as being 'earthly, unspiritual, devilish'.

3. The sign of its mischief

'For where you have envy and selfish ambition, there you find disorder and every evil practice' (v. 16).

James is a great believer in the law of cause and effect. We saw this when he wrote, 'Then, after desire has conceived, it gives birth to sin; and sin, when it is full-grown, gives birth to death' (1:15). Later in the same chapter we found him writing, 'But the man who looks intently into the perfect law that gives freedom . . . will be blessed in what he does' (1:25). Then he reminded us that 'Judgement without mercy will be shown to anyone who has not been merciful' (2:13). So here James says that the same law operates: envy and selfish ambition produce certain inevitable results and he names two of them.

1. 'Disorder'. The original word is *akatastasia*, which comes from the same root as a word James has used twice before. The first occasion was when he wrote of a double-minded man being '*unstable* in all he does' (1:8) and the second when, earlier in the section we are studying at the moment, he spoke of the tongue as '*a restless* evil' (3:8). The word carries with it various shades of meaning and may therefore bear more than one application. James may be referring to rows, divisions and disorder in the church, what the Bible calls 'dissension among brothers' (Proverbs 6:19). What is absolutely clear is that when these unholy wars come about as the result of envy and ambition, God is not to blame, for 'God is not a God of disorder but of peace' (1 Corinthians 14:33). The other, more personal, application is the tragic truth that the envious, ambitious man is never at rest. There is always someone else to envy, another mountain to climb, another position to attain. There is an unholy restlessness about a man who is eaten up with envy and selfish ambition. He never has what Anna Laetitia Waring calls 'a heart at leisure from itself'.

2. 'Every evil practice'. These words are a serious reminder to us that no sin is isolated or benign. Sin is a malignant disease that spreads its tainted tentacles far and wide. Envy and selfish ambition certainly are. It was through selfish ambition that Satan fell. It was through envy that Cain killed Abel. It was ambition that gripped Absalom and drove him to steal the hearts of the men of Israel. It was envy that drove Haman to erect what was to prove his own scaffold. It was because of envy that the religious leaders delivered Jesus to Pontius Pilate. There is almost literally no limit to the sins that have followed envy and selfish ambition. We have been warned!

Yet it is interesting to notice that the word 'evil' which James uses here is not one of the more usual Greek words, *kakos*, but *poneros*, which has a primary meaning of 'trivial' or 'worthless'. Is there not a lesson here? Whatever we achieve as a result of envy or selfish ambition proves at the end of the day to be worthless. A Holywood film star once said, 'I did everything I could to get to the top of the tree, and when I got to the top I discovered that there was nothing there.' When we use worldly wisdom in trying to do God's work, when we use nothing more than our own natural ingenuity to gain our ends or settle arguments in our favour, the end result is uncannily disappointing, and not only does it come to nothing on earth, but it will lead to nothing in heaven, because it will be among those things that will be 'burned up' (1 Corinthians 3:15). The wisdom that comes from hell will get us nowhere in heaven!

24.

Wisdom from heaven

> *'But the wisdom that comes from heaven is first of all pure; then peace-loving, considerate, submissive, full of mercy and good fruit, impartial and sincere'* (James 3:17).

From his penetrating analysis of false wisdom, James now turns to the wisdom that is spiritual and godly, the kind for which every Christian should constantly pray and which he should seek to exhibit in his daily life. Our understanding of what James is saying will obviously come from a straightforward study of each of the words he uses to describe true wisdom, but it will be helpful to prepare for this with a brief introduction.

1. The contrast with false wisdom
'But the wisdom that comes from heaven . . .'

To begin reading this verse is like taking a sudden, giant leap from night to day. After all the darkness and deception of the three previous verses we now move into an entirely different atmosphere. The contrast is complete and flows entirely from the fact that the source of the 'wisdom' concerned in each of the two passages is totally different. In the previous verses, James writes of a 'wisdom' that 'does *not* come down from heaven'; here, he writes of 'the wisdom that *comes* from heaven'. Again, the NIV translators are supplying the obvious meaning of the Greek word *anothen*, which literally means 'from above'. But we can even take this one step further and say that 'above' and 'heaven' are equally obviously being used as synonyms for God. What James is saying is that false wisdom does *not* come from God – in fact, it is 'earthly, unspiritual, of the devil' –

whereas true wisdom *does* come from God. It is what James himself would call a 'good and perfect gift . . . coming down from the Father of the heavenly lights' (1:17).

It is important to underline this and to be crystal clear in our minds that true wisdom is the free gift of a gracious God and in no way the result of man's own scheming, imagination or effort. The Bible insists on this truth. Old Testament writers put it like this: 'God gave Solomon wisdom and very great insight, and a breadth of understanding as measureless as the sand on the seashore' (1 Kings 4:29); 'For the Lord gives wisdom, and from his mouth come knowledge and understanding' (Proverbs 2:6); 'To the man who pleases him, God gives wisdom, knowledge and happiness' (Ecclesiastes 2:26). The New Testament writers testify to the same truth and Paul speaks for them all when he says, 'We . . . speak a message of wisdom among the mature . . . God has revealed it to us by his Spirit' (1 Corinthians 2:6, 10). James does not develop this point in any way, so neither shall we. The characteristics of true wisdom will come to light one by one as we go through this verse and as they do they will in themselves be powerful illustrations of the truth contained in James's opening words, that true wisdom is not man-made, it is God-given. It 'comes from heaven'.

2. The criterion of this gift
'. . . first of all pure . . .'

In this verse, James is to use eight adjectives about the 'wisdom that comes from heaven', but he draws specific and primary attention to one and says that this wisdom is '*first of all* pure'. In speaking of wisdom in the terms he does, James is obviously referring to those who possess it, so that when he says that 'wisdom' is 'first of all pure' he means that this is the thing that is fundamentally true of those who are truly wise; it is the criterion by which the person claiming to be wise can be tested.

Then we should notice that what James chooses as the fundamental criterion of wisdom is not an outward expression, but an inner experience. He examines our hearts before he looks at our hands. He is primarily concerned with what we *are* and only then with what we *do* – and this is the man who is renowned for being so 'practical'! But what does James mean by being 'pure'? The particular Greek word used – *hagne* – basically means 'undefiled' or 'uncontaminated' and the most important thing to grasp is that this is an adjective applied to God himself. Writing of the certainty of Christ's return to the earth, John says, 'Everyone who has this hope in him purifies himself, *just as he is pure*' (1 John 3:3). This takes us to the heart of what James is saying. The purity of which he is speaking does not primarily refer to outward behaviour (though it is obviously closely connected) but to an attitude of heart towards God. There is an obvious echo here of the promise Jesus made: 'Blessed are the pure in heart, for they will see God' (Matthew 5:8). The emphasis stated there, and implied by James, is on the heart, the very centre of the personality and the source of all outward activity. It is here first of all, in what the Bible calls 'the wellspring of life' (Proverbs 4:23) that God demands purity. And what is this purity? I believe that we would be capturing the spirit of what both Jesus and James meant if we called it unmixed devotion, an undivided love for God burning on the altar of a man's heart. This seems to be confirmed by the fact that James is telling us that purity is the criterion of true wisdom, in contrast to the false wisdom which was characterized by envy and selfish ambition. False wisdom puts self at the centre of life; true wisdom puts God at the centre and in that sense is 'pure', being both undefiled and undivided. The man who is 'pure in heart' is the man who can truthfully pray in the spirit of these words by Antoinette Bourignon:

> Oh, let thy sacred presence fill,
> And set my longing spirit free!
> Which pants to have no other will,
> But day and night to feast on thee.
> Henceforth may no profane delight
> Divide this consecrated soul;
> Possess it thou, who hast the right,
> As Lord and Master of the whole!

3. The characteristics of this gift

'. . . then peace-loving, considerate, submissive, full of mercy and good fruit, impartial and sincere.'

The little word 'then' is particularly important here, because it provides a vital link between what has gone before and all that is to follow. It is only when a man's heart is 'pure', when it is undivided in its devotion, that the characteristics James now lists will follow. These qualities are the consequences of a pure heart, not its cause. They do not *make* a man wise; they *mark* him as being so. James mentions seven characteristics of true wisdom here. Let us look at each of them in turn.

1. It is 'peace-loving'. It is interesting to notice that this characteristic is mentioned immediately after James has said that true wisdom is 'pure', because we have exactly the same order in the Beatitudes, where the promise to the pure in heart is immediately followed by the words, 'Blessed are the peacemakers, for they will be called sons of God' (Matthew 5:9). 'Peace-loving' sounds a very comfortable, almost compromising word, but it is far from that. It does not refer to a spineless anonymity that does not want to get involved. It breathes action, not apathy. It seeks to preserve peace where it exists and to promote peace where it does not exist. It unites where false wisdom divides and reconciles where false wisdom rips apart. Let me give just one illustration of this attitude. John Wesley and George Whitefield were both mighty men of God, yet on certain theological issues they were diametrically opposed. One of these issues came to a head when Wesley published a sermon entitled 'Free Grace'. On Christmas Eve 1740 Whitefield wrote a long letter to Wesley. It was clear, firm and decisive, and plainly showed that they stood in opposite doctrinal camps. Yet towards the end of that letter Whitefield wrote, 'Nothing but a single regard for the honour of Christ has forced this letter from me. I love and honour you for his sake; and when I come to judgement will thank you before men and angels for what you have, under God, done for my soul.' What a beautiful, peace-loving spirit that showed! And how different it is from the militant spirit shown by some Christians towards those who disagree with them!

2. It is 'considerate'. This is one of many words used in English versions of the Bible to translate the Greek *epieikes.* It carries with it the sense of being prepared to see the best in even the worst of people and of being willing to forgive when one has the right to condemn. The story is told of Dr William Trumbull, who was travelling by train one day when a drunken man got into the same compartment. After a while, he drew a bottle of liquor from his pocket and offered Dr Trumbull a drink. Dr Trumbull replied, 'No thank you, I don't drink.' After taking some himself, the man settled back in his seat. Some time later he took the bottle out again and offered Dr Trumbull a drink. He got exactly the same reply: 'No thank you, I don't drink.' After the same thing had happened a third time, something suddenly seemed to bring the man to his senses. Looking at Dr Trumbull, he said, 'You must think I'm a beast.' 'On the contrary,' Dr Trumbull replied, 'I think you are very generous.' That was being what James calls 'considerate'! Dr Turnbull could have adopted a 'holier than thou' attitude towards the man; he could have lobbed texts at him like moral hand grenades; he could have simply walked out in disgust. Instead, he gave up what we might call his legal rights, made all the allowances he could for the man's weakness and sought to see the best he possibly could in him. The result was that the man was eventually led to Christ, his heart broken open by Dr Trumbull's courteous attitude. Are you considerate? Or are you reluctant to forgive, to overlook weaknesses, to make allowances? Commenting on this word, Robert Johnstone says, 'The Christian man loves to make allowances for the ignorance and weakness of others, knowing how great need he stands in constantly of having allowance made for himself both by God and man.'

3. It is 'submissive'. This is the only place where this particular word occurs in the New Testament. The Greek word is *eupeithes*, which in turn is made up of two words meaning 'easy, or well' and 'to be persuaded'. However, this does not mean that the person who is *eupeithes* is a spineless weakling, a 'pushover', someone who is without convictions or moral courage. What it does mean is that he is open to reason. He is not so obstinately entrenched in his own opinions that he refuses to listen to any alternative view – like the man who during a presidential election in the United States put a sticker on the back of his car which read: 'My mind is made up. Don't confuse me with facts'! This is the kind of person the Bible has in mind when it says, 'The sluggard is wiser in his own eyes than seven men who answer discreetly' (Proverbs 26:16). Even when outnumbered seven to one, this man obstinately refuses to listen to any opinion except his own; nothing will make him change his mind. It is tragic to see that kind of attitude in churches, societies, committees and other groupings of Christians. Some people are so rigid, so determined not even to listen to the other side, that they give the impression of being self-constituted arbiters of the whole counsel of God. It is true that Jesus never changed his mind, or took advice, or revised his opinions, but he was God incarnate. It is both tragic and pathetic when a Christian acts as if he was nothing less. Wisdom has exactly the opposite spirit. It is submissive, open to reason.

4. It is 'full of mercy'. This seems to have the double meaning of a spirit of forgiveness towards those who have wronged us and practical help to those in need, and it is surely significant that James reinforces this particular quality by saying that true wisdom is '*full* of mercy'. The Christian should never be miserly with his mercy – not least because he has received so much of it from God's good hand.

5. It is 'full of good fruit'. This is closely linked with 'mercy', and is exactly what we would expect James to include in his list of the virtues characterizing true wisdom. It takes us back to the place where he exposed the scandal of a person in desperate need being callously dismissed with the pious advice: 'Go, I wish you well; keep warm and well fed' (2:16). An ounce of help is said to be worth a ton of pity. We might use the same formula here and say that an ounce of fruit is worth a ton of feeling! There used to be an advertising slogan that ran: 'Where there's need there's the Salvation Army'; I think James would have approved of that! Thomas Manton says, 'It is the great fault of some that when they begin to be religious, they leave off to be human,' but that is a travesty of New Testament Christianity. A Christian should not only be growing in his knowledge of God; he should also be the best neighbour a man could have. When there is an accident or sickness in a neighbour's home, when some crisis arises, when some need appears, the Christian should be the first to offer help, because godly wisdom has provided him with a store of 'good fruit'.

6. *It is 'impartial'.* This translates another word which only James uses in the whole of the New Testament. The word is *adiakritos*, which literally means 'not divided'. It is difficult to know precisely what James has in mind here, but it may well be that he is underlining an earlier point that Christians should not 'show favouritism' (2:1). Some time ago I found these words written on the wall of a church in Wiltshire: 'O God, may the door of this house be wide enough to include all who need divine love and human friendship; narrow enough to shut out all envy, pride and strife. May its threshold be smooth enough to be no stumbling block to children or to straying feet, yet rugged enough to turn back the tempter's power.' That is a fine prayer for any church and its spirit expresses something of what James means when he says that true wisdom is 'impartial'.

7. *It is 'sincere'.* The Greek word here is *anupokritos*, which literally means 'without hypocrisy'. Does James put this word at the end for emphasis, because man is so prone to hypocrisy? When someone told Emperor Frederick III of Germany that he was going to travel to some far country where no hypocrites lived, the emperor replied that he faced a very long journey, because as soon as he arrived in a country there would be at least one hypocrite there! 'Hypocrisy' originally meant a dialogue, then playing the part of an actor, and its history vividly illustrates its meaning, which is to pretend to be something that one is not.

The Bible gives us many instances of this particular sin and tells us that there was even an occasion when an apostle was guilty of it. This came about when the question arose in the early church as to whether Gentile converts should be circumcised, or simply accepted on their profession of faith and treated as equals with Jewish Christians. A special meeting called at Jerusalem ruled in favour of the second alternative, opening the way for full fellowship between Christians from both backgrounds. The apostle Peter duly obeyed this ruling and met freely with the Gentile converts, eating with them, mixing with them and accepting them as equals in every way. However, when a group of hardliners came from Jerusalem and began to apply all the old pressures about the issue, we read that Peter broke off his links with the Gentile converts 'because he was afraid of those who belonged to the circumcision group'. The Bible then adds, 'The other Jews joined him in his hypocrisy, so that by their hypocrisy even Barnabas was led astray' (Galatians 2:12, 13). Peter's action is called 'hypocrisy' because he acted contrary to his beliefs. He accepted the ruling of the special meeting at Jerusalem, but acted as if he had changed his mind. That is hypocrisy and we can be sure that Peter repented of it as firmly as James rebukes it.

Of course, in dealing with the question of sincerity, James is right back to the heart of things. What we *are* is all-important. Reality banishes hypocrisy as surely as hypocrisy disguises reality. It is better to be ingenuous than ingenious! William Shakespeare once wrote, 'This above all, to thine own self be true; then it must follow, as the night the day, thou canst not then be false to any man'; a greater than Shakespeare was able to say, 'Our conscience testifies that we have conducted ourselves in the world, and especially in our relations with you, in the holiness and sincerity that are from God. We have done so not according to worldly wisdom but according to God's grace' (2 Corinthians 1:12).

May God give us the same grace!

25.

Peace and righteousness

'Peacemakers who sow in peace raise a harvest of righteousness' (James 3:18).

Some commentators have seen great difficulties in establishing a clear link between this verse and those which immediately precede it, but there seem to me to be two obvious connections. The first is that having said that 'peace-loving' is the first practical characteristic of 'the wisdom that comes from heaven' (v. 17), James now rounds off his section of teaching on the subject of wisdom by emphasizing the matter of peace; he begins and ends on the same note. The other connection is even clearer. In summing up his teaching on false wisdom, James said that the restlessness of envy and selfish ambition produced 'every evil practice' (v. 16); now, in summing up his teaching on true wisdom, he says that peace-loving true wisdom produces 'a harvest of righteousness'.

The other comment to be made by way of general introduction is that James's fine-sounding aphorism seems to contradict a statement made in the Old Testament. In essence, James is saying that the fruit of peace will be righteousness, but we read earlier in Scripture that 'The fruit of righteousness will be peace' (Isaiah 32:17). That seems a useful piece of ammunition for the person who wants to pick holes in the Bible! However, close examination proves otherwise. There seems little difficulty in understanding what Isaiah meant: when men obey the will of God and act towards each other with justice, fairness, love, honesty and humility, the result will be the harmonious happiness that can rightly be called peace. Then does James turn Isaiah's truth on its head and say the opposite? Let us turn to the text and find out. Its most practical application will come across as we see James saying three things about peace in the space of these few words.

1. The right actions
'Peacemakers . . .'

That one word makes a very important point, and that is that peace is something that needs to be *made*! It is not something that exists naturally in the world. In fact, it would be difficult to think of a single word in the dictionary about which the world says so much and of which it experiences so little. It has been calculated that in the last 4,000 years there have been only 300 without a major war somewhere or other. Nor can we take refuge in the thought that things are gradually improving. In 1967 Britain's Defence Minister said, 'This has been the most violent century in history. There has not been a single day since the end of World War II when hundreds of people have not been killed by military action.' We live in a world aflame with passion, anger and violence. Within individual nations, too, peace is among the rarest of commodities. In spite of the fact that there has never been so much machinery for negotiation and arbitration in the field of industrial relationships, it is also true that there have never been so many strikes, disputes and disorders. In wider community life, we find almost endless wrangling, in-fighting and bitterness. Again, we live in a world when our young people seem to be in a state of unprecedented ferment. A cynic might be forgiven for thinking that the purpose of attending university was to hold sit-ins, or strike, or refuse to eat, or hold protest marches, or tear the gates down – in fact, to do almost anything but study! Family life is in chaos, with the divorce rate leaping upwards every year and an untold number of other homes where there is distrust, disharmony and strife. The French philosopher Albert Camus said that every century was characterized by one special emphasis. He then went on to say that the seventeenth century was characterized by mathematics, the eighteenth century by physical science, the nineteenth century by biology and the twentieth century by fear. What a terrible comment on a century in which man has made so much outward progress! In spite of all his advances elsewhere, man seems incapable of stabilizing himself; his life is increasingly characterized by fear, insecurity, unrest and turmoil – a lack of peace.

All of this provides us with a more than adequate background for the need to apply James's words in today's world. Take his agricultural analogy. Can you imagine a farmer spending all his time sitting in an armchair reading glossy magazines about seeds, equipment, fertilizers, farming techniques and the like? He would have little to show for it if he did! If the farmer is to raise a harvest he must work for it, and the same is true for the Christian. It is an interesting coincidence that every single chapter in the Epistle of James ends with a call to action. James insists that a man must prove the reality of his faith by doing good. True wisdom is not only 'peace-loving' (v. 17), it is peace-making, and it is important to notice that Jesus and James are agreed that peace-making is an evidence of biblical faith. In a promise we noted in our last study, Jesus said, 'Blessed are the peacemakers, for they will be called sons of God' (Matthew 5:9). Now there is obviously no suggestion here that people become Christians as a result of being peacemakers, but rather that Christians prove the reality of their relationship to God by their concern for peace. One of the Bible's titles for God is to describe him as 'the God of peace' (Hebrews 13:20), but this is not just a passive characteristic. It sent the Son of God into the world 'to guide our feet into the path of peace' (Luke 1:79) and so that we might have 'peace with God through our Lord Jesus Christ' (Romans 5:1). Christians are therefore called upon to prove their parenthood by following their Father's example and pursuing his policy. In William Hendriksen's notable phrase, they are 'God's "peace corps"'. The Bible indicates at least three ways in which we should take action as far as peace is concerned.

1. We should preserve it. We have a particular responsibility here as citizens of the country in which we live and the Bible is uncompromisingly clear on the issue: 'Everyone must submit himself to the governing authorities' (Romans 13:1). Unless there is a direct conflict with what God clearly reveals in Scripture, the Christian should peacefully submit to the law of the land. Then we have a particular responsibility within the church: 'Be completely humble and gentle; be patient, bearing with one another in love. Make every effort to keep the unity of the Spirit through the bond of peace' (Ephesians 4:2, 3). Both in civic circles and within the closer community of the church, Christians are called upon to keep the peace.

2. *We should promote it.* Let me put this particular challenge in the form of a multiple question: does the general flow of your life tend to promote peace, or do you tend to be prickly, touchy, difficult to get on with? Francis of Assisi has a beautiful prayer that points us in the right direction:

> Lord, make me an instrument of your peace!
> Where there is hatred, let me sow love;
> Where there is injury, pardon;
> Where there is doubt, faith;
> Where there is despair, hope;
> Where there is darkness, light;
> Where there is sadness, joy.
> O Divine Master, grant that I may not so much seek
> To be consoled, as to console;
> To be understood, as to understand;
> To be loved, as to love.
> For it is in giving that we receive;
> It is in pardoning that we are pardoned;
> It is in dying that we are born to eternal life.

3. *We should pursue it.* The Bible uses this precise word: 'Turn from evil and do good; seek peace and *pursue* it' (Psalm 34:14). The same call to energetic determination comes across elsewhere. Paul says, 'Let us therefore make every effort to do what leads to peace and to mutual edification' (Romans 14:19), while the writer of Hebrews urges us to 'make every effort to live in peace with all men' (Hebrews 12:14). But somebody may say that such a thing is impossible, that human nature being what it is there are some people with whom peaceful co-existence is quite impossible. Well, we need to be careful about using the word 'impossible' when the grace of God is at work, but the Bible actually makes provision for just such an argument. Paul says, '*If it is possible,* as far as it depends on you, live

at peace with everyone' (Romans 12:18). Yet far from excusing us, this verse examines us. It recognizes the difficulty of living at peace with some people, but asks whether we are pursuing the possibility with every power at our disposal. Jesus said of the woman who anointed him with expensive perfume in the house of Simon the leper, 'She did what she could' (Mark 14:8). Could that be said of us? Are we doing all we possibly can to preserve peace, promote it, pursue it?

The Bible's challenge obviously extends to every area of life, but there is one particular activity in which we have a very special responsibility to act as peacemakers, and that is by evangelism. One of the special duties of an ambassador is to pass on to the citizens of the alien country in which he is living the messages sent to him from his own ruler. Now Christians are said to be ambassadors and it is instructive to notice the context in which they are given this title: 'Therefore, if anyone is in Christ, he is a new creation; the old has gone, the new has come! All this is from God, who reconciled us to himself through Christ and gave us the ministry of reconciliation: that God was reconciling the world to himself in Christ, not counting men's sins against them. And he has committed to us the message of reconciliation. We are therefore Christ's ambassadors, as though God were making his appeal through us. We implore you on Christ's behalf: Be reconciled to God' (2 Corinthians 5:17–20). At the end of the day, the greatest single thing a Christian can do to promote peace in the world is to share with others what the Bible calls 'the gospel of peace' (Ephesians 6:15). Dr W. E. Sangster once described evangelism as 'the sheer work of the herald who goes in the name of the King to the people who, either openly or by their indifference, deny their allegiance to their rightful Lord. He blows the trumpet and demands to be heard. He tells the people in plain words of the melting clemency of their offended King and of the things that belong to their peace.'

History teems with most marvellous illustrations of the way in which the gospel has brought peace where all else has failed. In the late 1960s Nigeria was a bloodbath, with tribal, social and political hatred erupting into the most appalling violence, yet there was a period then when the officers of the Scripture Union in Nigeria were drawn from three opposing tribes: the president was a Hausa from the north, the chairman a Yoruba from the west and the secretary an Ibo from the east. The gospel brings peace between man and God and between man and his fellow men and if we are truly anxious to be peacemakers we will seek to be involved in one way or another with the glorious work of evangelism.

2. The right attitudes

'. . . who sow in peace . . .'

These words clearly have an importance all their own, or the Holy Spirit would have not moved James to write them. What they seem to say is that the Christian should not only do the right thing, but should do it in the right way, in other words he should not only have the right actions but the right attitudes. Let us look at just two of these.

1. A spirit of courtesy. What an important element this is! And we can link it directly back to the matter of evangelism. It is possible to preach the gospel very faithfully, and yet to do so in a militant, harsh kind of way that all but obliterates its loveliness. We must sow the message of peace in a spirit of peace. Yet perhaps the area in which we must be particularly careful to exercise a spirit of courtesy is when people do exactly the opposite to us – when we are attacked, maligned, criticized or opposed. The Bible is so clear as to what our attitude should be in that kind of situation: 'A gentle answer turns away wrath, but a harsh word stirs up anger' (Proverbs 15:1); 'Calmness can lay great errors to rest' (Ecclesiastes 10:4); 'Therefore, as God's chosen people, holy and dearly loved, clothe yourselves with compassion, kindness, humility, gentleness and patience. Bear with each other and forgive whatever grievances you may have against one another. Forgive as the Lord forgave you. And over all these virtues put on love, which binds them all together in perfect unity' (Colossians 3:12–14). Whenever we are offended, reviled, wronged, abused or slandered, we have a special opportunity to be peacemakers, and the greater the sin committed against us, the greater the opportunity of demonstrating the power of the grace of

God. Many years ago a man called John Dickenson, who lived in Birmingham, was known as 'the peacemaker'. It was said of him that 'Such was his anxiety to keep the bonds of peace from being broken . . . and to heal the breach when made, that he would stoop to any act but that of meanness, make any sacrifice but that of principle, and endure any mode of treatment, not excepting even insult and reproach.' To act like that is to sow in peace!

2. A sense of urgency. Thomas Manton writes, 'Whatever we do in this life is seed,' and adds, 'Have a care of the season; it is the seed-time,' and in both cases he is right. All our activity is sowing and so is our inactivity. It is seed-time for the young; it is seed-time for the middle-aged; it is seed-time for the elderly. All of life is a process of sowing—and who is able to say with certainty how many more handfuls of seed he has left to sow? Do you see the relevance of this in the context of peacemaking and of sowing in peace? Is there an apology you ought to make? A letter you ought to write? A restitution you ought to pay? A hand you ought to offer? A misunderstanding you ought to correct? A breach you ought to heal? A gift you ought to make? Then do it *quickly,* while it is still seed-time. Remember that 'Night is coming, when no one can work' (John 9:5).

These two elements, a spirit of courtesy and a sense of urgency, are brought together by Paul: 'Be wise in the way you act towards outsiders; make the most of every opportunity. Let your conversation be always full of grace, seasoned with salt, so that you may know how to answer everyone' (Colossians 4:5, 6). To act like that is to sow in peace, with the right attitudes.

3. The right aim

'. . . raise a harvest of righteousness.'

Here is the outcome of everything James has been saying in this section, and we can bring home its practical application by looking at it as an aim. The word 'righteousness' used to be spelled 'rightwiseness' and in context means those things that are pleasing to God. The point is important. We are not simply called to pursue peace as an end in itself, and we are certainly not called to seek peace at any price.

We are not to buy peace at the expense of truth, for instance; there is such a thing as the sin of tolerance. The Bible links peace and righteousness together, and we dare not tear them apart. In a verse we quoted earlier, we are told, 'Make every effort to live in peace with all men and to be holy' (Hebrews 12:14).

But what about that apparent conflict between James and Isaiah? Isaiah says that peace is the harvest produced by righteousness, while James says that righteousness is the harvest produced by peace. Who is right? The answer is that both are! When men live together in a way that is righteous, when their behaviour towards each other is godly, the result will be harmonious relationships – so Isaiah is right. When men live peaceably together, actively concerned for harmony and unity, then the result will be righteousness, because they will be living in obedience to the will of God – so James is right. Righteousness promotes peace and peace promotes righteousness; they form what we might call a virtuous circle.

But to complete the biblical picture, we must add one further thing. Although the Bible commands us to aim at righteousness, it is not righteousness in a self-contained vacuum, but as being wrapped up in what we could dare to call the greater aim of the glory of God. In a wonderful messianic chapter, which also speaks of the church, God's work in the lives of his people is said to be such that 'They will be called oaks of righteousness, a planting of the Lord for the display of his splendour' (Isaiah 61:3). That is the ultimate aim of wisdom, peace, righteousness, and every other virtue mentioned in the pages of Scripture. Katie Barclay Wilkinson captures this perfectly in this simple verse of her well-known hymn:

> May his beauty rest upon me
> As I seek the lost to win,
> And may they forget the channel,
> Seeing only him!

26.

The root of the trouble — I

'What causes fights and quarrels among you? Don't they come from your desires that battle within you?' (James 4:1)

As even those with only a superficial understanding of the Bible will know, its division into chapters and verses came many years after the last of the New Testament books was written. This means that although this 'editing' often has a sense of rightness about it, we must not treat it as infallible, or allow it to interrupt the flow of the original author's writing.

The end of James 3 and the beginning of James 4 provide us with a good illustration of what I mean, for while our anonymous editor decided that we should take a break after James 3:18, there is in fact a direct link between that verse and the opening words of James 4, which are now before us, and the link is the very obvious one of contrast. Chapter 3 ends with the words: 'Peacemakers who sow in peace raise a harvest of righteousness,' while chapter 4 begins with the words: 'What causes fights and quarrels among you?' James is clearly contrasting the ideal (peace-making) with the attitude and approach they should have as Christians and he now turns to demonstrate how far short of those they sometimes fall. We shall not be long before discovering how relevant his findings are to our twentieth-century situation! Two headings will sum up the contents of this verse.

1. The condition he diagnosed
'What causes fights and quarrels among you?'

As James looked at the world of his day, and in particular

at the lives of his readers, he was deeply saddened. Far from working together in a spirit of peace, people were constantly in conflict. In this opening phrase, James points out three things he saw.

1. Something that was general. 'What causes fights . . .?' The word 'fights' translates the Greek *polemoi*, meaning a continuous state of war. In the Bible, the word is most widely used in Revelation. Here are three examples: John speaks of a titanic conflict involving Michael, the dragon and hosts of angels as 'war in heaven' (Revelation 12:7); later, he prophesies that terrible forces of evil 'will make war against the Lamb' (Revelation 17:14); and in another momentous passage he writes of 'the beast and the kings of the earth and their armies gathered together to make war against the rider on the horse [previously identified as the glorified Christ] and his army' (Revelation 19:19). Surely there is something significant here? The very climax of earthly humanity is coloured by conflict; right to the end, man is seen to have belligerence in his bones, to have lived out history in a state of chronic hostility.

Was James right to make that kind of diagnosis in his day? He certainly was! He probably wrote this letter in Jerusalem, a name meaning something like 'the possession of peace', but how little peace it had known! Quite apart from its long and bloody Old Testament history, it was invaded by Antiochus IV about 168 B.C., Judas the Maccabee led a revolt there a few years later, Roman forces overthrew it in 63 B.C. and again in 54 B.C., the Parthians plundered it in 40 B.C., and Herod the Great fought a bloody battle for its possession in 37 B.C. The most recent of these conflicts would have taken place while the parents of James's original readers were alive – and even as he wrote Jewish ferment was leading up to the city's invasion by the Roman Emperor Titus in A.D. 70, a holocaust in which 1,100,000 people were massacred. This, then, was the background against which James wrote of men being in a continuous state of unrest.

And what of the centuries since then? In his book *The Study of War*, Professor Quincey examines the period from 1480 to 1941 and says that during this time nations were engaged in the following numbers of major wars: Great

Britain 78, France 71, Spain 64, Russia 61, Austria 52, Germany 23, The United States of America 13, China 11 and Japan 9. Today, we have had to invent a new phrase, 'the cold war', to describe the continuous state of international tension. Addressing a gathering of the United Nations on 26 September 1961, U.S.A. President John F. Kennedy said, 'Every man, woman and child lives under a nuclear sword of Damocles, hanging by the slenderest of threads, capable of being cut at any moment by accident, miscalculation or madness.' To ensure what is chillingly called a 'balance of power', the U.S.A. possesses enough aerosol nerve gas to kill all living matter on an area eight times the size of the world and the destructive equivalent of 10,000 tons of TNT for every human being on the face of the earth!' Two thousand years ago Jesus prophesied a time of 'wars and rumours of wars' (Matthew 24:6), grippingly relevant in today's world!

2. Something that was individual. He speaks not only of 'fights', but of 'fights and quarrels'. It may be that his complete phrase should be translated as two separate questions: 'What causes fights?' and 'What causes quarrels?' as the words are not identical. 'Quarrels' is the Greek word *machai*, meaning individual conflicts rather than a general state of war. The Amplified Bible translates it 'conflicts, quarrels and fightings'. In adding this phrase James is bringing the issue right home to the lives of his individual readers and there is a deeply personal application here which we dare not miss today. The fiercest, bloodiest, costliest wars have begun with one man's festered heart. The longest wars have begun with a single blow. That being so, we should seek never to behave in such a way that in our homes, our places of work, our churches, or our social lives, we strike that first blow that eventually leads to untold pain, injury and sorrow. There is something here that is inescapably individual. The Christian is called to fight against fighting!

3. Something that was shameful. 'What causes fights and quarrels among *you*?' I am quite sure that my italics capture James's intention! You see, he was writing to Christians, to those who claimed to have found what the Bible calls 'the path of peace' (Luke 1:79), yet here they were fighting and squabbling with each other. There is ample evidence of that kind of behaviour, even in the early church. Paul had to write to the church at Philippi, 'I plead with Euodia and I plead with Syntyche to agree with each other in the Lord' (Philippians 4:2). He told the church at Corinth, 'Some from Chloe's household have informed me that there are quarrels among you' (1 Corinthians 1:11), and a little further on he added, 'If any of you has a dispute with another, dare he take it before the ungodly for judgement instead of before the saints?' (1 Corinthians 6:1.) In a later letter he wrote, 'For I am afraid that when I come I may not find you as I want you to be . . . I fear that there may be quarrelling, jealousy, outbursts of anger, factions, slander, gossip, arrogance and disorder' (2 Corinthians 12:20).

What a catalogue of contention! And surely these are shameful things to find among Christians? But before we condemn these people, let us examine our own churches, our own fellowship and our own hearts! Are we without sin in these areas? Are we always gentle, peaceable, mild? Or is the following parable tragically nearer the mark? There was trouble in the carpenter's workshop and the tools were having a row. One of them said, 'It's the hammer's fault. He is much too noisy.' 'Nonsense,' the hammer protested, ' I think the blame lies with the saw. He keeps going backwards and forwards all the time.' The saw shouted, 'I'm not to blame. I think it's the plane's fault. His work is so shallow, he does nothing but just skim the surface.' The plane objected loudly: 'I think the real trouble lies with the screwdriver, always going round in circles.' 'That's ridiculous,' the screwdriver said, 'the whole trouble began with the ruler, because he is always measuring other people by his own standards.' The ruler was furious: 'Then what about the sandpaper? Surely he is always rubbing people up the wrong way?' 'Why pick on me?' said the sandpaper, 'I think you ought to blame the drill for being so boring.' Just as the drill was about to protest, the carpenter came in and began to work. Using every one of those tools, he eventually built a beautiful pulpit, from which the gospel of peace was eventually preached to thousands of people.

That is just a fable, of course, perhaps no more than a children's story, but beware of missing its point! In his surprising grace God does use imperfect instruments, but we all have a solemn responsibility to 'make every effort to live in peace with all men' (Hebrews 12:14) and, especially as Christians, to 'live in peace with each other' (1 Thessalonians 5:13). So much for the condition James diagnosed.

2. The cause he discovered

'Don't they come from your desires that battle within you?'

In view of the widespread nature of the disease he has diagnosed, James's report of the cause is surprisingly concise. With clinical precision he puts the trouble down to 'your desires that battle within you' – yet that brief phrase tells us four things about the cause of men's conflicts.

1. It is pleasure-seeking. '. . . your desires . . .' The original Greek noun here is *hedonon*, from which we get our English words 'hedonism' and 'hedonistic', and in the New Testament it always has a sinister meaning. Apart from James 4:3, which we shall study in our next chapter, Jesus spoke of the devastating effects when a man was 'choked by life's worries, riches and pleasures' (Luke 8:14); Paul wrote of people 'enslaved by all kinds of passions and pleasures' (Titus 3:3); and Peter condemned those whose 'idea of pleasure is to carouse in broad daylight' (2 Peter 2:13). A pleasure-seeking, hedonistic spirit of life says that if a thing is enjoyable it must be good; if it is good I must have it, and I must have it whenever I want it. But let us apply this in context. Why does James say that this kind of thing produces 'fights and quarrels'? The simple answer is surely that a man can only satisfy all of his own self-centred desires by conflicting with the desires of other people. One of the fundamental bases for unity and harmony is that, as part of our total submission to God's Word, we should be concerned about 'the interests of others' (Philippians 2:4) and we ignore this principle at our peril. For all of man's so-called progress, emancipation and sophistication, the fact remains that he cannot please himself without cost. What a telling truth! Take a man who says, 'I am going to ignore God, the Bible and religion in any way, shape or form. I am going to live my life my way. I can afford to be extravagant. I can indulge myself sexually without risk. I will do everything I want to do whenever I want to do it.' Now the terrifying thing is that when a man acts like that, there is a price to be paid and almost inevitably part of the price will be conflict with other people. Arrogant self-assertion is never the way to peace and it is exactly at this point that the advocates of our so-called 'permissive society' display the most guilty ignorance of all. But there is more to it than that. When a man determines that his philosophy is 'I will please myself' then he automatically moves God from the centre of the stage. If self-satisfaction comes first, then even at best God can only come second and when God comes second in a man's life, that man has problems! At a time when he was an atheist, Malcolm Muggeridge said, 'The pursuit of happiness, however conceived, is the most foolish of all pursuits.' It is not only futile, but fatal, because whenever you have seeking without finding, you have the ingredients of unrest and turmoil – which is exactly what James is saying.

2. It is persistent. '. . . your desires that battle . . .' Notice that vivid verb! The Greek word is *strateumenon*, the same militant word used by Peter when he writes of 'sinful desires which war against your soul' (1 Peter 2:11). As with the word 'fights' earlier in the verse we are studying, the picture is one of a continuous state of war, not a single, hit-and-run raid. The doctrine of sinless perfection may be preached by some, but it is experienced by none! The Christian is a walking civil war. As Professor R. V. G. Tasker puts it, 'The human personality has . . . been invaded by an alien army which is always campaigning within it.' He goes on to say that our self-seeking desires 'are permanently on active service' and that our human nature 'is in the grip of an overwhelming army of occupation'. Our trouble is persistent!

The fourteenth-century poet and humanist Francesco Petrarch once wrote, 'Five great enemies to peace inhabit with us: avarice, ambition, envy, anger and pride. If these enemies were to be banished we should infallibly enjoy perfect peace.' But the sober truth is that they will never be banished this side of heaven. The enemy is entrenched within us and will fight to the last gasp. One thing more: in our frantic twentieth century, which makes such tremendous demands on our time, our skills and our nervous physical energies, it is perhaps a natural corollary that pleasure for pleasure's sake should be one of the universal creeds of our generation. Let us be aware of its dangers!

3. It is personal. '. . . *your* desires that battle within *you*'. The words I have emphasized underline the fact that James is identifying a factor common to all Christians. We cannot escape the impact of his words by retreating into the orthodoxy of our theology or the success of our church. This is a personal issue – '*your* desires that battle within *you*'. The point is surely obvious. The world consists of nations, nations consist of communities, communities consist of families and families consist of individuals. It is so easy to moralize, to discuss doctrine, to pass judgement on others, even to read the Word of God and draw an accurate line of difference between good and evil; it is quite another thing to admit our own self-centred sin.

When the prophet Nathan went to King David with a story of a rich man who stole a poor man's only ewe lamb to provide a meal for a guest, David had no problem in assessing the moral issue and in passing judgement: 'As surely as the Lord lives, the man who did this deserves to die' (2 Samuel 12:5). It was simple – an open and shut case. But when Nathan replied, '*You* are the man,' David was shaken to the core. *He* was the man, guilty of the very sin he had so clinically condemned! The courageous Nathan then went on to underline God's word of condemnation until David cried out, 'I have sinned against the Lord.' Only then was the prophet able to bring the precious word of cleansing: 'The Lord has taken away your sin.' The lesson is surely impossible to miss. Beware of judging others and failing to recognize the subtle sin in your own heart. And remember that these 'desires' may not appear grossly sinful. They may even be camouflaged with the colours of legitimacy, but anything that puts self before God is sin of the deepest dye.

4. It is penetrating. '. . . your desires that battle *within* you'. Four centuries before Christ was born, the philosopher Plato said, 'The sole cause of wars and revolutions and battles is nothing other than the body and its desires.' But although Plato was a wise man, he only knew what the Bible calls 'the wisdom of the wise' (1 Corinthians 1:19) and he was a long way from the truth when he rooted man's troubles in 'nothing other than the body and its desires'. He was making the fatal mistake of saying that the body was evil in itself. But that is not what the Bible teaches. A man once had these words engraved on his tombstone: 'Here lies the part of Thomas Wood that kept his soul from doing good.' Now that is very neat, and perhaps even appealing as an excuse for failure, but it is totally unbiblical. It is rhythmic but wrong. The Bible does not teach that the body is the part of us that prevents us from doing good. That is the false assumption made by those who seek to elevate the spirit by starving or punishing their bodies. Physical discipline is excellent in its place, but it will never win spiritual battles. The real conflict for the Christian is between his old, sinful nature and the Holy Spirit dwelling within him. In other words, the Christian's body (I am including in that word all of his personality and faculties) is not so much an evil, defiled thing as occupied territory.

I remember returning as a teenager to my native island of Guernsey after World War II. Evidence of the German occupation was everywhere – concrete bunkers, gun emplacements, German signposts and so on, mute reminders of the fact that for five years the island was occupied territory. I was evacuated a few days before the invasion, but thousands of Guernseymen remained as the enemy moved in. Now they did not despise their native island because an enemy had penetrated it. It was still something very precious to them. They cherished it, yearned for its welfare and longed for its freedom. That is a far from perfect illustration, but perhaps it will help in applying the truth of what James is saying to our own attitudes and actions. The cause of our trouble is not just outward or external or circumstantial. It is inward, personal and penetrative.

In threading through this one verse we have studied the condition James diagnosed – 'fights and quarrels among you' – and the cause he discovered – 'your desires that battle within you', selfish forces that are pleasure-seeking, persistent, personal and penetrative. It would be natural to expect him to follow a condition and a cause with a cure, but he does not deal directly with this until verse 6. However, in order to close this particular study on a positive note rather than a negative one, let us be clear about one thing. The only answer to persistent attack from an entrenched enemy engaging us in a continual state of war and penetrating every part of our personality lies along the lines of determined resistance and vigilance. This is the consistent scriptural answer to those who would claim that there is some kind of once-for-all experience that a Christian can have which will lift him into a state where he is incapable of sinning, or unlikely to do so. I must say, in all charity towards those who seem to hold that kind of view, that I do not find it taught anywhere in the Bible. What I do find is that some of the greatest of men committed their worst sins at the peak of their spiritual maturity. We could scarcely have better evidence of the need for unrelenting prayerfulness, discipline and vigilance. Charles Wesley, in one of his magnificent hymns, puts it like this:

Leave no unguarded place,
No weakness of the soul;
Take every virtue, every grace,
And fortify the whole:
Indissolubly joined, to battle all proceed;
But arm yourselves with all the mind
That was in Christ, your Head.

27.

The root of the trouble — II

'You want something but don't get it. You kill and covet but you cannot have what you want. You quarrel and fight. You do not have because you do not ask God. When you ask, you do not receive, because you ask with wrong motives, that you may spend what you get on your pleasures' (James 4:2, 3).

In these two verses James continues to expose the root cause of the fractured relationships he has described as 'fights and quarrels' and moves on to show at least one way in which they seriously affect a vitally important part of a person's life. Two general headings sum up his description of what happens when men give free rein to their self-centred desires.

1. Their passions become destructive

'You want something but don't get it. You kill and covet but you cannot have what you want. You quarrel and fight' (v. 2a).

I have deliberately stopped the quotation there because, as we shall see later, the remainder of this verse and the whole of the next hang together as one piece.

The first point to make in studying this verse is to notice that even in the excellent NIV which we are using as our basic text, the wording seems strangely awkward. In the second sentence, for instance, it seems odd to find the words 'covet' and 'want' coming after the word 'kill'. Surely we would expect the order to be 'want', 'covet' and 'kill', building up to an obvious climax? Yet an obvious solution to this tangle suggests itself if we simply see the problem as one of punctuation. Originally, of course, there were no punctuation marks in the text – in fact, even the words were joined together – so we cannot blame James for the confusion! The way to produce a logical construction of the passage is to arrange the punctuation so that the words 'kill' and 'fight' are each seen to be the natural climax of the sentence in which they occur and this can be done very simply. By keeping the words in exactly the same order and inserting two little conjunctions (allowed by the force of the original text), the passage would read as follows: 'You want something but don't get it [so] you kill. You covet but you cannot have what you want [so] you quarrel and fight.' That is surely much clearer! Now we can examine the meaning and application of what James is saying.

Perhaps the best way to do this is to notice that in this passage there are three 'parallel' groups of words. In the first group we have 'you want something' and 'you want'; in the second group come the words '[you] don't get it' and 'you cannot have what you want'; thirdly, there are the phrases 'you kill' and 'you quarrel and fight'. The sequence of the groups is obvious: one can almost feel the tension building up as they move towards their terrible climax. Let us look at them in turn.

Firstly, *'you want something'* and *'you want'.* Although in the same general area of meaning, the phrases are not identical. The first 'want' is the Greek *epithumeite* and means 'to set your heart on' a thing. The second is the Greek *zeloute*, which is translated 'envy' in James 3:14 and 16. The link between the two phrases is obvious and here, surely, we are at the root of the trouble. It begins with a thought, an idea, an envious look, but gradually the desire grows until it becomes a raging passion that fills the heart.

Jesus used a similar expression in the Sermon on the Mount: 'You have heard that it was said, "Do not commit adultery." But I tell you that anyone who looks at a woman lustfully has already committed adultery with her in his heart' (Matthew 5:27, 28). The thought is as guilty as the deed; in fact, it is the parent of it. It has been said that a man is not what he thinks he is; but what he thinks, he is.

That being so, it is vitally important that our minds should be fed and filled with the right material. How many troubles and tragedies have begun, festered and gathered their mad momentum in the mind – especially a mind that is lazy, undisciplined, unguarded! The biblical defence in this area is clear. Writing to the Colossians, Paul says, 'Since, then, you have been raised with Christ, set your hearts on things above, where Christ is seated at the right hand of God. Set your minds on things above, not on earthly things' (Colossians 3:1, 2); while in his letter to the Philippians he says, 'Finally, brothers, whatever is true, whatever is noble, whatever is right, whatever is pure, whatever is lovely, whatever is admirable – if anything is excellent or praiseworthy – think about such things' (Philippians 4:8). In that second verse, the Amplified Bible adds the phrase 'fix your minds on them', and that helps to hammer home the sense of discipline built into Paul's words. Even in our sophisticated twentieth century we have not altogether lost the art of study; indeed, a great deal of study is often necessary in order to obtain technical qualifications. But many Christians have lost the deeper discipline of meditation. Only as the mind is filled with the mingled fruits of both study and meditation will the springs of our desires be kept clean. John Owen once wrote, 'If I have observed anything by experience, it is this: a man may take the measure of his growth and decay in grace according to his thoughts and meditations upon the person of Christ, and the glory of Christ's Kingdom, and of his love.'

Secondly, we have the two phrases *'[you] don't get it'* and *'you cannot have what you want'*. In these terse yet telling words, James reminds us of a simple fact of life: it is one thing to want something, but quite another thing to obtain it. Nobody can disagree with that! James is to give a reason for this later, but just for the moment he states the simple, pathetic fact that desire does not satisfy. It is important to remember that he is speaking primarily about evil desires, about putting self before God, and the point he is driving home is that even when a man does everything he pleases, he is still not satisfied. 'Satisfaction' is a much longer word than 'self' and satisfaction is a much bigger thing than the passion for self-pleasing. Dr Samuel Johnson, the famous eighteenth-century man of letters, once said, 'Of all that have tried the selfish experiment, let one come forth and say that he has succeeded. He that has made gold his idol, has it satisfied him? He that has toiled in the fields of ambition, has he been repaid? He that has ransacked every theatre of sensual enjoyment, is he content? Can any answer in the affirmative? Not one!' As John Macmurray succinctly put it, 'The best cure for hedonism is the attempt to practise it'!

Yet no comment on this issue is more devastating than the Bible's own words. Read carefully these words by an Old Testament preacher: 'I thought in my heart, "Come now, I will test you with pleasure to find out what is good." But that also proved to be meaningless. "Laughter," I said, "is foolish. And what does pleasure accomplish?" I tried cheering myself with wine, and embracing folly – my mind still guiding me with wisdom. I wanted to see what was worthwhile for men to do under heaven during the few days of their lives. I undertook great projects: I built houses for myself and planted vineyards. I made gardens and parks and planted all kinds of fruit trees in them. I made reservoirs to water groves of flourishing trees. I bought male and female slaves and had other slaves who were born in my house. I also owned more herds and flocks than anyone in Jerusalem before me. I amassed silver and gold for myself, and the treasure of kings and provinces. I acquired men and women singers, and a harem as well – the delights of the heart of man. I became greater by far than anyone in Jerusalem before me. In all this my wisdom stayed with me. I denied myself nothing my eyes desired; I refused my heart no pleasure. My heart took delight in all my work, and this was the reward for all my labour' (Ecclesiastes 2:1–10).

In those ten verses the words 'I', 'me', 'my' and 'myself' occur over thirty times. The entire passage is saturated by self. Yet what did all this raging desire achieve? The answer comes in the very next words:

> 'Yet when I surveyed all that my hands had done
> and what I had toiled to achieve,

> everything was meaningless, a chasing after the wind;
> *nothing was gained* under the sun'
> (Ecclesiastes 2:11).

My italics are hardly needed; the words themselves speak with devastating impact of the destructive nature of man's self-centred passions.

Thirdly, we come to the climax of these groups of phrases that James uses: *'you kill'* and *'you quarrel and fight'*. Bear in mind the progression of thought there has been in this section. James has written firstly of thoughts and desires; then of the dissatisfaction these bring when selfishly pursued; now he sees the situation breaking out into quarrelling, fighting, even killing. Is he overstating the case? Some people have thought so and have tried to solve what they saw as a problem by an interesting suggestion. The word 'kill' translates the Greek *phoneuete*, very similar to the word *phthoneite*, which means 'envy'. Even giants like John Calvin, Martin Luther and William Tyndale felt that somewhere along the line there had been an understandable error in translating the text. Yet surely we can hold to the word 'kill' exactly as we have it by bearing two things in mind. The first is that there is no need to think that James is referring to wholesale murder going on within the Christian community – that is surely unthinkable. What he is doing is to warn his readers that unbridled, selfish passion knows no limits; it will do anything to achieve its ends. The second thing to bear in mind is that in saying that envy and selfishness can lead to murder, James had history on his side, and his readers would remember at least two famous Old Testament stories of people whose selfish desires eventually led them to commit murder. The first classic case is told in 2 Samuel 11, the story of David, Bathsheba and Uriah the Hittite. The other is in 1 Kings 21, the story of the rich King Ahab, the wicked Jezebel, and the innocent Naboth, who was eventually killed in order that Ahab could add his one small vineyard to his other possessions.

The lesson here is clear. Never underestimate the terrible power of human desire. Adam must have been created with a tremendously strong desire, one that kept him utterly pure and obedient to the will of God, perhaps for a very long time.

Now that man is fallen, his desire is twisted, warped and perverted, but it is still almost unbelievably strong. It seeks to rip aside anything that stands in its way. Unfulfilled desire produces tension, strife, irrational actions and can even go as far as murder. We have been warned!

We might add one other point here. The word 'kill' could possibly be translated 'destroy', a solemn reminder to us that we can 'murder' a person in our heart as well as with our hands. Jesus said, 'You have heard that it was said to the people long ago, "Do not murder, and anyone who murders will be subject to judgement." But I tell you that anyone who is angry with his brother will be subject to judgement. Again, anyone who says to his brother, "Raca," is answerable to the Sanhedrin. But anyone who says, "You fool!" will be in danger of the fire of hell' (Matthew 5: 21, 22). The apostle John says bluntly, 'Anyone who hates his brother is a murderer' (1 John 3:15). According to the Bible, a word can be just as penetrating as a knife, a thought just as deadly as a gun, and a criticism just as corroding as poison. Make no mistake about it – character, reputation, the progress of Christian work, the prospect of a special effort, harmony in the home – all of these things can be destroyed, killed, because of our desire to put self first. This is the climax James reaches in this part of his letter. He shows his readers that their passions could become destructive. So can ours, and we must therefore seek to ensure that they are consecrated to the Lord, that we are mastered by one desire only, the desire to do his will. James now moves on to say a second thing about those who give free rein to their self-centred desires.

2. Their prayer becomes defective

'You do not have because you do not ask God. When you ask you do not receive, because you ask with wrong motives, that you may spend what you get on your pleasures' (vv. 2b–3).

There is something quite devastating in the way James writes here. He is brief, blunt, but utterly realistic. He speaks of the prayer of self-centred men being defective in four ways.

1. Its content. 'You do not have because you do not ask

God.' To put it in the simplest possible language, one reason why these people did not obtain certain things was that they did not pray for them. Their prayer was defective in its content because its content was nil! Of course, there may have been a simple reason why they did not pray for certain things, namely that they knew perfectly well that they could not honestly do so. The things they wanted were things about which it would have been useless to pray because they were wrong, or their desire to have them was wrong. There is a simple but clear principle here: if you cannot pray about it, then you will not profit from it. That principle can be written across the whole of life. If we cannot pray about it, then we cannot profit from it. If we cannot say, 'Lord, bless me as I do this thing,' we ought not to be doing it at all. Of course, all prayerlessness leads to failure in obtaining, as Joseph Scriven wrote in his famous hymn:

> Oh, what peace we often forfeit,
> Oh, what needless pain we bear,
> All because we do not carry
> Everything to God in prayer!

Is there any measure in which that can be said of you? Is your prayer defective in its content? Are there whole areas of your life about which you never pray? Are there issues which you never take to the throne of grace? Is it therefore surprising that things do not seem to work out? Of how many good, legitimate, godly things, of how many blessings for yourself and other people could it be said: 'You do not have because you do not ask God'?

2. Its consequence. 'When you ask you do not receive.' Notice the pathetic refrain in these two verses: 'you don't get it', 'you cannot have what you want', 'you do not have', 'you do not receive'. These verses are marked not only by intense desire but by immense disappointment. Two little phrases in the story of the prodigal son bring out this same acute sense of unfulfilment. In the early part of the story his whole attitude is summed up in two words: 'give me' (Luke 15:12); but before long his condition is crystallized in two vastly different words: 'in need' (Luke 15:14). Here are the same two elements, intense desire and immense disappointment. He got what he wanted but it was not what he needed; it failed to satisfy him. Here, surely, is a lesson we must never stop learning. Just as a triangle will never fill a circle, so a man's selfish desires will never fill his deepest needs. The world may meet some of man's needs at a certain level and for a limited time, but at the end of the day he will remain unfulfilled.

Matthew Henry once wrote, 'It should kill these lusts to think of their disappointment,' but the unspiritual man is a fatal optimist; he goes on hoping, trying, scheming, striving. There are few clearer evidences of the presence and persistence of indwelling sin than the futile and fatal pursuit of that which cannot satisfy. This is brought out so poignantly in the patient appeal of God's Word: 'Why spend money on what is not bread, and your labour on what does not satisfy?' (Isaiah 55:2.) There are times when God's sternest rebuke is to allow us the things for which we ask, in order that we might learn that they do not satisfy us; and there are times when his greatest love is shown in his refusal to give us those things we crave.

3. Its conception. '. . . because you ask with wrong motives . . .' Perhaps no phrase in the whole of this epistle has wounded me more often than this one, stating as it does one of the main reasons for what we call 'unanswered prayer'. The phrase 'with wrong motives' perfectly captures the sense of the Greek word *kakos*, which would literally be translated 'out of place'. James is not concerned here with people who do not pray, nor even with those who ask for the wrong things, but with those who ask in the wrong way. There is a good illustration in the well-known story of the Pharisee and the tax-collector, which Jesus told in Luke 18. Jesus never condemned the Pharisee for his honesty, generosity, moral purity and so on. He was condemned because he gave these things the wrong value. He was not wrong in being honest, generous and moral, but he was wrong to bring these things into his prayer as a basis for boasting. Nothing that James says about prayer is more important than the point he is making here, namely that our motive must be right. The Bible tells us that at the end of the day there is one overruling condition for answered prayer: 'This is the confidence we have in approaching God: that if we ask anything *according to his will*, he hears us' (1 John 5:14). That is crucial and we are not praying according to God's will when we pray with the object of feathering our own nests, promoting our own causes, gaining our own ends. As John Calvin says, 'James meant briefly this – that our desires ought to be bridled; and the way of bridling them is to subject them to the will of God.'

But all of this leads us into another truth, and that is that we are to be as dependent upon God for our prayers as we are for his answers. Paul says quite clearly that 'We do not know what we ought to pray for' (Romans 8:26). Prayer is not just a concoction of words said with our knees bent and our eyes closed. We need more than bent knees and closed eyes. We need open, broken, humble, dependent, thirsting, believing hearts, and above all we need an overwhelming concern that God's will should be done. The Scriptures are certainly crystal clear that there is no such thing as an automatic answer to words said in prayer:

> '[God] does not answer when men cry out
>   because of the arrogance of the wicked.
> Indeed, God does not listen to their empty plea;
>   the Almighty pays no attention to it'
>
> (Job 35:12, 13);

> 'When you spread out your hands in prayer,
>   I will hide my eyes from you;
> even if you offer many prayers,
>   I will not listen.
> Your hands are full of blood;
>   wash and make yourselves clean'
>
> (Isaiah 1:15, 16);

> 'Then they will cry out to the Lord,
>   but he will not answer them.
> At that time he will hide his face from them
>   because of the evil they have done'
>
> (Micah 3:4);

'If I had cherished sin in my heart,
the Lord would not have listened'
(Psalm 66:18).

These verses all underline the negative side of a clear biblical principle, yet we must not press the point so logically that we think that we can earn ourselves the right to be answered because of our obedience. Let us be careful here. It is certainly true that we cannot get the gratification of evil, wrongly motivated desire just by praying for it. But we cannot press the reverse so far that we believe in God answering our prayer because our obedience has earned us the right to be answered. We have been examining God's law, but we must place it alongside God's love, and when we do that we discover that when God answers our smallest prayer, at our finest moment, then he only does so by overwhelming our unworthiness with his grace. And if that does not make sense, it is because God's ways are higher than our ways. It may not pacify the logical mind, but it satisfies the longing heart!

4. Its concern. '. . . that you may spend what you get on your pleasures.' The word 'pleasures' here is the same as the one translated 'desires' in verse 1. It speaks of man's instinctive appetite for self-gratification and unmasks the real concern of the kind of prayer that James has shown to be totally defective. It is said that the following prayer was found among the papers of John Ward, a Member of Parliament who owned part of Dagenham:

> 'O Lord, thou knowest that I have mine estates in the City of London, and likewise that I have lately purchased an estate in the county of Essex. I beseech thee to preserve the two counties of Middlesex and Essex from fire and earthquake; and as I have a mortgage in Hertfordshire, I beg of thee likewise to have an eye of compassion on that county. As for the rest of the counties, thou mayest deal with them as thou art pleased.'

No doubt the inhabitants of the counties concerned would have been grateful if they had known of his prayers, but his concern was not for them, but for himself! His motive was wrong.

It is possible to pray for many good things in the wrong way. For instance, it is possible to pray for the conversion of one's parents or children primarily because it would be so much better to live in a Christian home. It is possible to pray for the conversion of a workmate because he is a difficult fellow with whom to work and life would be so much more comfortable if he was converted. It is possible to pray for a missionary need to be met in order to avoid the pressure of the need. It is possible to pray for the success of your church, your fellowship, your Christian work or organization because that would increase its stature. What is your concern when you pray? When you pray for missionaries, when you pray for your church, when you pray for your home, your parents, your children, what is your *first* concern? What could you write above your prayer time that would sum up exactly the primary concern of your intercession? Incidentally, there is a link between concern and consequence, in that the word 'spend' that James uses here is the same word that is used in Luke 15, when we are told that the prodigal son '*spent* everything . . . and began to be in need', and of the woman in Mark 5 who had been ill for twelve years and who, despite numerous visits to the doctors, had '*spent* all she had, yet instead of getting better she grew worse'. It indicates the terrible emptiness which follows selfish praying. God's promise is to supply our need, not our greed. Prayer is not asking God for what we want, it is asking God for what *he* wants!

Man's ruin began in the Garden of Eden, when in spirit the first Adam said, 'Not your will, but mine be done.' Man's rescue came towards its consummation when in another garden the second Adam said, 'Not my will, but yours be done' (Luke 22:42). That is the spirit that should characterize all of our praying. That should be our one dominating concern. When we pray, we should have a single eye to the glory of God, regardless of what it might cost us, regardless of our own plans, regardless of whether our particular church or missionary society or other Christian organization thrives and flourishes or is allowed to subside so that God might work in other ways and through other channels. When we pray like that, our prayer will be truly effective and God will be glorified.

28.

Backsliding unmasked

> *'You adulterous people, don't you know that friendship with the world is hatred towards God? Anyone who chooses to be a friend of the world becomes an enemy of God. Or do you think Scripture says without reason that the spirit he caused to live in us envies intensely . . .?'* (James 4:4, 5).

In the first three verses of this chapter James has exposed the root cause of strife and unrest in the world at large, in communities, in churches and in the lives of individuals. He now turns to take an even closer look at people whose lives are characterized by the self-centred sins he has so roundly condemned. Two general headings will help us to grasp the impact of his words.

1. Their conduct is exposed

'You adulterous people, don't you know that friendship with the world is hatred towards God? Anyone who chooses to be a friend of the world becomes an enemy of God' (v. 4).

It is important to remember that James is writing to Christians; but it is obvious that at this point he has in mind believers who are backsliders, people whose whole approach to life, and especially their self-centred attitudes and actions, show their practical Christianity to be tragically deficient. Towards the end of chapter 3, James showed us the difference between spiritual, heavenly, godly wisdom and the false wisdom of the world, with the clear inference that Christians who put their trust in earthly wisdom are in fact backsliding. That kind of wisdom, James told us in no uncertain fashion, 'is earthly, unspiritual, of the devil'

(3:15). In the verse now before us James rips aside all the rationalism that men use to defend their actions and exposes their backsliding for what it really is. Each of the three descriptions he uses is vivid in its language and deeply challenging in its implications.

1. It is adultery. 'You adulterous people . . .' The first point to make here is that there is not necessarily any suggestion of physical adultery having been committed. In the best of the ancient manuscripts, this phrase is rendered by the one Greek word *moichalides*, which means 'adulteresses'. The question to ask is why James is obviously including both men and women in this one terrible word of condemnation. To answer it, we have to go back to the Old Testament and to one of the most wonderful pictures the Bible gives us of God's relationship to his people. Here are three of the places where we find it used: 'For your Maker is your husband – the Lord Almighty is his name' (Isaiah 54:5); '"Return, faithless people", declares the Lord, "for I am your husband"' (Jeremiah 3:14); '"But like a woman unfaithful to her husband, so you have been unfaithful to me, O house of Israel," declares the Lord' (Jeremiah 3:20). The picture we have in these passages is of the Lord as the Husband of his people, his people as the wife, the bride of their Lord and Master. We find the same picture in the New Testament and of the new, spiritual Israel. Paul writes, 'So, my brothers, you also died to the law through the body of Christ, that you might belong to another, to him who was raised from the dead, in order that we might bear fruit to God' (Romans 7:4); and again, 'I am jealous for you with a godly jealousy. I promised you to one husband, to Christ, so that I might present you as a pure virgin to him' (2 Corinthians 11:2); and again, 'Now as the church submits to Christ, so wives should submit to their husbands in everything. Husbands, love your wives, just as Christ loved the church and gave himself up for her, to make her holy, cleansing her by the washing with water through the word, and to present her to himself as a radiant church, without stain or wrinkle or any other blemish, but holy and blameless' (Ephesians 5:24–27). John gives us the same picture as he records the voice of a great multitude in heaven crying,

'Let us rejoice and be glad
  and give him glory!
For the wedding of the Lamb has come,
  and his bride has made herself ready'
(Revelation 19:7).

It is probably no exaggeration to say that nowhere in the Bible do we find more wonderful imagery of the relationship between Christ and his church than this – the Bridegroom and the bride! In the marriage service in the Book of Common Prayer, the bride is asked whether, in taking her husband, she will 'forsaking all other, keep thee only to him as long as ye both shall live', to which she answers, 'I will.' Here is the solemn vow that lies at the heart of holy matrimony and when that vow is broken we say that adultery has been committed. Whether it is once or often, whether it is discovered or not, regardless of whether there are extenuating circumstances, the fact of the matter is that with that sin the relationship is fractured. Now in drawing a spiritual analogy, let us be very careful to guard against saying three things. Firstly, that a person becomes a Christian by making a vow to God, by making a promise to the Lord Jesus Christ. Nobody becomes a Christian by making promises to God. Secondly, that one remains a Christian by keeping promises to God. That would remove salvation from the realm of grace altogether. Thirdly, we must guard against saying that committing one sin or many sins puts a Christian outside of God's family, in other words cancels out his salvation. Let us not make any of those three mistakes, but let not any of our carefulness in avoiding those errors allow us to avoid the impact of the point that James is making here, which is that worldliness, or backsliding, is spiritual adultery. It is loving something or someone else more than your rightful Husband, the Lord himself. The Amplified Bible translates the phrase: 'You are like unfaithful wives having illicit love affairs with the world and breaking your marriage vows to God!'

I remember a young man coming to me after a service and saying, 'I shall never be the same again after tonight. I now realize that for a long time I have been flirting with the world.' He was admitting that although he was sure he was a Christian, part of the bride of Christ, he had been carrying on a dishonouring relationship with the world. In the heart of the Old Testament, Elihu asked these two penetrating questions: 'If you sin, how does that affect him? If your sins are many, what does that do to him?' (Job 35:6.) In terms of your relationship to Christ, the answer is here in the Epistle of James: you break his heart because you break your vow; you commit spiritual adultery. For the Christian, wilful sin is as serious as that.

2. It is antagonism. '. . . don't you know that friendship with the world is hatred towards God? Anyone who chooses to be a friend of the world becomes an enemy of God.'

One of the most terrible things the Bible says about unconverted people is that they are incapable of pleasing God. As Paul puts it, 'The sinful mind is hostile to God. It does not submit to God's law, nor can it do so. Those controlled by the sinful nature cannot please God' (Romans 8:7, 8). Unconverted people can please themselves, they can please their worldly friends, they can even please certain elements within the church, but what they cannot do is to please God; indeed, as Paul so trenchantly puts it, their minds are actually hostile to him, even if they do not realize it. Paul underlined the point when writing to the Colossians, reminding them that before their conversion they, too, were 'enemies in your minds because of your evil behaviour' (Colossians 1:21). The same was true of all Christians, of course, before their conversion, yet in God's amazing grace that enmity, that Adamic hostility to God with which they were born was overwhelmed in the saving death of the Lord Jesus Christ on their behalf, so that Paul can tell the Christians at Rome, 'When we were God's enemies, we were reconciled to him through the death of his Son' (Romans 5:10). Notice the precise wording here. Paul does not say that although we were once God's enemies, we brought ourselves to a better frame of mind and put matters right. It was *when* we were enemies, while we were *still* enemies, that God reconciled us to himself. It was while we were literally hell-bent that God worked the miracle of reconciliation for us in the death of his Son. In Anne Steele's words,

Dear Lord, what heavenly wonders dwell
In thy atoning blood!
By this are sinners snatched from hell,
And rebels brought to God!

Now what James is saying is this: backsliding or worldliness is going back in spirit to what we were before we were converted. It is going back to the place where we were antagonistic to God. To put it more vividly, it is standing at Calvary uncommitted to Christ, fingering the nails, helping to make the crown of thorns, passing a hammer to the Roman soldier. Is that language too strong? Not according to the apostle John, who said, 'Do not love the world or anything in the world. If anyone loves the world, the love of the Father is not in him' (1 John 2:15). Not according to Paul, who wrote of those who were 'treacherous, rash, conceited, lovers of pleasures rather than lovers of God' (2 Timothy 3:4). Not according to Jesus, who said, 'No one can serve two masters. Either he will hate the one and love the other, or he will be devoted to the one and despise the other' (Matthew 6:24). Not according to James, who says that friendship with the world is hatred towards God.

One final point here: notice the phrase 'chooses to be'. The verb here is the Greek *boulomai*, which means 'to have a deliberate purpose and intention'. James is not speaking of a moral accident, or an unconscious drift into sin. He is speaking of the deliberate choice of the way of the world instead of the way of God and he is saying that that kind of attitude and action is nothing less than antagonism against God. In the light of that fact and of the staggering truth of our reconciliation through the death of Christ, we must make up our minds, not only conclusively but continually, whether we are hungering to be transformed or happy to be conformed. The Bible tells us that 'Christ died and returned to life so that he might be the *Lord* . . .' (Romans 14:9). When we deny his rightful lordship in our lives we are guilty of antagonism.

3. It is audacity. 'Or do you think Scripture says without reason . . .?' Before going any further, I ought to warn you that the remainder of the section we are studying at this moment is one of the most tortuously difficult in this epistle, if not in the whole of the New Testament, so we will need to tread carefully!

In the version we are using, the complete sentence reads: 'Or do you think Scripture says without reason that the spirit he caused to live in us envies intensely?'

If this is exactly what James had in mind, then the phrase about Scripture obviously refers to the words which follow. That may well be so, but it is possible that the phrase refers to what came before. If this is the case, we could paraphrase what James is saying like this: 'Do you think Scripture is meaningless when it speaks about worldliness as being spiritual adultery and enmity against God?' Incidentally, the point as to whether the phrase applies to verse 4 or the second part of verse 5 does not affect the application in any way, because in point of fact neither verse 4 nor the second part of verse 5 appear in the Old Testament Scriptures at all. In using the phrase, James is not introducing a specific verse of Scripture. What he is saying is that the spirit of his words appears throughout Scripture, and he assumed that his readers would know this perfectly well. Paul uses the same formula when he writes,

> 'This is why it is said:
> "Wake up, O sleeper,
> rise from the dead,
> and Christ will shine on you" '
> (Ephesians 5:14).

In fact, we have no scripture that uses that precise phrase, but its spirit is there again and again.

I have chosen the word 'audacity' here because there may be an important link between the phrase 'don't you know' in verse 4 (perhaps inferring that they know perfectly well) and the phrase 'Or do you think Scripture says without reason . . .?' in verse 5. The point would be that those people knew what the Bible said, and James's withering criticism was that, having read God's Word, and understood its meaning, they were deliberately disobeying it and allowing its truth to go no further than their heads. If James is moving along these lines, then it is surely not difficult to apply what he is saying to our own lives. Let us beware of reading the Bible, understanding what it means and then giving it less than the wholehearted obedience it demands. That is tantamount to saying that the Bible is no more than a collection of empty words – and that is sheer audacity! The truth of the matter is that 'All Scripture is God-breathed' (2 Timothy 3:16) and as such all its teaching is valid, all its promises are true, and all its warnings are real.

Here, then, is the backslider unmasked: he is guilty of spiritual adultery by sinning against God's love; he is guilty of antagonism by sinning against God's law; he is guilty of audacity by sinning against God's light. We can now move on to the final phrase in this section.

2. A challenge is extended

'. . . the spirit he caused to live in us envies intensely'.

The first challenge in this phrase comes to anyone who attempts to explain it! The sixteenth-century Dutch humanist Desiderius Erasmus, who prepared a complete text of the New Testament, once said, 'There are wagon-loads of interpretations of this passage'! Let me illustrate its difficulties. In studying the one word 'spirit' I looked at eighteen different translations and discovered that nine of them take the word to mean the Holy Spirit, six take it to refer to the spirit of man, that is man's human nature, and three were completely ambiguous as to what they meant! Even the translators of our excellent New International Version have found it necessary to revise their original translation of this phrase and also to add two alternative renderings as footnotes: 'God jealously longs for the spirit that he made to live in us' and 'the Spirit he caused to live in us longs jealously'. Nor do our problems end there, because within the phrase itself nearly every word has been subject to various interpretations over the years. At moments like this, I can certainly identify with Solomon, who cried out, 'I am only a little child and do not know how to carry out my duties'! (1 Kings 3:7.) In a study as brief as this, perhaps the most helpful thing would be to look at just three translations, covering what seem to me to be the most likely areas of James's meaning. As we do so we will discover that in each case – though in different ways – a challenge is extended.

Firstly, there is the New English Bible, which translates the phrase like this: 'The spirit which God implanted in man turns to envious desires.' This would take up the point James made in verse 1, when he referred to 'your desires that battle within you'. If so, the challenge is to face up to the sobering reality of the continuing power of our residual fallen nature – to recognize that the spirit which God implanted in man, originally good but corrupted by the Fall, is still, even after conversion, liable to break out into 'envious desires'. As Thomas Manton wrote, 'We commit sin, as heavy bodies move downward, not from an impression without, but from our own spirit and nature.'

I remember reading with great interest the story of Dr Christian Barnard, the first man in the world to perform a heart transplant operation. On one occasion, he was talking to one of his transplant patients, Dr Philip Blaiberg, and suddenly asked, 'Would you like to see your old heart?' Blaiberg said that he would. At eight o'clock one evening the men stood in a room of the Groote Schuur Hospital, in Johannesburg, South Africa. Dr Barnard went up to a cupboard, took down a glass container and handed it to Dr Blaiberg. Inside that container was Blaiberg's old heart. For a moment he stood there stunned into silence – the first man in history ever to hold his own heart in his hands. Finally, he spoke and for ten minutes plied Dr Barnard with technical questions (Blaiberg himself was a dentist). Then he turned to take a final look at the contents of the glass container and said, 'So this is my old heart, that caused me so much trouble.' He handed it back, turned away and left it for ever.

Now the point of that illustration is this: conversion is not a transplant. Our old heart (or nature) is not taken away and replaced by a new one, so that we can look back and say, 'There was a day when I had an old heart, an old nature, but now it has been taken away and can never again cause me any trouble.' The fact of the matter is that our old nature remains entrenched within us, incurably antagonistic to the things of God and constantly promoting 'envious desires'.

Secondly, there is the paraphrase by J. B. Phillips, which translates the paraphrase like this: 'Do you imagine that this spirit of passionate jealousy is the Spirit he [that is, God] has caused to live in us?' If this is something like the right translation, then the meaning is clear. James is asking his readers, 'Do you seriously think that the Holy Spirit, who came to dwell within you at your conversion, can be blamed for the way you are choosing to live, the things you are choosing to do? Is he responsible for your passionate jealousy?' Now if that is the correct interpretation, then James is taking up a point he made in chapter 1: 'When tempted, no one should say, "God is tempting me." For God cannot be tempted by evil, nor does he tempt anyone' (1:13). We cannot offload on to God the responsibility for our own failures, not even by sheltering behind the high doctrine of his absolute sovereignty over the entire universe. As Thomas Manton brilliantly puts it, 'God can by no means be looked upon as the direct author of [sin] . . . for his providence is conversant about sin without sin, as a sunbeam lighteth upon a dunghill without being stained by it'!

Thirdly, there is the second of the alternative renderings in the New International Version: 'the Spirit [God] caused to live in us longs jealously'. This seems to me to be very much preferable to the wording chosen by the NIV translators for the main body of the text and it produces a clear and challenging meaning by bringing us face to face with the jealousy of God. In present day use, the word 'jealousy' has an almost totally bad connotation, but we are quite wrong to cramp its meaning in this way. As Alec Motyer has said, 'Jealousy, properly considered, is an essential element of true love: it is . . . an unceasing longing for the loved one's welfare.' The Greek verb is *epipothei*, which speaks of intense longing or desire, and when the Bible uses it of God, it is not the jealousy of self-centred possessiveness or carnal desire, but of loving concern for the welfare of his people. Here are some places in which we find this expressed. In the course of the Ten Commandments, God required unadulterated obedience on the grounds that 'I, the Lord your God, am a jealous God' (Exodus 20:5); later, he tells Moses, 'Do not worship any other god, for the Lord, whose name is Jealous, is a jealous God' (Exodus 34:14); while his message to Zechariah included the statement: 'I am very jealous for Zion; I am burning with jealousy for her'

(Zechariah 8:2). In closing our study of this section of James's message, let us mark three things about God's jealousy.

1. It is an intense jealousy. This comes across with particular vividness in the quotation from Zechariah, where God speaks of 'burning with jealousy'. In his book *Blessings out of Buffetings*, Alan Redpath says, 'The jealousy of God . . . is the greatest flame that burns in the heart of deity . . . a concern for the purity, the holiness, the greatness, the glory of his people.' What a marvellous, humbling thing it is that God should have a passionate concern that we should be a pure, holy, great and glorious people!

2. It is an infinite jealousy. Because God's jealousy is one of his attributes, it must be infinite and eternal. It is not something acquired, it is not something developed, it is not something prompted by circumstances, it is not something suggested by anything that we are, anything that we have, anything that we become, any obedience that we tender, any sacrifice we make or any faith we exercise. Are you a Christian? Then let me apply this to you personally. It is a jealousy of the divine Lover of his people, the one who loves you with an everlasting love, who was jealous for you the moment you first drew breath upon this earth, who was jealous for you when you were groping for the first hold on life, who was jealous for you when you took those first conscious steps into sin, jealous for you when you first heard his name, jealous for you when you rejected him, jealous for your salvation as he brought the gospel to you in one way and another, through one person and another, through one means and another, until finally he broke through in the power of the Holy Spirit and brought you to living faith. What is more, he is jealous for you now, jealous for your spiritual welfare, jealous for you in every temptation and in every trial, jealous lest you should be robbed by covetousness, compromise, worldliness, prayerlessness or disobedience in any shape or form. He is jealous that you should have that fulness of blessing, those riches of grace that he longs to bestow upon every one of his people. When we speak about the jealousy of God we mean at least all of this, for his is an infinite jealousy.

3. It is an intimate jealousy. Notice James's phrase that the

Holy Spirit has been 'caused to live *in us*'. God's jealousy, his passionate concern for our welfare, is not exercised by 'remote control'. He yearns for our deepest well-being from within the deepest well of our being, because he himself, in the person of the Holy Spirit, has come to dwell within our hearts. As Harriet Auber has it in one of her hymns,

And his that gentle voice we hear,
Soft as the voice of even;
That checks each fault, and calms each fear,
And speaks of heaven.

And every virtue we possess,
And every conquest won,
And every thought of holiness
Are his alone.

I suggested that in the phrase we have been studying a challenge is extended, and surely it is! If interpreted in the first way, it challenges us to recognize the presence and power of the old nature; if the second interpretation is correct, then the challenge is to accept personal responsibility for our failures; and if the third interpretation is right, we are challenged to respond to the Holy Spirit's passionate yearning that we should walk in the paths of righteousness and obedience. We may have to admit difficulty in grasping the precise intention of James's words, but at the end of the day we cannot escape their impact!

29.

Amazing grace!

'But he gives us more grace. That is why Scripture says: "God opposes the proud but gives grace to the humble"' (James 4:6).

'The religion of the Bible is a religion of grace or it is nothing . . . no grace, no gospel.' Every Christian will echo that statement by Dr James Moffatt in his book *Grace in the New Testament*. One's mind runs immediately to Paul's matchless words: 'For it is by grace you have been saved, through faith – and this not from yourselves, it is the gift of God – not by works, so that no one can boast' (Ephesians 2:8, 9). Then there is his word to the elders at Ephesus when he describes his life's ministry as 'testifying to the gospel of God's grace' (Acts 20:24). Peter, too, attributes the Christian's salvation entirely to 'the God of all grace' (1 Peter 5:10).

There is a case for saying that other than the divine names and titles, there is no greater word than 'grace' in the whole Bible. That being so, we shall take an overall look at its place in the Bible as a whole before concentrating on James's use of it here. Two headings will cover our complete study.

1. How it is given

It has been said that 'The essence of the doctrine of grace is that God is for us,' and the Bible underlines this in at least three ways.

1. Common grace. In Christian circles, we usually think of grace in terms of the crisis of salvation or the process of sanctification, but the Bible teaches us that God's grace covers a much wider area. David says, 'The Lord is good to all; he has compassion on all he has made' (Psalm 145:9) and later adds, 'You open your hand and satisfy the desires of every living thing' (Psalm 145:16). Is that not obviously true? The smallest bird, the tiniest animal, the most microscopic fish all have their needs met by their Creator. They exist and survive only by his grace. In the same way all of humanity benefits from God's common grace, regardless of whether or not they respond to it in any way. Paul tells us that God is 'the Saviour of all men, and especially of those who believe' (1 Timothy 4:10). This is obviously a crucial verse on the subject of common grace, because Paul says that God 'is the Saviour of all men'. What does he mean? Obviously he does not mean that he is their Saviour in the evangelical sense of saving them from sin and giving them eternal life, because in the first place that would teach the unbiblical doctrine of universalism (that all men will eventually be saved) and in the second place it would render completely unnecessary Paul's next phrase 'especially of those who believe'. Then in what sense can we say that God is the Saviour of all men? If we were to take time to study the biblical development of the word 'saviour', we would discover that some of its fundamental meanings include 'preserver' and 'deliverer', and if we apply Paul's words with those definitions in mind we come to a perfectly satisfying explanation. God *is* the Saviour of all men. Every moment that a man enjoys the benefits of a healthy body, God is saving him from illness; if a man is sane, God is saving him from a diseased mind; to whatever degree a man knows the truth about any subject whatever, God is saving him from error; when a man has food to eat and water to drink, God is saving him from starvation; every moment of good in a man's life is possible because God is saving him from the forces of evil; every thought, word and deed that has the slightest element of rightness about it is possible because God is at work saving that man from utter and complete corruption; in every moment of life, God is saving him from death. As William Hendriksen says, 'He provides his creatures with food, keeps them alive, is deeply interested in them, often delivers them from disease, ills, hurt, famine, war, poverty, and peril in any form. He is, accordingly, their *Soter* (Preserver, Deliverer, and in *that* sense Saviour).'

This is common grace, in the sense that God pours it out upon all men regardless of their faith or infidelity. As Jesus himself put it, 'He causes his sun to rise on the evil and the good, and sends rain on the just and the unjust' (Matthew 5:45). God pours out this common grace upon all men without distinction, upon the downright sinner as well as the upright saint! To quote Hendriksen again, 'There is no one who does not in one way or another come within reach of his benevolence.'

2. *Covenant grace.* This is what Paul means when he speaks of 'this grace in which we [as Christians] now stand' (Romans 5:2). Unlike common grace, this is not given indiscriminately to all men, but only to those whom God calls and causes to receive his free gift of salvation. The first time the word occurs in the Bible is where we read that 'Noah found favour in the eyes of the Lord' (Genesis 6:8). (The word 'favour' translates the Hebrew *chen* which has the same meaning as 'grace'.) The immediate result was Noah's physical salvation, but the deeper truth is clear and the whole context shows it to be a covenant word, as it is when used of God's dealings with Abraham, Isaac and Jacob. Indeed, the Old Testament teems with the idea of covenant grace, brought out in words such as 'mercy', 'kindness' and 'love'.

Turning to the New Testament we come across the surprising fact that Jesus never once used the word! Yet, of course, he had no need to, for he was the very personification of the grace of God. As John put it, 'Grace and truth came through Jesus Christ' (John 1:17). This does not mean that God did not reveal his grace and truth before the birth of Christ, but that he displayed them in their fullest form. As Thomas Parker puts it in *Baker's Dictionary of Theology*, 'We may say that grace means Jesus Christ and Jesus Christ means grace.'

The word 'grace' is a translation of the Greek *charis* and it will help us to grasp its meaning in terms of salvation if we look at one particular verse in which it is used. This is where Paul says, 'For the wages of sin is death, but the gift of God is eternal life in Christ Jesus our Lord' (Romans 6:23). Now Paul's word 'gift' is the Greek *charisma,* which means a gift that is free and unmerited. It stands in direct contrast to 'wages', which are worked for, earned, deserved, and makes it crystal clear that the Christian's salvation is his entirely as the result of the free, unmerited, covenant grace of God. In William Jenkyn's brilliant phrase, 'Grace is not native but donative.'

Few Christians have as dramatic a testimony as John Newton. A deserter, slave trader and infidel, the turning point in his life came when he miraculously survived the terrifying Atlantic storm that struck the trading ship the *Greyhound* in March 1748. After his conversion, he taught himself Greek and Hebrew, became a minister of the gospel and had a decisive influence on William Wilberforce, who was to lead the successful campaign for the abolition of the slave trade. Newton also wrote a number of fine hymns and one of the best-known gives poetic expression to so much of what the Bible says about covenant grace:

Amazing grace! (how sweet the sound!)
That saved a wretch like me!
I once was lost, but now am found;
Was blind, but now I see.

'Twas grace that taught my heart to fear,
And grace my fears relieved;
How precious did that grace appear,
The hour I first believed!

Through many dangers, toils and snares,
I have already come;
'Tis grace has brought me safe thus far,
And grace will lead me home.

The Lord has promised good to me,
His word my hope secures:
He will my shield and portion be,
As long as life endures.

Yes, when this flesh and heart shall fail,
And mortal life shall cease;
I shall possess, within the veil,
A life of joy and peace.

The earth shall soon dissolve like snow,
The sun forbear to shine:
But God, who called me here below,
Will be for ever mine.

3. *Continuing grace.* This is the sense in which James is using the word when he writes, 'But [God] gives us more grace.' He is using the word 'grace' to speak of the God-given help a Christian needs moment by moment if he is to counter the devastating forces of his old nature. At this point, let us try to link this in to the previous verse. Now what is the link between what James said in verse 5 and his statement that '[God] gives us more grace'? If we accept the first interpretation of verse 5 that we considered, then James is saying that in contrast to our covetous, envious old nature the Holy Spirit's nature is to give. If the second interpretation is correct, James is saying that far from being responsible for our sins of jealousy, envy and covetousness, the Holy Spirit longs to pour in his continuing grace to enable us to overcome these very things. If we accept the third interpretation, which tells us of God's yearning for our holiness, then James is adding this reminder that God alone can empower us to achieve it. In Thomas Manton's fine phrase, 'Grace is nothing but an introduction of the virtues of God into the soul.'

Yet regardless of alternatives, the statement is axiomatic: 'God gives us more grace,' and of that continuing grace we can add two further comments.

The first is that it is *according to God's nature.* The verb 'gives' is the Greek *didosin*, a present indicative which implies giving which never ends. There is a story about an artist who submitted a painting of the Niagara Falls to an exhibition, but forgot to give it a title. Faced with the need to supply one in the artist's absence, the organizers chose just three words: 'More to follow'. Do you see why? Those surging waters had poured down for countless years and had been harnessed to bring light, heating, power and comfort to multitudes of people, yet there was more to follow. So with the grace of God; although multitudes have drawn on it for untold centuries, there is still more to follow from the hand of the one who can truly be described as 'the giving God' (1:5, Amplified Bible).

The second is that it is *according to our need.* The Amplified Bible has this wonderful elaboration of Hebrews 4:16: 'Let us then fearlessly and confidently and boldly draw near to the throne of grace – the throne of God's unmerited favour to us sinners; that we may receive mercy for our failures and find grace to help in good time for every need – appropriate help and well-timed help coming just when we need it.' Surely that is a truth written into the experience of all the children of God? Just as God supplies food for all his creatures 'at the proper time' (Psalm 104:27), so he supplies perfectly measured grace to meet the needs of the godly. For daily need there is daily grace; for sudden need, sudden grace; for overwhelming need, overwhelming grace. God's grace is given wonderfully, but not wastefully; freely but not foolishly; bountifully but not blindly. Annie Johnson Flint has perfectly captured the spirit of this in these well-known lines:

> He giveth more grace when the burdens grow greater;
> He sendeth more grace when the labours increase;
> To added afflictions he addeth his mercy,
> To multiplied trials his multiplied peace.
>
> When we have exhausted our store of endurance,
> When our strength has failed ere the day is half done;
> When we reach the end of our hoarded resources,
> Our Father's full giving is only begun.
>
> His love has no limits, his grace has no measure,
> His power has no boundary known unto men;
> For out of his infinite riches in Jesus,
> He giveth, and giveth, and giveth again.

So much for our brief study of how grace is given. Now let us turn to the remainder of the text.

2. How it is governed

'That is why Scripture says: "God opposes the proud but gives grace to the humble."'

The essence of this statement is taught throughout the Old Testament, but James seems to have Proverbs 3:34 in mind: '[God] mocks proud mockers but gives grace to the humble' (also used by Peter in 1 Peter 5:5). James's point in quoting these words here is surely to show us how we can know this amazing grace of God of which he has been writing, or as Spiros Zodhiates puts it, 'to provide direction for the finite to participate in the infinite'. Now the grace of God is infinite, boundless, limitless, yet its application is governed by very specific laws. That may seem contradictory, but because those laws are divine, they are perfectly consistent with the freedom of the grace being given. God's mind is not in conflict with his heart. James now tells us two ways in which the grace of God is governed.

1. The proud in spirit are resisted. 'God opposes the proud.' The verb here is the Greek *antitassetai,* which literally means 'to arrange against'. It is a military term which could be translated 'to set in array as in a battle', and the picture it conjures up is vivid and terrifying. Whereas the humble, godly man has the hosts of God encamped around him, the arrogant, godless man has the God of hosts arrayed against him! James is saying nothing less than that. But is his language too strong? Is he overstating the case? Not in the least! The Bible even goes so far as to say that 'The Lord detests all the proud of heart' (Proverbs 16:5). But why is pride singled out for such terrible condemnation? Thomas Manton sums up the Bible's answer to that question like this: 'Other sins are more hateful to man, because they bring disgrace . . . but the Lord hateth it because it is a sin that sets itself most against him. Other sins are against his law, this is against his being and sovereignty. Pride doth not only withdraw the heart from God, but lifteth it up against God . . . Besides, pride is the cause of all other sins.' To recognize this is to understand precisely why the Bible speaks so clearly of God's implacable hatred of pride and his unyielding resistance to it.

How then does God resist the proud? He does so in many ways. To quote Thomas Manton again, 'The proud man hath his tactics, and God hath his anti-tactics.' His quaint wording is remarkably up to date in our world of missiles, anti-missiles and anti-missile missiles! Try as he will, man's pride will never get the better of God. How does God resist proud men? The Bible gives us a number of answers to that question.

God resists the proud *by refusing to speak.* Recording one of the trials Jesus faced before his crucifixion, Luke writes, 'When Herod saw Jesus, he was greatly pleased, because for a long time he had been wanting to see him. From what he had heard about him, he hoped to see him perform some miracle. He plied him with many questions, but Jesus gave him no answer' (Luke 23:8, 9). Herod was an Edomite, a descendant of Esau, and noted for his pride. But the king's arrogance was met by the Master's silence. There are some terrible and more widely applicable examples of this in Romans 1, where Paul describes people who 'claimed to be wise' (v. 22), 'worshipped and served created things rather than the Creator' (v. 25), 'did not think it worth while to retain the knowledge of God', and were 'insolent, arrogant and boastful' (vv. 28, 30). And what was God's reaction to such people? He 'gave them over' (vv. 24, 26, 28). In other words, there came a time when he had nothing more to say to them, did nothing to stop them, had nothing more to do with them. It is impossible to imagine anything more terrible than that.

Then God resists the proud *by ridiculing their schemes.* One single passage from Scripture makes this clear:

> 'Why do the nations conspire
>   and the peoples plot in vain?
> The kings of the earth take their stand
>   and the rulers gather together against the Lord
>   and against his Anointed One.
> "Let us break their chains," they say,
>   "and throw off their fetters."
> The One enthroned in heaven laughs;
>   the Lord scoffs at them'
>
> (Psalm 2:1–4).

This kind of language is known as anthropomorphism – using human terms to describe God's attributes or actions – and how telling it is! While men and nations proudly plot their independence of God, he remains totally unmoved except to derisory laughter and whenever he chooses he brings their schemes to nothing.

God also resists the proud *by ruining their success.* In 2 Chronicles 26 we are told something of the story of King Uzziah. His amazing success as a ruler, administrator and commander-in-chief takes us right through to verse 15, where we read, 'His fame spread far and wide, for he was greatly helped until he became powerful. But after Uzziah became powerful, his pride led to his downfall. He was unfaithful to the Lord his God, and entered the temple of the Lord to burn incense.' Now the burning of incense was exclusively reserved by divine law for the Levitical priests, God having added the clear warning: 'Anyone else who comes near the sanctuary must be put to death' (Numbers 18:7). The arrogant Uzziah decided to override God's law, but even as he stood in the sanctuary, defying the courageous priests who remonstrated with him, the deadly disease of leprosy broke out on his forehead and his reign was at an end.

Finally, God resists the proud *by removing their status.* Like Uzziah, King Belshazzar was successful, opulent – and arrogant. He also had recent history as a warning, for Daniel reminded him that although the king's father, Nebuchadnezzar, had been equally exalted, 'When his heart became arrogant and hardened with pride, he was deposed from his royal throne and stripped of his glory' (Daniel 5:20). Refusing to learn from history, Belshazzar was doomed to repeat it and in the midst of his careless revelry he was violently done to death. Let us learn the lesson that God has power both to give and to take away. None of our positions, in business, social or church life, are so secure that God cannot end them, and if we do not hold them in humility we may be forced to leave them in humiliation.

This then, is the first law by which grace is governed – the proud in spirit are resisted.

2. The poor in spirit are rewarded. 'But gives grace to the humble.' This law applied both to unbeliever and believer; it applies both to entering the kingdom of heaven and being a member of it. Both applications can be seen in these words spoken by Jesus: 'I tell you the truth, unless you change and become like little children, you will never enter the kingdom of heaven. Therefore, whoever humbles himself like this child is the greatest in the kingdom of heaven' (Matthew 18:3, 4). Notice first that to enter the kingdom of heaven a man must become as a little child, he must humble himself, he must abandon all trust in his own goodness and throw himself as a spiritual bankrupt on the mercy of God. The very first of the Beatitudes says, 'Blessed are the poor in spirit, for theirs is the kingdom of heaven' (Matthew 5:3), and the particular word translated poor – the Greek *ptochos* – does not mean having very little, it means having *nothing.* Grace can only flow into empty hands. The only way into the kingdom of heaven is in the spirit of Augustus Toplady's well-known words:

> Nothing in my hand I bring,
> Simply to thy cross I cling;
> Naked, come to thee for dress;
> Helpless, look to thee for grace;
> Foul, I to the fountain fly;
> Wash me, Saviour, or I die!

Then notice that the second part of the quotation from Matthew 18 shows humility as the key to spiritual greatness *within* the kingdom of heaven. This underlines what Jesus said elsewhere: 'For he who is least among you all – he is the greatest' (Luke 9:48). In Christian circles we often tend to estimate a man by his gifts, of oratory, organization, leadership, knowledge and so on. But God thinks most of the man who thinks himself least. In William Bridge's lovely words, 'If you lay yourself at Christ's feet he will take you into his arms.'

We shall look more closely at the subject of humility in chapter 32. For the moment, let us leave this particular section of James's epistle with the assurance that in the deepest spiritual sense, the Bible's words are unshakeably true: 'Humility and the fear of the Lord bring wealth and honour and life' (Proverbs 22:4).

30.

Victory secrets

'Submit yourselves, then, to God. Resist the devil and he will flee from you' (James 4:7).

As a young Christian, I used to get very excited by the second part of this verse. Looking back to my unconverted days, I knew the devastating impact the devil could have in a person's life, while my Bible study was teaching me more and more about his supernatural power and cunning. Yet here was the Bible promising that I could actually know the experience of seeing the one described as 'the ruler of the kingdom of the air' (Ephesians 2:2) running away from me in defeat. I could hardly believe my eyes! However, a closer look at the text and my growing experience as a Christian soon taught me the important truth that victory over the devil was conditional; other things would need to come first!

This is the consistent scriptural picture. Paul speaks about being 'able to stand your ground' (Ephesians 6:13), but only if we 'put on the full armour of God'. Again, he promises that as Christians we can 'extinguish all the flaming arrows of the evil one' (Ephesians 6:16), but only if we 'take up the shield of faith'. In other words we must meet particular requirements before we can expect promised results. Let us study this verse with that pattern in mind.

1. The requirements

'Submit yourselves, then, to God. Resist the devil . . .' There are two clear requirements here and we can examine them just as they stand.

1. 'Submit yourselves, then, to God.' The philosophy of submission can hardly be said to be popular in this latter part of the twentieth century. We live in what may be an age of unparalleled rebellion. Children rebel against parents, scholars against teachers, students against tutors, workers against management. All over the world this has led to disturbance, violence, bloodshed and even death. It seems to be the very spirit of the age in which we live, a spirit of arrogance, assertion and self-seeking. Today's slogan is not 'submit yourselves', but 'assert yourselves' – stand up for yourselves, promote your own ends and be prepared to destroy anything that stands in your way. During trouble at a British university, a student leader said, 'We will stop at nothing. Our aim is to destroy the system.'

Yet what a different spirit we find required of us in the Bible, and supremely in the perfect example of the life of Jesus! Rising into his teenage years, and living with his parents in Nazareth, we read that he was 'obedient to them' (Luke 2:51). Coming where it does, that phrase is very significant, for two reasons: firstly, because Jesus, as a Jewish boy, had reached his majority on his twelfth birthday and was therefore no longer legally bound to his parents as he had been in his earlier years, and secondly, because he knew that Joseph was not his father and could not enforce all the rights of a normal parent. Yet within that home the eternal Son of God lived in humble obedience and gentle submission.

The word 'obedient' comes from the same root as James's word 'submit' – the Greek *hupotasso*, which means 'to place oneself in order under' – and it is deeply instructive to notice how the Bible uses this precise word to direct our behaviour in so many areas of life.

In *civic life*, for instance, we are commanded: 'Submit yourselves for the Lord's sake to every authority instituted among men . . .' (1 Peter 2:13). In simple terms, this means that a Christian should be a model citizen, submitting to the laws and regulations of his country, knowing that they are basically intended for the promotion of men's welfare.

In *church life*, the same principle is meant to apply. After commending those who had devoted themselves to the service of the church, Paul urged the Christians at Corinth to 'submit to such as these' (1 Corinthians 16:16). God-ordained offices and officers within the church are to be treated with deference and respect.

In *family life*, the Bible says, 'Wives, submit to your husbands, as is fitting in the Lord' (Colossians 3:18). This in no way infers the wife's inferiority, nor does it give the husband licence to exercise an unspiritual dictatorship; what it does is to underline the biblical principle that, in William Hendriksen's words, 'God made the human pair in such a manner that it is natural for the husband to lead, for the wife to follow.'

In *business life*, the Bible commands servants to 'submit yourselves to your masters with all respect' (1 Peter 2:18). What a revolution that kind of spirit would bring about in today's rebellious, assertive world!

Yet there is one other, clinching use of the same word. The overall commandment to 'be filled with the Spirit' (Ephesians 5:18) is followed by a series of participles, the last general one of which says, 'Submit to one another out of reverence for Christ' (Ephesians 5:21). The inescapable point here is that the mark of a Spirit-filled man is not assertion but submission. He does not strut around boasting of his spiritual superiority; instead, he has a spirit of humility. In its biblical context, submission is a mark of spirituality.

Now if this principle of submission is right in our relationships with each other, it must clearly be right in our relationship with God, for three reasons.

The first is *because he is the Lord.* Writing of the sheer incongruity of man resisting God's will, Paul says, 'But who are you, O man, to talk back to God? Shall what is formed say to him who formed it, "Why did you make me like this?"' (Romans 9:20.) Paul is using the illustration of a potter making a vessel out of a lump of clay, and asks whether it is rational that the finished vessel should rise from the potter's wheel and complain about its size, shape or intended use. Why, Paul infers, the thing is ludicrous, unthinkable! When the potter takes that clay in his hands he has the right to do with it whatever he wants. He is the undisputed master of the situation. In a much deeper sense, because God is not only the moulder of our human clay but its Maker, he has the indisputable right to demand our submission and obedience.

The second is *because of his law.* What I have in mind here is not merely the clear law contained in the very words, 'Submit yourselves, then, to God,' but the outworking of the law or principle that we found in verse 6, namely that 'God opposes the proud.' Now that is a law; God deliberately sets himself in array against arrogance. Think of the simplest possible illustration. An unconverted man hears the gospel, in which he is told that there is nothing he can do to earn his salvation, which is entirely by grace. Instinctively he rebels and says, 'I don't accept that. I am going to earn my own salvation, and trust that at the end of the day God will accept me on the basis of my own efforts.' Now when a man takes that attitude, God resists him – and rejects him! God has nothing to say to the proud, self-sufficient sinner.

But the same law operates in the life of the Christian. He can never forfeit his salvation, of course, but he can lose a great deal of blessing and fruitfulness as a result of his deliberate failure to submit to God. This surely explains the little word 'then' in our verse: 'Submit yourselves *then*, to God', that is, because God has laid down an unchangeable law that he resists those who do not submit. Submission to God is not only expressly scriptural, it is eminently sensible!

The third is *because of his love*. This is another point of contact with verse 6, where James wrote not only about God resisting the proud but giving grace to the humble. Here, the emphasis is on the tenderness and mercy of God, his longing to bless, strengthen and guide his people. Having been told that God is longing to pour out his gracious blessing on all those who yield him humble obedience, we should not be surprised to find James adding, 'Submit yourselves, then, to God.'

These are some of the reasons why we should submit to God, but we need to take the matter further and apply the general principle in some specific areas.

We must submit to his doctrines. As we read the New Testament, it is obvious that the teachings of Jesus drew varied reactions. At one stage we are told that 'The large crowd listened to him with delight' (Mark 12:37), but that was not always the case. On another occasion 'Many of his disciples said, "This is a hard teaching. Who can accept it?"' (John 6:60.) Fully aware of their murmuring, Jesus went on to develop the point he was making, namely that nobody could be saved unless God granted him the gift of faith. The result? 'From this time many of his disciples turned back and no longer followed him' (John 6:66). Now that is a most significant statement! When people use the word 'disciples' they are nearly always thinking of a handful of people in the New Testament, all of them committed Christians. But if we limit the word in that way we soon find ourselves in trouble, because here were 'disciples' who 'no longer followed him', which would mean that as Christians they took a course of action which lost them their salvation – something the Bible teaches is impossible. We begin to unravel the problem when we realize that the word 'disciple' very simply means 'learner' and was a common word in New Testament times. There were disciples of Greek philosophers, Jewish rabbis and many other teachers or professors. They were learners, interested in what these people had to teach, but there was not necessarily a personal commitment. If a time came when they could no longer accept the teaching they were being given, they would leave their teacher, perhaps to become a disciple of someone else. That is just what happened here. Multitudes flocked to hear what Jesus was teaching and while he was performing miracles, healing the sick, feeding the hungry and raising the dead, I have no doubt that there were many of them who were 'disciples', at least on the surface. But when Jesus began to teach doctrines that stripped away the pride and the arrogance of man, when he began to show that a man could only be saved when he cast himself wholeheartedly on the grace and mercy of God, many of them drifted away, never to return. They were disciples, they were learners, they were listeners; but they set limits on what they were prepared to accept and believe. Is the point becoming clear? A true disciple must be governed by what he is taught. He must submit to it, and to submit to God includes submission to his doctrines. As Jesus himself put it, 'If you hold to my teaching, you are *really* my disciples' (John 8:31). Submission to his doctrine was the seal of their discipleship. When we come to the Bible, we are to stand under it even when we cannot understand it!

Martin Luther was able to say, 'My conscience is captive to the Word of God.' Every true Christian disciple must be able to say the same.

We must submit to his disciplines. This vital issue is almost totally ignored in many circles today, with the result that many untaught Christians seem to think that in some vague way God is responsible for all the pleasure there is in the world and the devil is responsible for all the pain, that God is responsible for the happy experiences of life and the devil for the harrowing ones, that God is responsible for life's delights and the devil for life's difficulties. But that is a very long way removed from the teaching of the Bible. In the first place, God is in control of everything that happens in the world. There are no accidents as far as God is concerned. In the second place God often uses disciplines, the hard things of life, pain, sorrow and deprivation, to bring about his glory and his people's good.

Yet the teaching of Scripture is plain enough: 'Know then in your heart that as a man disciplines his son, so the Lord your God disciplines you' (Deuteronomy 8:5).

> 'Blessed is the man whom God corrects;
> so do not despise the discipline of the Almighty'
> (Job 5:17).

> ' "My son, do not make light of the Lord's discipline,
> and do not lose heart when he rebukes you,
> because the Lord disciplines those whom he loves,
> and he punishes everyone he accepts as a son" '
> (Hebrews 12:5, 6).

To submit to God's discipline is nothing less than an act of worship – a recognition of his right to deal with us as he wishes, and of his rightness in doing so.

There are two extraordinary examples of this in the Old Testament. The first concerns Eli, who was the priest at Shiloh. His two sons, Hophni and Phinehas, served in the temple but were guilty of the most appalling sin, sin in which their father shared because of his failure to restrain them. Divinely inspired, Samuel forecast a terrible visitation from God, during which both of Eli's sons would be killed in one day. When he heard this, Eli replied, 'He is the Lord; let him do what is good in his eyes' (1 Samuel 3:18). We can hardly commend Eli for conniving at his sons' blasphemous behaviour, but what a remarkable response to the Lord's hand of discipline upon him!

The other example is Job, a man 'blameless and upright' and who 'feared God and shunned evil' (Job 1:1). Yet his integrity was no proof against pain and in one terrible day he lost all of his vast flocks and his ten children died in a hurricane. Job's response to the news was staggering:

> 'At this, Job got up and tore his robe and shaved his head. Then he fell to the ground in worship and said:
> "Naked I came from my mother's womb,
> and naked I shall depart.
> The Lord gave and the Lord has taken away;
> may the name of the Lord be praised"'
> (Job 1:20, 21).

And the Bible adds with great significance to the point we are making here, 'In all this, Job did not sin by charging God with wrongdoing' (Job 1:22). In other words, he submitted to his disciplines, even to the point where he could mingle praises with his tears.

I remember speaking to Czechoslovakian pastors who had been imprisoned during the era of Stalin in Moscow and Novotny in Prague and they told me, 'In prison, we learned not to ask "Why?" but just to say, "Praise the Lord".' Can we begin to match the submission of Eli or Job or those brave believers in Eastern Europe? Our circumstances may never match theirs, but life does have its disciplines, and we must face up honestly to the question in Josiah Conder's great hymn:

> The Lord is King! Who then shall dare
> Resist his will, distrust his care,
> Or murmur at his wise decrees,
> Or doubt his royal promises?

Is it not simply and sadly true that we often moan and groan at the slightest inconvenience, difficulty or restriction?

Too often we chafe and complain at even the minor disciplines of life. We can all shout, 'Praise the Lord!' when the sun is shining and the sky is blue, but when difficulties come into our lives, then we begin to complain, to grow bitter and even at times to doubt whether God is in control of our circumstances. To do that sort of thing is to despise the discipline of the Almighty.

We must submit to his demands. This hardly needs saying in view of all that has gone before, but one scriptural illustration will pinpoint the principle. When the wine ran out at the wedding feast at Cana, the servants must have been at their wits' end, but the mother of Jesus knew where the answer lay: 'Do whatever he tells you' (John 2:5). There is the very essence of submitting to God, which is immediate, wholehearted, unquestioning obedience to all of God's revealed will for you. There is a great deal of the will of God for your life that is obviously unknown to you at this moment – it lies in the future – and there is therefore no practical way in which you can submit to it. But there are things that God *has* revealed to you in your life and the crucial question is whether at this moment you are consciously obedient to that which God has revealed to you through his Word, by his Spirit, through the fellowship and counsel of other Christians, or in some other way.

In all of this, we have been looking at the first requirement for victorious Christian living: 'Submit yourselves, then, to God.'

2. *'Resist the devil.'* The verb here is the Greek *antistete*, a military term that literally means 'take your stand against', and there are two things about it that are particularly important in grasping its significance here. The first is that it is a *defensive* word. This comes across clearly when Peter writes, 'Your enemy the devil prowls around like a roaring lion looking for someone to devour. *Resist* him, standing firm in the faith . . .' (1 Peter 5:8, 9). The Christian never has to pick a fight with the devil, because the devil is constantly attacking him. The Christian was born a child of the devil and an enemy of God; at his conversion he became a child of God and an enemy of the devil. The Christian is a marked man, always in the devil's sights; his responsibility is to resist.

The second point to make about the word 'resist' is that it is *active* and not passive. It is defensive, but not docile! 'Let go and let God' may be a comfortable-sounding cliché used in certain circles, but it has no part in the biblical doctrine of sanctification. An army does not assume an effective defensive formation by lying around doing nothing; nor can a Christian effectively resist the devil without earnest effort. As someone has rightly said, 'A godly life is characterized by its conflicts with sin.'

It is no coincidence that the command to 'resist the devil' comes immediately after the words: 'Submit yourselves, then, to God.' Consecration and conflict go together, and the greater your determination to submit to God, the greater will be the intensity of the enemy's opposition. If you are content to be a careless, slipshod kind of Christian, then the devil will not need to waste much powder and shot on you, but if you are determined to comply with the Word of God, consecrate yourself to the will of God and commit yourself to the work of God, then the devil will attack you again and again. As Paul puts it, 'Everyone who wants to live a godly life in Christ Jesus will be persecuted' (2 Timothy 3:12). The godly Christian spends his life in an arena, not in an armchair.

Then we need to remember that we are to resist him all along the line. We are to resist his *arguments,* for they are always dishonest. When we realize that in his first recorded words – in Genesis 3 – the devil disputed the truth of God's words, it is hardly surprising that Jesus said of him, 'When he lies, he speaks his native language'(John 8:44). We are to resist his *attractions*, for they are always deceptive. Paul warns us that there are times when the devil 'masquerades as an angel of light' (2 Corinthians 11:14) and this is true in matters of belief and behaviour. There is something satanically attractive about false teaching, while his promises of liberty in the realm of morals and ethics lead only to slavery and corruption. Our resistance, then, must be total. But how are we to resist him? The Bible gives us several clear directions, all of them essential as we face the enemy.

The first is *to know his tactics.* Paul was able to write to the Corinthians, 'We are not unaware of his schemes'

(2 Corinthians 2:11). The context concerned a scandalous sin committed by a member of the church at Corinth, who had been excommunicated some time earlier. Paul said that the offender had now suffered sufficient punishment and ought to be restored to fellowship in a spirit of love. He then added the assurance of his own forgiveness, 'in order that Satan might not outwit us' (2 Corinthians 2:11). He knew perfectly well that if hatred of the offender's abominable sin had festered into unforgiving hatred of the man himself, then Satan would have achieved a great victory. The lesson is that our minds need to be stored with the recorded biblical history of the tactics, devices and arguments which Satan has used down the years.

The second is *to take decisive action.* Writing to the Ephesians, Paul says, 'Do not let the sun go down while you are still angry, and do not give the devil a foothold' (Ephesians 4:26, 27). The argument is somewhat similar to the previous one. To have a grievance is one thing, but to nurse it is to make it grow into something bigger and therefore something worse. Sins seldom go alone; with terrible certainty one leads to another. The other sense in which we are to prevent the devil getting a foothold is by carefully avoiding things, places or situations that bring obvious pressures at our personal points of weakness. Remember that the devil knows where your Achilles heel is.

The third is *to wear the armour God has provided.* The axiomatic teaching on this is, of course, to be found in Ephesians 6 and should be studied in depth by every Christian. To do so here would require another volume, but let us just remind ourselves of the words as they stand: 'Put on the full armour of God so that you can take your stand against the devil's schemes. For our struggle is not against flesh and blood, but against the rulers, against the authorities, against the powers of this dark world and against the spiritual forces of evil in the heavenly realms. Therefore put on the full armour of God, so that when the day of evil comes, you may be able to stand your ground, and after you have done everything, to stand. Stand firm then, with the belt of truth buckled around your waist, with the breastplate of righteousness in place, and with your feet fitted with the readiness that comes from the gospel of peace. In addition to all this, take up the shield of faith, with which you can extinguish all the flaming arrows of the evil one. Take the helmet of salvation and the sword of the Spirit, which is the word of God. And pray in the Spirit on all occasions with all kinds of prayers and requests' (Ephesians 6:10–18).

These, then are the two requirements. We are to submit ourselves to God and we are to resist the devil. Only then will we be able to claim the promise in the second part of the verse we have been studying.

2. The result
'. . . he will flee from you'.

Although we have approached this point very slowly, the promise is still there in plain, straightforward language: 'He *will* flee from you'! There are three important inferences we can draw from these exciting words.

1. The devil is vulnerable. In his book *The Invisible War*, Donald Grey Barnhouse has a section on 'The ignorance of Satan' in which he argues that although the devil is 'the wisest creature ever to come from the Word of God' and has 'retained the wisdom of Lucifer, in a perverted sense, he most certainly is not omniscient'. Barnhouse goes on to say that there are at least two things Satan does not know: 'He does not know what goes on within the mind and heart of man, and he does not know the future.' Whether or not one agrees with the examples Barnhouse gives, he is surely right to speak of 'the ignorance of Satan'. There are things Satan does not know and there are things he cannot do. That makes him vulnerable! He is strong, but not supreme; he is potent but he is not omnipotent. He can be beaten back, forced to give ground. He is vulnerable!

2. We must be vigilant. After describing his temptation of Jesus in the desert, Luke records that 'When the devil had finished all this tempting, he left him until an opportune time' (Luke 4:13). Faced with the devastating impact of the Word of God, the devil turned and ran. But notice that it was a temporary retreat, not a permanent defeat. It was a strategic withdrawal; later, he could attack again. As Christians we have the Bible's promise that the day will come when God will 'crush Satan under your feet' (Romans 16:20), but that will not happen during our earthly lifetime. William Grimshaw once said, 'I expect to lay down my life and my sword together,' and the Christian must maintain constant and concentrated vigilance if he is to avoid a constant succession of damaging wounds and to know anything of the personal experience of the promise contained in this verse.

3. We can be victorious. In our lifelong conflict with the devil we are to be defensive but not defeatist. Many of today's protest songs are variations on the theme 'We shall overcome some day.' Sometimes, depending on the cause being championed, that hope sounds so vague, so improbable and so far distant. The Christian, on the other hand, is able to say, 'I *can* overcome *today*.' We can be 'more than conquerors through him who loved us' (Romans 8:37). We *can* be victorious, we can know the joy of temptation overcome, of new heights gained, progress made, victories achieved. And when we do, let us remember to give all the praise to God. For God to defeat the devil demonstrates his greatness; for God to enable us to defeat him demonstrates his grace.

Charles Wesley gives us just the words with which to close this study:

> Jesu's tremendous Name
> Puts all our foes to flight:
> Jesus the meek, the angry Lamb,
> A Lion is in fight.
> By all hell's host withstood,
> We all hell's host o'erthrow;
> And conquering them, through Jesu's blood,
> We still to conquer go!

31.

The Christian's walk with God

> *'Come near to God and he will come near to you. Wash your hands, you sinners, and purify your hearts, you double-minded. Grieve, mourn and wail. Change your laughter to mourning and your joy to gloom'* (James 4:8, 9).

There are two views the Christian ought to covet more than any other: one is the devil's back and the other is God's face – and James promises that he can enjoy both! At the end of verse 7 he writes, 'Resist the devil, and he will flee from you'; now he adds, 'Come near to God and he will come near to you.'

In studying the last section of this epistle, we saw the need to submit ourselves to God – to his doctrines, disciplines and demands. Yet we must remember that the Christian life is not a matter of slavishly following a set of rules or a code of conduct, but of developing an intimate, personal relationship with the living God. The two verses now before us tell us four things that should characterize the Christian's walk with God; three of them stated by way of commandments and one in the nature of a promise.

1. Communion

'Come near to God (v. 8).

As these words are written to Christians, we might usefully take a moment to clear away two possible areas of difficulty arising from these words.

Do not be puzzled. Taking the words at their face value, an untaught Christian might well ask, 'Why am I being told to come near to God? Surely I have already done that? That was how I became a Christian. I was "brought near through the blood of Christ" (Ephesians 2:13). Why am I being asked to come near to God?' The answer is that the Bible is prolific in the number of pictures it paints and the analogies it draws to describe the Christian's position. For example, Paul tells us that a Christian is 'in Christ' (2 Corinthians 5:17), but elsewhere he speaks of 'Christ in you, the hope of glory' (Colossians 1:27). At first glance, those two statements seem to contradict each other – but each is perfectly accurate and holds a wealth of spiritual truth for the believer. To illustrate the point in another way, the Bible describes the church as 'the bride, the wife of the Lamb' (Revelation 21:9); elsewhere it speaks of 'the church, which is [Christ's] body' (Ephesians 1:22, 23); and in another place says of Christians that 'Jesus is not ashamed to call them brothers' (Hebrews 2:11). Now in human terms, those titles are mutually exclusive. You cannot at one and the same time, or indeed at any time, be a person's bride, body and brother! Yet each of these statements is gloriously true. So we need not be puzzled by being commanded as Christians to 'come near to God'. It has a meaning, as we shall see.

2. *Do not be presumptuous.* The very fact that we are commanded as Christians to 'come near to God' should teach us a very clear lesson, and that is that we have a constant need to do so. We are not to assume that because we belong to a sound church, read the Bible every day and pray regularly, we are automatically walking closely with the Lord. It is possible to be diligent in our religion and distant in our relationship. Take the illustration of marriage again. The marriage itself takes place in a moment of time, but that marriage bond will need to be cultivated or the relationship will cool. So in the Christian life we need to 'draw near to God with a sincere heart in full assurance of faith' (Hebrews 10:22), and we need to do so continually. As Thomas Manton puts it, 'Drawing nigh to God is not the duty of an hour . . . but the work of our whole lives.' Not least in the context of his lifelong battle against the world, the flesh and the devil, every Christian needs to pray daily in the spirit of Leila Morris's hymn:

Nearer, still nearer, close to thy heart,
Draw me, my Saviour, so precious thou art;
Fold me, Oh, fold me close to thy breast,
Shelter me safe in that haven of rest!

2. Cleansing

'Wash your hands, you sinners, and purify your hearts, you who are double-minded' (v. 8).

As with the previous phrase, these words can obviously be applied to people who are unsaved, but again we must see them as being addressed to those who were already Christians. James's use of the word 'sinners' implies, however, that they were Christians living sub-standard lives. They were saved by grace, but sinners by disgrace, and James urgently calls them back to an obedient walk with God.

James's language here is almost identical with that used by David when he asks,

'Who may ascend the hill of the Lord?
   Who may stand in his holy place?
He who has clean hands and a pure heart . . .'
(Psalm 24:3, 4).

Here is a principle written on every page of Scripture: as far as a man's relationship with God is concerned, there can be no communion without cleansing. James now emphasizes the fact by pinpointing two serious defects.

1. Dirty hands. 'Wash your hands . . .' This has nothing to do with personal hygiene! It is a reference to the actions performed by the Old Testament priests, who before entering the tabernacle went through an elaborate ritual of washing their hands in the sight of the people. This was an unmistakable visual aid, showing that no man could enter into God's holy presence with dirty hands, that is to say, with unconfessed sin. The same principle remains true today, and it is interesting to notice that Paul uses the same imagery of the hands when dealing with the subject of prayer: 'I want men everywhere to lift up holy hands in prayer, without anger or disputing' (1 Timothy 2:8). The crucial point here is not that the hands must literally be raised in the air. There is biblical warrant for praying in numerous physical positions, but no particular merit is claimed for any of them. The all-important word is 'holy' – the person seeking to draw near to God must do so in a spirit of confession and repentance. Better to pray with your hands hanging down but with a penitent heart than to wave them around in some kind of superficial ecstasy and to have unconfessed sin nullifying it all. Paul is not calling for a physical performance but for spiritual penitence; his point is not that you should lift up your hands, but that your hands should be holy, in other words that your sin should be confessed.

Incidentally, the Bible's usual word for 'confess' comes from two words meaning 'same' and 'speak'. To confess sin to God is to speak about it in the same way that he does, to call it by the same name. We are right to insist on the glorious truth of justification by faith, but we dare not forget that God is concerned about particulars. It is so easy to pray, 'O God, forgive my sins!' and to leave it at that, but we dare not be content with wrapping up our confession in generalities. We sin in particular, specific ways. There are specific words we speak, specific things we do, specific thoughts that pass through our minds, and it is only as 'we confess our sins' that we will be able to claim God's gracious promise that he will 'forgive us our sins and purify us from all unrighteousness' (1 John 1:9).

2. Divided hearts. '. . . and purify your hearts, you who are double-minded.' This speaks not so much of outward actions as of inward affections, and shows us something of James's deep understanding of life. He begins by speaking about the 'hands' – outward, individual, specific sins; but then reaches into men's 'hearts', where the real source of the trouble lies. Jesus taught that 'Out of the heart come evil thoughts, murder, adultery, sexual immorality, theft, false testimony, slander' (Matthew 15:19), which is precisely why the Bible says, 'Above all else, guard your heart, for it is the wellspring of life' (Proverbs 4:23). I find so often when counselling people in spiritual need that the trouble lies not so much in specific sins but rather in the depths of an unspiritual attitude. James describes it as being 'double-minded', a word only he uses (here and at 1:8). The Greek word is *dipsuchoi*, which literally means 'having two souls'. The picture is not of an out-and-out, unconverted sinner, but of a Christian who finds himself constantly torn in his affections between God and the world. Yet that is nothing less than what Alec Motyer calls 'the sin of being two-faced with God', and James insists that it must be rooted out, that the heart must be cleansed, consecrated.

It was precisely at the moment when the devil was trying to divide his heart that Jesus reminded him of God's fundamental requirement to 'worship the Lord your God, and serve him only' (Matthew 4:10). Here is a clear command to yield God our undivided allegiance, and it is the bedrock upon which all the rest of the Bible's commands are based. Yet we must add a necessary word of caution here. In urging people to commit themselves unreservedly to the Lord, some preachers thunder out this kind of challenge: 'Are you 100% for God?', or 'Are you 100% for Christ?' Whenever I hear that kind of thing I must say that I cringe, not because I know the sad answer I must give, but because the question is unbiblical. The Christian life is not a matter of percentages; it is a living, growing relationship, and because one of the partners is fallible then it is an imperfect relationship and will remain so until both partners are united in heaven. If you fail to grasp this you will find yourself in an area of 'perfectionism' that will prove cruelly damaging to your Christian health and growth.

Nevertheless, we need to be sure that we do not have divided hearts, that we are continually coming to the Lord in the spirit of these words by Frances Ridley Havergal:

> Jesus, Master, whose I am,
> Purchased thine alone to be;
> By thy blood, O spotless Lamb,
> Shed so willingly for me;
> Let my heart be all thine own,
> Let me live to thee alone.

3. Concern

'Grieve, mourn and wail. Change your laughter to mourning and your joy to gloom' (v. 9).

Whatever else we may discover to be true about this phrase,

it is certainly a long way removed from the spirit of the age in which we live. 'Eat, drink and be merry for tomorrow you die,' is for many the whole philosophy of life. We live in an age in which the pursuit of pleasure has become a social obsession. For an increasing number of people, the selfish pursuit of enjoyment is taking up more and more time, energy, money and concern. But the phrase is also a long way removed from a widespread emphasis in some Christian circles today where the all-important goals are joy, peace and happiness, where it is a sin not be singing all the time, where a man's standard is measured by his smile and his godliness by his grin, and it is almost the unforgivable sin not to be bubbling over in the prescribed manner. Yet this sort of thing can be so superficial and unreal. The Christian life is happy, but not funny.

On the other hand this verse is not a call to a morbid misery, nor is it a blanket prohibition on pleasure, or the enjoyment of life. The Bible nowhere takes that line. Speaking of God delivering his people from captivity, David wrote, 'Our mouths were filled with laughter, our tongues with songs of joy' (Psalm 126:2) and Bildad promised Job: '[God] will yet fill your mouth with laughter and your lips with shouts of joy' (Job 8:21). The Christian who can never smile, never have a happy sense of enjoyment, is missing a dimension of life God intends him to have.

Then what does James mean? Although there are no less than five separate injunctions in this verse, it may be that James is basically saying just one general thing, and that is that if we are to walk closely with God our approach to life will be characterized by a seriousness that we can rightly call *concern.* This concern will cover many areas, both of our own lives and the lives of others. Here are some of them.

1. Unrepented sin. Remember that this whole section of the epistle is being directed to Christians who are out of step with God, to backslidden believers. One of the surest signs that a Christian is in that state is when he treats sin carelessly and, if he ever gets around to confessing it, does so in a mechanical, unfeeling way in which there is no true spirit of repentance. What a contrast James calls for! Take the vivid expressiveness of his first three words, for instance.

'Grieve' is the Greek *talaiporesate*. This is the only place in the New Testament where the verb occurs, but Paul uses the same root when he cries out, 'What a *wretched* man I am! Who will rescue me from this body of death?' (Romans 7:24.) This helps us to understand the meaning of the word, because Paul is clearly groaning under the burden of indwelling sin. 'Mourn' is the Greek *penthesate*, and is exactly the word we use for the kind of sorrow that surrounds death. 'Wail' is the Greek *klausate*, the word we would use for the outward weeping of a broken-hearted mourner. Taken together, these words call for a deep, broken-hearted sorrow for sin. Do they find any place in your life? When did you last groan, mourn and weep over a particular sin, your lukewarmness of heart, your divided affections? Thomas Manton calls this 'a holy exercise, by which the soul is every day more and more weaned from sin, and drawn out to reach after God'. In this sense, surely every Christian's life should be marked by a deep concern.

2. Unrecognized sovereignty. Frederick and Arthur Wood, the founders of the National Young Life Campaign, were walking through a town one day when they were engulfed by a crowd of young people coming in the opposite direction. When they finally emerged through the crowd, Arthur noticed that there were tears in his brother's eyes. 'Why are you crying?' he asked. Frederick hung his head and said slowly, 'They don't know my Saviour.' He was not judging them harshly, but there was something about their behaviour, their language, their attitude that convinced that sensitive man of God that they were unbelievers, that they were lost. When did you last weep over anyone who did not know your Saviour? When was there last a single tear in your eye over one person dead in trespasses and sins? When did you last weep with concern over someone within your own home, someone in your family, someone with whom you work, someone with whom you mix socially and who is away from God and but for a miracle of divine grace will spend eternity in hell? You may say that you care, you may pass on literature, you may witness to them, you may do all the outward things, but is your heart breaking with concern? Can we honestly say that we are walking with God when we have no concern for the lost, who do not recognize their rightful Sovereign? David was able to say, 'Streams of tears flow from my eyes, for your law is not obeyed' (Psalm 119:136). Can we say that? Of course, even in its lawlessness the world has its laughter, but can the Christian share in it? Much of the world's humour today is drawn from drunkenness, immorality, crime in general and blasphemy. The world laughs at these things, makes fun of them. Can the Christian happily join in? The man who gets his humour from the world does not give honour to the Lord.

Not only should the Christian mourn over the Lord's unrecognized sovereignty in the world, but he should mourn when he sees the same thing in the church. Paul was able to write to the church leaders of his day, 'Remember that for three years I never stopped warning each of you night and day with tears' (Acts 20:31). The apostle was concerned for the church's welfare to the point of weeping. Have we any tears for the church today? Are we broken-hearted when we see it split by heresy, crippled with compromise and torn by carnal divisions that show that Christ is not recognized as its Sovereign?

3. Unrelieved suffering. This is not directly stated in the text, but the ever-practical James would surely approve of us drawing it into the general need for seriousness and concern in the Christian's life. As I was writing these very words, news came through of a plane crash in Spain, with over a hundred British holidaymakers perishing on a lonely mountain. It was a dramatic reminder to me that we live in a world of pain, sorrow, tragedy, agony, disease and disaster – in other words a world of unrelieved suffering. But do we care? Do we see all suffering as being the ultimate result of man's original sin? Are we concerned about 'man's inhumanity to man', about injustice and oppression? The Bible tells us that we are to 'mourn with those who mourn' (Romans 12:15); can we say that we are walking closely with the Lord when we have no tears for a suffering world? As R. V. G. Tasker puts it, 'The mourning of penitence and the sorrow of sympathy must be among the Christian's most deeply felt emotions.'

4. Confidence

'. . . and he will come near to you' (v. 8).

So far, our study of this section has been cast in a negative mood, but we can end it on this positive note of confidence. Moses once told the people of Israel, 'What other nation is so great as to have their gods near them the way the Lord our God is near us whenever we pray to him?' (Deuteronomy 4:7) and that same truth runs like a vein of gold right through the Bible. 'The Lord is with you when you are with him. If you seek him, he will be found by you . . .' (2 Chronicles 15:2); 'Return to me, and I will return to you' (Zechariah 1:3; Malachi 3:7).

The Christian's walk can properly be described as communion; there will need to be continual cleansing; there should be genuine concern; but let us be no less certain that it can be a walk of joyful confidence, based on the unchangeable promise of God that 'The Lord is near to all who call on him, to all who call on him in truth' (Psalm 145:18). The aorist tenses James uses in this passage should help to teach us that when sin is confessed and forgiven that should be the end of the matter. If we have fulfilled the conditions on which God has promised to forgive a sin, we have no right to drag it back to life, worry over it and confess it all over again. Although we must always have a spirit of godly concern, we must not fall into the devil's trap and believe his deadly lie that we can never have a settled sense of forgiveness, cleansing and communion with God. We can! This is the radiant message shining through the solemn words in these two verses.

One of Basilea Schlink's books has the arresting title *Repentance – the joy-filled life.* That title captures so well what Jesus meant when he said, 'Blessed are those who mourn, for they will be comforted' (Matthew 5:4). Nothing can shake the truth of those words. As you seek to deepen your communion with God, as you seek his cleansing from every sin the Holy Spirit reveals to you, as you share a godly concern for the sin and suffering in people's lives, so you may walk the Christian way with confidence, knowing that as you come near to God he will come near to you.

32.

Humility

'Humble yourselves before the Lord, and he will lift you up' (James 4:10).

One of the greatest theologians in the history of Christendom was undoubtedly Aurelius Augustinius, better known as St Augustine, who was converted in the year 387 and later became Bishop of Hippo in North Africa. One of his memorable sayings was this: 'For those who would learn God's ways, humility is the first thing, humility is the second, and humility is the third.' That may at first sound like an unwarranted exaggeration, but it is surely an echo of these words in the Old Testament:

'[God] has showed you, O man, what is good.
 And what does the Lord require of you?
To act justly *and to love mercy*
 and to walk humbly with your God'
(Micah 6:8).

The words I have emphasized pinpoint a truth found throughout the Bible, namely that the only way in which a man can walk closely with God is to walk humbly with him. As Dennis Tongue puts it in *The New Bible Dictionary*, 'The emphasis placed on pride, and its converse humility, is a distinctive feature of biblical religion unparalleled in other religions or ethical systems.' It should therefore be no surprise to find James referring to humility in a section which directly concerns the Christian's walk with God, and he does so by means of a principle and a promise.

1. The principle that is stressed
'Humble yourselves before the Lord'.

In the course of his epistle, James makes many references, both directly and indirectly, to the merit of humility and the menace of pride. The point to notice here is how the principle of humility is stressed.

1. In a straightforward manner. 'Humble yourselves . . .' With the ultimate economy of words, James gets straight to the point. There is no beating about the bush; no exceptions are made; no excuses tolerated; no alternatives accepted. 'Humble yourselves,' he says, 'get down from your pedestal! Cross out the capital "I"!' I wonder whether there are two words in all the New Testament epistles we need more than these. If we were to remove all the texts which festoon our houses and replace them by the two words, 'Humble yourselves', so that when we sat down to a meal, or to talk to other people, or went into the study to work, we were faced with those same two words, what an impact they might have! Certainly if they were obeyed they would revolutionize our homes, our churches, our Christian service, indeed the whole of our lives.

Many years ago there was a famous correspondence in *The Times* under the subject 'What is wrong with the world today?' The best letter of all was also the shortest and read: 'Dear Sir, I am, Yours faithfully, G. K. Chesterton.' That devastating declaration showed a profound insight into man's universal malaise and I believe that it can teach us a deeply challenging lesson. I am convinced that throughout the Christian church there are problems, difficulties and frustrations that would begin to dissolve immediately if only some Christians would be honest enough to answer the question: 'What's wrong?' with the words, 'I am'!

Coming as they do in a passage which speaks of the need for a continuous attitude of repentance and faith, perhaps the first thing James's words do is to remind us that even these must not be tainted with pride. The reason, of course, is that both repentance and faith are gifts. Peter told the authorities at Jerusalem that God had raised Jesus from the dead and 'exalted him to his own right hand as Prince and Saviour that he might *give* repentance and forgiveness of sins to Israel' (Acts 5:31), while Jesus said plainly that

'No one can come to me unless the Father has *enabled* him' (John 6:65). Repentance and faith are graces we have received, not goals we have achieved.

And the same principles hold true as we move on in the Christian life. While we should certainly be growing in knowledge, maturity, power and usefulness, we should never be proud of our progress. The very fine balance here is seen perfectly in Paul's testimony to the Corinthians: 'By the grace of God I am what I am' (1 Corinthians 15: 10). He could not deny that his life had been changed, but he could claim no credit for it. The growth had been by grace.

There is yet another important truth that emerges from James's straightforward treatment of the subject, and that is that the original Greek word – *tapeinothete* – is in the passive voice, which means that its literal translation is 'be humbled'. Grammatically, the point is that the power to bring about this humbling comes from outside of ourselves, that is from God; practically, the point is that we cannot even boast of our humility! Humility is a gift of God, the gracious work of the Holy Spirit in our hearts.

That is the general teaching inherent in James's command, 'Humble yourselves,' and as I have already hinted, there is no part of life in which it is not relevant. Yet perhaps there is one area in particular in which its message is constantly needed and that is the realm of designated Christian service. The Christian church is bulging at the seams with organizations, committees, councils, boards and offices, and, the human heart being what it is, men sometimes think more of the position they hold than of the Saviour they profess to serve. John wrote of Diotrophes that he 'loves to be first' (3 John 9). That was his main concern, to be in the forefront, to be noticed. He had an insatiable appetite for appreciation. Does that find a tragic echo in your own heart? What a contrast we find in the lives of men who were truly great! George Whitefield has been called 'the greatest preacher that England has ever produced', yet in 1771 Charles Wesley wrote of him:

Though long by following multitudes admired,
No party for himself he e'er desired;
His one desire, to make the Saviour known,
To magnify the Name of Christ alone.
If others strove who should the greatest be,
No lover of pre-eminence was he.

There would be a marvellous transformation within many of our Christian structures if that could be said of all who hold office within the church.

2. With a supreme motive. '. . . before the Lord'. The original word translated 'before' is *enopion* and carries the sense of having a thing or person in mind. The same word was used by Peter, when he quoted David as saying, ' "I saw the Lord always *before* me" ' (Acts 2:25). What Peter was telling the crowd at Jerusalem was that in the face of all his trials and troubles their great forefather was sustained by constant meditation on the presence and power of God. Here, James gives us the same motive for exercising a spirit of humility in all that we do.

People have sometimes written about 'practising the presence of God' and perhaps others have felt that that kind of phrase was too pietistic to be of any practical value. Yet surely there is nothing more practical in all the world than practising the presence of God? Perhaps we can best understand this if we think of God in terms of the Lord Jesus Christ. Now let me seek to apply James's words in the most personal and practical way possible, taking his word about holding the Lord in mind to mean exactly the same, in practical terms, as bearing in mind that he is present with you. Remember his presence in your home, when you sit down to a meal, switch on the television set, gather in conversation, open a book, speak about a person who is not there. Bear his presence in mind in your family relationships, with your husband, wife, parents or children. Remember his presence in your business life, when you transact that business, pick up the telephone, write that letter, drive that vehicle, operate that piece of machinery, handle those goods, deal with those people. Remember his presence in your relationships with your employer or employees. Then there is your church life. Remember his presence when you sit in church, teach that Bible Class, sit at that committee meeting, mount those pulpit steps. Can you catch the spirit of what James is saying? Dare you act arrogantly in any of these areas when *he* is there?

The whole issue is so serious, so searching, that perhaps a word of warning would be helpful. Some people may fear that to dwell too deeply on the Lord's continual presence is so overwhelming as to become demoralizing, frightening, depressing. The knowledge of their own weakness and their frequent failures might tend to drive them to despair. To such people, let me say that exactly the opposite should be the case! David was a man deeply conscious of his own weakness, yet in a psalm in which he specifically contemplated the fact that God knows his every word, thought and deed he wrote these words:

> 'Such knowledge is too wonderful for me,
> too lofty for me to attain.
> Where can I go from your Spirit?
> Where can I flee from your presence?
> If I go up to the heavens you are there;
> if I make my bed in the depths, you are there.
> If I rise on the wings of the dawn,
> if I settle on the far side of the sea,
> even there will your hand guide me,
> your right hand will hold me fast'
> (Psalm 139:6–10).

David did not despair at the Lord's presence, he delighted in it, for he knew that the Lord was there to strengthen and sustain him. That positive note takes us on to the second part of our verse.

2. The promise that is stated
'. . . and he will lift you up.'

A brief look at these precious words exactly as they occur will show us that the promise is stated in four specific ways.

1. In provisional terms. '. . . *and* he will lift you up.' The word 'and' is obviously the link with the first part of the verse and makes it clear that the promise is provisional. It is only to the humble. Martin Luther once said, 'It is God's nature to make something out of nothing, that is why he cannot make anything out of him who is not yet nothing.' Mark that! The reason some people are ineffective in their Christian service is that they are doing it in the energy of the flesh and with their own glory as the aim. There must be genuine humility of spirit before the promise of this verse can be claimed.

2. In powerful terms. '. . . and *he* will lift you up.' In practical terms, pride is so often an attempt to lift ourselves up. We so often want to justify ourselves, or prove ourselves to be superior in one area or another, even in the godly graces the Bible exhorts us to have. But there is no need for such pathetic behaviour. There is no need for this straining and striving; in fact they are folly, for God alone can lift us to a place of true spiritual exaltation. There is no point in the Christian resorting to worldly behaviour in order to 'get somewhere' in the church, or in life in general. The only places worth getting to are places to which only God has the power to lift us.

3. In positive terms. '. . . and he *will* lift you up.' Just as there is no escaping the condition, so there is no denying the promise, and it is one stated so often in Scripture that the problem is to know when to stop quoting! It is interesting to notice that on three separate occasions Jesus thrust home the point in almost identical terms, once in the context of salvation, once in the context of service and once in the context of social life. On the first occasion, he ended the story of the Pharisee and the tax collector by saying, 'For everyone who exalts himself will be humbled, and he who humbles himself will be exalted' (Luke 18:14). On the second occasion he told the ostentatious Pharisees who loved to parade their religion before others: 'For whoever exalts himself will be humbled, and whoever humbles himself will be exalted' (Matthew 23:12). On the third occasion he taught the wisdom of taking the lowest place when invited to a social occasion and added, 'For everyone who exalts himself will be humbled, and he who humbles himself will be exalted' (Luke 14:11). Here is one of the bedrock laws of the kingdom of God, and we ignore it at our peril.

4. In practical terms. '. . . and he will *lift you up*.' The original word translated 'lift you up' is *hupsei.* Figuratively it means to raise to a position of dignity and blessing, and as it is obviously meant in this sense we can apply it in two ways.

There is a blessing *at present*, that is to say in this present life. Sometimes that blessing is conscious and simultaneous. Paul's testimony was 'When I am weak, then I am strong' (2 Corinthians 12:10). The consciousness of his own weakness was matched by the certainty of God's strength; in other words the humility and the lifting up flowed together as a simultaneous experience. At other times, the outworking of the promise may be delayed for some divinely ordained reason, but it can never be denied. God's lifting up will follow our casting down. It is one of the self-governing principles of the grace of God. Someone has said, 'God's mercy seeks the guilty, his power the weak, his wisdom the ignorant and his love the lost.' To those great truths we can add this further one: God's grace seeks the humble. Just as water constantly pours itself into the lowest part of the earth that is accessible to it, so God pours his healing, strengthening, sanctifying grace into the lowly heart.

There is a blessing *in prospect*, that is to say in the future life. Matthew Henry once said, 'The highest honour in heaven will be the reward of the greatest humility on earth.' The Bible gives us the perfect illustration of this when it says,

> 'Your attitude should be the same as that of Christ Jesus:
> Who, being in very nature God,
> did not consider equality with God something to be grasped,
> but made himself nothing,
> taking the very nature of a servant,
> being made in human likeness.
> And being found in appearance as a man,
> *he humbled himself*
> and became obedient to death – even death on a cross!
> *Therefore God exalted him* to the highest place
> and gave him the name that is above every name,
> that at the name of Jesus every knee should bow,
> in heaven and on earth and under the earth,

> and every tongue confess that Jesus Christ is Lord,
> to the glory of God the Father'
> (Philippians 2:5–11).

Eternally co-equal with God the Father, Jesus humbled himself to share the frailties of human flesh and even to experience physical and spiritual death. But that amazing humility resulted in his exaltation 'to the highest place'. Now just as we cannot match his perfect humility, so we will never equal his unspeakable glory; throughout eternity he will remain the object of our praise and worship. Nevertheless, Scripture sets him before us as the supreme example of the truth it states so often.

Peter has a passage very similar to the words of James which we have been studying. He writes, 'Clothe yourselves with humility towards one another, because, "God opposes the proud but gives grace to the humble." Humble yourselves, therefore, under God's mighty hand, that he may lift you up in due time' (1 Peter 5:5). In some measure, that promise is fulfilled in the earthly lifetime of the humble Christian; in its fullest measure, God's 'due time' will come at the end of time, when those who have walked humbly with him on earth will receive their promised reward in heaven.

33.

Mind your language!

'Brothers, do not slander one another. Anyone who speaks against his brother, or judges him, speaks against the law and judges it. When you judge the law, you are not keeping it, but sitting in judgement on it. There is only one Lawgiver and Judge, the one who is able to save and destroy. But you – who are you to judge your neighbour?' (James 4:11, 12.)

In these two verses James returns to one of the major themes in his epistle – the use of the tongue. Dr James Moffatt suggests that these verses should come immediately after James 2:13, but I see no need to transplant them in this way. James could certainly switch to a totally different subject at this point, but it is surely not difficult to link this section directly on to what has gone before. After all, James has been writing about pride and humility and so often it is with our words that we betray the presence of one and the absence of the other. We justify ourselves by judging others; we seek to lift our reputation by lowering theirs and to promote ourselves by demoting them. Jesus told the story of the Pharisee and the tax-collector specifically to teach an important lesson to people who 'were confident of their own righteousness and looked down on everybody else' (Luke 18:9). For James to follow a passage on pride with teaching about the wrong use of the tongue seems perfectly natural. He does so by issuing one clear-cut commandment backed up by four reasons why it should be obeyed.

1. The commandment that is urged

'Brothers, do not slander one another' (v. 11).

The Greek verb translated 'slander' is *katalaleite*, which literally means to talk against other people in a disparaging way, with the intention of 'putting them down'. Now, of course, there is no suggestion here that we are prohibited from speaking about a fellow Christian, or even from pointing out some error or fault. What James is condemning is a spirit of negative criticism, a spirit of judgement and condemnation. The word also has woven into its meaning the thought of careless gossip, indulged in by those who have what has been called 'a keen sense of rumour'! It is also interesting to note that William Tyndale (and others who followed him) used the word 'backbite', with the obvious meaning of an injury caused when a person's back is turned, in other words, in his absence.

All of this gives the word sufficient colour to understand why it is so roundly condemned in the Bible. The people of Israel were told, 'Do not go about spreading slander among your people' (Leviticus 19:16). Paul feared that when he returned to the church at Corinth, he would find 'factions, slander, gossip, arrogance and disorder' (2 Corinthians 12:20) – and the grouping is not without significance! – while Peter urged his readers: 'Therefore, rid yourselves of all malice and all deceit, hypocrisy, jealousy and slander of every kind. Like newborn babies, crave pure spiritual milk, so that by it you may grow up in your salvation' (1 Peter 2:1, 2). In passing, notice Peter's point that even someone relatively young in the faith – 'a newborn babe'– should cut out that kind of behaviour. On a human level, quality of speech is one of the marks of a child's progress; a mother will joyfully announce that 'Johnny has begun to talk' or that 'Mary can now put a whole sentence together,' with the inference that the baby is making progress. So in Christian terms, the quality of our speech is often an indication of our spirituality – or lack of it.

There is another point we should make here. So often we say of our critical words: 'Of course there is nothing personal in this; it is a matter of principle.' Yet that is often a blatant lie. There *is* something personal in it. There is an intention to wound or weaken. Not only that, but there is the thinly veiled suggestion that we are guiltless in the thing we are condemning, so that, to use John Calvin's words, we are 'fondly exalting ourselves by calumniating others'.

All of this breeds one of the deadliest diseases in the Christian church, which is tale-bearing – the passing on of a juicy rumour or tantalizing titbit of gossip – something that has caused untold sorrow, harm and division. Yet there is decisive action we can take here. What would you do if someone passed on to you a counterfeit coin, one that had no commercial value? If you were honest, you would immediately take it out of circulation. You would not pass it on to someone else and transfer its uselessness to them. Then surely we should do the same with the kind of thing we have been examining here. We should take it out of circulation by refusing to pass it on. Nor is this merely a pious platitude. The Bible states very clearly that 'the accuser of our brothers' (Revelation 12:10) is one of the names attributed to the devil himself. This means that when a Christian passes on gossip or rumour about a fellow believer, or speaks about him in a way calculated to cause harm, he is guilty of nothing less than doing the devil's work for him. There can be little wonder that James warns us so strongly against all such behaviour.

2. The considerations that are used

'Anyone who speaks against his brother, or judges him, speaks against the law and judges it. When you judge the law, you are not keeping it, but sitting in judgement on it. There is only one Lawgiver and Judge, the one who is able to save and destroy. But you – who are you to judge your neighbour?' (vv. 11, 12.)

James now goes on to give four reasons, or considerations, why we should not slander our fellow Christians.

1. Because of the partnership it spoils. Notice James's use of the words 'brothers', 'brother' and 'neighbour' in this section. He is clearly appealing to his readers on the basis that they are bound together in a spiritual relationship or partnership and that malicious gossip and harsh criticism can only bring harm where there should be harmony. We dare not miss his message today. There is a shameful amount of slander that goes on within our Christian organizations today and the result is always marred relationships. The work may seem to go fairly well, there may be certain signs of blessing; but something essential and powerful is missing. What a desperate need there is for honest confession and wholehearted forgiveness in this whole area! It is interesting to notice how when Paul appeals to Christians to do nothing that offends a fellow believer, he refers to him as 'your brother for whom Christ died' (Romans 14:15) – a vivid reminder that Christians are blood brothers and that their relationship was formed at Calvary. What a tragedy when that relationship, that partnership, is spoilt by criticism, backbiting or rumour!

2. Because of the principle it smashes. 'Anyone who speaks against his brother or judges him, speaks against the law and judges it.' James's reference to 'the law' would seem to mean the law of God in general, but particularly what he had earlier described as 'the royal law found in Scripture, "Love your neighbour as yourself"' (2:8). In Mark 12:31, Jesus summed up God's requirements with regard to man's personal relationships by encapsulating the last six of the Ten Commandments in exactly the same words, and Paul underlined the point that in this one principle 'the entire law is summed up' (Galatians 5:14).

We can now see what James is getting at. 'The law' says we should love one another, that is act and speak in a way which aims at each other's blessing and welfare. But slander, gossip and negative criticism are all calculated to bring about the exact opposite and in engaging in these things we smash the principle the law of God lays down. The clear remedy is this: 'Do not let any unwholesome talk come out of your mouths, but only what is helpful for building up others according to their needs, that it may benefit those who listen' (Ephesians 4:29).

We also need to notice that the verb 'to speak against' which James uses twice here is the same one – *katalaleo* – translated 'slander' earlier in the verse, a reminder that it carries with it the sense of disparagement. What he is therefore saying is that the person who reads God's law of love and then deliberately disobeys it is virtually saying that the law is not worth obeying, that he can break it with impunity. There could hardly be a more devastating condemnation than that!

3. *Because of the prerogative it seizes.* 'When you judge the law, you are not keeping it, but sitting in judgement on it. There is only one Lawgiver and Judge, the one who is able to save and destroy.' The first of these two sentences continues the point James has just made. God's law has not been given for our opinion, but for our obedience. The man who does not set himself under the law of God sets himself above it. But James adds another powerful point to his argument: 'There is only one Lawgiver and Judge, the one who is able to save and destroy.' James is saying that if a man refuses to submit to the law, he is saying in effect that the law need not have been given and will not be enforced; but the only one with the right to decide what the law is, and to pass judgement on men's reaction to it, is God, and it is madness to act as if one could seize that prerogative from him. This is the kind of picture we have when the King of Syria sent Naaman to the King of Israel, asking him to get Naaman healed of his leprosy. On receiving the message, the King of Israel cried out, 'Am I God? Can I kill and bring back to life?' (2 Kings 5:7.) What he meant was that life and death were God's prerogatives, matters that were ultimately in his power alone. In bringing in this argument, James is reminding his readers of two things.

The first is *God's authority*: 'There is only one Lawgiver and Judge . . .' James lived, as we do now, in a structured society, with kings, rulers, presidents, ministers and public officers of many kinds, and the Christian's response to this situation is clearly laid down in Scripture: 'Everyone must submit himself to the governing authorities, for there is no authority except that which God has established. The authorities that exist have been established by God' (Romans 13). If God is the ultimate source of all lesser authorities, how dare we treat his law lightly?

The second is *God's ability*: '. . . the one who is able to save and destroy.' The *fact* of what James is saying here is beyond dispute. All of Scripture bears testimony to the fact that the eternal destinies of all men are in the hands of God. The *point* of what he is saying seems to be that if all judgement is ultimately in the hands of God, who are we to strut around picking and choosing which parts of God's law we will obey and passing our arrogant judgements on other people? Is there not something pathetic about people who act as if they have a personal responsibility to put the world straight? Let us beware of that and remember instead the words of the Lord Jesus: 'Do not judge, or you too will be judged. For in the same way you judge others, you will be judged . . .' (Matthew 7:1, 2).

4. Because of the presumption it shows. 'But you – who are you to judge your neighbour?' What exquisite use of sanctified sarcasm! Having spoken of God's sovereign authority and ability to judge the whole of humanity, James now questions a man's authority and ability to judge even one 'neighbour'! There are many reasons why we are disqualified for doing so. Let us close this particular part of our study by noting two of them.

The first is *our lack of perfect information.* It has been said that 'to know all is to forgive all', and I have often had to reverse my opinion about a person or situation on hearing the other side of the story. Even a High Court judge, with hundreds of pages of evidence before him, can be misled by false or incomplete evidence and there have been classic cases of miscarriage of justice. We run the same kind of risk when we pass hasty judgements on the basis of our limited knowledge. Warning people of this very thing, Paul wrote, 'Therefore, judge nothing before the appointed time; wait till the Lord comes. He will bring to light what is hidden in darkness and will expose the motives of men's hearts' (1 Corinthians 4:5).

The second is *our lack of personal integrity.* It is John who tells us the story of a woman caught in the act of adultery. In no time at all a crowd had gathered, ready to stone her to death. But when Jesus said, 'If any one of you is without sin, let him be the first to throw a stone at her' we read that 'Those who heard began to go away one at a time, the older ones first, until only Jesus was left . . .' (John 8:7–9). The inference was obvious: they recognized that they had forfeited their rights by their wrongs! As Dr Louis H. Evans asks, 'Is there that blamelessness in us, that purity of motive, that perfection, that overflowing charity, that love of the sinner that makes us like Christ and so qualifies us for unprejudiced judgement? James challenges us to a sense of humility in this whole area.'

Jesus drove home the same challenge in the Sermon on the Mount when he spoke of the incongruity of a man trying to remove a speck of dust from someone else's eye while a plank of wood was sticking out of his own. To set oneself up as a critic of other people betrays both arrogance and ignorance. As somebody once very cleverly put it, 'The critic who starts with himself will have no time to take on outside contracts'! The Bible's word to each one of us could not be clearer: 'Therefore let us stop passing judgement on one another'(Romans 14:13).

These verses have been necessary, but negative. They have told us what *not* to do. These words by James Whitcomb Riley will help us to grasp the other, obvious side of the truth that James has been teaching:

When over the fair frame of friend or foe
The shadow of disgrace shall fall; instead
Of words of blame, or proof of so and so,
Let something good be said!

No generous heart may vainly turn aside
In ways of sympathy; no soul so dead
But may awaken strong and glorified,
If something good be said.

And so I charge thee, by the thorny crown,
And by the cross on which the Saviour bled,
And by our own soul's hope for fair renown;
Let something good be said!

34.

D.V.

'Now listen, you who say, "Today or tomorrow we will go to this or that city, spend a year there, carry on business and make money." Why, you do not even know what will happen tomorrow. What is your life? You are a mist that appears for a little while and then vanishes. Instead, you ought to say, "If it is the Lord's will, we will live and do this or that." As it is, you boast and brag. All such boasting is evil' (James 4:13–16).

The longer I have studied James's writings, the more I have come to see the close integration of sections that appear at first glance to be totally disassociated, and these verses give us a good example of what I mean. The previous section we studied (vv. 11, 12) had to do with judging other people, with backbiting, criticism and rumour-mongering. The verses now before us seem to be addressed to businessmen planning their diaries, and there seems no obvious connection! But there is – the deadly sin of *pride*. In the earlier section, pride caused people to pronounce on the sins of other people; here, pride causes these men to presume upon their own lives. Two general headings will help us to grasp what James is saying.

1. The arrogance he condemns

'Now listen, you who say, "Today or tomorrow we will go to this or that city, spend a year there, carry on business and make money . . ." As it is, you boast and brag. All such boasting is evil' (vv. 13, 16).

The Jewish penchant for business is well known the world over and James undoubtedly had businessmen in mind here, but not all businessmen! He is not condemning industry and commerce out of hand. The Bible never condemns honest initiative, hard work or profit-making. James has only certain businessmen in mind and isolates them with the phrase beginning with the words: 'you who say . . .' We can safely assume that the words, 'you who say', refer to spirit as well as speech. Their words were outward signs of their whole attitude of life and that attitude was one of total arrogance. They strutted around as if they owned the place! The idea of failure, the thought that their plans might come unstuck, never entered their heads. They acted as if nothing could possibly come between them and the schemes they had worked out for the future. Notice the number of things that filled their minds.

1. The plan. 'Today or tomorrow . . .' Here were men looking into the future and making specific plans as to what was going to happen. As the father of a large family, I often listened to my children excitedly discussing some future event, such as a family holiday. As the day drew near, so they would get more and more enthusiastic about all the wonderful things they were going to do and any thought that their plans might come unstuck would never once enter their young heads. But the people to whom James was referring were not children; they were mature men, they were men of the world, men used to what are called the changes and chances of everyday life. They must have experienced ups and downs in the past, they must have known failure, frustration and disappointment at times and yet they went blithely on, planning their future without any thought that their plans might not materialize. Like others before them their attitude to life was 'Tomorrow will be like today, or even far better' (Isaiah 56:12).

2. The place. '. . . we will go to this or that city . . .' The original Greek is in fact more specific than this and a better translation would be 'this city'. We can imagine them poring over a map, discussing density of population, trade routes and other relevant factors before choosing one particular city for their next business venture. Travelling by train on one occasion, I remember a group of businessmen doing just this sort of thing. Their general language and behaviour told me that they were not Christians, but the particular thing that struck me about their conversation was their monumental arrogance. They spoke as if they ruled the world! They spoke about plans and projects, deals and developments as if nothing in the world could stop them happening. That is the kind of thing James is getting at here.

3. The period. '. . . spend a year there . . .' Although their lives hung on a heartbeat, they were confidently forecasting their activities twelve months ahead. The idea that their lives might be cut short before then, or that there might be an economic recession, or that some other factor might upset their timetable, never seems to have entered their heads. In Thomas Manton's words, their hearts were 'stupidly secure, and utterly insensible of the changes of providence'. Let us never be guilty of the same sin. We do have all the time in the world, but how much time does our world have?

4. The programme. '. . . carry on business . . .' Notice again how much was being taken for granted. They assumed they would have money to use, goods to sell, customers to charge. Remember that all these phrases are prefaced by the words 'we will'. There was no question about it! They were arrogantly confident not merely of spending time in a certain city, but of securing trade there. We can imagine them developing the details of just how they would persuade people to do business with them, confident that they had the know-how to handle them successfully.

5. The purpose. '. . . and make money.' This was clearly the whole object of the exercise. The plan, the place, the period and the programme all led up to this specific purpose — to make money. The particular Greek word used here is *kerdesomen.* The root noun is *kerdos*, which can mean not only making money but the love of making it. Peter speaks of those who were 'experts in greed' (2 Peter 2:14) and this is what James has in mind here. These men were not merely making prudent business arrangements; they had a passion for profit. Everything was geared to that one end.

Yet even their greed was not the fundamental flaw for which James condemned them. Their greatest sin was not that gain had too big a place in their lives, but that God had no place at all. The Bible tells us to walk humbly with God; these men chose to walk proudly without him. One phrase could sum up their whole existence – life with God left out. Yet that is the tragic truth about the majority of people in the world today. They are what I would call practical atheists. Let me illustrate what I mean. Some time ago I was speaking to several hundred schoolchildren. They were unusually restless and inattentive and in an attempt to get their attention, I suddenly asked them an apparently ridiculous question: 'Have you ever seen a pig saying grace before a meal?' There was a short burst of laughter and then a puzzled silence. 'Well,' I went on, 'what is your answer to the question? Give me the answer all together.' Needless to say, there was a universal roar of 'No!' 'Now', I went on quickly, 'let me ask you another question. Do *you* say grace before meals?' There was no laughter this time, just silence, which I broke by saying, 'Would you now answer that question all together?' Again it seemed that everyone in the building shouted out the same word: 'No!' 'Thank you,' I replied, 'that is of great help to me. You see, I have never been to this school before and I had no idea what kind of people you were. Now I know – you are on the same level as the pigs!' Shock tactics, if you like! But they worked, and from then on I had a close hearing, perhaps for the simple reason that, however reluctantly, those young people realized that what I had said was true. They were living life with God left out. As I had so bluntly put it, they were living like animals. They got up in the morning, washed (presumably!), ate their meals, did their work, enjoyed their play, met with their friends, went to bed at the end of the day, closed their eyes in sleep and did not give God one thought from beginning to end. That is life with God left out and Christians with a burden for the lost need to recognize that that is the experience of people all around them.

James clinches his condemnation of this kind of behaviour in verse 16: 'As it is you boast and brag. All such boasting is evil.' The particular words James uses are very significant. 'Boast' is the Greek *kauchasthe*, which is sometimes used in a good sense (Paul says that Christians are to '*boast* in the

Lord' (1 Corinthians 1:31), but here carries the meaning of loud-mouthed arrogance. 'Brag' is hardly the best word for the Greek *alazoneiais*, which is in the plural. The root of the word was originally used of a wandering charlatan and it carries with it the sense of making a false claim. Building all this into the context, James is accusing these men of boasting in their false assumption that even without God they are making a success of life. 'All such boasting', says James, 'is evil', and its greatest evil of all lay in the fact that it was quite literally godless.

It is instructive to notice that James says these things in the context of writing about a group of apparently successful businessmen, because it is often when things are going well that men tend to forget God. After painting a wonderful picture of the promised land that was before the children of Israel, Moses told them, 'When you have eaten and are satisfied, praise the Lord your God for the good land he has given you. Be careful that you do not forget the Lord your God . . . You may say to yourself, "My power and the strength of my hands have produced this wealth for me." But remember the Lord your God, for it is he who gives you the ability to produce wealth . . .' (Deuteronomy 8:10–18).

The Bible's warning is clear: when things are going well, beware lest you forget God! It is said that when Napoleon Bonaparte was considering invading Russia, a friend tried to dissuade him, saying, 'Man proposes, but God disposes.' Bonaparte's reply was 'I dispose as well as propose.' A Christian who heard of this said, 'I set that down as the turning-point of Bonaparte's fortunes. God will not suffer a creature with impunity thus to usurp his prerogative.' As all the world knows, that forecast was absolutely true. The Russian campaign marked the beginning of Napoleon's downfall. Man proposes, but God disposes. For us to go through life, or to conduct any part of our lives, without reference to God, smacks of arrogance, and arrogance is something that the Bible everywhere, and not least in the Epistle of James, condemns outright.

2. The attitude he commends

'Why, you do not even know what will happen tomorrow.

What is your life? You are a mist that appears for a little while and then vanishes. Instead, you ought to say, "If it is the Lord's will, we will live and do this or that"' (vv. 14, 15).

Having condemned the arrogance of these godless businessmen as being thoroughly evil, James goes on to show them the right attitude they ought to have to life, and he does so by drawing their attention to two things.

1. The point they ought to remember. 'Why, you do not even know what will happen tomorrow. What is your life? You are a mist that appears for a little while and then vanishes.' The simple point they seemed to forget was the brevity of life. They said, 'we will'; God said, 'you do not even know'. They planned for a whole year; God said they could not be sure of the next day. They thought they were independent; God said they were ignorant. All of this reflects what the Bible says elsewhere. As an Old Testament writer put it, 'Do not boast about tomorrow, for you do not know what a day may bring forth' (Proverbs 27:1) and just like James he linked the brevity of life with the folly of boasting.

The apostle now drives his point home with the simple but devastating question, 'What is your life?', which he answers with the vivid illustration: 'You are a mist that appears for a little while and then vanishes.' The Bible's pictures of life are numerous and luminous: 'Our days on earth are like a shadow' (1 Chronicles 29:15); 'My days are swifter than a weaver's shuttle' (Job 7:6); 'Remember, O God, that my life is but a breath' (Job 7:7); 'My days are swifter than a runner' (Job 9:25); 'You have made my days a mere handbreath' (Psalm 39:5); 'For my days vanish like smoke' (Psalm 102:3); 'My days are like the evening shadow; I wither away like grass' (Psalm 102:11); 'All men are like grass, and all their glory is like the flowers of the field; the grass withers, and the flowers fall . . .' (1 Peter 1:24). Even with all our civilization, sophistication and medication, life is brief and death is certain, and the Bible's statement that 'The length of our days is seventy years — or eighty, if we have the strength . . .' (Psalm 90:10) remains a remarkably accurate comment on the average span of life, with nearly a third of it gone by the time we reach the end of our teens.

There is really no need to illustrate James's illustration:

the point about a quickly-vanishing mist is unmistakable. The moment a man is born he begins to die, and that death could come about at any time, by design, disease, decay or disaster. Man is not here to stay; he is here to go! Yet James's word 'appears' is particularly interesting. In the original, it is *phainomene*, which could literally be translated 'shines', in the sense of attracting attention. The application now becomes even more pointed. A man's life may be full of show, noise, activity and boasting, but in a pathetically short time it is all over. In the words of Thomas Gray's famous elegy, 'The paths of glory lead but to the grave.'

Jesus spoke of a businessman who would have done well to remember that. Things were going so well on the farm that his barns were bursting at the seams. Brimming with confidence, he decided to pull them down, build bigger ones, get his bumper crop safely in. Then, with 'plenty of good things laid up for many years', he could afford to 'take life easy; eat, drink and be merry' (Luke 12:19). But he had forgotten the brevity of life, and God said to him, 'You fool! This very night your life will be demanded from you' (Luke 12:20). Here was a man more concerned with harvest than with heaven or hell. He was so busy with his accounts that he forgot he was accountable.

Life is not meant for self or for earthly gain. It is meant for God, for holiness and for heaven; and because it is so brief, so uncertain, so fragile, we should constantly ask God's help to 'number our days aright, that we may gain a heart of wisdom' (Psalm 90:12).

2. The providence they ought to recognize. 'Instead, you ought to say, "If it is the Lord's will, we will live and do this or that."' These men had left God out of their lives altogether; now notice how James brings him right into the centre of things. They could not even live, let alone do 'this or that', unless their living was in the providential will of God. Now of course James was not suggesting that they just sit back and do nothing. He was not condemning their business but their boasting; not their industry but their independence; not their acumen but their arrogance. What he is telling them is that the right attitude to life is to recognize that God is in sovereign control of it all, and that it should be yielded in humble submission to his divine will.

Two things about this attitude will help us to hold James's words in perspective.

The first is that *it is biblical.* The sovereignty of God is woven throughout the whole fabric of Scripture, but nowhere more clearly than where Paul says that God 'works out everything in conformity with the purpose of his will' (Ephesians 1:11). There are no accidents with God, no unforeseen circumstances, no surprises. God has a plan, not only for the world in general, but for individual lives. The writer of the Epistle to the Hebrews speaks of life as 'the race marked out for us' (Hebrews 12:1) and Paul says that Christians are 'God's workmanship, created in Christ Jesus to do good works, which God prepared in advance for us to do' (Ephesians 2:10). Nor was this mere theory on Paul's part. Although he was a man of intense dynamism and drive, he always recognized the providence of God which must overrule any plans of his own. 'I will come back', he promised the Christians at Ephesus, 'if it is God's will' (Acts 18:21). He wrote to the church at Rome, 'I pray that now at last by God's will the way may be opened for me to come to you' (Romans 1:10). He promised the Corinthians: 'I will come to you very soon, if the Lord is willing' (1 Corinthians 4:19) and 'I hope to spend some time with you if the Lord permits' (1 Corinthians 16:7). Even this human dynamo recognized that all his hopes and plans had to be stamped 'D.V.', *Deo Volente*, God willing! We dare not make any plans of our own in any other spirit. That is the first thing James says about the right attitude to life.

The second is that *it is beneficial.* This flows naturally from the fact that it is biblical. Here is God's answer to the fretting, the fury, the frenetic scrambling of our twentieth century. Jesus said, 'Do not worry about tomorrow, for tomorrow will worry about itself' (Matthew 6:34), while Paul added, 'Do not be anxious about anything' (Philippians 4:6), and those commands become sane rather than simplistic when we realize that it is pointless for us to be fretfully anxious about the future when that future is entirely in the hands of an all-wise God who has a loving concern for his people. To grasp this is to steer clear of two great dangers. One is planning recklessly without reference to God and the other is living carelessly in the hope that

'Things will all come right in the end.' Planning for the future is clearly sensible, but we should plan prayerfully. It is not enough to make our plans first and then ask God to bless them. We should seek God's will *before* we make our plans and act when we have an assurance that we are doing so according to his will. As Alec Motyer puts it, '[James] would have us empty our lives of proud planning which does not fear and bow to the will of God and submit all things to his ordering hand.' If we do, our lives will be marked by the conviction and confidence expressed by W. F. Lloyd in the words of this hymn:

My times are in thy hand,
My God, I wish them there;
My life, my friends, my soul I leave
Entirely to thy care.

My times are in thy hand,
Whatever they may be,
Pleasing or painful, dark or bright,
As best may seem to thee.

My times are in thy hand,
Why should I doubt or fear?
A Father's hand will never cause
His child a needless tear.

My times are in thy hand,
Jesus the crucified;
The hand my cruel sins had pierced
Is now my guard and guide.

My times are in thy hand;
I'll always trust in thee,
And after death at thy right hand
I shall for ever be.

35.

Knowing and doing

'Anyone, then, who knows the good he ought to do and doesn't do it, sins' (James 4:17).

To the casual reader, this verse may seem to be no more than an appendix to the chapter. Some might even go further and say that, like a physical appendix, it serves no useful purpose and could be removed without loss. Yet it is one of the most penetrating verses in the whole of the epistle. The basic lesson hardly needs any comment. If you know that a thing is right, but fail to do it, then you have committed a sin of omission. Much more lies beneath the surface, as we shall discover, but before going into its detail, notice that this is a very telling verse in what we could call the 'sinless perfection' issue. It strikes a mortal blow at the extreme viewpoint that says it is possible to live without sin of any kind. But this verse shows that in order to do so, a man would not only have to avoid doing everything that was sinful, he would *always* have to do *everything* that he knew to be good. I will begin to believe that doctrine when I meet someone who can testify to knowing that experience!

1. Establish the connection

First, let us establish the connection with the preceding verses. Some say that there is no connection at all, presumably inferring that James just dropped the words in at this point because he had nowhere better to put them — the kind of exegisis I find decidedly unsatisfying! Dr James Moffatt felt that another transplant was necessary and in his own translation put this verse after 2:21, an operation for which he had no reliable authority. Yet surely there is a connection. The word 'then' is the Greek *oun*, which could equally well be translated 'therefore', and on that basis alone we at least have a connection in the wording. But is there a connection of thought, of meaning? Does the teaching of this verse in any way flow in with what has gone before? I believe it does for the following reason.

In the preceding verses, James has been condemning the attitudes and actions of businessmen who planned their lives without any reference to God. They were not intellectual atheists, believing there was no God; they were practical atheists, behaving as if there was none and aggravating their sin by boasting in their success. Now that alone would give contextual meaning to what James is saying here in verse 17. These men were not totally ignorant pagans. They knew of the existence of God. They knew that life was brief. They knew that their powers were limited by providence, and to know these things but ignore them in practice was clearly sinful.

But there is another possibility that is equally valid. The phrase, 'the good he ought to do' reminds one of what Peter said of the Lord Jesus, that 'He went around doing good' (Acts 10:38). What a vivid contrast with these worldly businessmen! They must have known the difference between greed and generosity; they must have seen something of the poverty and need of others; they must have known something of their responsibility to give help where they could. In fact, the particular word 'knows' comes from the Greek root *oida* which means 'to know perfectly well'. Then surely that clinches the connection? Knowing perfectly well that they should make their plans with a consciousness of the providence of God and that they should share their wealth with those in need, these men persisted in their arrogant selfishness. That seems to me to establish the connection.

2. Emphasize the comparison

Next, let us see the comparison with the general drift of New Testament teaching. To begin with, this verse bears close comparison with other parts of the epistle. Here are some examples: 'Do not merely listen to the word, and so deceive yourselves. Do what it says' (1:22); 'faith by itself, if it is not accompanied by action, is dead' (2:17); 'As the body without the spirit is dead, so faith without deeds is dead' (2:26).

But this verse also fits into the wider teaching of the New Testament as a whole, where sins of omission are treated just as seriously as sins of commission. Notice the way Jesus castigated some of the religious leaders of his day: 'Woe to you, teachers of the law and Pharisees, you hypocrites! You give a tenth of your spices – mint, dill and cummin. But you have neglected the more important matters of the law – justice, mercy and faithfulness. You should have practised the latter, without neglecting the former' (Matthew 23:23). Jesus did not condemn them for the things they did, but for the things they neglected to do. The same principle is underlined in the parable of the talents. Before leaving on a journey, a man gave one of his servants five talents, another two and another one. On his master's return, the man who was given five talents was able to show an increase of five and was rewarded accordingly. The man with two talents had also made 100% profit and again his master was delighted to reward him. But the man given only one talent confessed that he did not use it at all; he just kept it buried for safety's sake. That man was roundly condemned, not for doing something wrong, but for failing to do something right. It was a sin of omission. The very next passage in Matthew 25 tells of the Day of Judgement, of the dividing of all men as 'sheep' and 'goats'. To the 'goats' God says, 'Depart from me, you who are cursed, into the eternal fire prepared for the devil and his angels' (Matthew 25:41). But why were they cast out? Had they committed murder, adultery, robbery or some such sin? No! They were condemned for the omission of good deeds. They gave the hungry no food, they gave the thirsty no drink, they gave the stranger no shelter, they gave the naked no clothing and they gave the prisoner no company. They were condemned for sins of omission.

In fact, we could go a step further than that. Everyone who ultimately misses heaven does so because of a sin of omission. Talking about his coming into the world to save sinners, Jesus said, 'Whoever believes in him is not condemned, but whoever does not believe stands condemned already because he has not believed in the name of God's one and only Son' (John 3:18). Again, here is a sin of omission – the sin of not believing. This whole question of sins of omission is not just a casual and unimportant one, something out of the circumference of biblical teaching. For the unbeliever it is literally a matter of life and death. For the Christian it is something that needs constant monitoring because, in R. V. G. Tasker's words, 'It is probably true to say that we more often leave undone the things we ought to have done than do the things we ought not to have done.' Throughout the Bible that is condemned as sin. Recognizing that, we can now turn to our third task in studying James's words.

3. Extend the context

This clearly needs to be done because while we have made out a case for establishing a connection between this verse and those preceding it and have noted its comparison with the general teaching of the New Testament, we dare not leave it without allowing it to speak to us in direct and specific terms. Question 14 in the Westminster Assembly's Shorter Catechism asks, 'What is sin?', and the answer given is 'Sin is any want of conformity unto, or transgression of, the law of God.' It is interesting to notice that the ancient divines who drew up this historic document gave such an important place to 'any want of conformity unto . . . the law of God', in other words to sins of omission, *any* of which were clearly defined as sin. With that principle in mind, it becomes a very salutary experience to take the Bible in one hand and a mirror in the other! Some years ago I read Dr W. E. Sangster's booklet *A Spiritual Checkup* on a day when I underwent a medical examination, and there is no doubt as to which was the more important – or the more painful! In extending the context of James's words, let me turn doctor and close this study by asking you whether in any of the following areas of your life there is a 'want of conformity', a sin of omission.

1. Prayer. When Jesus told the parable of the persistent widow, he did so for the specific purpose of teaching that we should 'always pray and not give up' (Luke 18:1).

Ignoring other possible defects in your prayer life for the moment, how do you measure up to that? Are you guilty of praying and giving up? What about that missionary for whom you promised to pray? Or that sick friend? Or that person's financial need? Or that church member's spiritual need? Or that unsaved friend, relative or neighbour? Have you given up praying for them? Jesus said we should 'always pray', not that we should be praying all the time, but that we should continue to pray and not give up and lose heart. We live in an age of short-term commitments, crash courses and push buttons. Have you lost out on the costly responsibility to keep on praying? Are you guilty of the sin of omission here?

2. Meditation on the Scriptures. I do not mean Bible reading, because I assume in normal circumstances that every Christian reads his Bible daily. But for too many people reading the Bible is just a daily ritual. It is formal, cold, mechanical. I believe that there would be a revolution in the life of the church if Christians made an honest examination in this particular area and had a fresh approach to the Scriptures altogether, one that led them to meditate on the Word of God and not just to read it. Dr A. T. Pierson once said, 'If you want to understand the Bible, get on your knees and read it on your knees; or if you do not literally search it on your knees, let your soul be bowed down before God. You will learn more in one hour of prayerful communion with the Spirit than in a thousand years in all the schools of human culture.' The psalmist says of the righteous man that 'His delight is in the law of the Lord, and on his law he meditates day and night' (Psalm 1:2). How much do you meditate on God's Word? Are you content merely to read it, or to study it in an academic way? George Swinnock linked these first two areas together and said, 'Meditation is the best beginning of prayer, and prayer is the best conclusion of meditation.' Failure to do either as we should is a sin of omission.

3. Relationships in the home. One of the most sinister elements in the malaise of our present-day society is the disintegration of family life. Much of it, of course, happens where all the members of the family are unbelievers, but Christian homes are by no means exempt and it would not be difficult to prove that much of the trouble is caused by sins of omission, members of the family failing to do what the Bible says they should do. We can see this by looking briefly at what someone has called 'The Bible's Ideal Home Exhibition' in Colossians 3, where Paul lays down the basic building blocks of a secure family life.

The ladies are mentioned first. Paul says, 'Wives, submit to your husbands, as is fitting in the Lord' (Colossians 3:18). We hear a great deal today about 'Women's Lib.' and the spirit of the world has infiltrated the home with disastrous results. For a woman to lead the home and dominate the marriage partnership is contrary to God's law. As we saw in an earlier study, there is no question here of the wife being inferior to the husband; she is his rightful equal, sharing with him all the glorious liberties granted to the Christian. As Bishop H. C. G. Moule has it, they are 'sacredly one'. Nevertheless, the wife's clear duty, and the greatest contribution she can make to the harmony of the home, is that of glad co-operation with the husband's divinely ordained leadership. If you are reading this as a wife, does this teaching find you out? Are you guilty of a sin of omission here?

Then Paul comes to the men, and says, 'Husbands, love your wives and do not be harsh with them' (Colossians 3:19). It is so easy for a husband to be unsympathetic towards his wife, to feel that her problems are so trivial by comparison with his. After all, he has to run the whole world, while she only has to worry about footling things such as the sink and the supermarket! Whole volumes could be written on this area of family life, but the general point is clear. Are you a husband? Then do you love your wife? Are you gentle, understanding, caring, sympathetic towards her and especially bearing in mind the multitude of day-to-day responsibilities that concern her? If not, you are guilty of a sin of omission.

Next come the younger members of the family, to whom Paul says, 'Children, obey your parents in everything, for this pleases the Lord' (Colossians 3:20). We seem to live in an age of restlessness and revolt and so often the seeds are sown in the home, with children flatly refusing to obey their parents' wishes. But revolting children are revolting!

And their behaviour strikes terrible blows at the harmony of the home. Does this apply to you? Are you refusing to submit to your parents' leadership and guidance? Then you are guilty of a sin of omission.

Then the parents come back into the picture and Paul says, 'Fathers, do not embitter your children, or they will become discouraged' (Colossians 3:21). The word 'fathers' could legitimately be rendered 'parents', but leaving it as it is points up a necessary emphasis. Busy about so many other things, a father can sometimes give the impression that he feels it is the mother's job to raise the children. When he is called in to deal with a problem he almost resents it as taking up time he ought to be spending doing something else. He begins to think of his children as a headache and not as a heritage, a problem and not a privilege. But the Bible points us in other directions. The husband has a responsibility to love his children, to spend time with them, to accommodate their mistakes, to be patient to them, to be kind to them, not to treat them in such a way that they become fretful and discouraged. Hendriksen again puts it very well: 'Fathers should create an atmosphere which will make obedience an easy and natural matter, namely the atmosphere of love and confidence.' Are you a father? If so, where do you stand here? Are you guilty of sins of omission?

4. *Stewardship of money.* It has been said that the unconsecrated wealth of Christians is the greatest hindrance to Christian progress. I have been able to look at that issue from so many angles – as an 'ordinary' Christian in the pew, as a voluntary worker in a Christian organization, as a full-time preacher dependent on the gifts of others for my own income and as a council member of a number of Christian organizations. The result is that I am inclined to agree with that assessment. Unconsecrated Christian wealth is one of the greatest hindrances, humanly speaking, to the bringing in of the kingdom of God. Many solidly evangelical Christians have never honestly faced up to the issue of tithing, for instance. Have you? Have you come to a settled conviction about the meaning of Malachi 3:8–10? Look it up *now*! And do not turn from it until you are convinced that you are making an honest response to its

demands. When did you last sit down and honestly examine your stewardship of money in the light of your total (and perhaps steadily increasing) income, the urgency of the hour and above all in the light of 'the grace of our Lord Jesus Christ' who though immeasurably rich became unspeakably poor 'so that you through his poverty might become rich'? (2 Corinthians 8:9.) Is there a serious sin of omission in this area?

5. *Practical help to those in need.* The Bible's teaching is crystal clear: 'And do not forget to do good and to share with others, for with such sacrifices God is pleased' (Hebrews 13:16); 'Therefore, as we have opportunity, let us do good to all people, especially to those who belong to the family of believers' (Galatians 6:10). We live in a world of need, pressure and hardship. There is a huge grey mass of human need all around us and as Christians we should be turned towards it and involved in it. We should be known as those who are always the first to lend a helping hand, to comfort a sufferer. And remember the impact here – that to know a thing is good and right to do and to fail to do it is *sin.* Remember too James's point about the brevity of life. Does that not add an urgency to all of these things? It has been said that delayed obedience is disobedience and we need to be as urgent about our response to God's revealed will to us as Christians as we urge sinners to be about their response to the gospel.

Perhaps these words, though a little light in touch, will help to bring the whole point home:

> He was going to be all that a mortal could be – tomorrow.
> No one would be kinder or braver than he – tomorrow.
> A friend who was troubled and weary, he knew,
> Who'd be glad of a lift – and he needed it too;
> On him he would call and see what he could do –
> tomorrow.

Each morning he'd stack up the letters he'd write –
tomorrow.
And think of the folk he would fill with delight –
tomorrow.
It was too bad indeed, he was busy today,
And hadn't a moment to stop on his way;
More time he would have to give others he'd say –
tomorrow.

The greatest of mortals this man would have been –
tomorrow.
The world would have known him, had he ever seen
tomorrow.
But the fact is, he died, and he faded from view,
And all that was left when his living was through,
Was a mountain of things he intended to do –
tomorrow!

As we should expect, James's words prove on examination to be intensely practical and inescapably personal. The last words of Archbishop James Ussher, who died in 1656, were these: 'Lord, forgive my sins, especially my sins of omission.'

In the light of all that James has said, we dare not leave that prayer that late!

36.

The madness of materialism

> *'Now listen, you rich people, weep and wail because of the misery that is coming upon you. Your wealth has rotted, and moths have eaten your clothes. Your gold and silver are corroded. Their corrosion will testify against you and eat your flesh like fire. You have hoarded wealth in the last days. Look! The wages you failed to pay the workmen who mowed your fields are crying out against you. The cries of the harvesters have reached the ears of the Lord Almighty. You have lived on earth in luxury and self-indulgence. You have fattened yourselves in the day of slaughter. You have condemned and murdered innocent men, who were not opposing you'* (James 5:1–6).

There seems little doubt that in this particular section of his letter James turns aside to address one specific group of people – wealthy, unbelieving Jews. There is no doubting that he has wealthy people in mind, because he identifies them as 'rich people' (v. 1). It also seems pretty clear that they were not Christians, not only because of the terrible judgement that he pronounces on them, but also because he does not once address them as 'brothers', an affectionate term which he uses no less than fifteen times and in virtually every other section of his letter when addressing his fellow Christians. They would also seem to have been Jews, because in the course of his outburst against them, James calls God 'the Lord Almighty' (v. 4), a distinctively Jewish title taken from the Old Testament.

For all of these reasons, there might be a temptation for

many people to skim over this passage on the assumption that it is not likely to be of much value to them. The average Christian, for instance, might be tempted to glance at these words and say, 'This passage has not really got anything to say to me. After all, I am a Christian and this is written to non-Christians; I am not rich and this is specifically written to people who are; this is written to Jews and I am a Gentile.' But there is an important principle that must always govern our reading of Scripture and if we remember this principle we will never bypass this kind of passage for that kind of reason. Put in a nutshell, the principle is this: not all Scripture is written *to* us, but all Scripture is written *for* us. To give an obvious example of what I mean, take the words of Moses, which were clearly written and spoken to the people of Israel. Now most Christians today do not belong to the ethnic race of Israel, but does that mean that we can jettison the Ten Commandments and say that they were not written *for* us? Or take Paul's letters to the Corinthians. We do not live in Corinth, nor in the first century, so those letters were not written *to* us, but does that mean that his teaching on the Lord's Supper in 1 Corinthians 11, or on love in 1 Corinthians 13, or on the resurrection in 1 Corinthians 15 is not written *for* us? Surely not! So with this letter written by James. The epistle at large was originally written to the *diaspora*, Jews scattered abroad in times of persecution, but who can have studied its pages thus far and felt that it was not written *for* us? If we apply this same principle to the passage now before us, we will discover that it has a relevant message for our times and for our lives. As Paul himself put it, quoting David's words in Psalm 69 as an example, 'For everything that was written in the past was written to teach us' (Romans 15:4).

Turning now to the text, we can divide our study into three separate sections.

1. The wickedness he denounces

'You have hoarded wealth in the last days. Look! The wages you failed to pay the workmen who mowed your fields are crying out against you . . . You have lived on earth in luxury and self-indulgence. You have fattened yourselves in the day of slaughter. You have condemned and murdered innocent men, who were not opposing you' (vv. 3–6).

In the course of these few brief sentences James lists a veritable catalogue of crime that was being committed by these people. Four words will give us a summary of the offences to which James drew their attention.

1. Covetousness. 'You have hoarded wealth in the last days.' The phrase 'hoarded wealth' comes from the Greek verb *thesaurizo*, which means to store away in a safe place. It is the root of our English word 'thesaurus', which basically means a collection, and this points to what James has in mind here. He is thinking of those people who seem bent on hoarding together every penny they possibly can and yet who seem to have an insatiable appetite to get even more.

When Jesus told the parable of the rich fool (at which we looked in an earlier study) he told it to illustrate the folly of this very thing. In the prelude to the story he said, 'Watch out! Be on your guard against all kinds of greed; a man's life does not consist in the abundance of his possessions' (Luke 12:15). Pressing home the application of the parable he added, 'This is how it will be with anyone who stores up things for himself but is not rich towards God' (Luke 12:21). Notice the two words that reveal all – 'for himself'. The rich farmer's motives in his energetic expansion policy were totally selfish and covetous, and the Bible denounces covetousness as a sin. In fact, it even goes so far as to speak of 'greed, which is idolatry' (Colossians 3:5). Greed of gain is nothing less than the deification of self and if our minds are set on hoarding wealth for ourselves then we are being idolatrous. Yet the Bible is wonderfully balanced here. It nowhere condemns a good business sense or industry or hard work. Nowhere in the Bible is profit or wealth condemned in absolute terms – but hoarding wealth for our own selfish enjoyment is something that is denounced in no uncertain manner.

Then notice that James also condemns the actions of these people as not only sinful but foolish, because they were hoarding wealth 'in the last days'. There has been a great deal of discussion about the precise meaning of these words. Did James mean the last days of the people concerned, that is to say their old age? Or did he have in mind the wider truth that ever since Christ's birth at Bethlehem we have been living in 'the last days'? (Acts 2:17.) In a study of this kind it is probably pointless to probe further, but just to make the obvious general point that covers both interpretations and that is that they were feverishly hoarding wealth for a shrinking and uncertain future. It is interesting to notice that these words come not very long after James's comment about the brevity of life and it is literally true that there is no man for whom these days are not the last days, because the earlier ones have already gone! In the light of that solemn and obvious truth, let us be on our guard against covetousness, greed or an inordinate preoccupation with wealth; and in case we still have a distant feeling that all of this applies only to those who are already wealthy, let us heed Matthew Henry's wise words that 'Poor people are as much in danger from an inordinate desire towards the wealth of the world as rich from an inordinate delight in it.'

2. *Corruption.* 'Look! The wages you failed to pay the workmen who mowed your fields are crying out against you.' We shall look at the last part of this phrase a little later on. For the moment, we are just concerned to pinpoint the second indictment James has against these rich unbelievers and we can sum it up in one word – corruption. Having presumably agreed to pay their farm labourers a certain wage for harvesting their fields, they now refused to pay them. The verb translated 'failed to pay' is *aphusteremenos*, which literally means 'being kept back'. The biblical law for the payment of such wages was 'Do not hold back the wages of a hired man overnight' (Leviticus 19:13) and the reason for this comes out clearly in another passage, where the law said, 'Do not take advantage of a hired man who is poor and needy . . . Pay him his wages each day before sunset, because he is poor and is counting on it' (Deuteronomy 24:14, 15). The poor labourer was dependent on getting his money day by day, so that he could keep body and soul together, but rich landowners would be tempted to delay payment and then no doubt to haggle over the exact amount that was due. But all of this chicanery was in direct contravention of the law of God, which roundly condemned dishonesty of any kind.

Any Christian employer should take very serious note of the Bible's insistence on scrupulous honesty in dealing with an employee. Jesus taught that 'The worker deserves his wages' (Luke 10:7) and Paul made it clear that even slaves were to be provided with 'what is right and fair' (Colossians 4:1). There is a crying need for a rebirth of uncomplicated honesty in our land today, a liberation from the tangled web of double-thinking into clean, plain, straightforward, above-board dealing, and it is symptomatic of our age that we have lost that spirit. For the Christian, honesty is not the best policy; it is the only one. To be other than honest is to be guilty in some measure of the sin of corruption.

3. Carelessness. 'You have lived on earth in luxury and self-indulgence. You have fattened yourselves in the day of slaughter.' Notice that this takes their indictment a little further. Having feathered their own nests by swindling the poor, these men now lived in idle ease and luxury, utterly careless of the needs of the rest of the world. But again, that kind of thing is roundly condemned in the Bible. Take this word from Amos, for instance:

> 'Woe to you who are complacent in Zion,
>   and to you who feel secure on Mount Samaria,
> you notable men of the foremost nation,
>   to whom the people of Israel come!
> Go to Calneh and look at it;
>   go from there to great Hamath,
>   and then go down to Gath in Philistia.
> Are they better off than your two kingdoms?
>   Was their land larger than yours?
> You put off the evil day
>   and bring near a reign of terror.
> You lie on beds inlaid with ivory
>   and lounge on your couches.
> You dine on choice lambs
>   and fattened calves.
> You strum away on your harps like David
>   and improvise on musical instruments.
> You drink wine by the bowlful
>   and use the finest lotions,
>   but you do not grieve over the ruin of Joseph.
> Therefore you will be among the first to go into exile;
>   your feasting and lounging will end'
>
> (Amos 6:1–6).

What a devastating condemnation of the self-indulgent, careless spirit that James is pointing out in the words we are studying!

Perhaps there are few of us who feel that we can afford to live in luxury and we may be tempted to think that this particular indictment is one that hardly applies to us at all and from which we find it difficult to draw any relevant lesson. But a spirit of careless self-indulgence can so easily creep in. The man who deals in hundreds can be infected by it just as deeply as the man who deals in tens of thousands. Few things test a man's spirituality more accurately than the way he uses money and to guard against even the beginnings of sin in this whole area we need to remember with Thomas Manton that 'God gave us wealth for another purpose than to spend it in pleasure.'

James's reference to 'a day of slaughter' is a little difficult to pinpoint, but it would fit in perfectly with his apocalyptic warnings to see this as the Day of Judgement. With terrible scorn, he sees these men resembling a herd of cattle grazing contentedly away in the fields, oblivious to the fact that in fattening themselves they are hastening the certainty of their destruction!

It is a simple fact of history that wicked men, when raised to great wealth and power, have repeatedly oppressed the poor and been prepared to press their persecution even to the point of shedding blood, and there is a dreadful degree of truth in Lord Acton's famous aphorism that 'All power corrupts and absolute power corrupts absolutely.' It would seem to be instances of this kind of thing that James has in mind here, and it ties in exactly with something he wrote earlier: 'You want something but don't get it. You kill and covet, but you cannot have what you want' (4:2). When we were studying that particular passage we referred to a case that would spring immediately to the minds of James's readers – the story of King Ahab and Naboth's vineyard. Here was a classic example of a man who was covetous, corrupt, careless and cruel and was even prepared to shed innocent blood in order to satisfy his greed. It is a striking example, but by no means an isolated one, and history before and since that sad episode records the stories of many who rose to power as cruel, heartless despots.

But there is something in this sentence that calls for our attention – the phrase 'who were not opposing you', which R. V. G. Tasker sees as bringing it to an end 'on a note of majestic pathos'. The picture is on the one hand of rich, vicious oppressors and on the other of poor, unresisting victims. Now it may be that James was thinking of a corrupted judiciary that would make it impossible for the poor to exercise any redress in a case of rough justice. On the other hand, he may be compounding the sin of the oppressor by reminding him that in refusing to answer violence with violence, his victim was following the example of the Lord Jesus Christ who, 'When they hurled their insults at him, he did not retaliate; when he suffered, he made no threats. Instead, he entrusted himself to him who judges justly' (1 Peter 2:23). If this is the case, the implied lesson is there for us all!

To sum up, then, we can say this: to oppress any man is sin. We are to treat men with the dignity of their humanity. Not all men are the children of God by regeneration, but they are all nevertheless God's creatures and one of the things that the Bible so challengingly teaches is that we should treat all of our fellow men, regardless of their beliefs or behaviour, in the light of that special dignity that God has placed upon them as men. In his own inscrutable wisdom God has separated them from all the rest of his creation and we act against the mind of God when we treat men as animals. On the other hand, when we as Christians are oppressed or wronged, the right attitude is not to seek for vengeance but humbly to commit our cause to God and to ensure that our response, in thought or action, never adds any other kind of sin to the one being committed against us.

2. The warning he delivers

'Now listen, you rich people, weep and wail because of the misery that is coming upon you. Your wealth has rotted, and moths have eaten your clothes. Your gold and silver are corroded. Their corrosion will testify against you and eat your flesh like fire . . . The wages you failed to pay . . . are crying out against you' (vv. 1–4).

The terrible nature of James's warning can be sensed from his opening words and especially the two expressions 'weep and wail' which when taken together speak of deep anguish of spirit. The second verb is actually a present imperative (the Greek *ololuzontes*) and the phrase literally reads 'weep-wailing', a construction which indicates not an occasional pang of sorrow but a continuous agony of heart. But why should these men do that? James says that it is because 'of the misery that is coming upon you'. The Greek word translated misery is *talaiporiais*, which is actually a plural word carrying the meanings of hardship, suffering and distress, and there may be a dual reference here. The first is the destruction of Jerusalem which took place in A.D. 70, perhaps only ten years or so after James wrote. The bloody siege led by the Roman general Titus claimed over a million lives and the richest men were those who were the first targets for the looters and murderers. But there is a wider and more likely reference that would apply to wealthy, corrupt cruel men of every nationality and of every generation, and that is the Day of Judgement. Typically, these men live as if there was no God, no judgement, no eternity, no heaven and no hell, but James warns of a 'misery that *is coming*'. The story is told of a godless American farmer who wrote to his local newspaper, 'I have been conducting an experiment in one of my fields. I have ploughed it on Sundays, sowed the seed on Sundays, watered and weeded it on Sundays, and gathered the harvest on Sundays – and I want to tell you that this October I have the finest crop of Indian corn in the whole neighbourhood.' The editor published the letter, but added this footnote: 'God does not settle all his accounts in October!' There *is* such a thing as a judgement to come and we shall have this second meaning in mind as we look in greater detail at the 'misery' James promises to his rich but rotten readers.

1. There will be a transformation. 'Your wealth has rotted, and moths have eaten your clothes. Your gold and silver are corroded' (v. 2). The verbs here are in the perfect tense and it seems best to understand that as being in what is sometimes called 'the prophetic perfect', that is to say, to refer to events which have not yet taken place but which are so certain that they can be spoken about as if they had. In James's day, three things in particular were tokens of a man's wealth – food, clothing and precious metals – and it is interesting to see that he may be alluding to all of them here. In warning the rich man of the folly of hoarding riches, he urges him to look ahead to the Day of Judgement and to see what a transformation there will have been in the things he clutched at here on earth. Firstly, 'Your wealth has rotted.' The verb is *sesepen*, exactly the word one would use about food that falls to pieces as putrefaction sets in. Secondly, 'Moths have eaten your clothes.' Even the finest clothing, owned by the richest man, would eventually fall prey to the tiny moth. Thirdly, 'Your gold and silver are corroded.' Here, James's language is obviously metaphorical, because gold and silver do not in fact corrode. The point he is making is that even gold and silver, those apparently imperishable status symbols of wealth, will be as worthless on the Day of Judgement as a heap of rusty metal. The point about worthlessness is underlined by both the sense and the tense of the verb *katiotai*, which the Amplified Bible helpfully translates as 'completely rusted through'.

What a transformation, then, in these things which had once been so valuable! No wonder the Bible says that 'Wealth is worthless in the day of wrath'! (Proverbs 11:4.) Things thought imperishable and unaffected by time are found to be utterly worthless in eternity.

2. There will be testimony. In gathering his wealth, exploiting the poor and enjoying his ill-gotten gains, the rich called the tune, but James says that the day is coming when he will have to listen to other voices, each of which will give testimony against him.

The first is the testimony of *their unused possessions:* 'Their corrosion will testify against you.' What powerful language this is! Surrounded by the poor while living on earth, these men had nevertheless covered themselves with wealth that could have been used to meet the needs of others. Now, their rusted riches would be eloquent – evidence of their sinful stupidity.

The second is the testimony of *their ill-gotten gains:* 'The wages you failed to pay . . . are crying out against you.' James mentions this one particular instance, but his words have a much wider application. Our vices have voices! The day is coming when they will give testimony and point unerring fingers at the guilty. The verb translated 'are crying out' is *krazei*, which in context means they shriek to God for vengeance – a terrible illustration of the impending doom of all those who come to the Day of Judgement as impenitent sinners.

The third is the testimony of *those they have defrauded:* 'The cries of the harvesters have reached the ears of the Lord Almighty.' There is an important point here and it is reinforced by two other biblical examples of the voices of the wronged crying out. The first is where God tells the murderer Cain: 'Your brother's blood cries out to me from the ground' (Genesis 4:10). Cain had stopped Abel's blood from circulating but he could not stop it speaking! Then we are told that towards the end of their captivity in Egypt, 'The Israelites groaned in their slavery and cried out, and their cry for help because of their slavery went up to God' (Exodus 2:23). James has the same picture here – and what a terrifying prospect he is predicting for the ungodly men he has in mind! Those they had wronged had cried out to God; God had heard their cry and registered their protest; and one day God would ask those voices to repeat their damning evidence. The point is made even stronger by the fact that James reminds his readers that the God to whom the oppressed had appealed is 'the Lord Almighty'. This particular title translates the Greek *kurion sabaoth*, which may originally have meant 'the Lord of armies', but later came to mean 'the Lord of hosts', that is to say, the Lord of the whole universe. The picture is one of awesome power and there seems little doubt that James deliberately uses it, as someone has suggested, 'to strike terror into those who think that the poor have no protector'.

3. There will be torment. 'Their corrosion will . . . eat your flesh like fire.' The precise wording here may be somewhat difficult to understand but the general implication is obvious and ominous. The Bible's constant references to hell as a reality mean that we dare not think of it as a fantasy. Jesus spoke of a place 'where the fire never goes out' (Mark 9:43) and even the gentle John spoke of 'the lake of burning sulphur' (Revelation 20:10) and 'the lake of fire' (Revelation 20:14). The eternal, conscious punishment of the ungodly is clearly taught in the Bible and James joins his voices to those of many others in warning men of its appalling implications.

3. The worth we can draw

We have now covered all the words of the text in these opening six verses of James 5, but it may be helpful if we take a moment to sum up some of the lessons we can learn, if only by inference, from James's searing indictment of the ungodly men to whom he was writing.

Firstly, there is not a word here against riches as such, but only against the ungodly way in which they are gained and used. The Bible does *not* say that money is the root of all evil, but that 'The love of money is a root of all kinds of evil' (1 Timothy 6:10). The Bible never condemns a man for being wealthy; what it does condemn him for is gaining wealth by ungodliness and failing to use his wealth for the good of others.

Secondly, there is not a word here against business, industry, ingenuity, skill, effort, a good commercial instinct or hard work. On the contrary, the Bible says, 'Go to the ant, you sluggard; consider its ways and be wise' (Proverbs 6:6). What the Bible condemns is not industry but indolence.

Thirdly, the whole passage teaches not only the madness but the menace of materialism. As Thomas Manton says, 'There is not a vice which more effectually contracts and deadens the feelings, which more completely makes a man's affections centre in himself and excludes all others from partaking in them, than the desire of accumulating possessions.' There is a deadly danger in 'things' and Paul is by no means overstating the case when he says that 'People who want to get rich fall into temptation and a trap and into many foolish and harmful desires that plunge men into ruin and destruction' (1 Timothy 6:9). We have been warned!

Fourthly, the passage implies the responsibility and reward of wise stewardship. We have all heard the saying, You can't take it with you.' Now that is obviously true, but James's words about hoarded wealth testifying against us teach an even more challenging truth, and that is that things to which men have clung selfishly here on earth *will* in effect be there on the other side of the grave – giving evidence against their previous owners on the Day of Judgement! That is the chilling prospect facing those who have led greedy, self-indulgent lives.

It is precisely in this context that Jesus pointed us to a

better way: 'I tell you, use worldly wealth to gain friends for yourselves, so that when it is gone, you will be welcomed into eternal dwellings' (Luke 16:9). How are we to use our material possessions? We are clearly not to hoard them up; we are not to treasure up these things for ourselves. Nor are we to squander them on pleasure; that would be equally wrong. Jesus said that we were to use our worldly wealth in quite another way, and I believe that the essence of what he meant was this – that we are to use our means to help in the spreading of the gospel throughout the world, so that at the end of life there will be those in heaven who will welcome us because we gave of our perishable, material possessions here on earth. I can think of few things more exhilarating than to realize that material possessions – and I am thinking in particular of bits of paper and metal – can help towards the conversion of other people, that things which are themselves perishable can be used by God to bring about an imperishable miracle in the lives of people we may never see until the day we reach heaven. Imagine that lovely moment when someone will come up to you and say, 'Welcome to heaven. I have some wonderful news for you. Do you remember that gift you sent regularly to that missionary society? Well, I was converted through the preaching of a missionary who would not have been in my part of the world if it had not been for your giving. You sent him out to preach the gospel, and I am in heaven as a result.' What a wonderful experience that will be – the perfect fulfilment of Jesus' command to 'store up for yourselves treasures in heaven, where moth and rust do not destroy, and where thieves do not break in and steal'! (Matthew 6:20.)

Let all that James has to say about the madness of materialism help to teach us the sanity of stewardship.

37.

Live looking up!

'Be patient, then, brothers, until the Lord's coming. See how the farmer waits for the land to yield its valuable crop and how patient he is for the autumn and spring rains. You too, be patient and stand firm, because the Lord's coming is near. Don't grumble against each other, brothers, or you will be judged. The Judge is standing at the door! Brothers, as an example of patience in the face of suffering, take the prophets who spoke in the name of the Lord. As you know, we consider blessed those who have persevered. You have heard of Job's perseverance and have seen what the Lord finally brought about. The Lord is full of compassion and mercy. Above all, my brothers, do not swear – not by heaven or by earth or by anything else. Let your "Yes" be yes, and your "No", no, or you will be condemned' (James 5:7–12).

In the opening six verses of this chapter, James has been exposing and challenging the lives of wealthy, ungodly men who defrauded and persecuted the poor and who lived in self-indulgent luxury. Now, he turns from the oppressors to the oppressed, tells them how they should behave under pressure and encourages them to look for the day of deliverance that will one day be theirs.

Notice how his change of tone is focused in his reversion to the word 'brothers', which he uses in verses 7, 9, 10 and 12. Here is a word of sympathy and identification. In turning to the Christians suffering under the tyranny of their ungodly oppressors, James writes with tenderness and affection. He feels personally involved in all their afflictions and wants to stand with them, comfort them, encourage them. He feels their anguish as if it were his own. Is this not an immediate challenge to our own hearts? Do we identify with the suffering, oppression and persecution which Christians are bearing in some parts of the world today? Richard Wurmbrand, a Rumanian pastor, spent fourteen years in a Communist jail, three of them in solitary confinement. Today, he is dedicating himself to the spread of the gospel in the land of his tormentors and elsewhere behind the Iron Curtain. He has an almost tangible burden for the thousands of Christians who are being persecuted for the faith in Eastern Europe today, and in seeking to arouse the consciences of Christians in the free West he often asks, 'Why, if you are members of the same body, do you not feel the pain when these people suffer?' That is a deeply challenging question and one whose principle can be extended throughout the world-wide fellowship of the church. If we are part of one body, surely we should feel the pain when Christians suffer? We should identify with the hurt inflicted by every blow struck at the body of Christ, whether it be by a Communist regime, a religious edict or a critic's tongue.

Moving now on to the body of the text, notice that James has three words for these oppressed Christians.

1. A word of expectation

'. . . the Lord's coming' (v. 7); **'. . . the Lord's coming is near'** (v. 8); **'The Judge is standing at the door!'** (v. 9).

These three phrases form the context in which the whole passage is framed, and we shall capture the spirit of it by noting just one thing each of them says about the second coming of the Lord Jesus Christ to the earth.

1. It was clear. 'Be patient, then, brothers, until the Lord's coming.' This is James's first reference to the Second Coming and it is simple, concise, straightforward and uncluttered. He could hardly have put as great a truth in fewer words and the inference of that seems clear. No long explanation was needed because the Christians to whom he was writing already knew and believed it. It was a familiar doctrine in the New Testament church. It has been calculated that there are 1,835 references in the Bible to the Second Coming and it is certainly true that there are about 300 references in the New Testament alone, one for every thirteen verses from Matthew to Revelation. But whatever the statistics, the fact of Christ's return was clear to James and equally clear to his readers.

There are three main Greek words used in the Bible to describe the second coming of Christ. The one used here is *parousia*, which one would use about the arrival of an emperor or king. It speaks of authority and power. It was the word used by Jesus when he spoke of 'the coming of the Son of Man' (Matthew 24:27). It was the word Paul used when he spoke of 'the coming of our Lord Jesus Christ' (1 Thessalonians 5:23). It was the word Peter used when he spoke of 'the coming of our Lord Jesus Christ' (2 Peter 1:16). It was the word John used when he said that we should live in such a way that when Christ returns to the earth 'we may be confident and unashamed at his coming' (1 John 2:28). The main thrust of the word is to indicate a person's physical presence, and this makes it easy to see why James uses the word here. These persecuted Christians were no doubt comforted by the spiritual presence of Christ, but they longed for the fulfilment of his further promise, and in the midst of all their anguish James assures them that Christ *will* come. Do we have the same settled certainty? The Puritan preacher John Trapp once wrote, 'This is pinned as a badge to the sleeve of every true believer – that he looks for and longs for Christ's coming to judgement.'

2. It was comforting. '. . . the Lord's coming is near'. Here again, let us remember the context. Some of these Christians – perhaps those who suffered most – must have wondered if there would ever be an end to the persecution and oppression. James's answer to their unasked question was to point out that the return was not only getting closer all the time but could actually be described as being 'near'. Surely this reminder would have been a comfort to them! They were not to know exactly *when* Christ would return, but they could be sure that each day brought it closer. The practical implications of this were that the time of their suffering was getting shorter, not longer; it was moving towards an end. The day of their release was getting nearer, and even the worst of their agony should be seen in the light of the glory that was to come. This was exactly the spirit that nerved Paul when he wrote that 'Our light and momentary troubles are achieving for us an eternal glory that far outweighs them all' (2 Corinthians 4:17).

3. It was challenging. 'The Judge is standing at the door!' Notice a significant change of wording here, from 'the Lord' to 'the Judge'. Why does James use that particular word? We might have expected him to use it when addressing the ungodly, but why does he do so when writing to his oppressed Christian brothers? The answer, of course, lies in the context and it is important to notice that he prefaces this particular statement with the command: 'Don't grumble against each other, brothers, or you will be judged.' We shall look at those words a little later, but the point to grasp here is that alongside the clarity and the comfort of the Second Coming, James now brings this element of challenge.

You will often have heard preachers saying something like this: 'One day you will come face to face with Jesus Christ. Will you meet him as your Saviour or as your Judge?' Now the point of saying that is clear. People are being faced with the matter of whether they are right with God, whether they have ever been converted. But a closer look at the issue shows that in fact the question is not thoroughly biblical unless it is explained, because the truth of the matter is that we shall *all* meet him as Judge. As Paul says so clearly, 'For we must *all* appear before the judgement seat of Christ' (2 Corinthians 5:10) and while the Christian's salvation will not come into question on that great day, the issue of his reward most certainly will. His life will come under God's solemn review, and 'be shown for what it is, because the Day will bring it to light. It will be revealed with fire, and the fire will test the quality of each man's work' (1 Corinthians 3:13). There is no escaping the fact that when James speaks of 'the Judge' here, he is addressing Christians in the context of their behaviour.

Let us carefully understand what this means. We are to be judged according to our works as Christians. Our reward or lack of reward will be in direct relationship to the things we have thought, said and done while here on earth. Our prayer lives, our stewardship of time, our use of money, our behaviour within the church, our domestic lives, our business ethics – all will be revealed. What a challenge this is! On his ninetieth birthday George Bernard Shaw said, 'Our conduct is influenced not so much by our experience as by our expectations,' and there is surely more than a measure of truth in that. How differently we would behave if we knew how certain events would turn out! Then the certainty of the second coming of Christ in judgement should touch and tincture every part of our daily behaviour. Martin Luther once said, 'I preach as though Christ died yesterday, rose from the dead today and was coming back tomorrow.' How different our lives would be if we lived them in that spirit! All of this comes across as part of the challenge raised by James's word of expectation.

2. A word of exhortation

'Be patient, then, brothers' (v. 7); **'You too, be patient and stand firm'** (v. 8); **'Don't grumble against each other, brothers'** (v. 9); **'Above all, my brothers, do not swear – not by heaven or by earth or by anything else. Let your "Yes" be yes, and your "No", no, or you will be condemned'** (v. 12).

Reading through these four imperatives, which are scattered throughout the passage we are studying, we can separate our distinct exhortations – two negative and two positive. Let us look at them in that order.

1. A warning against intolerance. 'Don't grumble against each other, brothers, or you will be judged.' The root word for 'grumble' is the Greek *stenazo*, which literally means 'to groan' and primarily denotes a feeling that is internal and unexpressed. With that in mind, it is not difficult to see why James uses it here. Here were Christians under severe pressure and beginning to fray at the edges. Soon they would begin to grumble at their circumstances and then, tragically, start directing their grumbling at each other. What deep spiritual insight James shows here! So often the first people to suffer when we begin to crack under the strain are our fellow Christians. 'Divide and conquer' is not only a well-known military tactic, it is one Satan uses with repeated success. One of the greatest things Satan can do to forward his purposes is to cause division among Christians, to make them complain, murmur, fight, bicker and grumble against each other. The devil has achieved a great victory when he gets Christians at loggerheads. James has already warned us about this kind of thing, when he wrote, 'Brothers, do not slander one another' (4:11) and he considers the point serious enough to come back to it here.

When reminding the Corinthians of the fate of many Israelites in the wilderness, Paul wrote, 'And do not grumble, as some of them did – and were killed by the destroying angel' (1 Corinthians 10:10). It is always a tragedy when a Christian 'blows his top' and doubly tragic when he does so within the fellowship of believers. We can be so terribly unforgiving on the one hand and so terribly demanding on the other with those who are nearest and dearest to us, those in our own family and others with whom we are in close fellowship. Why? Because the devil loves to wreck a relationship that is likely to bring glory to God. That is something we need to remember very carefully. I remember the first visit that I made to Eastern Europe, travelling by car with two other evangelists. It is not for me to suggest their opinions about their companion on the journey, but they were delightful Christians, men I still love dearly in the Lord. We met together one evening in a town in the south-east of England and the next morning drove to Dover to catch the cross-channel ferry. We were in something of a hurry, and were already driving when we started to pray for the whole journey – for our safety, for fruitful contacts, effective ministry and, above all, the glory of God. But before long the devil was hard at work, doing his utmost to wreck the fellowship within that car. Great blessings were minimized, little problems were magnified and we found ourselves needing to look to the Lord hour by hour for his protection and for his enabling to overcome the pressures that were being exerted against us. To his great glory the whole of that long, arduous journey was a happy triumph for the love of God 'poured . . . into our hearts by the Holy Spirit' (Romans 5:5) and, as we have since discovered, the ministry in those days helped significantly in laying the foundation for a great work being carried on in Europe today. But the devil's tactics were clear. Let us learn and relearn the lesson!

2. *A warning against irreverence.* 'Above all, my brothers, do not swear – not by heaven or by earth or by anything else. Let your "Yes" be yes, and your "No", no, or you will be condemned.' This is a somewhat difficult passage and it will probably be best if we concentrate on the central thing that James is saying here. The background to it is that oaths formed a very important part of Jewish religious and civil life. For instance, the writer of Hebrews says this: 'When God made his promise to Abraham, since there was no one greater for him to swear by, he swore by himself' (Hebrews 6:13) and later adds that in order to make the unchanging nature of his purpose clear, God 'confirmed it with an oath' (Hebrews 6:17). Paul also swore by an oath: he wrote to the Corinthians, 'I call God as my witness that it was in order to spare you that I did not return to Corinth' (2 Corinthians 1:23). Throughout the Bible, and especially in the Old Testament, we find godly people swearing by an oath. Then why does James appear to forbid it here?

To discover the answer, we need to probe the background a little further. To put it as simply as possible, oath-taking had fallen into disrepute, in two ways. In the first place, some people used oaths so frequently that they lost all significance. On the other hand there were others who divided oaths into two categories, those that were binding and those that were non-binding. For example, an oath was binding if the name of God was brought into it, but not if a man swore by any other name. A man could swear by heaven, or by earth, or by Jerusalem, or even by the hair on his head, and as long as he did not invoke the name of God then that was a non-binding oath! Something that had always been treated seriously and often sacredly had degenerated into a farce and a disgrace and in that kind of situation there was obviously a need for the Christian's attitude to be clarified, and it is not difficult to sense the need to be even greater in times of crisis and pressure, when tempers tended to get frayed.

One should also add that in giving this direction James is not forbidding the taking of an oath in a court of law. Of course, there should be no need to take an oath in a court of law; a man should be able to stand in the witness box and have every word of his evidence believed at its face value. But we live in an imperfect world and the legal structure of oath-taking, with its sanctions against perjury, has become necessary in some measure to guard the accuracy of what is said. It is a concession to the imperfect world in which we live. Oaths have become necessary because of man's inherent dishonesty. But the real lesson here is that in our everyday dealings, with our fellow men, we should be so honest, so straightforward and unambiguous that no oath or underlining of any kind should ever be necessary. The Amplified Bible puts part of this verse like this: 'Let your yes be a simple yes and your no be a simple no.' That is the way we should deal with each other. There should be no need to underline our words, or swear by anything, or to say 'cross my heart' or 'Boy Scouts' honour' or anything else. Our 'yes' ought to be 'yes', and our 'no' ought to be 'no', beyond any kind of contradiction or compromise or ambiguity. We ought never to need to emphasize that we are telling the truth, because we should never do anything else! In Curtis Vaughan's fine phrase, 'One's mere word should be as trustworthy as a signed agreement attested by legal witnesses.'

The other element which seems to be woven into what James is saying here is a stern prohibition against the terrible possibility of taking God's name in vain by using it lightly whether in oath or otherwise. Any use of God's name other than in holy reverence is condemned by God himself and to understand that is to understand why James prefaces this particular injunction with the words: '*Above all,* my brothers . . .' As R. V. G. Tasker says, 'There are few spheres of conduct in which the young Christian today needs to take the injunction of the Epistle of James more to heart than in this matter of frivolous and indiscriminate oaths and the thoughtless mention of the Divine name in general conversation.'

These, then, are the two negative exhortations we find in this passage: a warning against intolerance and a warning against irreverence. Now we can turn to the two positive exhortations.

1. A call for restraint. 'Be patient, then, brothers . . . You too, be patient . . .' In the original Greek, the root verb is *makrothumeo*, which literally means 'to be long-tempered' and is a much stronger word than our general usage would suggest. It carries with it the thought of restraining anger and resentment regardless of the provocation, being 'long-tempered' with people. Is there any Christian who would not be challenged by James's words here? Are our lives marked by an inner restraint that bears calmly with injury and insult alike? Few things test us more clearly than our attitude to life's pressures and problems and especially those which involve personal offence. No wonder the Bible says, 'Clothe yourselves with . . . patience' (Colossians 3:12).

2. A call to resolution. '. . . stand firm . . .' A word for word rendering of the original Greek would read 'establish the hearts of you' and it is the first word that is obviously the key to the meaning of the whole phrase. The Greek word is *sterexate* and one particular use of the same verb elsewhere in the New Testament provides us with a vivid illustration of its meaning. This is where we read that Jesus 'resolutely set out for Jerusalem' (Luke 9:51). Do you see the picture? Jesus knew what was going to happen in Jerusalem. He knew that the pressures were mounting and that his enemies were growing in number and ferocity. He knew that ahead lay desertion, trials, blood, sweat, tears, torture and agonizing death. But he knew something else. He knew that beyond all of these lay the resurrection, the ascension and eternal glory at the right hand of his Father, so he resolutely set out, refusing to yield to the pressure around him.

This is exactly the spirit in which the writer to Hebrews says we are to live the Christian life: 'Therefore, since we are surrounded by such a great cloud of witnesses, let us throw off everything that hinders and the sin that so easily entangles, and let us run with perseverance the race marked out for us. Let us fix our eyes on Jesus, the author and perfecter of our faith, who for the joy set before him, endured the cross, scorning its shame, and sat down at the right hand of the throne of God' (Hebrews 12:1, 2). The Bible does not speak of patience as waiting for something to happen, but rather as resolute endurance while things are happening and pressing on regardless of what may happen. Biblical patience is not rooted in fatalism that says everything is out of control. It is rooted in faith that says everything is in God's control.

3. A word of example

'See how the farmer waits for the land to yield its valuable crop and how patient he is for the autumn and spring rains' (v. 7); **'Brothers, as an example of patience in the face of suffering, take the prophets who spoke in the name of the Lord. As you know, we consider blessed those who have persevered. You have heard of Job's perseverance and have seen what the Lord finally brought about. The Lord is full of compassion and mercy'** (vv. 10, 11).

As well as words of encouragement and exhortation, James also mingles into this particular passage in his letter three examples of people who in differing circumstances illustrate what he is saying about the virtues of patient endurance.

1. The farmer. 'See how the farmer waits for the land to yield its valuable crop and how patient he is for the autumn and spring rains.' Here is a simple illustration of the principle James has been hammering home. The NIV translators have exceeded their responsibilities in giving us the words 'autumn' and 'spring', which should really read 'early' and 'latter', though in fact they have explained what James meant. The autumn rain would be the first to fall after the sowing of the crop and would germinate the seed, and the latter rain would fall in the spring and help to swell the grain before harvest. Knowing that both would come in good time, the farmer faithfully sowed, carefully cultivated and then patiently waited for God to fulfil his promise. That is the point James is making here. In Alec Motyer's felicitous phrase, 'In the farming world, patience is a fruitful virtue.'

2. The prophets. 'Brothers, as an example of patience in the face of suffering, take the prophets who spoke in the name of the Lord. As you know, we consider blessed those who have persevered.' The persecution of the prophets was a fact of history, so much so that at his martyrdom Stephen cried out, 'Was there ever a prophet your fathers did not persecute?' (Acts 7:52.) If you were a prophet you were persecuted; it was a byword. In Hebrews 11 there is a spine-chilling list of the ways in which God's special messengers had been persecuted: by tortures, flogging, chaining, imprisonment, stoning and banishment from society. Even those chosen by God for positions of special honour and service had not been exempt, in fact quite the reverse. They had been singled out for the worst outrages. Yet what is our assessment of them now? Do we consider that they are to be pitied? Not at all! As James rightly says, these are the very people 'we consider blessed'. These are our heroes in the Christian church, people we admire, and we rejoice that they have passed victoriously through all their trials to receive the crown of life. But we are called to do more than that. James points to the experience of these heroes as 'an example' and an example is to be copied, not just complimented. If they suffered so much and were persecuted so greatly, yet endured so courageously, should we not be encouraged to bear our smaller burdens with the same resolute faith? The example, the challenge and the reward are all caught up in these words from the Sermon on the Mount: 'Blessed are you when people insult you, persecute you and falsely say all kinds of evil against you because of me. Rejoice and be glad, because great is your reward in heaven, for in the same way they persecuted the prophets that were before you' (Matthew 5:11, 12).

3. Job. 'You have heard of Job's perseverance and have seen what the Lord finally brought about. The Lord is full of compassion and mercy.' Even today we speak of 'the patience of Job', though the NIV has correctly registered the fact that Job's particular quality was not *makrothumia* ('patience') but *hupomone* ('perseverance'). The difference lies in the fact that *hupomone* is not so much a matter of patience with people (Job did not in fact excel in that department) but rather a steadfast endurance of adverse circumstances in the settled assurance that they were all being governed by the overruling providence of God. Job was not perfect. He made mistakes at times. He 'lost his cool' with some of those with whom he discussed his problems, but throughout it all he retained his steadfast faith in God. At the end of that terrible day when he lost his entire family and all of his thousands of animals, we read that 'He fell to the ground in worship and said: "Naked I came from my mother's womb, and naked I shall depart. The Lord gave and the Lord has taken away; may the name of the Lord be praised"' (Job 1:20, 21). Later, when the pressures had become even greater, his trust in God was so firm that he could say, 'Though he slay me, yet will I hope in him' (Job 13:15). Do we begin to match that kind of faith, that kind of trust, that kind of perseverance under trial?

Finally, notice James's own comment on Job's story. He says that his readers 'have seen what the Lord finally brought about' and adds, 'The Lord is full of compassion and mercy.' Job's story only begins to make sense when we realize that through it all God was at work and that his ultimate purposes were loving and kind. Without this golden thread holding it together, it collapses in a meaningless heap of pain, suffering, sorrow and heartache, but when we see what the Lord finally brought about we can see even the worst of Job's disasters in their right light. As John Calvin comments, 'Afflictions ought ever to be estimated by their end', and in Job's case the end was glorious. In material things, for example, we are told that 'The Lord made him prosperous again and gave him twice as much as he had before' (Job 42:10). But Job was blessed at a level altogether higher than the material. His character was completely vindicated and his spiritual experience and understanding enriched beyond measure. It may seem strange that God should have allowed his servant to experience such darkness, but we can reverently say that the end justified the means and proved, in James's own words, that 'The Lord is full of compassion and mercy.'

Here is the right note on which to end our study of this section. We live in a world of affliction, pressure and persecution of one kind or another. There are problems beyond our understanding. There are times when we are tempted to despair, to throw in the towel, to turn aside from the pathway of obedience. When we are, let us encourage ourselves by remembering that the Lord is coming; that we are going to be with him for ever and that at the end of the day we will be able to look back even on our darkest hour and confess that the Lord has been full of compassion and mercy. Let us learn to say in faith,

> 'Surely goodness and love *will* follow me
> all the days of my life,
> and I *will* dwell in the house of the Lord
> for ever'
>
> (Psalm 23:6).

To live with that conviction is to live looking up!

38.

A God for all seasons

'Is any one of you in trouble? He should pray. Is anyone happy? Let him sing songs of praise' (James 5:13).

Ralph Waldo Emerson, the American essayist, once wrote, 'We do not live an equal life, but one of contrasts and patch-work; now a little joy, then a sorrow, now a sin, then a generous or brave action.' There is nothing very profound about those words, but they do crystallize for us something we all know to be true, and that is that life is never the same for very long. It is seldom a motionless plateau, with nothing happening or changing. Life is full of variety. There are mountain tops and valleys, clouds and sunshine, pain and pleasure, and sometimes they all seem thrown together in hopeless confusion.

Generations of philosophers, teachers, thinkers and leaders of men have wrestled with the problem of how to cope with the changeability of life, with all its triumphs and disasters, yet whatever the distilled wisdom of the ages might say, at the end of the day it is only the Christian who has the ultimate answers, because only the Christian has the resources necessary to cope with the questions.

It is these two factors — life's changeability and the Christian's attitude to life — that the down-to-earth James now brings together. There are two obvious parts to what he is saying here and in each of them he describes a condition and then gives counsel as to how Christians should react. By looking carefully at what he has to say we will discover that we truly do have a God for all seasons.

1. In times of pressure
'Is any one of you in trouble? He should pray.'

It would be difficult to imagine how a more penetrating diagnosis of a human condition and a more powerful prescription for its cure could possibly be contained in fewer words. There are only five in the original Greek, yet they probe the very depths of our daily need and point to the all-sufficient provision that is ours as children of God.

1. The condition. 'Is any one of you in trouble?' Everything obviously hinges on the meaning of the word 'in trouble'. The Greek word is *kakopathei*, which in turn is made up of the noun *kakos* ('evil') and the verb *pascho* ('to suffer'). Spiros Zodhiates says that the compound verb means 'to suffer the evil blows of the outside world' and that would certainly give the perfect picture of what James has in mind here. He is speaking of all of those blows that rain in upon us as Christians as we live out our lives in this alien world. But what are the blows? Many centuries before James, David wrote, 'A righteous man may have many troubles . . .' (Psalm 34:19) and it is surely not difficult to prove the truth of that statement.

There are *natural troubles.* There is a sense in which these cover all others, because all man's troubles are ultimately brought about by the entry of sin into the world. Paul even dares to say that 'The whole creation has been groaning as in the pains of childbirth right up to the present time' (Romans 8:22) and while the detailed meaning of that amazing statement is beyond our understanding, what it clearly teaches is that the whole universe is somehow out of joint as a result of man's sin – and many of man's troubles come in turn from the disorganization and disease of nature. Not only is man not what he was meant to be, and not as he was when God created him, but neither is the natural world in its pristine condition. The whole created universe has become disorganized, with the end result that all men, Christians included, suffer from a host of what we have called natural troubles.

There are *physical troubles.* This moves us into the particular realm of man's physical flesh, his body. In his original state, man was without disease or disorder of any kind. Not only was Adam made in God's moral likeness, but he was without any physical defect, deformity or weakness. But the entrance of sin brought about the onset, for the very first time in man's experience, of disease, disorder, decay, deterioration and ultimately death. In that fateful moment, every fibre of man's physical being became prone to disease, a terrible transformation which was part of the fulfilment of God's solemn warning to Adam that if he disobeyed God's word, he would 'surely die' (Genesis 2:17). From that time on, not one atom of our physical being has been exempt from the ravages of disease and the onset of death. Of course, modern medicine has harnessed scientific discovery in many brilliant ways, so that there are some diseases fatal just a few years ago which can now be cured almost without risk, and we can praise God for that, but the fact remains that 'Man is destined to die' (Hebrews 9:27) and death is sometimes preceded by the most savage agony or the torture of lingering pain. There are physical troubles.

There are *mental troubles.* It has been estimated that 50% of the hospital beds in Great Britain today are occupied by people who are suffering from mental problems of one kind or another. Another estimate says that one in five of the present population of Great Britain will eventually suffer from some kind of marked mental disorder. When we widen the angle a little and take in all those other mental troubles and pressures that do not take us to the psychiatrist's couch or the doctor's surgery, how few people today totally escape any kind of mental trouble? The whole Western civilization in which we live today is geared to success and speed, regardless of the cost in human terms. We live in a rat race. We speak of the law of the jungle as if it were something that was put away when man discovered concrete, but in fact the law of the jungle exists today just as much as ever it did. The weakest goes to the wall. Success too often belongs not merely to the hard-working, but to the ruthless and the brutal, and the unquestionable result is that mental pressures of stress and anxiety and fear build up to the most terrifying proportions. Yet again, as with the other troubles, the Christian finds himself caught up in that situation. Do you not sometimes feel the effect of that kind of pressure in the world in which we live? Are you under increasing pressure to succeed, to work harder, to move faster, to cover more ground, to meet an increasing demand? That pressure can come not only at work but at home, and in our church fellowships, in fact, wherever our lives take us, and the result, often unnoticed, and at times more serious, is what we can put under the general heading of mental troubles.

There are *spiritual troubles.* I have grouped mental, physical and spiritual troubles under different headings, yet it is important for us to remember that they are not in water-tight compartments. In a remarkable little book called *None Of These Diseases*, Dr S. I. McMillen says, 'Medical science recognizes that emotions such as fear, sorrow, envy, resentment and hatred are responsible for the majority of our sicknesses. Estimates range from 60% to nearly 100%.' Here is the inevitable mingling of the physical, mental and spiritual within our human frames and personalities.

But spiritual troubles can also be looked at from a distinctly separate angle. Paul reminds us that, as Christians, 'Our struggle is not against flesh and blood, but against the rulers, against the authorities, against the powers of this dark world and against the spiritual forces of evil in the heavenly realms' (Ephesians 6:12). While the implications of that statement overlap into the natural, physical and mental worlds, it is with the spiritual realm that we usually associate it. In facing the sombre reality of spiritual troubles in the world, we need to recognize that we are not merely up against blind circumstances, an unthinking fate or plain 'bad luck'. We are opposed by a living, intelligent, powerful and implacable enemy, the devil, who 'prowls around like a roaring lion looking for someone to devour' (1 Peter 5:8). No wonder we have spiritual troubles!

There are *special troubles.* I have chosen that phrase quite deliberately, because the Bible clearly shows it to be true – the Christian faces special troubles. This comes across very clearly in Paul's correspondence to Timothy. At one point he encourages his young friend to 'join with me in suffering for the gospel' (2 Timothy 1:8), and the word he uses – *sunkakopatheo* – is a cognate of James's word. Yet Paul's emphasis is not on the trouble as being physical, or mental, or spiritual, but rather on its association with 'the gospel'. As Kenneth Wuest puts it, 'The sufferings are those that are a natural accompaniment of the preaching of the gospel.' Mark those words! Preaching the gospel is likely to bring trouble to the preacher! Later in the same letter he tells Timothy to 'endure hardship with us *[sunkakopatheo]* like a good soldier of Christ Jesus' (2 Timothy 2:3). Further on, he speaks of 'my gospel, for which I am suffering *[kakopatheo]* even to the point of being chained like a criminal' (2 Timothy 2:8, 9). Finally, he exhorts Timothy to 'endure hardship *[kakopatheo]*, do the work of an evangelist, discharge all the duties of your ministry' (2 Timothy 4:5). The clear inference in all of these statements is that there are special troubles associated with dedicated Christian living and with the proclamation of the gospel. Broadening that just a little, there are troubles that are peculiar to Christians. People sometimes speak rather loosely about 'bearing a cross'. Sometimes they mean a physical illness, or a tyrant of a boss, or a rebellious child, or a nagging wife, or even a chronic headache. But this is playing fast and loose with biblical teaching. Strictly speaking, a cross is something you bear because you are a Christian that you would not have to bear if you were not a Christian. It is a special trouble reserved for God's people.

Let me add something else here. As we have seen, every Christian is in a battle, every Christian is locked in combat with the world, the flesh and the devil. Yet there is a sense in which the full-time Christian worker is in the front line of that battle. I am sure there are times when that is not always understood in the church at large. For instance, one has sometimes heard unthinking criticism about 'the glamour of evangelism', with the sinister inference that itinerant evangelists live very comfortably, with more pleasures and fewer problems than other Christians. But that kind of statement is both ignorant and iniquitous. Of course, there are those who misuse their office, but the essential truth is that there is no glamour in the gospel. There is no glamour in the ministry of a true man of God, whether his ministry is itinerant or settled. The more I read of Scripture and history, the more convinced I become that the man who is determined to live for God, to work for God, to set his face against the world, to give the main thrust of his life to the spread of the gospel is certain to suffer these 'special troubles'. Paul himself makes this clear when he writes, again to Timothy, that 'Everyone who wants to live a godly life in Christ Jesus will be persecuted' (2 Timothy 3:12).

There is an interesting link here with what James said a little earlier about those Old Testament prophets. He specifically made the point that they were 'an example of patience in the face of suffering' (5:10) and the word he uses is *kakopathias*. If there are special troubles that belong to the Christian, then we have to go one step further and say that there are extra-special troubles that belong to the man who dares to be a spokesman for God.

These, then, are some of the troubles that beset the Christian as he seeks to live for God in an alien world.

2. The counsel. 'He should pray.' The immediate thing to notice is that while the condition James exposes was capable of many different applications and interpretations, the counsel he gives has no diversity whatever; in the original Greek it is just one word – *proseuchestho*. The special significance of the word is that it is always used in a religious sense, it always refers to prayer directed to God, and the lesson hidden in all of this is that in the storms of life, prayer should be the Christian's first resort. As Robert Johnstone says, the Christian 'will always feel, if his faith be intelligent and vigorous, that nothing is so becoming and needful under trial as earnest wrestling with his heavenly Father'.

James has had a great deal to say on the subject of prayer earlier in his letter, and rather than go over ground already covered in the exposition of earlier verses, let me just concentrate on one aspect which is especially helpful in the context of what James says about the troubles which beset Christians, and that is the encouragement the Bible gives us to pray. For example, listen to David as he speaks of some of the troubles he has known in his own life. He speaks of 'the cords of death' and 'the torrents of destruction' (Psalm 18:4); 'the cords of the grave' and 'the snares of death' (Psalm 18:5). Then comes the turning-point:

'In my distress I called to the Lord;
I cried to my God for help.
From his temple he heard my voice;
my cry came before him, into his ears'
(Psalm 18:6).

Now read on through the rest of that psalm and you will discover that it is almost entirely given over to the marvellous outcome of that prayer:

'He reached down from on high and took hold of me;
he drew me out of the deep waters. He rescued me
from my powerful enemy,
from my foes, who were too strong for me'
(Psalm 18:16, 17);

'The Lord was my support'
(Psalm 18:18);

'It is God who arms me with strength'
(Psalm 18:32).

The whole psalm is a glorious affirmation that God is personally and practically involved in the troubles of his people.

The same truth shines through elsewhere in Scripture, too. After Israel had endured over 400 years of slavery, God told Moses, 'I have indeed seen the misery of my people in Egypt. I have heard them crying out because of their slave drivers, and I am concerned about their suffering' (Exodus 3:7). God promised the psalmist: 'Call upon me in the day of trouble; I will deliver you, and you will honour me' (Psalm 50:15); Peter tells us that 'The eyes of the Lord are on the righteous and his ears are attentive to their prayer' (1 Peter 3:12). What a wonderful encouragement all of this is! God is looking, God is listening and God is longing to deliver his people from their troubles, longing to bless them, guide them, strengthen them, comfort them. Days of darkness in our lives are no more an indication that God is absent than clouds indicate that the sun has left the sky and, as John Calvin so beautifully puts it, 'There is no time when God does not invite us to himself.' No wonder James's counsel to the Christian facing trouble of any kind is so direct: 'He should pray'!

In 1924 two climbers by the name of Mallory and Irvine were members of an expedition that set out to conquer Mount Everest. Both were lost and after the failure of the expedition the party returned home to England. Addressing a meeting in London, one of the survivors described the ill-fated venture, then turned to a huge photograph of Mount Everest mounted on the wall behind him. 'Everest,' he cried, 'we tried to conquer you once, but you overpowered us. We tried to conquer you a second time, but again you were too much for us. But Everest, I want you to know that we are going to conquer you, for you can't grow any bigger, and we can!'

Do you see a spiritual parallel? There is a sense in which our afflictions can never grow any bigger. They can certainly never grow any bigger than God allows. But by the grace of God we can 'grow bigger'. We can 'grow bigger' by the power of prayer. Isaiah tells us that 'Those who hope in the Lord will renew their strength' (Isaiah 40:31). Our problems *can* be faced; our mountains *can* be climbed. We can say to the Everests we face, 'You can't grow any bigger, but I can,' and we can do so as we lay hold of God's power. Joseph Scriven's well-known words are exactly to the point:

> Have we trials and temptations?
> Is there trouble anywhere?
> We should never be discouraged:
> Take it to the Lord in prayer.
> Can we find a friend so faithful,
> Who will all our sorrows share?
> Jesus knows our every weakness:
> Take it to the Lord in prayer.

2. In times of pleasure

'Is anyone happy? Let him sing songs of praise.'

As he did when writing to the Christian under pressure and facing the troubles of life, James has a word to describe the condition of his reader and then gives him a word of counsel.

1. The condition. 'Is anyone happy?' Again, the key is the meaning of just one word, in this case the word 'happy'. The original word is *euthumei*, which is made up of the preposition *ue* ('well' or 'good') and the verbal form of the noun *thumos* ('soul' as the principle of life and feeling). Putting all of this together, the word denotes not a superficial euphoria, but a deep inner sense of well-being. The root of the word James uses occurs only four other times in the New Testament and it is instructive to look them up. The first is where Paul, grasping the opportunity to give his testimony before Felix, said, 'I gladly *[euthumos]* make my defence' (Acts 24:10). Then the basic word occurs three times in the story of the shipwreck during Paul's voyage to Rome. After several days' sailing in the teeth of the storm, most people on board had given up all hope of being saved, but Paul was told by an angel that there would be no loss of life, so he turned to them and said, 'I urge you to keep up your courage *[euthumein]*' (Acts 27:22), adding a moment later, 'So keep up your courage *[euthumeite]* men, for I have faith in God that it will happen just as he told me' (Acts 27:25). On the fourteenth night Paul again urged them not to panic, and we read that they 'were all encouraged *[euthumoi]*' (Acts 27:36).

The interesting thing to notice is that in each of these cases the word occurs in difficult circumstances, yet faced with either the tyrant or the tempest Paul had a deep, inner sense of joy, rooted in an unshakeable faith in God. There is surely a lesson here. It is the devil's lie that the Christian life is meant to be morbid, dreary or dull. The Christian life is certainly not funny — the issues are much too serious for that — but it should be wonderfully happy! The Bible says that God 'richly provides us with everything for our enjoyment' (1 Timothy 6:17) and that 'the kingdom of God is . . . righteousness, peace and joy in the Holy Spirit' (Romans 14:17). Life does have its problems and pressures, and the Bible never seeks to hide the fact. But it is equally insistent that they should never crush the joy from the Christian's heart. The story is told of a Christian lady who was very poor and yet radiantly happy in her assurance of salvation and in her joyful expectation of going to heaven when she died. A sceptic was speaking to her one day and asked, 'But supposing you never get there?' 'But I am sure

I will,' the lady replied, 'because God has promised it in his Word.' The sceptic persisted: 'But what if you were to reach the very gates of heaven and at the very last moment were refused entry?' The lady thought for a moment and then said, 'Well in that case I would walk around the walls of heaven all day shouting what a wonderful time I had had on the way there!' Whatever its theological imprecision, there was the genuine joy of her Christian experience. Laughter and a happy heart are not out of place in God's world.

Here, then, is the condition that James supposes some to be in; he pictures people with a settled sense of well-being. What should they do?

2. The counsel. 'Let him sing songs of praise.' Again, this is just one word in the Greek, and in this case the word is *psalleto*. Originally it meant 'to twang or twitch a stringed instrument with the hands', but later it developed to include wider aspects of sacred music and singing and, of course, it is the root of our English word 'psalm'. But to cut across the technicalities, James's counsel is perfectly clear; if you have an honest reason to be genuinely happy, then praise God! All through the Bible that same counsel is given by example and directive. David says,

> 'Give thanks to the Lord, call on his name;
> make known among the nations what he has done.
> Sing to him, sing praise to him;
> tell of all his wondrous acts.
> Glory in his holy name;
> let the hearts of those who seek the Lord rejoice'
> (1 Chronicles 16:8–10).

The psalms themselves are full of exhortations to praise God, with words like these: 'Come, let us sing for joy to the Lord; let us shout aloud to the Rock of our salvation. Let us come before him with thanksgiving and extol him with music and song' (Psalm 95:1, 2). The early church was a singing church: after the ascension the disciples 'returned to Jerusalem with great joy. And they stayed continually at the temple, praising God' (Luke 24:53). Joyful singing is meant to be a continuing characteristic of church life.

Paul's directions to the Colossians included this: 'Let the word of Christ dwell in you richly as you teach and admonish one another with all wisdom, and as you sing psalms, hymns and spiritual songs with gratitude in your hearts to God' (Colossians 3:16).

In today's technical, austere, brittle, science-orientated world all this emphasis on singing and praising may seem to some to be utterly irrelevant. But we dare not be wiser than God in these things and if he finds a place for them in his Word we have no right to rule them out of our lives. But we can go further than that and find an even wider biblical basis for obeying James's injunction.

In the first place, *it identifies the Christian.* Let me put that negatively to begin with. Paul saw that among the marks of ungodly men was the fact that even when they acknowledged the existence of God, 'They neither glorified him as God nor gave thanks to him' (Romans 1:21). That is one of the marks of an impenitent sinner – he refuses to praise God. But if that is the mark of the sinner, then praise is the mark of the saint. The Christian gratefully acknowledges that the Lord's compassions are 'new every morning' (Lamentations 3:23) and in Thomas Manton's words, recognizes that 'Every new mercy calls for a new song.' Never a day should pass in the Christian's life without him lifting his heart and voice in joyful praise to God for all his greatness and goodness. As someone has rightly said, 'It is amazing that man is not always praising God, since everything around him invites praise.'

In the second place, *it counteracts pride.* Humanly speaking, what are the things that are likely to produce a happy heart? The answer is obvious – a calm sea, a blue sky, good health, success in business, popularity, comfort. When things are going well a man tends to be happy in his heart. But pleasure brings peril, and there is no greater peril in pleasure than that there can be a tendency to forget God. He begins to set his mind on 'earthly things' (Colossians 3:2). He begins to get proud and self-centred and to act as if he achieved all his success and comfort and prosperity and happiness by his own efforts, and God gets pushed into the background. Yet the Bible anticipates this very thing. As they made their way through the wilderness to the promised land of Canaan, the children of Israel were warned again and again to 'be careful that you do not forget the Lord, who brought you out of Egypt, out of the land of slavery' (Deuteronomy 6:12). Arrogance and adoration cannot possibly live together and one of the surest antidotes to pride is to praise the Lord.

In the third place *it brings glory to God.* This follows on from what we have just seen, and again the Bible gives us the clear direction we need: 'He who sacrifices thank-offerings honours me, and he prepares the way so that I may show him the salvation of God' (Psalm 50:23). What a marvellous encouragement to offer our praise, adoration, worship and thanksgiving to God, to give him 'the glory due to his name'! (Psalm 96:8). Our attitude of heart, our words, our music, could never be bent to higher use than to bring honour to God. No wonder David cries out, 'Glorify the Lord with me; let us exalt his name together'! (Psalm 34:3.) Commenting on this last verse, Matthew Henry says this: 'We cannot make God greater or higher than he is; but if we adore him as infinitely great, and higher than the highest, he is pleased to reckon this magnifying and exalting him.' We surely need no higher incentive than that!

To sum up, then: in times of pressure we are to pray and in times of pleasure we are to praise. Here is counsel that is eminently practical yet deeply spiritual, down to earth yet up to heaven. When the world is on top of you, pray; when you are on top of the world, praise. In Alec Motyer's words, 'Our whole life, as we might say, should be so angled towards God that whatever strikes upon us, whether sorrow or joy, should be deflected upwards at once into his presence.'

We have a God for all seasons!

39.

This question of healing

> *'Is any one of you sick? He should call the elders of the church to pray over him and anoint him with oil in the name of the Lord. And the prayer offered in faith will make the sick person well; the Lord will raise him up. If he has sinned, he will be forgiven'* (James 5:14, 15).

We come now to some of the most controversial words in the whole of James's letter. For centuries Christians have been radically and sometimes heatedly divided on their meaning, significance and relevance and these divisions have not merely been between major historical groupings (such as the Eastern and Western churches) but often between Christians who would be united on most other scriptural issues.

It may help to study these two verses in three sections, the first by way of introduction, the second to point out some of the many interpretations of the verse that have been suggested and the third to outline some basic principles that seem to me to emerge from the text.

1. The paradoxes that are so confusing

Before we turn to anything approaching an exposition of the text, it must be obvious that the words before us raise at least two paradoxes. The first is that while the directions James gives seem so clear, the church as a whole tends to ignore them. Take the first two sentences, for instance. James posits a situation in which a member of the church is taken ill. The degree of illness is irrelevant at this point, but what we cannot escape is that in this situation James directs that certain action must be taken both by the sick man and by 'the elders of the church'. He must call for them and they must come to him, pray for him and anoint him with oil. The instructions are concise and apparently perfectly clear. They are as specific and direct, for instance, as those which Paul 'received from the Lord' (1 Corinthians 11:23) with regard to the Lord's Supper. But how many churches today give them equal weight? Do James's words here form an uncomplicated part of the general teaching and practice of the church at large today? The answer must surely be in the negative.

It has been suggested that with today's huge strides in medicine and surgery, and with the social provisions of the welfare state, the need for this kind of ministry by the elders of the church has been greatly reduced if not entirely eliminated, and one can understand the reasoning behind the suggestion. But surely that cannot explain the widespread historical retreat from James's simple words? After all, there has never been an age in which sickness has not wreaked the most terrible havoc and even today lingering and agonizing diseases still hold sway over multitudes of people, including those living in the most technically advanced nations of the world. Without any further attempt to discuss the matter at this stage, this is surely a puzzling paradox: the Bible is apparently offering a straightforward solution to one of man's greatest problems, and the church is largely ignoring it!

The second paradox does not concern its use or non-use, but the effect produced. Again, James is so uncomplicated: 'The prayer offered in faith will make the sick person well; the Lord *will* raise him up.' But is that the universal testimony of all those who have seemingly obeyed the instructions? Again, there can be only one honest answer: 'no!' Sometimes, there has been instantaneous and astonishing healing; sometimes, the cure has been so gradual and prolonged as to be scarcely identifiable with the scriptural instructions; at other times, the patient has continued to deteriorate and eventually died of his illness. Now that, surely, is a paradox. It seems to say, 'The Bible is true, but when we obey it, it does not always work,' and that statement poses a host of practical and theological problems. Again, let us not attempt any discussion of the matter at this stage. Let us just acknowledge that this is the second paradox that faces anyone coming to these verses with an open mind.

2. The propositions that are so conflicting

Commenting on these verses Thomas Manton wrote, 'This scripture hath occasioned controversy. Though in this exercise I would mainly pursue what is practical, yet when a matter lieth obvious and fair, like the angel in the way of Balaam, it cannot be avoided without some dispute and discussion.' His words may seem quaint, but we take his point! Down the years, these two verses have been interpreted in a multitude of ways and used to support many different quasi-medical practices in the Christian church. While some of the lines followed have seemed sane and spiritual, some have been patently absurd, while others have stretched all the rules of honest exegesis to breaking-point and beyond. Let us look at some of the propositions that have been made. In doing so, we will still not come to the actual words of the text in order, but we can easily bear them in mind as we go along, will refer to them often and will look at them in a more positive context later. Here, then, are some of the propositions that have been made about James's words.

1. That they find expression in extreme unction. Extreme unction is one of seven sacraments recognized by the Roman Catholic Church. The priest anoints with oil a person who is *in extremis* (that is, at the point of death) and prays for the remission of his sins. In its present form the sacrament was not introduced until the twelfth century, but the ultimate question to ask is whether it has any scriptural basis in these words by James. The merest glance provides the answer. Extreme unction is only administered when the sick person is expected to die, whereas James is speaking of someone who is expected to recover. There could hardly be a greater discrepancy! In spite of the footnote to these verses in the Douai Version of the Bible which says that they provide 'a plain warrant for the Sacrament of Extreme Unction', the proposition falls flat on its face at the very first glance.

2. That they are the basis for 'divine healing' ministries.

Some churches that emphasize this question of healing give a large place to specific people with 'a gift of healing'. This sometimes forms a major part of an itinerant ministry which includes 'divine healing crusades' and the like. With no space to comment on these in detail, we can surely say that these words of James cannot possibly form a valid basis for them. In the first place, there is no suggestion by James that anybody in the situation had 'a gift of healing'. The sick man was to call for 'the elders of the church', who are seen in the New Testament to be called and equipped by the Holy Spirit to serve the church in various capacities and in general to be 'overseers' and 'shepherds of the church' (Acts 20:28). They were to be so qualified that they were able to 'encourage others by sound doctrine and refute those who oppose it' (Titus 1:9), but in not a single case are we told of an elder having 'the gift of healing' or of being a miracle-worker. In the second place, it is quite plain from the text that James has in mind a normal domestic church situation and not a special event when a 'healer' arrives in town to conduct a special event. As Frank Gabelein puts it, 'Whatever else it was, the scene James described was intimate and personal, not a public display.' These verses, then, have no direct relationship to 'divine healing' ministries.

3. That they were only intended for the apostolic age and are no longer relevant or applicable. While this view would be held with certain variations, its general line has many weighty supporters. In the seventeenth century, John Trapp said that anointing with oil, 'an extraordinary sign of an extraordinary cure,' was only used 'as an outward symbol and sign till miracles ceased'. John Howe, one-time chaplain to Oliver Cromwell, limited the use of James's words to the age when it was 'necessary that frequent miracles should be wrought for the confirmation of Christianity'. The great Matthew Henry wrote tersely, 'When miracles ceased, this institution ceased also.' Matthew Poole said that the outward rite was only relevant while the gift of miracles lasted, 'but the gift ceasing, it is vainly used'. John Calvin's judgement was that 'As the reality of the sign continued only for a time in the church, the symbol must have been only for a time.'

Those are impressive statements, yet to endorse their view without qualification raises many questions. Can we agree flatly that miracles have ceased? Are there no places in the world today where 'signs' would be out of place for 'the confirmation of Christianity'? Can we say 'it is vainly used' and that there are no instances of it being used effectively? Can we overthrow the judgement and testimony of other godly men who would take the opposite view? The questions deserve very careful answers!

4. That this is the only divine prescription for healing and that every Christian should ask for healing in this way. This is a somewhat extreme view, but it demands to be looked at. The basic objection to this particular proposition is that it limits God to working in supernatural ways, without recourse to means of any kind. But surely this is manifestly untrue! In the foreword to his splendid book *Miraculous Healing*, Dr Henry W. Frost explains his choice of the title by saying that 'Healing of any kind is necessarily divine. A physician does not heal, nor medicine, nor a scientific diet, nor an improved environment, nor anything else that may be named. All creation or re-creation is from God; and hence, in every instance of healing, he is the one who heals, whether he acts directly through unknown laws or indirectly through known laws.'

We could elaborate on this. The complex healing mechanism of the body, which is triggered off by any illness, injury or disease, is a gift from God. Fresh air and sunshine are gifts from God. Vitamins and proteins are gifts from God. Medicine is a gift from God. The diagnostician's skill is a gift from God and so is the surgeon's. All these are means God uses to restore health and we actually limit God when we confine him to the miraculous.

A second objection to this particular proposition is that it runs counter to the words of Jesus. Answering those who queried his association with notorious sinners, Jesus said, 'It is not the healthy who need a doctor, but the sick' (Matthew 9:12). Here is a clear acknowledgement that those who are sick *do* need a doctor and that we are not to think of the medical profession as being in any way God's second-best.

There is the further objection that the proposition conflicts with the experience of the apostles. In one of his final letters Paul refers to 'our dear friend Luke, the doctor' (Colossians 4:14) with the clear inference that as a man of God he was honourably able to continue his medical practice. Again, sympathizing with his chronic illness, Paul advised Timothy, 'Stop drinking only water, and use a little wine because of your stomach and your frequent illnesses' (1 Timothy 5:23). But surely Paul would have instructed him to call the elders if their ministry was the only God-honouring means of restoration?

5. That no Christian need ever be ill, because there is healing in the atonement. Put very basically, this suggests that it is God's invariable intention that his people should always enjoy perfect health and they may therefore claim it as of right. Theologically this argument looks mainly to Matthew's note that the healing ministry of Jesus was carried out to fulfil Isaiah's words that 'He took up our infirmities and carried our diseases' (Matthew 8:17). The quotation is from Isaiah 53:4, where an alternative reading would allow the word 'sickness' to be brought in.

Now while it is undoubtedly true that Jesus took upon himself the divine judgement on his people's sins, including the penalty of physical death, it is clearly *not* true that Christians have immediate and complete possession here and now of *all* the benefits of his death. Ultimately, the Christian will be free from temptation, but for the moment he must still face it. Ultimately, there will be for the Christian no more tears, sorrow, crying or pain, but while he lives on this present earth, these remain facts of life. One day, the Lord will give the Christian a body 'like his glorious body' (Philippians 3:21), but for the moment he must live within his natural, physical limitations. Although death for the Christian has lost its sting, being swallowed up in the victory of Christ's resurrection, it is still something he must experience here on earth. It has not been removed from him by the atonement. The same is clearly true about bodily sickness. Paul says that while we already have 'the firstfruits of the Spirit', we still 'wait for . . . the redemption of our bodies' (Romans 8:23).

Put very simply, a dogmatic proposition about there being 'healing in the atonement' is found to prove too much and to raise more questions than it answers. Why, for instance, did Paul have to admit to Timothy, 'I left Trophimus sick in Miletus' (2 Timothy 4:20) instead of persuading his sick friend to claim healing as his right? Why did he allow his beloved fellow-worker Epaphroditus to become so ill that he 'almost died' (Philippians 2:27) instead of pointing him to the guaranteed remedy? Yet it is Paul himself who provides the clinching answer to the argument when he tells us of his 'thorn in the flesh' (2 Corinthians 12:7). Various suggestions have been made as to its precise nature, the most plausible being that it was some kind of eye disease. What we do know is that although he prayed three times for it to be removed, God did not grant his request, telling him instead, 'My grace is sufficient for you, for my power is made perfect in weakness' (2 Corinthians 12:9). This is obviously a key statement in the matter, for it shows that in his infinite wisdom God sometimes allows his children to suffer. While he undoubtedly *can* preserve or restore from sickness, it is clearly not always his *will* to do so.

The propositions at which we have looked briefly are only some of many, but to look at any more might only add to the sense that these two apparently straightforward verses by James have been little more than a theological and ecclesiastical battleground. Instead, let us try to gather together a positive line of interpretation that seeks to do justice both to history and to the actual text before us. In doing so, perhaps I should say that I shall not quote any 'case histories', as I incline to the view that individual cases make bad law, and can be made to prove almost anything. Many non-Christian religions could produce startling 'evidence' of healing; the devil himself is capable of 'counterfeit miracles, signs and wonders' (2 Thessalonians 2:9); and Jesus prophesied that there would be 'false Christs and false prophets' who would 'perform great signs and miracles' (Matthew 24:24). Instead, let us turn to the text of James's words for the third and major section of our study.

3. The principles that are so convincing

In view of all the controversy over this passage, it may seem bold to suggest that it contains any clear and convincing principles at all. But I believe that it does and that these will emerge as we go through the text in order.

1. The complaint. 'Is any one of you sick?' The Greek word translated 'sick' is *asthenei* which literally means 'without strength'. We can therefore be sure that James is not speaking of a minor discomfort such as a slight headache or an attack of indigestion but rather of a relatively serious condition. This is perhaps confirmed by the fact that the patient has to call for help, the inference being that he is not well enough to go and receive it.

2. The call. 'He should call the elders of the church.' As we have already seen, these elders held God-ordained positions of spiritual and practical leadership within the local church, but the important thing to notice here is that the human initiative comes from the patient. As John Bird says, 'There is no warrant in Scripture for people running around with bottles of oil healing anyone and everyone.' The responsibility rests first with the person who is sick. For reasons we shall see later, this responsibility is very serious.

3. The command. The elders were '. . . to pray over him and anoint him with oil in the name of the Lord'. Quite apart from any miraculous element, there is a warm, pastoral word here. As R. V. G. Tasker comments, 'While it is true that they could intercede for the sick man without being present at his bedside, nevertheless, by coming to the actual scene of the suffering and by praying within sight and hearing of the sufferer himself, not only is their prayer likely to be more heartfelt and fervid, but the stricken man may well become more conscious of the effective power of prayer . . .' There is surely an incidental word here for all those in positions of leadership and responsibility within the church? Let them remember that their duties are not primarily institutional, but personal. Their first concern should be for people, not things, and they should continually ask the Lord for that sensitive spirit that enables them with sincerity and understanding to 'rejoice with those who rejoice' and 'mourn with those who mourn' (Romans 12:15). Happy the church that is served by leaders with that kind of loving, selfless concern!

The responsibility of the elders continues with the

instruction that they are to 'anoint him with oil in the name of the Lord'. The use of oil for medicinal purposes was apparently common in biblical times. Isaiah speaks of bruises, sores and wounds that have not been 'soothed with oil' (Isaiah 1:6), and in the story of the Good Samaritan, part of the emergency first-aid given to the wounded man included 'pouring on oil and wine' (Luke 10:34). On the other hand, when Jesus sent the twelve apostles out into Galilee for an intensive ministry of preaching and healing, we read that 'They drove out many demons and anointed many sick people with oil and healed them' (Mark 6:13) and in this case we must surely assume that the oil was not used medicinally, but symbolically. The cures did not stem from the properties of the oil, but from the power of the Lord, working through the apostles. The oil was merely a 'visual aid', perhaps granted by the Lord to help in focusing the faith of the sufferers.

Jesus did much the same thing in the healing of a deaf and dumb man, when he 'spat and touched the man's tongue' (Mark 7:33), in the healing of a blind man, when he 'spat on the man's eyes' (Mark 8:23), and in the healing of a man blind from birth, when he 'spat on the ground, made some mud with the saliva, and put it on the man's eyes' (John 9:6). Bearing these incidents in mind, it would not be difficult to see that this could be the significance of the oil in the situation depicted by James. Incidentally, it is worth noting that Jesus did not always use these 'visual aids' in performing his miracles, nor did he give any instructions to the disciples to do so later in commissioning them for their ministry. This makes it additionally clear that the power did not rest in the means but in the Lord. As A. P. Waterson wisely writes in *The New Bible Dictionary,* 'Great care must be exercised in avoiding the magical in the search for the miraculous.'

4. The consequences. 'And the prayer offered in faith will make the sick person well; the Lord will raise him up. If he has sinned, he will be forgiven.' It could probably be said that it is the tone of these two sentences that lies at the heart of the controversy about James's teaching on the subject of healing. If we read, 'And the prayer offered in faith *may* make the sick person well' there would be little or no problem! But we do not read that. We are faced with the straightforward assertion that the person concerned *will* be healed. There are those who have sought to 'spiritualize' the words, either by suggesting that even in the absence of physical healing the sufferer will be given a greater measure of grace to bear his illness and could therefore be said to have been 'raised up', or by saying that as the Christian would go to heaven when he died he would be 'raised up' eventually, but neither of these explanations begins to satisfy the demands of James's simple words. He promises that there will be healing from physical illness.

Not only that, but James adds a second (but not secondary) consequence, namely that 'If he has sinned, he will be forgiven.' The use of the word 'if' does not, of course, mean that the sufferer might possibly be without sin at all; the Bible makes it clear that no such person exists. James is referring to the possibility of a direct link between the patient's sin and his sickness, the link of cause and effect, and this is completely consistent with the Bible's general teaching on the subject. All sickness is included in Paul's blunt statement that 'In Adam all die' (1 Corinthians 15:22). All human sorrow, pain and suffering stem from Adam's deadly sin. At the same time, not all sickness is a *direct* result of a person's sin. This can be the case, both by specific divine judgement (of which there are many examples in the Bible) or by the natural course of events (venereal disease being an obvious example). But this is not always the case. When the disciples asked Jesus whose sin was responsible for the tragic condition of a man blind from birth and he answered, 'Neither this man nor his parents sinned, but this happened so that the work of God might be displayed in his life' (John 9:3), he was not suggesting that these three people were sinless, but that their sin did not cause the man's blindness.

The connection between sickness and sin is sometimes shrouded in mystery, but there can be no doubting its reality. What James is saying here is that if in the case concerned some sin has caused or contributed to the sickness, either by way of divine chastisement or by what we might call 'natural causes', God will not only heal the person concerned of sickness, but will also graciously forgive the sin that caused or contributed to the trouble; and in case that begins to sound like the elders acting in some priestly, mediatorial capacity, with the ability to secure forgiveness for other people, we should add that there is the obvious assumption that the patient is truly repentant and that he is mingling his heartfelt prayers with theirs.

5. The conditions. '. . . in the name of the Lord' and '. . . the prayer offered in faith . . .' The more I have studied this section of James's letter, the more I have become convinced that these two phrases hold the key to their real meaning and significance, and I believe it would not be exaggerating to say that every historical, ecclesiastical and theological argument must eventually be settled in the light of their meaning. Let me illustrate why I believe they are so important. Two Christians fall ill and both call for the elders of the church. They are prayed over, and anointed with oil. One dies and the other is healed. Why? Hold their cases alongside James's words and see if there can be any scriptural explanation. In both cases, there are certain *visible* factors that can be checked off as identical in each case. Both are sick, both call for the elders, in both cases the elders come, in both cases the sufferer is prayed over and anointed with oil. But two things are missing from this visible check-list – the phrases 'in the name of the Lord' and 'the prayer offered in faith'. These are what we might call the *invisible* conditions, but as the visible conditions are met in the case of the patient who dies as well as in the case of the person who recovers, they obviously hold the key to the difference between success and failure. That being so, they deserve particularly close attention.

The first of these conditions is that the patient be anointed with oil *'in the name of the Lord'*. It must be obvious that this means much more than the mechanical repetition of a phrase such as 'We do this in your name,' which can be no more than an empty formula. The simple word 'name' contains the first clue we need. The Greek word is *onoma*, which is made up from the same root as the noun *nous* ('mind') and the verb *ginosko* ('to know'). This explains why many times in the Bible a person's 'name' identifies not only *who* a person is, but *what* he is. It is a revelation of his mind, his character, his personality. Applying this principle to the situation before us, 'the name of the

Lord' is equivalent to the active presence of God in his revealed nature and character. James himself gave an illustration of this a little earlier when he referred to prophets 'who spoke *in the name of the Lord*' (5:10). These men spoke under a divine mandate, according to God's will, on his authority, and it was only because they did so that their ministries were valid and effective. This point comes across in an Old Testament statement about the ministry of false prophets. People who wanted to know when a message had not in fact been spoken by the Lord were given this touchstone: 'If what a prophet proclaims in the name of the Lord does not take place or come true, that is a message the Lord has not spoken. That prophet has spoken presumptuously' (Deuteronomy 18:22). A message authentically spoken 'in the name of the Lord' would be bound to come to pass.

Now let us apply this principle to the question of healing. James is not saying that whenever a Christian falls ill he must immediately send for the elders to anoint him with oil. The calling of the elders and their response are not automatic, press-button procedures for healing. If they were, there would presumably be no need for Christians to die at all, as they could avert death whenever it threatened! The plain truth is that the actions James describes are only effective when carried out 'in the name of the Lord', that is to say in accordance with his mind; on his authority. There must therefore be a thoughtful, Spirit-directed conviction that it is right to call for the elders, and as 'God is not a God of disorder' (1 Corinthians 14:33) we may expect that when there is, the elders will have a similar conviction that the course of action is right. The caller and the called must act 'in the name of the Lord'.

The second 'invisible' condition is that there must be *'the prayer offered in faith'*. One is immediately reminded of the condition James attached to the prayer of the person seeking spiritual wisdom, when he said that 'He must believe and not doubt' (1:6), and as we shall see in a moment this fits in exactly with what we have already discovered about acting 'in the name of the Lord'. But what is the meaning of 'the prayer offered in faith'? The biblical answer comes across by a specific definition and a general principle. The specific definition is that in which Paul tells us that 'Everything that does not come from faith is sin' (Romans 14:23). The Amplified Bible gives this helpful elaboration: 'For whatever does not originate and proceed from faith is sin – that is, whatever is done without a conviction of its approval by God is sinful.' Applying this definition to what James is saying, 'the prayer offered in faith' is a prayer offered with the definite conviction that it has God's approval.

Turning from the specific definition to the general principle, we need to recognize that James's teaching on healing is part of a larger section concerned with the whole subject of prayer. He refers to prayers of intercession and thanksgiving (v. 13), prayer for the sick (vv. 14, 15), prayer for one another (v. 16) and, by way of example, the prayers of Elijah (vv. 17, 18). With that in mind, we must approach any interpretation of the passage on healing with the understanding that it must be subject to the biblical laws that govern the whole question of prayer. We cannot interpret one statement about prayer in a way that does violence to the general teaching of Scripture on the subject.

Now let us follow this line of thought in the light of the fact that James 'guarantees' the success of 'the prayer offered in faith'. Is there in fact a general law in Scripture that points just as certainly to answered prayer? Yes, there is, and there are at least seven occasions when it is stated. The first five come directly from the mouth of Jesus and the other two from John, and it will help if we see them all together. 'Again, I tell you that if two of you on earth agree about anything you ask for, it will be done for you by my Father in heaven. For where two or three come together *in my name*, there am I with them' (Matthew 18:19, 20); 'And I will do whatever you ask *in my name*, so that the Son may bring glory to the Father' (John 14:13); 'You may ask me for anything *in my name*, and I will do it' (John 14:14); 'You did not choose me, but I chose you to go and bear fruit – fruit that will last. Then the Father will give you whatever you ask *in my name*' (John 15:16); 'I tell you the truth, my Father will give you whatever you ask *in my name*' (John 16:23); 'Dear friends, if our hearts do not condemn us, we have confidence before God and receive from him anything we ask, because we obey his commands and *do what pleases him*' (1 John 3: 21, 22); 'This is the confidence we have in approaching God: that if we ask anything *according to his will*, he hears us' (1 John 5:14).

On that evidence (which merely supports the obvious truth that must follow from the Bible's revelation of the nature of God) it is clear that all the laws of prayer are eventually governed by this one principle: to be successful, prayer must be according to God's will. It is difficult to see that any Christian would wish to dispute that. Furthermore, we cannot alter God's will by our goodness, our persistence, nor even by our faith. This, incidentally, is the answer to the cruel assertion made by some people that anybody can be miraculously healed 'as long as they have enough faith'! That is plainly not true. We cannot alter God's will by an effort of faith, nor by 'claiming' something he has not promised or designed to do. As Spiros Zodhiates puts it, 'If God does not will a thing, neither medicine nor prayer will accomplish the results which we want. His results will come to pass, and happy is the man who is satisfied with the fulfilment of God's wishes rather than his own.'

We need to have this clearly in our minds if we are to have a sane grasp of these verses. As Henry Frost makes so clear, Jesus was sovereign as to the people he healed (he did not go everywhere and heal everybody); as to the conditions which he imposed upon men as a means of physical healing (he did not, for instance, always insist on their being disciples); in the limitations which he put upon himself in his acts of healing (he allowed many people to remain ill in spite of having the power to heal them); as to the persons to whom he gave the gift of healing (only eighty-two are recorded); and in making the Holy Spirit sovereign in his miracle administration (the Spirit granting his gifts according to his own will). From this overruling principle it would seem right to infer that 'the prayer offered in faith' is not something that man can produce at will, either by the repetition of certain words or in any other way, but is a gift from God, something that can only rightly be prayed when God gives assurance that its substance will be answered in accordance with his own sovereign purposes. As we shall see in our detailed study of verses 17, 18, the success of

Elijah's prayers, both for drought and rain, depended not on his own merit or effort, but upon God's determination to bring these things about, a determination he revealed to Elijah before the prophet turned to prayer. In other words, we could say that 'the prayer offered in faith' is circular in shape; it begins and ends in heaven, in the sovereign will of God.

From this we can go on to say that the primary thing in the whole situation is the glory of God, the working out of his will. Furthermore, we need to recognize that he can accomplish this in any of the circumstances that might follow a Christian's illness. Healing by the body's natural processes can be to the glory of God; healing by medical means can be to the glory of God; healing by supernatural intervention can be to the glory of God and so can the death of the sufferer. Notice how clearly this comes across in Paul's great statement to the Christians at Philippi, when he tells them that his over-arching concern is that 'Christ will be exalted in my body, whether by life or by death' (Philippians 1:20). The important thing is not health or sickness, but the glory of God.

In the light of all that we have seen, what should a Christian do when he is taken ill? Should he always and immediately go through the outward procedure of calling the elders and being prayed over and anointed, and then assess God's will by the outcome of the process? Surely not! While our faith in the omnipotent power of God will always encourage us with the possibility of praying for healing, the seriousness of the issues involved should prevent us praying recklessly.

The ultimate concern of this passage is not physical at all, but spiritual, and its most important theme is not the health of man, but the glory of God. As we have seen, 'the prayer offered in faith' is prayer made 'in the name of the Lord', that is, in accordance with his will. But how can we know his will? Paul admits quite frankly, 'We do not know what we ought to pray for' (Romans 8:26) and it would seem that Paul's prayers for deliverance from his thorn in the flesh constitute an example of this. Yet Paul also says that the Holy Spirit 'helps us in our weakness' and 'intercedes for us with groans that words cannot express' (Romans

8:26). Effective prayer (and notice how perfectly all of this holds together) is prayer that is God-initiated, God-energized. It is not meant to be a spiritual fire-engine brought in to deal with emergencies, but something that is the continuous expression of a Spirit-filled life. The Christian is therefore lovingly commanded to 'live by the Spirit' (Galatians 5:16) allowing him to direct and control every area of life, including the vital area of prayer.

When we do so, we will rejoice in being subject to the Lord's 'good, pleasing and perfect will' (Romans 12:2) and will instinctively recognize that, in Alec Motyer's fine words, 'The disposing of the welfare of a child of God cannot be left with greater confidence anywhere else than in the Father's hands, nor can any solution of the plight be more fitting, beneficial and glorious than that which he has in mind.'

40.

The power of prayer

'Therefore confess your sins to each other and pray for each other so that you may be healed. The prayer of a righteous man is powerful and effective. Elijah was a man just like us. He prayed earnestly that it would not rain, and it did not rain on the land for three and a half years. Again he prayed, and the heavens gave rain, and the earth produced its crops' (James 5:16–18).

There is a long-standing tradition that James was nicknamed 'Camel Knees' because his knees had become hardened and calloused through the amount of time he spent in prayer. There may be no way of confirming the legend, but one only has to read through his letter to know that he was deeply concerned with the matter of prayer and anxious to impress its importance on his readers. In the very opening part of his letter, he writes, 'If any of you lacks wisdom, he should ask God, who gives generously to all without finding fault; and it will be given to him. But when he asks, he must believe and not doubt . . .' (1:5, 6); later, in examining the reasons for men's failures in the matter of prayer, he says, 'You do not have, because you do not ask God' (4:2) and adds, 'When you ask, you do not receive, because you ask with wrong motives, that you may spend what you get on your pleasures' (4:3).

Now, as he comes towards the end of his letter, he returns to this vitally important subject. The whole of the section taking in verses 13–18 is concerned with prayer and might helpfully have been looked at as a whole, but the three verses now before us do have something specific to say: they speak to us of the power of prayer. We can examine the text under three headings.

1. A vital doctrine

'The prayer of a righteous man is powerful and effective' (v. 16).

This phrase not only lies in the centre of the wider section on prayer (vv. 13–18), but it lies at the very heart of everything the section teaches. It is the hub around which it all revolves, the rock on which it is built. It is the vital doctrinal basis from which all the practical implications flow. As we examine it closely, we can see three things.

1. The intensity of the asking. Perhaps the very first thing to be said about the sentence we are examining at the moment is that there is much more to it than meets the eye. This becomes clear from the great variety of words employed by the various English translations in trying to capture the meaning of the original language, and although the NIV is as smooth as any, it is hard-pressed to do justice to all that James wrote. The first sense that James is concerned with is the *power* of prayer that comes across in the particular word 'prayer' he uses here. It is not the most common New Testament word for prayer, which is *proseuche*; instead, James uses the distinctive word *deesis.* The significance of this is that whereas *proseuche* refers to what we could call prayer in general, *deesis* puts the emphasis on the sense of specific need. It has a feeling of urgency and importance about it. In ancient Greek it was commonly addressed to ruling kings and in the New Testament it is exclusively used in addressing God. Combining the greatness of the need and the greatness of the person to whom it is addressed, perhaps the English word 'supplication' comes nearest to capturing its precise nuance.

This already begins to point us in the right direction as we consider the quality of prayer that James says proves to be effective, but before we go any further it might be helpful to note some of the things that are *not* necessary to make prayer effective. For instance, it does not have to be phrased in religious language. An American lady is said to have visited Israel very late in life and on her return home to have started taking a course in Hebrew. When asked why she was taking up such a difficult language so late in life, she replied, 'Well, it will not be long before I die, and when I do I would love to greet my Maker in his native tongue'! But there is no need to pray in Hebrew, or Greek, or seventeenth-century English, or any other special 'religious' language in order for prayer to be effective. Nor does prayer have to be long in order to be effective. Although we do read of people spending nights and days in prayer, most of the prayers recorded in the Bible are very brief. Peter's 'Lord, save me!' (Matthew 14:30) could not have been briefer – nor more effective. The publican could only blurt out, 'God, have mercy on me, a sinner' (Luke 18:13), but he was saved as a result. Even the most magnificent prayer in the Bible, recorded in John 17, only takes a few minutes to read. The length of the prayer is not, therefore, the vitally important thing. Again, frequency of prayer is not the all-important thing. We are certainly told to 'pray continually' (1 Thessalonians 5:17), but the meaning is clearly not that we should never do anything else. Alongside that command we have to place the words of Jesus: 'And when you pray, do not keep on babbling like pagans, for they think they will be heard because of their many words' (Matthew 6:7). A multiplicity of words is clearly no guarantee of blessing.

Then what *is* important? There are many different answers to that question, and one of them is what I have called 'intensity', that is to say fervency, earnestness. There is a marvellous illustration of this in the Old Testament, when Jacob, wrestling with God himself in the form of a strange nocturnal visitor, cried out, 'I will not let you go unless you bless me' (Genesis 32:26). In the New Testament, Epaphroditus provides another example of the same spirit. Paul told the Colossians, 'He is always wrestling in prayer for you' (Colossians 4:12). Here is the vital difference between merely saying prayers and actually praying. It is relatively easy to say prayers, to go through a daily routine of repeating words with our eyes closed, but to be fervent in prayer is both difficult and costly. Yet such fervency is essential if our praying is to achieve its end. As Jim Elliot wrote in his diary, 'Cold prayers, like cold suitors, are seldom effective in their aims.'

The point I have been making is underlined by the fact that James uses the word 'powerful' to describe the kind of prayer he has in mind. This translates the Greek adjective *ischuei*, which when used in other contexts means strong in body and sound in health. It is a living, active, dynamic word. This comes across well in one particular instance recorded in Acts, where we are told that 'The word of the Lord spread widely and grew in power *[ischuen]*' (Acts 19:20). One only has to imagine those early Christians witnessing boldly for Christ in a hostile environment to sense the intensity of their efforts. There was a living dynamism about their evangelism. They were gripped by the truth that their message was a matter of life or death and they poured themselves into its proclamation with all their sanctified energies. Can the same spirit be said to be true of our praying? Is it not tragically true that all too often it is almost totally devoid of the spirit that would entitle it to be called 'powerful'?

2. The integrity of the asker. This next condition of effective prayer is stated quite clearly: the person praying must be 'a righteous man'. This is a truth so deeply embedded in scriptural teaching that when the Jews told Jesus, 'We know that God does not listen to sinners' (John 9:31), they seem to have been repeating some kind of proverb which was a counterpart of the Old Testament tenet: '[The Lord] hears the prayers of the righteous' (Proverbs 15:29).

But what does James mean by 'a righteous man'? The word 'righteous' is the Greek adjectival noun *dikaiou*, which comes from one of the most important families of words in the whole of the New Testament, a family that includes the great salvation word 'righteousness'. It is therefore important that we understand exactly how James is using the word here. Briefly, we can say that the Bible uses the word 'righteous' in two senses. It uses it in what we might call the spiritual sense and the moral sense. Let us take an example of each. When Paul says that 'There is no-one righteous *[dikaois]*, not even one' (Romans 3:10), he is clearly using the word in a spiritual sense and saying that there is not a single person on earth who is perfect in God's sight on the basis of his own qualities and efforts. On the other hand, when John writes that 'He who does what is right is righteous *[dikaois]*' (1 John 3:7), he is clearly using the word in a moral sense and saying that the quality of a man's life is an important test of whether or not he is truly right with God.

Now in what sense is James using the word here? Is it in the spiritual sense? Surely not, because if it is true that only the prayer of 'a righteous man' is powerful and effective, and no one is righteous, then no one can pray effectively. But let us take this a little further. Paul's terrible indictment that no one is righteous no longer holds against Christians, because as he himself is so careful to point out, 'Christ is the end of the law so that there may be righteousness for everyone who believes' (Romans 10:4). Then does this mean that because, as Paul says elsewhere, 'Christ Jesus . . . has become for us . . . our righteousness' (1 Corinthians 1:30), all our prayers are always powerful and effective? The answer is obviously in the negative and provides another reason for knowing that James does not have this spiritual righteousness in mind when he speaks of 'a righteous man'.

James is clearly using the word 'righteous' in a moral sense and showing its great importance in the matter of prayer. It is not enough for a person to be able to say, 'I am a Christian,' and look to his spiritual or positional righteousness as a guarantee of praying successfully; he must also be morally righteous. That simple truth is underlined throughout the Bible. The psalmist could testify to answered prayer, but he also indicated that it was conditional: 'If I had cherished sin in my heart, the Lord would not have listened' (Psalm 66:18). Isaiah's word to God's disobedient people emphasized the same principle: 'Surely the arm of the Lord is not too short to save, nor his ear too dull to hear. But your iniquities have separated you from your God; your sins have hidden his face from you, so that he will not hear' (Isaiah 59:1, 2). John states the same truth from a positive angle: 'Dear friends, if our hearts do not condemn us, we have confidence before God and receive from him anything we ask, because we obey his commands and do what pleases him' (1 John 3:21, 22).

There is a striking illustration of all of this included in the story of Joshua's leadership of the people of Israel. After the conquest of Jericho, they came to the comparatively insignificant town of Ai. After listening to the report of a reconnaissance party, Joshua decided that there was no need to deploy his whole army to deal with it; two or three thousand men would do the trick very nicely. But Joshua's men met with humiliating defeat at Ai and in the hour of humiliation Joshua did what we might reasonably expect a spiritual leader to do – he called Israel to prayer. All day long Joshua and the elders of Israel lay on their faces and called upon God. And what did God do? He stopped the prayer meeting! But why? Was praying not the most important thing Israel could do at that time? No! And God's word to Joshua explained why: 'Stand up! What are you doing down on your face? Israel has sinned; they have violated my covenant, which I commanded them to keep . . . That is why the Israelites cannot stand against their enemies' (Joshua 7:10–12). Recognizing the truth of the situation, Joshua began the investigations that eventually led to the execution of the guilty Achan and when that was done, but only then, the people of Israel went on to further victories. Only when there was moral, practical righteousness was Israel's prayer effective. We cannot expect to live defectively and pray effectively.

3. The immensity of the answer. James has just one word to describe this: he says that it is 'effective'. The particular word he uses here is the Greek *energoumene*, and the most important point to be made about it is that throughout the New Testament it is almost invariably used of God at work. To give just one example: Paul writes of the gospel as 'the word of God, which is at work in you who believe' (1 Thessalonians 2:13), showing that only God can apply his Word effectively to our hearts and lives. Applying the same line of truth to the matter of prayer, James is telling us that if our prayer is going to be truly effective it must be divinely energized. This will not necessarily entail any kind of spectacular or noisy manifestation – think of the vast energies at work in the rising of the sun or even the opening of a flower, which to the human ear happen in serene silence – but if our prayer is to be effective it must be energized by God himself, as part of the mysterious ministry of the Holy Spirit, who 'intercedes for us with groans that words cannot express' (Romans 8:26).

As to the immense power unleashed through prayer, one only has to read the Bible to agree with the verdict of one who expressed it like this: 'Prayer has divided seas, rolled up flowing rivers, made flinty rocks gush into fountains, quenched flames of fire, muzzled lions, disarmed vipers and poisons, marshalled the stars against the wicked, stopped the course of the moon, arrested the sun in its rapid race, burst open iron gates, released souls from eternity, conquered the strongest devils, commanded legions of angels down from heaven. Prayer has bridled and chained the raging passions of man and routed and destroyed vast armies of proud, daring, blustering atheists. Prayer has brought one man from the bottom of the sea and carried another in a chariot of fire to heaven. What has prayer *not* done?'

Prayer works! Or, to put it more accurately, God works through prayer. It is one of the means of grace he uses to bring about his sovereign purposes in the world. This is the vital doctrine James establishes in the words we have been studying.

2. A vivid demonstration

'Elijah was a man just like us. He prayed earnestly that it would not rain, and it did not rain on the land for three and a half years. Again he prayed, and the heavens gave rain, and the earth produced its crops' (v. 17, 18).

James could have chosen many Old Testament examples of the effective prayer of righteous men. He could have cited Moses, who 'lay prostrate before the Lord . . . forty days and forty nights' (Deuteronomy 9:25); or Samuel, who 'cried out to the Lord all . . . night' (1 Samuel 15:11); or Daniel, who 'three times a day . . . got down on his knees and prayed, giving thanks to his God' (Daniel 6:10). His reason for choosing Elijah was probably that to the Jews Elijah represented the prophets in the same personalized way that Moses represented the law. Be that as it may, two things stand out in the illustration James gives.

1. Natural weakness. James says that Elijah was 'a man just like us'. This is the first thing he wants to impress upon us. He is not using some kind of superman, some biological or spiritual freak, to help in making his point; instead, he is using someone 'just like us'. This translates the single Greek word *homoiopathes*, which literally means something like 'of the same experience' or 'of the same suffering'.

A similar word was used by Paul at Lystra when he protested to the mob seeking to worship him and Barnabas that 'We too are only men, human like you *[homoiopathesis]*' (Acts 14:15). James's point is clear. Elijah was a prophet, but he was not perfect. He was prone to all of our failures and weaknesses and sins. He was susceptible to all of our diseases. He was simply a man. We might say that in some senses he was no better than we are. He was in no way exempt by nature from temptation or trial, nor were these things in any particular way held back by God from striking at him. Nowhere in the story of Elijah does that come across more vividly than in the account of what happened after that tremendous victory at Mount Carmel over the prophets of Baal. With no attempt to gloss over the imperfection of one of the greatest Old Testament heroes, the Bible tells us that after his great triumph Elijah came face to face with the threat of the wicked Jezebel and ran for his life. The man who had defied hundreds of prophets now ran away from one devil-inspired woman, escaped into the wilderness, lay down under a juniper tree and cried out to God, 'Take my life; I am no better than my ancestors' (1 Kings 19:4). Yet it is precisely this element of weakness in Elijah that makes his story such an encouragement to us. The story of Elijah on the mountain, opposing the prophets of Baal, may make us feel that that is something right outside our kind of experience. If so, then we fail to grasp the point James is making. His concern is not to show Elijah as an extraordinary miracle-worker, but as an ordinary man who knew the humiliation of defeat and who could put his head between his knees and wish himself dead. But why should that encourage us? Because it is this man – this dejected prophet on the brink of suicidal depression – who had such power with God that, in Thomas Manton's words, he 'seemed to have the key to heaven, to open and shut it at pleasure'!

There is a great danger in reading in the Bible of outstanding incidents linked with certain men and women to think that the people involved lived as it were in a different world, breathing different air. But that is not so! They lived in our world. They were ordinary people with all of our human weaknesses, all of our propensity to sin. They were fallen and fallible. It is crucially important that we grasp this.

2. Supernatural power. Having reminded us that Elijah was an ordinary mortal, James summarizes two incidents to make his point: 'He prayed earnestly that it would not rain, and it did not rain on the land for three and a half years. Again he prayed, and the heavens gave rain, and the earth produced its crops.' The interesting thing to notice here is that neither of the prayers – one at the beginning of the drought and the other at the end of it – is actually mentioned in the Old Testament narrative. What we are told is that one day Elijah went to the idolatrous King Ahab and said, 'As the Lord, the God of Israel, lives, whom I serve, there will be neither dew nor rain in the next few years except at my word' (1 Kings 17:1). There is no mention of prayer, yet the implication seems clear: God revealed his intentions to Elijah. He told him that he was going to stop up the heavens for three and a half years and, in the light of God's revealed will, Elijah was able to pray earnestly and confidently for this very thing. When the drought did eventually come about, then it happened according to God's word, and according to Elijah's prayer.

After the drought began, Elijah went to hide in a ravine at Kerith, where ravens brought him food twice a day. Later, he went on to Zarephath, where there was an amazing incident of the jug of oil that never ran dry and the jar of flour that was never used up. In the third year after that (which would comfortably accommodate the 'three and a half years' to which James refers), God said to Elijah, 'Go and present yourself to Ahab, and I will send rain on the land' (1 Kings 18:1). Here we are no longer in the realm of conjecture. God did reveal to Elijah that the drought was going to end and there seems little doubt that when Elijah heard this he both praised God for his promise and prayed for it to be fulfilled. In other words, Elijah harnessed his prayers to the revealed will of God. This seems to be confirmed by the fact that when the rains did come, Elijah was praying on top of Mount Carmel – and stopping every few minutes to ask his servant for a weather report!

The story, then, is of an ordinary man and a succession of extraordinary miracles, and the link James points out is that Elijah 'prayed earnestly'. The construction here is a very interesting one. The literal translation of the original reads, 'he prayed in prayer' or 'he prayed with prayer', the noun being used to emphasize the force of the verb. Jesus used the same kind of language at the Last Supper, when he told his disciples, 'I have eagerly desired' (literally, 'desired with desire') 'to eat this Passover with you before I suffer' (Luke 22:15). The whole feeling is one of intensity, earnestness, passion. Elijah 'prayed earnestly' and his petitions remain as living examples of the kind of prayer that prevails.

3. A valuable directive

'Therefore confess your sins to each other and pray for each other so that you may be healed' (v. 16).

There is an obvious connection between these words and the teaching in verses 14 and 15 about praying for those who were sick. If prayer is such a powerful weapon against serious sickness, surely we should seek to use it in every area of our life where healing is needed? There has been a great deal of discussion as to whether in this particular sentence James is referring to physical or spiritual healing and there is no clear clue in the word 'healed' that he uses here – the Greek *iathete* – as it is used in both senses elsewhere in the New Testament. The Roman centurion, deeply concerned about his paralysed servant, told Jesus, 'Lord, I do not deserve to have you come under my roof. But just say the word, and my servant will be healed' (Matthew 8:8), and the connotation is obviously physical. On the other hand, Jesus said that one of the reasons he taught in parables was to fulfil Isaiah's prophecy about those who were wilfully blind to the gospel:

> 'Otherwise they might see with their eyes,
>   hear with their ears,
>   understand with their hearts and turn,
> and I would heal them'
>
> (Matthew 13:15)

and the connotation is obviously spiritual. There may well be a mingling of both meanings in James's use of the word, though the early emphasis on confession leads me to believe that it is spiritual healing he has in mind. In the Amplified

Bible's words, James is anxious that the people concerned should be 'restored to a spiritual tone of mind and heart'.

As with healing, the confession of sins is a matter that has given rise to many unwise extravagancies and excesses, and it is therefore important that we take careful note of the principles embedded in what James has to say.

1. The area in which confession should be made. '... confess your sins to each other ...' It is on these words that the Roman Catholic Church bases its doctrine of auricular confession – that is to say, confession of sins to a priest – which is obligatory for Roman Catholics at least once every year. Yet it seems perfectly obvious that James intends no such thing. There is no suggestion here that any man is to be the depository for the sins of a multitude of other people, nor that confession should be put on an organized basis. As Robert Johnstone rightly says, 'Whenever it becomes in any way methodized into a system, for periodical observance, then, as it seems to me, the desire for it is certainly a symptom of spiritual disease – a disease which the supposed remedy will only aggravate.'

All of this is confirmed by James's words about confession being made 'to each other', rather than that the many should confess to the few. Yet we must balance this by saying that James is obviously not suggesting that all Christians are to confess all their sins to all other Christians. The result would obviously be carnal chaos and the cause of even more sin. Glimpses of the dangers involved can be seen in the history of certain groups that have emphasized the confessional element in their personal relationships with fellow Christians and we would do well to learn the lessons. Then what is the area in which confession should be made?

The first clearly takes in those we have wronged. In the course of the Sermon on the Mount, Jesus said, 'Therefore, if you are offering your gift at the altar and there remember that your brother has something against you, leave your gift there in front of the altar. First go and be reconciled to your brother; then come and offer your gift' (Matthew 5:23, 24). Albert Barnes's comment on that verse sums up the lesson very well: 'The worship of God will not be acceptable, however well performed externally, until we are at peace with those that we have injured.' Here is an important biblical principle, yet one which is widely ignored. Who can possibly tell how much of our public and private worship is nullified because of our obstinate refusal to seek the forgiveness of fellow Christians we have offended in one way or another and with whom there is a festering sore of disagreement? We ignore James's words at our peril!

A second area which James's words would seem to suggest would be that in which we sense the need of someone else's counsel in dealing with a particular problem or failure. If there are times when we feel that because of his or her experience, knowledge of life, background, walk with God or knowledge of the Scriptures, a particular person would be able to help us in dealing with a particular weakness, failure or sin, then let us not be too proud to seek that person's help.

Finally – though probably just outside of James's immediate intention – there is the sad and serious case where sin has caused a public scandal which brings public discredit to the gospel. In this case, however costly it may be to do so, confession should be made to the whole church, so that the matter might be dealt with openly and honestly and in a way most likely to settle it once and for all.

2. The attitude in which confession should be made. '. . . and pray for each other . . .' These words are vitally important, because they remind us that James is not looking at the subject of confession in isolation, but rather including it in the wider context of prayer. It is the spirit of prayer that should condition confession. This is the attitude in which we should approach another Christian for help and in which we should listen to the confession and confidence of a fellow believer. We are not to confess our sins in a spirit of mock humility, nor as a perverted device to draw attention to ourselves. We are not to do it in any other attitude except that conditioned by the conviction that we need the prayerful counsel of the person whose help we seek. But the same attitude must govern the person whose help is sought. As Alec Motyer wisely puts it, 'There should be no hearing of someone else's admission of sin and need without a deliberate and single-minded intention to make it a matter of prayer. Only thus will we be delivered from the spirit of prying curiosity which, far from helping the needy out of his sin, would make the thing a matter of sin to the listener.'

3. The aim with which confession should be made. '... so that you may be healed.' The importance of these words cannot be over-emphasized. The whole aim of the making and hearing of confession of sin is that the person seeking help might be healed. This is the whole object of the exercise and must therefore be uppermost in the minds of all concerned. The aim of confessing and of hearing confession should be the healing of the spiritual situation, forgiveness, blessing, restoration of the spiritual glow, renewed usefulness in God's service. When the aim of confession is along those lines, it is hardly possible to conceive of a more valuable spiritual exercise, nor of a more heart-warming demonstration of the power of prayer.

Just one footnote: for all of its importance, there is one other factor which makes it clear that confession to other Christians is not a *sine qua non* for the forgiveness of sins in every case – and that is that it is God who forgives, not the person to whom the confession is made. The religious experts' question, 'Who can forgive sins but God alone?' (Mark 2:7), received no answer, because there is none that can be given. The Bible makes it transparently clear that most of our sins are to be confessed privately and to God alone. But woven into the biblical picture is this valuable directive by James and others, encouraging us to seek the pardon of those we have wronged and the counsel of those who are qualified to give it in order that we might be restored to spiritual health and vigour.

41.

One last word

'My brothers, if one of you should wander from the truth and someone should bring him back, remember this: Whoever turns a sinner from the error of his way will save him from death and cover over a multitude of sins' (James 5:19, 20).

As we come to the end of James's letter, it is fascinating to reflect on the tremendous amount of ground he has covered in such a comparatively short space. He has written on subjects ranging from the sovereignty of God to the use of the tongue, from the doctrine of election to the stewardship of money, from Bible reading to temptation, from prayer to criticism. Far from being a minor book in the Bible, we have seen that it is a treasure-house of divine truth, deeply spiritual and eminently practical all the way through.

Now James comes to his last word. Some people have suggested that his ending is abrupt and disconnected, but nothing could be further from the truth. In keeping with the whole tenor of his letter, the words now before us breathe an air of loving concern for the good of the church as a whole and fit in perfectly well with the theme with which he dealt in the verses immediately preceding them.

One obvious thing James's final phrase has in common with almost every section of his letter is his use of the words, 'my brothers', in introducing it. He addresses his readers in this way nearly twenty times in the course of his letter and there is surely something very significant in this. When he is teaching them, it is as brothers. When he is scolding them, it is as brothers. When he is challenging them, it is as brothers. When he is encouraging them, it is as brothers. When he is warning them, it is as brothers. Few of James's characteristics shine through his writing more clearly than his deep, sympathetic, warm, practical understanding of the needs of the church and his willingness to identify with them. Can we casually side-step that challenge? Do we share a similar concern for the church of Jesus Christ? It is so easy to be critical of 'the church' and to spend time sniping and judging and pontificating about it in a negative and unhelpful way, but that kind of thing is doing the devil's work for him. It is no part of our function as Christians to provide ammunition for the enemies of the church: instead, we should remember that 'Christ loved the church and gave himself up for her' (Ephesians 5:25) and our concern should be to nourish and encourage the church in every way we can. We can all learn from the attitude of E. Stanley Jones, who once said, 'I know that the church has its stupidities and inanities and irrelevancies; but I love my mother in spite of her weaknesses and wrinkles!' The church is a divine institution with which we should identify at every opportunity, about which we should speak with affection and concern, and against which we should refuse to offer public and unguarded criticism.

Turning to the text before us, it is immediately obvious that, as well as being warmly pastoral, it is eminently practical, and these two features become even more striking as we examine in detail its two main lessons.

1. A danger of which we should be aware

'My brothers, if one of you should wander from the truth . . .' (v. 19).

To underline a point made clear in an earlier study, notice immediately that James is addressing these final words to Christians: 'My *brothers*, if one of *you* should wander from the truth . . .' He is not writing to people outside of the church, those who have never come to the truth in the first place. Instead, he is pointing out a very real danger for Christians, and it is one that must be faced soberly by every believer. James's words pinpoint two things about this danger.

1. It is subtle. '. . . if one of you should wander from the truth . . .' The Greek verb is *planethe*, and in the New Testament it and its cognates are used to describe irregularities in both doctrine and practice. To give an example of both: John tells us how we may distinguish between 'the Spirit of truth and the spirit of falsehood *[planes]*' (1 John 4:6), while Jude speaks of those who have 'rushed for profit into Balaam's error *[plane]*' (Jude 11). We must be careful, however, of drawing too rigid a distinction between errors in doctrine and errors in practice, as in experience they are both intertwined, as they undoubtedly are in the warning James is giving here. Yet it is the NIV's literal rendering of *planethe* as 'wander' that most clearly helps us to capture the subtlety of the danger. The picture is not of a sudden, impulsive U-turn, an impetuous, violent rebellion, a headlong rush into sin. James is speaking of a wandering, an almost gentle straying, a subtle loosening of one's doctrinal or moral moorings. It is not a sudden, violent jerk of the helm; it is a slow drifting with the tide.

Surely the lesson and the warnings are obvious! Backsliding never begins with a loud bang; it never begins with an outrageous, scandalous sin. It always begins quietly, slowly, subtly, insidiously. Is it any wonder that the New Testament teems with warnings about this kind of danger? There are at least sixty occasions when we are specifically warned to be on our guard against this kind of deviation from living the truth, and all of them could be summed up in one particular warning Paul gave the Corinthians. Having reminded them of the disasters that befell their ancestors in the desert, he added, 'So, if you are thinking you are standing firm, be careful that you don't fall!' (1 Corinthians 10:12.) The permanent presence of the old nature guarantees that in the Christian life there is no victory without vigilance; in Thomas Watson's words, 'A wandering heart needs a watchful eye.' We have seen this truth stated earlier in James's letter, but it needs to be underlined here. No man is so far advanced along the Christian pathway, so knowledgeable in the Scriptures, so experienced in Christian service, so prominent in church affairs, that he is beyond the reach of Satan or the treachery of his own heart. The deadly subtlety of sin should constantly drive us to our knees.

2. It is serious. '. . . if one of you should wander from *the truth* . . .' It goes without saying that no backsliding is trivial – and the reason it is not trivial is because it is a deviation from what James calls 'the truth', and exactly in line with something we saw a moment ago. The New Testament makes it clear that this kind of deviation is possible in matters of doctrine and moral behaviour. In the matter of doctrine, we have the example of Hymenaeus and Philetus; Paul told Timothy that these two had 'wandered away from the truth' (2 Timothy 2:18) by teaching that there would be no bodily resurrection. In the matter of moral behaviour, Paul told the Galatians of those who 'were not acting in line with the truth of the gospel' (Galatians 2:14).

Taking these examples together, one clear principle emerges, and that is that every deviation from truth is to be regarded as extremely serious. There is no such thing as a small error, because truth is never small. What is more, we must underline in our minds the fact that it is possible to wander from the truth in an almost endless variety of ways. It is possible to wander doctrinally, by a failure to apply oneself to Scripture; it is possible to wander morally, by letting one's standards slip; it is possible to wander in one's identification with the church, by failing to contribute properly to its work and worship; it is possible to wander in terms of Christian service by becoming what Paul calls 'weary in doing good' (Galatians 6:9); it is possible to wander in one's home life, by failing to discharge biblical responsibilities as a parent or a child; and it is possible to wander in the inner recesses of one's own soul and to find with dismay that the flame of one's love for Christ has died into a flicker.

Here, then, is a danger that is serious, because in every case it is a straying from God's saving and sanctifying truth. In his little book on the Epistle of James, *Faith that Works*, John Bird had such an excellent section on this that with his kind permission I quote it at length. He wrote, 'We are living at a time when people are saying, "Doctrine does not matter. We must be tolerant to all and big-hearted enough to let all speak their minds and to hold their own opinions." Consequently, there is much confusion in the religious world. Doctrine matters greatly, for what a man believes will determine how he behaves. Our creed governs our conduct. Let a man deviate from the faith delivered unto the saints, and it will not be long before that man, morally and spiritually, strays in his ways. In the course of my ministry I have had appointments with a number of people whose lives have been marred and broken at one point or another. I have discovered that many of these, earlier in their lives, possessed an evangelical faith. They believed in the authority and inspiration of the Word of God, but at some point departed from that faith and soon lowered the standard of living and their lives caved in. When we turn aside from the doctrine of the sovereignty of God, we are soon left with no anchor and with very little assurance. We begin to question the purpose of things and lose the true perspectives of life. If we turn aside from the doctrine of the Lordship of Christ, it will not be long before we compromise our position as Christians and begin to live worldly lives. When the doctrine of sin is lost sight of, we begin to excuse ourselves for some of the things we do, and our ethical and moral standards are lowered. When the reality of the doctrine of hell is passed over and the doctrine of universalism is substituted, we miss the true meaning of Christ's death and lose any compassion we may have had for the dying souls of men. When we neglect the doctrine of the Holy Spirit, then we begin to work in the energy of the flesh and our power in service is lost. When we fail to recognize the doctrine of the meaning and function of the church, we become sectarian and treat it as if it were a religious club. When we treat scantily the doctrine of prayer, we go to battle without any weapons, thus losing the fight against the adversary of our souls. And when we do not study the doctrine of sanctification we become content with second-rate, mediocre, Christian living. So I may go on. We cannot gather grapes of thorns, nor figs of thistles, and we cannot expect our lives to be right if our doctrine is wrong.'

What a brilliantly clear exposition of the subtle and serious danger of which James speaks! Let us take its lessons to heart and apply ourselves with renewed diligence to the study of the Word of God and to obeying it in our daily lives.

2. A duty to which we should be alert

'My brothers, if . . . someone should bring him back, remember this: Whoever turns a sinner from the error of his way will save him from death and cover over a multitude of sins' (vv. 19, 20).

From the subtle and serious danger that even in the best of circles there is the possibility of a Christian wandering astray from doctrinal and moral truth, James now turns to the matter of how such lapses should be dealt with.

1. The responsibility of this duty. '. . . if . . . someone should bring him back'. It is immediately important to point out that the word 'someone' is a very general word which needs to be seen in the wider context of James's previous teaching about the healing of the sick and the confession of sin. In the case of healing James taught that particular responsibilities belonged to the elders of the church. In the case of confession of sin, on the other hand, he indicated that any member of the church might be involved, and he opens the door just as widely here. He is not speaking of a particular group of church officers and certainly not of one particular leader. There is no hint here of a special priesthood within the church, either individual or corporate, with the power of restoring those who have strayed. Rather, the responsibility of restoring those who have wandered is potentially placed fairly and squarely on the shoulders of each one of those who has not, though with biblical qualifications that we shall see in a moment.

That one general statement alone is immediately challenging. What a difference there would be in our churches if instead of barren, negative criticism we had a loving, pastoral concern for those we saw straying from the truth! I sense that our hearts are such that if people are making progress in the faith, if Christians are running well, submitting to the discipline of the church, attending the meetings, beginning to witness, then we find it easy to love them. Our hearts are warmed towards them. We are genuinely thrilled at the progress they are making. But if people are not making progress, if they are not submitting to the discipline of the church, if they seem to be going backwards rather than forwards, if they are being awkward rather than amenable, our attitude so often tends to be unloving and critical. Soon we begin to neglect them, to pass them by and, as a result, we miss out the very thing that James is saying here. His clear inference is that whenever anyone in the church begins to wander there is a general responsibility to seek to bring him back to the pathway of obedience and blessing.

This responsibility strikes home in another way, too, for while we have seen that the work of restoring the wanderer is not confined to one particular leader or group of leaders within the church, there are qualifications which must be met before a person has the right to engage in the work. This is how Paul puts it: 'Brothers, if someone is caught in a sin, you who are spiritual should restore him gently. But watch yourself, or you also may be tempted' (Galatians 6:1). The responsibility of caring for the wanderer is matched to the more searching responsibilities of spirituality, gentleness and personal vigilance. The person who seeks to rescue a fellow Christian who has strayed from God must himself be walking closely with him.

One other point needs comment in this particular part of the text, and that is James's statement that by his ministry to a wandering brother, a Christian can 'bring him back'. Now the strict truth is that this is something that no Christian can possibly do in his own strength or ability. We can no more correct an error of belief or behaviour in another Christian's life than we can persuade anyone to become a Christian in the first place. Then what does James mean? Surely this: that our commitment to the task of restoring the backslider is to be so complete, our identification with it so total, that we can actually speak of it as being something that we do. There is a vivid illustration of this kind of thing in the New Testament story of Onesimus, who ran away from his master Philemon and was converted to Christ under Paul's ministry at Rome. Sending him back to his rightful owner, Paul wrote of 'my son Onesimus, who became my son while I was in chains' (Philemon 10). Now nobody in Scripture is more insistent than Paul on the fact that regeneration is the lonely and sovereign work of God, yet he uses language that says in effect, 'I gave spiritual birth to Onesimus'! Yet surely his meaning is obvious? He was so totally identified with the event that he could gratefully speak of it as if he had brought it about. Elsewhere, he says that God will judge men's secrets through Jesus Christ, 'as my gospel declares' (Romans 2:16), and again the daring language reflects not insolence, but identification and involvement.

So here, our responsibility is so serious and our involvement is to be so total that James can say of our ministry to the wanderer that *we* 'bring him back'. Let us take the message to heart! With love, sympathy and tender concern, let us seek to restore the wanderer to the place of obedience and blessing.

2. The rewards of this duty. '. . . remember this: Whoever turns a sinner from the error of his way will save him from death and cover over a multitude of sins.' James's very last word, like his first, is one of warm encouragement. He says that when a backslider is brought back from his wandering two great things are achieved.

In the first place, *someone is rescued.* James says that when a Christian turns a wandering brother back into the way of truth he 'will save him from death'. What does he mean? There are those who say that this is a clear inference that Christians can wander so far from the truth that they can be eternally lost after being saved. The argument runs like this: James is speaking of a Christian who has wandered from the truth, and if by being brought back he is saved from death (which obviously means eternal death) then he would not be saved from such a death if he was not brought back. Now that argument seems logical, but it is not biblical, and we can see this by looking at the three passages of Scripture on which those who claim that Christians can be lost after being saved lean most heavily.

The first is this: 'It is impossible for those who have once been enlightened, who have tasted the heavenly gift, who have shared in the Holy Spirit, who have tasted the goodness of the word of God and the powers of the coming age, if they fall away, to be brought back to repentance, because to their loss they are crucifying the Son of God all over again and subjecting him to public disgrace' (Hebrews 6:4–6). The second is as follows: 'If we deliberately keep on sinning after we have received the knowledge of the truth, no sacrifice for sins is left, but only a fearful expectation of judgement and of raging fire that will consume the enemies of God' (Hebrews 10:26, 27). The third is as follows: 'If they have escaped the corruption of the world by knowing our Lord and Saviour Jesus Christ and are again entangled in it and overcome, they are worse off at the end than they were at the beginning' (2 Peter 2:20).

Now those are admittedly difficult passages and I will not attempt to unravel them here. But I am certain that they provide no basis whatever for saying that when James speaks about a Christian being saved from death when he is restored from a backsliding condition, he is endorsing the possibility of being lost after being saved. Why? Because if you look closely at the three passages I have quoted, you will see that in each case the reference is to a situation that is beyond recovery. We are told that 'It is impossible to be brought back to repentance', that 'No sacrifice for sin is left, but only a fearful expectation of judgement' and that those concerned will be 'worse off at the end than they were at the beginning'. In other words, all three passages speak of people as being beyond all hope of restoration. But the whole point of what James is saying here is that a wandering Christian *can* be restored! The cases are therefore as different as chalk from cheese; the writers are obviously not speaking about the same thing at all.

Then why does James say that when a person is brought back from wandering he is saved from death? The phrase is notoriously difficult, but there are at least two interpretations that would fit. One is that in referring to 'death' James is speaking about punishment for sin in a general sense; that while he has a penal element in mind, he is not thinking of final and irreparable loss. Rather, he is speaking of punishment for sin here on earth and of loss of reward in heaven. Is that what James means? One can certainly see that a Christian walking at a distance from God, and slipping further and further away, is missing out so much on the blessings of obedient Christian living that we could almost say that he is in a state of death, but it seems difficult to see why James uses the word 'death' to describe the loss of reward in heaven.

The second interpretation is well summed up by Alec

Motyer: 'Now, the present verses in James are not written from the point of view of what God knows about us, nor from the point of view of what we know about ourselves, but from the point of view of our fellow Christians observing our lives and hearing our talk. To them the evidence of backsliding in our lives must call in question whether we are truly Christ's or not.'

To elaborate, when James writes about a soul being saved from death, God knows that in fact the Christian never has to be saved all over again from final, spiritual death, because he is eternally secure. But other people look at our lives, see us living in a certain way, and begin to call into question whether we are really converted at all. And if, following that, the Word of God is brought home to our hearts, the Holy Spirit works in our lives and some fellow Christian helps to bring us back into that live, warm, virile and happy fellowship that we once knew, then people looking from the outside would say that our soul had been saved from death. One has often heard Christians refer to a stage in their lives when, some time after their conversion, there was a period of serious regression in their lives, followed subsequently and sometimes dramatically by a moment when they were brought back to the Lord. Sometimes, they can remember that moment as clearly as they can remember the day of their initial conversion. Looking at it from the outside, there would be many people who would even go so far as to say that that was the moment when their soul was saved from death. This interpretation, which would certainly underline the one central point being made, is that to restore a backslider is to rescue him from great harm, terrible loss and serious danger. That reward alone gives us a sufficient motive for seeking to be concerned and involved!

In the second place, *someone is restored.* James says that when a Christian brings a wanderer back to the truth he will not only save him from death but will also 'cover over a multitude of sins'. The verb here translates the Greek *kalupsei*, which literally means to cover over so that no trace can be seen, and is deceptively important because, although it is used in many different contexts, it is also one of the Bible's great salvation words, speaking of God's gracious covering over of man's sin by the sacrificial death of Christ. This 'covering over' of sin is what secures forgiveness for the sinner and the two concepts are brought together perfectly by David when he cries, 'Blessed is he whose transgressions are forgiven, whose sins are covered' (Psalm 32:1).

There are two main aspects of forgiveness mentioned in the Bible. One is the forgiveness that a person receives as part of his once-for-all, unrepeatable experience of justification, when in terms of his judicial standing with God all of his sins, past, present and future, are put out of the reckoning for ever. The second is the continuing need for the Christian to seek God's forgiveness of those sins which he commits in the course of his daily life, and it seems clear that this is what James has in mind here.

This being so, it is not difficult to see that he is right in saying that to bring a wanderer back to the truth is to 'cover a multitude of sins'. When a wanderer is brought back to the truth, a multitude of sins is covered, however vast the multitude may be. However great the defection, however persistent the rebellion, however grievous the sin, however serious the error, however damaging the action, however erroneous the belief, however distant the drift, when God forgives he forgets. God's forgiveness is complete and intractable. His own word is that 'I, even I, am he who blots out your transgressions, for my own sake, and remembers your sins no more' (Isaiah 43:25). Yet even this is not the end of the story, because with the forgiveness of sins comes a renewal of fellowship and the answer to the penitent's prayer: 'Restore to me the joy of your salvation' (Psalm 51:12). The returning backslider can have no greater delight than to know that that prayer has been answered and the Christian who helps him to return can share in the rejoicing. As Albert Barnes puts it, 'When we come to die, as we shall soon, it will give us more pleasure to be able to recollect that we have been the means of saving one soul from death, than to have enjoyed all the pleasures which sense can furnish, or to have gained all the honour and wealth which the world can give.' That being so, how earnestly we should give ourselves to the study of God's saving and sanctifying Word and to the sacred task of ministering its truth to all those in need! As we turn with humbled hearts from all that James has said, let our response be in the spirit of these magnificent words by Charles Wesley:

My talents, gifts and graces, Lord,
Into thy blessed hands receive;
And let me live to preach thy Word,
And let me to thy glory live;
My every sacred moment spend
In publishing the sinner's Friend.

Enlarge, inflame and fill my heart
With boundless charity divine:
So shall I all my strength exert,
And love them with a zeal like thine:
And lead them to thy open side,
The sheep for whom their Shepherd died.